THE END OF EQUALITY

THE END OF EQUALITY

MICKEY KAUS

A New Republic Book
Basic Books
A Member of Perseus Books, L.L.C.

Portions of this book have appeared previously in different form in *The New Republic.*

Designed by Ellen Levine

Library of Congress Cataloging-in-Publication Data

Kaus, Mickey, 1951–
    The end of equality/Mickey Kaus.
        p.   cm.
    Includes index.
    ISBN 0–465–09814–2 (cloth)
    ISBN 0–465–09816–9 (paper)
    ISBN 0–465–09829–0 (second edition paper)
    1. Equality—United States.   2. Liberalism—United States.   3. So-
cial classes—United States.   I. Title.
JC575.K38   1992   91–50880
320' .01' 1—dc20   CIP

98 99 00 LP 9 8 7 6 5 4 3 2

CONTENTS

PREFACE TO THE 1995
PAPERBACK EDITION

This book was published in hardcover the week that Bill Clinton received the 1992 Democratic nomination for president. The first paperback edition went to the printers a few months after Clinton took office in 1993. I remember fretfully searching the paperback galleys for passages that a successful Democratic presidency would soon render obsolete. The book, after all, claims that the "house of liberalism" needs "more than repainting [or] remodeling," that it needs to be ripped down and rebuilt on a different foundation. If President Clinton revived Democratic politics without that painful reconstruction, the book's liberals-are-in-deep-trouble tone would seem more than a bit foolish.

There was, it turns out, no need to worry. If anything, liberalism now may be in even deeper trouble than when the following chapters were written. The first two years of Clinton's term—the long-awaited swinging of the pendulum back to "affirmative government," Arthur Schlesinger, Jr., told us—were a political disaster. In the 1994 midterm elections, Democrats lost control of both houses of Congress for the first time in four decades. What's more, they lost to Republicans of a particularly conservative, antigovernment tendency.

Why did the Democrats fail? Not surprisingly, I believe that at bottom they failed because they refused to come to terms with the broad economic trends outlined in these pages. In particular, three themes of *The End of Equality* were central themes of the 1994 elections: First, the trend toward rising inequality of income and wealth, which meant that many voters found they did not benefit even from a growing economy. Second, the "meritocracy" problem, which manifested itself most obviously in the social gap between the skilled and the unskilled (especially the now-famous "angry white males"). Finally, the persistence of a largely urban, largely black "underclass," sustained by what Rep. Newt Gingrich, leading the successful Republican campaign, anathematized as the "liberal welfare state." This preface will address recent developments in each of these areas, with particular attention to the ongoing debate over welfare.

I.

The End of Equality proposes that liberals make the pursuit of social equality their central, explicit purpose. This is the "more secure foundation" on which, the book argues, a political movement needs to be built. It is to be preferred, in particular, to the more familiar liberal pursuit of greater material equality. The first three chapters suggest that the redistributionist enterprise was always in large part a means for achieving the "real" end of social equality. At any rate, a strategy that relies on diminishing material differences—Money Liberalism—is doomed in an era when income disparities are growing due to deep, structural changes in the economy.

The first half of Clinton's presidency helps prove the point. As candidate and president, Clinton has been unusually explicit in his embrace of money egalitarianism. During one campaign debate he asserted bluntly that "what we want is more income equality." The text of Clinton's original 1993 economic plan, which was accompanied by elaborate distributional charts, not only railed against the 1980s ("the richer you were, the better you did"), but also pledged to "redress" the "alarming rise in inequality."

What Clinton lacked was a plausible plan for accomplishing this goal. The inequality trend, as is now widely recognized, was not produced by Republican tax policies in the 1980s. It's the product of deep, long-term changes in the economy, changes that result in skilled workers being paid more and unskilled workers being paid relatively less. The big winners have been college-educated brainworkers—lawyers, investment bankers, and other "symbolic analysts," to use Robert Reich's term. But even among highly skilled workers with graduate credentials, inequality has grown, as the very best performers take home superstar salaries (the "Hollywood effect").

Economists debate whether the pay-for-skills trend is in turn caused mainly by international trade (unskilled labor can now be performed more cheaply abroad) or autonomous technological changes (computers demand skilled operators). But the trend itself is unmistakable. Less-skilled men, especially, have seen large wage drops in absolute as well as relative terms. According to Bureau of the Census statistics, the weekly earnings of a man in the middle of the wage distribution dropped about 15 percent between 1973 and 1992.

Statistics on income inequality during the first years of Clinton's term are still sketchy, but there is no reason to think that the general inegalitarian trend reversed itself. Even during the "white collar" recession of 1989–91, the earnings gap between college graduates and high school graduates continued to grow, according a study by Frank Levy, Richard Murnane, and Lijing Chen. The recession did hit the rich relatively hard, but over the 1989–92 period the top fifth of the income distribution actually increased its share of the nation's income, according to many measures. Meanwhile, the income share claimed by the bottom 40 percent of families continued to decline. Census data from 1993 show another big jump in the top fifth's share (though the Census changed its survey method in 1993, so there is some uncertainty as to what this increase means).

Clinton, of course, didn't always phrase his economic goals in terms of reversing inequality. He typically pledged to "restore the middle class." Perhaps that ambiguous promise referred to absolute, not relative, living standards. And Clinton may have thought he would achieve at least such an absolute improvement if he could keep the economy growing. In fact, the economy grew at a healthy 3 percent rate in 1993, and faster still in the first three quarters of 1994.

But, thanks to the inequality trend, even robust economic growth does not necessarily translate into higher living standards for many workers. Reich, Clinton's secretary of labor, lamented after the 1994 election that the bulk of income growth was going to the "top fifth of American households." In the middle of the distribution, stagnation was the norm. Indeed, the Census Bureau reported an actual decline in the median household income—from $31,583 to $31,241—between 1992 and 1993. Given these statistics, many have noted, the riddle of why Clinton didn't get more credit for the recovery doesn't look like such a riddle. Clinton's promise to "restore the middle class" proved hollow, not because he failed to revive the economy, but because while the economy revived he failed to reverse the inequality trend.

If the argument of chapter 5 is right, Clinton and the Democrats have, in fact, no realistic hope of reversing that trend, at least not without reinforcing the invidious correlation of high income with skills and smarts.

One traditional redistributive technique is progressive taxation. But, as chapter 5 notes, the top 1 percent have gotten so rich that it would take an effective tax rate of more than 50 percent to cut their income share back down to what it was in 1977. Clinton's 1993 economic package did manage to raise the effective tax rate on this top percentile—from 28 percent to 33 percent. Nice try. Clinton also dramatically increased the Earned Income Tax Credit for the working poor to a maximum of about $3,500. But it isn't clear that this credit can be expanded much further without either producing a significant work disincentive or encouraging widespread fraud.

Taxes, however, are not Clinton's favorite anti-inequality strategy. Training is. "You want to reverse income inequality in this country," he told a Democratic audience in December 1994. "There is an education premium, and we had better give it to every American who is willing to take it. That is the only way to do it." So far, Clinton's training program—championed most visibly by Reich—remains largely unrealized. (During his first two years, Clinton mainly proposed rearranging existing federal programs.)

The difficulties confronting the "training cure" are also discussed in chapter 5. Skills training may well be a sensible way to spend tax dollars. Yet even a large, successful training program would take a long time to produce a significant change in income distribution. As Lawrence Mishel of the Economic Policy Institute points out, even if training expenses were boosted by 1 percent of payroll, and even if a quarter of that investment were returned every year in the form of higher wages, it would take a generation just to make up the 17 percent decline in wages suffered between 1979 and 1993 by men with only a high school education.

That leaves one final inequality "cure" from the "intelligent Money Liberal's agenda": profit sharing. As of this writing, Clinton has yet to make a major effort in this area. But after the 1994 election, Democratic Minority Leader Richard Gephardt embraced the idea as his main solution to the problem of wage stagnation. Gephardt called for "special incentives" to "encourage companies to let the workers share in the profits," a program he called "Pay for Productivity." As noted in chapter 5, profit sharing may well boost incomes at the bottom. But will the effect be big enough to overcome the pay-for-skills trend? According to Douglas Kruse, a Rutgers University economist who published a comprehensive study of the subject, profit sharing plans seem to produce a one-time productivity increase averaging 4 or 5 percent. That's a sizable gain. But even if it could be achieved nationwide and returned in equal shares to low-level workers, it would only make up for a fraction of the increase in inequality since the mid-1970s. "The most diehard advocates wouldn't say profit-sharing is going to solve the problem of income distribution," says Kruse.

It would be odd if income inequality kept on getting worse forever. Some economists, such as Stanford University's Paul Krugman, are already speculating that technological advances will someday render highly educated "symbolic analysts" obsolete, as "tax lawyers are replaced by expert systems software." But there is little reason to think that the inequality boom of the mid-1970s and 1980s will be undone in our lifetimes. And unless inequality at least stops getting worse, even impressive growth may not be enough to generate large income gains in the middle of the distribution—meaning that the Clinton-Reich promise to "restore the middle class" will remain irredeemable.

II.

The decline in the wages of the unskilled, especially unskilled men, is certainly is one reason why the "angry white male" voters of 1994 might have been so angry. But it is not the only reason. Dennis Farney, writing about these voters in the *Wall Street Journal,* noted that "something beyond economics" was happening. Specifically, "what happened was cultural backlash against a professional and managerial 'knowledge class'" by the less educated and less well-off.

This wasn't such a new phenomenon, of course. Barbara Ehrenreich, in her book *Fear of Falling,* recounts in delicious detail the media's discovery of angry blue-collar workers in the late 1960s after the surprising success of the presidential campaign of George Wallace (who attacked "over-educated ivory-tower folks with pointed heads"). Ultimately, chapter 4 argues, this social division can be traced to the meritocratic sorting of citizens by skills, education, and brains—and to an economy in which those differences increasingly coincide with differences in income.

This meritocratic phenomenon is independent of the level of income equality. It's one thing, chapter 4 notes, to have an economy in which the distribution of income is unequal. It's another to have an income distribution based ever more rigorously on schooling and ability, in which those on top can implicitly claim not just that they have more money but that they are more skilled, more knowledgeable, smarter. That is a recipe for social inequality—and for resentment of the well-off meritocratic elite— regardless of precisely how well-off the elite is. The Wallace campaign, remember, tapped antimeritocratic resentments at a time when incomes were actually *more* equal than they've been before or since. It's not surprising that, after twenty-five years in which the link between income and education has gotten stronger, those resentments have surfaced again in our politics.

Even if a Clinton-Reich training program succeeded in reducing income inequality, it would not lessen this *social* inequality created by the increased value of skills. In fact, it would almost surely make those social divisions worse. The "lifelong learning" regime Clinton and Reich envision is, in essence, one more expansion of meritocracy, offering a world in which each citizen can rise to precisely the level that his or her applied ability justifies. But if you're offered elaborate training and you still can't climb into the middle class, how does that make you feel? Even if income differences diminished, those that remained would have a more poisonous bite.

I'm not saying that the Democrats lost the 1994 election because the voters rebelled against the meritocratic stratification implicit in Clinton's "training cure" for income inequality. I am suggesting that the voters may have sensed that Clinton's "smart work, high-wage" future might, in some sense, be a nastier place than the *un*skilled, high-wage past they had lost—and that this may help explain why the electorate wasn't whipped into a populist fervor by the Clintonites' talk of "skill standards" and "one-stop career centers." (Populists usually get votes by attacking educated elites, not by proposing to create them.) Reich described the "old American bargain" as: "If you work hard an play by the rules, you'll get ahead." He said the "new middle class" would be built on a "refinement" of that bargain: "You take responsibility for working hard, you get a chance to work smart." Voters can be forgiven if they found the old version more appealing.

An elaborate training program would also be a giant step in the direction of the late Richard Herrnstein's depressing syllogism, which holds that the more success is based on mental abilities that are to some degree inherited, the more success will also be inherited. Herrnstein's ideas have now received wide attention with the publication of *The Bell Curve,* the book he coauthored with Charles Murray. Nothing in that book alters the views on Herrnstein that are expressed in chapter 4. I still believe that something like the "Herrnstein scenario" is in fact transpiring— that is, even if success is still primarily a matter of luck, it is now passed genetically from generation to generation more than it used to be. (This has nothing to do with the question of whether black-white differences in measured intelligence are inherited, a more controversial subject discussed with deep disingenuousness in the Herrnstein-Murray book.) The possibility of a more durable, inherited class structure is also suggested by evidence from Robert Mare of the University of Wisconsin confirming the troubling trend toward "assortative mating"—people marrying others in their own class.

That would not be good for social equality even if incomes weren't getting more unequal. But they are. Meanwhile, the common space in which Americans of all classes rub shoulders keeps shrinking. For example, data from the 1990 census reveal that (as suspected) residential segregation by economic class is increasing, among whites as well as blacks. Paul Jargowsky of the University of Texas at Dallas found that "the phenomenon is incredibly widespread, affecting virtually every metroplitan area." The division of Americans by money and merit continues to assume a physical form.

The following chapters may not convince many readers that this is a terrible thing. The book does not really present an argument that justifies an overriding concern with social equality, certainly not an argument that starts from first principles. Rather, it attempts to work through the implications of social-egalitarian values it assumes the reader shares. Nothing in the text is likely to change the minds, for example, of people who rather enjoy elaborate gradations of civil status. But I have confidence they remain a small minority of Americans.

For those who do value social equality, the book suggests a strategy that does not rely on a futile campaign to somehow redress the rise in income inequality. That alternative, Civic Liberalism, would attempt to restrict the sphere of life in which money (and merit) matters while expanding the public sphere in which income differences are ignored. The continuing failure of Money Liberalism under Clinton, and the continuing stratification of Americans by smarts and skills, make a Civic Liberal strategy more appealing than ever. Let liberals use the power of "affirmative government" to neutralize the divisive implications of the new skills-based economy—and to incubate and spread a countervailing egalitarian culture.

III.

The sturdiest basis for such an egalitarian culture, chapter 9 argues, is work. The work ethic poses a test that anyone, rich or poor, smart or stolid, can pass. Many Democratic strategists (including many currently surrounding Clinton) seem to believe that the only way to win over struggling middle-class workers is to deliver tangible economic benefits—if not higher wages, then tax cuts, or training, or health insurance. But another way to appeal to underpaid workers is to honor their work by dishonoring those who do not work, including those who could work but instead rely on welfare.

In fact, 1994's victorious Gingrich Republicans didn't campaign by talking about the economic hardship of the middle class. Gingrich talked about the "liberal welfare state" and the "culture of poverty" it sustained. Democrats who hadn't lifted a finger to reform welfare tried to beat back the Republican assault by posing as antiwelfare crusaders themselves. When NBC and the *Wall Street Journal* polled voters right after the election, reforming welfare was the issue most often listed as a top priority for the new Congress. Health care reform came in a distant second. *Journal* reporter Gerald Seib, in follow-up calls to Democrats and independents who voted Republican, was surprised to find that they spontaneously raised the welfare issue.

I used to worry I'd overdone it in emphasizing the political salience of welfare reform in chapter 11. I don't anymore. How, after all, did Bill Clinton get elected president? By promising to "end welfare as we know it." That was the main message of the television ads his consultants ran in contested states. ("Those who are able must go to work," the ads declared). Indeed, as Al From of the Democratic Leadership Council points out, when it briefly appeared that Clinton had stolen the welfare and crime issues from the Republicans, there was talk in the press that he was on the verge of redefining American politics in his favor. I don't think it is much of an exaggeration to say that if in 1994 Clinton had pushed for welfare reform instead of his health plan, we now might be talking about a Democratic realignment rather than a Republican realignment.

How can welfare be so important? After all, the two biggest "welfare" programs—Aid to Families with Dependent Children (AFDC) and food stamps—still only add up to about 3 percent of the federal budget. But it's a crucial 3 percent. Pollsters will tell you that welfare is a "values" issue. Food stamps and AFDC are the only major components of our "welfare state" that flout the work ethic by offering to support able-bodied Americans whether or not they work. Social Security's retirement benefits, in contrast, go only to workers. And Social Security is immensely popular, while AFDC is despised. AFDC also seemingly undermines families, because it is available, by and large, only to single parents.

This is not simply (or even largely) a question of symbolism, because welfare is deeply implicated in America's biggest social problem: the existence of whole neighborhoods, mainly urban, mainly African American, where there are precious few intact, working families. Welfare may or may not have caused this underclass, but (as chapters 7 and 8 argue) welfare is what sustains it. And the underclass, in turn, drives the crime problem, the race problem, the drug problem, the "urban crisis," the general sense of social decay. Clinton made this connection in several speeches he gave after the 1992 Los Angeles riots, when he explicitly spoke of welfare reform as a way to "break the culture of poverty and dependence" in the ghettos. But it was Gingrich who made the connection in the months leading up to the 1994 election—talking about "twelve-year-olds having babies, fifteen-year-olds killing each other," pointing out that welfare reform would do far more to reduce crime than Clinton's "crime bill."

Given the manifest perverse consequences of welfare spending, it's not surprising that it has become a sort of threshold test of government efficacy. The AFDC program, in particular, is probably the most conspicuous ongoing example of the government "not working." If politicians are willing to keep spending 3 percent of the budget on such a crazy program, why trust them with even bigger sums for other liberal projects, such as national health insurance? Yet many Democratic leaders—Reich, for one—continue to dismiss public antipathy to welfare as a case of scapegoating, a by-product of declining middle-class paychecks. The anger of the economy's "losers," Reich explains, is "easily manipulated. . . . Today the targets of rage are immigrants, welfare mothers. . . . Who will be the targets tomorrow?" The condescension here is breathtaking. Isn't it possible that the voters' anger at welfare is anger at welfare—justified anger?

Welfare sits at the center of this book because transforming welfare is what opens up the possibility of a Civic Liberal alternative. It's not just that work is the common necessity that unites street sweepers and "symbolic analysts." The underclass that welfare sustains is also (chapter 7 argues) what "most obviously sets in motion the vicious circle in which the degradation of public life in cities encourages the flight" to class-segregated suburbs. The great hope of a Civic Liberalism would be that rich and poor can occupy the same neighborhoods and use the same local institutions (especially schools). But there is no hope of mixing classes if that means asking suburbanites to accept an underclass in their midst. Without neighborhood integration, Civic Liberals must rely heavily on the creation of intrusive new public institutions like the draft or an egalitarian national health system (both of which seem increasingly remote possibilities).

The welfare reform proposal in chapter 8 would completely replace cash welfare for the able-bodied with a system of WPA-style low-wage public jobs. As the reader will discover, this is a very expensive scheme, because the jobs would be available to all comers, and because it costs more to offer someone a job than simply to send them a check. (A job requires supervision, tools, and day care for the children of working mothers). I still believe this is the only plan that would 1) completely remove the economic basis of underclass culture, 2) guarantee that no American willing to work had to live in poverty, and 3) avoid the inevitable perverse effects of providing work or training only to those—mainly single mothers—who now go on AFDC. It's worth noting that Gingrich advanced a nearly identical plan a few years ago, presumably for these same reasons.

President Clinton's initial welfare proposal, as expected, drew on the "time limit" idea advanced by Harvard researcher David Ellwood, who became a co-chair of Clinton's welfare reform task force. During the 1992 campaign, Clinton pledged that after two years on welfare "those who can work will have to go to work, either by taking a job in the private sector or through community service." A critical discussion of this approach (the "Ellwood Plan") may be found in note 38 to chapter 8. Suffice it to say that I still think a rigorously enforced, Ellwood-style time-limit would have a significant effect in "breaking" the culture of poverty. A life on welfare, in a household separated from the world of regular work, would simply become impossible. Young girls—seeing neighbors or older sisters whose time was up—would know that if they made the disastrous decision to become unwed mothers, they would soon have to juggle mothering and a job. They might then begin to make better choices: staying in school, postponing childbirth, getting married.

In fact, Clinton's plan was surprisingly strict. As introduced, belatedly, in June 1994, it fudged the two-year limit a bit through various deferrals and exemptions. Clinton also held down the plan's expense by phasing it in so that it applied only to the youngest third of the caseload. But it applied to *all* of that younger cohort (most importantly, it would discourage young girls who hadn't yet become single mothers from going on the dole). The penalty for repeatedly failing to work after the time limit was reached was loss of all AFDC benefits. The Clinton plan also promoted the radical notion of "work for wages"—meaning that once time had expired welfare checks would simply stop coming. Any further income would have to come from work. In this respect the Clinton plan resembled the WPA-style scheme in chapter 8 more than it did traditional "workfare," in which a recipient keeps getting a welfare check while the government tries to sanction her if she doesn't "work it off." Press accounts characterizing Clinton's plan as "modest" simply missed the story.

All of which makes Clinton's failure to capitalize on antiwelfare sentiment seem almost willful. At a time when Clinton's approval rating was 42 percent, a *Los Angeles Times* poll put the approval rating of Clinton's two-years-and-go-to-work scheme at 90 percent. Even when voters were told the plan would cost them $50 billion over ten years, it drew 69 percent support. House Republicans initially promoted a time-limit bill similar to Clinton's, yet the president failed to push for legislation.

Why? The official reason is that health care reform took priority; the unofficial reason is that congressional liberals didn't support the plan, in part because of its tough sanction against those who refused to work, in part because, as expected, public employee unions lobbied against it, fearing competition from "community service" workers. Imagine how the midterm election might have looked if Clinton had spent 1994 pushing this tough, popular proposal—standing up to his paleoliberal opponents, overcoming "gridlock," et cetera. Instead, he not only lost control of Congress, he lost control of welfare reform.

Early in Clinton's term, Republicans such as Rep. Jan Meyers were calling it "political suicide" to help a Democratic president reform welfare. And, in late 1993, Republicans began moving away from an Ellwood-style solution, a movement that assumed two somewhat contradictory forms: first, a preference for cutting off benefits rather than enforcing work requirements; second, an impulse to send the welfare issue back to the states.

Just as Democrats were finally learning to embrace the old Reaganite idea of putting welfare recipients to work, Republicans began to abandon it. "I don't care how many women go to work," said Charles Murray, who lobbied Congress against the Ellwood plan. The core problem, said Murray, was the rise in illegitimate births, which "drives everything else." The solution was abolishing welfare, not enforcing work. Former education secretary William Bennett endorsed the Murray view in early 1994, writing that the "point of welfare reform" was "not to ensure tougher work provisions." GOP strategist William Kristol declared, "The problem is not that a single mother isn't working, it's that that single mother is a single mother."

As a matter of pure policy, this seemingly radical doctrinal shift was difficult to explain. After all, the problem with underclass culture is clearly the disastrous combination of families headed by single, often never-married, women *and* non-work. (Would conservatives be happy with a world of intact families on the dole?) What's more, the Clintonites hadn't ignored the illegitimacy issue. They clearly saw a work requirement, in part, as a way to deter unwed motherhood.

But the new "anti-illegitimacy" doctrine did neatly solve the political dilemma facing Republicans. It gave them a seemingly profound reason for failing to support Clinton's plan. It let them avoid the reality that the "workfare" reforms they'd been advocating for years required new government spending and new government bureaucracy. It gave them something to say ("Pull the plug," urged Bennett) that even New Democrats were unlikely to parrot. And it defused the contradiction between welfare work requirements and the traditionalist right-wing view that mothers should stay at home rather than go to work.

By the time of the election, Gingrich's followers had backed away from the two-years-and-go-to-work model and embraced a harsher combination of cutoffs and budget caps. The Republicans' 1994 "Contract with America" proposed a lifetime ban on AFDC and housing benefits for illegitimate children born to mothers younger than eighteen. Those mothers who qualified for welfare would still be required to work in community service jobs within two years. But after a maximum of five years they would be cut off for life—no AFDC, and no "community service" job either. Another provision stripped AFDC and food stamps of their "entitlement" status, making them subject to annual appropriations (and cuts) in Congress.

Yet the GOP contract also allowed states to opt out of these requirements if they wished, converting federal welfare money into a "block grant" and using it to finance programs of their own design. Here was the second Republican impulse: to dissolve the welfare question into the federalism question. Many governors urged this approach, voicing objections to "one-size-fits-all" federal rules, including the cutoff rules in the contract. They argued, in essence, that what works in Michigan won't necessarily work in, say, Florida. But the forces responsible for creating the underclass—segregation, the migration of jobs and the middle class from the cities to the suburbs, welfare itself—are more or less the same everywhere. What works in Michigan probably *will* work in Florida.

While the "block grant" solution would give states the freedom to experiment, it is not in itself reform. Some governors might go wild, ending all effective assistance, impoverishing the disabled, and so on. But there is a greater danger they won't go wild enough. When it comes to welfare, governors have not been radical reformers. (During Clinton's first two years, only three or four governors proposed statewide changes as bold as those embraced by the president.) In particular, governors tend resist expensive solutions like community service jobs. Will they adopt costly work programs when there is no money from Washington to pay for them? No. Most will simply continue the current system while making a few minor—if well-publicized—changes.

It's not clear, as of this writing, what the current welfare reform debate will produce. What *should* it produce? Assuming a plan like that in chapter 8 is (wrongly) deemed too expensive even for the federal government, three principles of reform suggest themselves.

The first proposition is that any reform should base itself squarely on the work ethic. That means no long-term cash assistance for able-bodied Americans, mothers included. Instead, after no more than a limited period of cash aid, they would have to work for what they receive. Work could be enforced either through a "requirement" (workfare) or the termination of welfare checks and the substitution of low-wage jobs ("work for wages").

A corollary to this work principle, however, is that those who *are* willing to work shouldn't be left out in the cold. The "Contract with America" violated this principle by requiring states to cut off even indigents willing to work in community service jobs. The business cycle has not yet been repealed. If there are no jobs to be had in the private economy, do we really want a low-skilled single mother who has been cleaning up parks in a subminimum-wage community service job to be left on her own? Why not let her keep cleaning the parks? As long as the wage for community service work is kept sufficiently below the lowest wage in the private sector, the danger that people will refuse private sector jobs will be minimized. (A moderate increase in the private sector minimum wage would help maintain this desirable differential.)

Shouldn't the work principle be supplemented by direct attempts to engineer "family values"—for example, by denying aid to unwed mothers? The premise of chapter 8 is that such a potentially harsh step is unnecessary—that if you restore the general work imperative, the family will take care of itself, since the family is the natural response to that imperative. Why run yourself ragged trying to raise a kid while working in a $10,000-a-year job when you can marry another worker and either stay at home or live on two incomes?

Enforcing the work ethic will cost money, at least in the short run. Expensive, last-resort public service jobs are the only sure, fair way to assess claims that there "just aren't jobs available" in the private sector, to put those making such claims to a test of whether they are or aren't willing to work. Enforcing work will save billions eventually—perhaps sooner than eventually, if a work requirement helps purge the rolls of thousands of recipients who are currently working under the table. But for the moment extra expense must be anticipated. The point of welfare reform is to solve a social crisis, not a budget crisis.

Which brings up a second principle of reform: big spending, or at least adequate spending. It's not simply that if there isn't enough money, there aren't enough public jobs, and the work test can't be enforced. Money is also needed to take care of those who *fail* the work test. Under virtually any work-based reform, some erstwhile recipients will refuse to work and lose cash support. Some will wind up on the streets. What happens to them and their children? A responsible plan would prepare a place for them. Paying for an expansion of the foster care system is one alternative. Even more expensive would be an attempt to develop group homes that allow mother and child to stay together while offering them food, shelter, and counseling. It wasn't irresponsible of Newt Gingrich to raise the possibility of orphanages as a necessary institution of last resort. It *is* irresponsible to recognize this need and then fail to provide the money to pay for it.

Of course, nobody is sure which type of institution is best. We don't know how many welfare recipients would fail a rigorously enforced work test. For that matter, we don't really know which work test is best—whether "work for wages" can avoid the complications of "workfare," for example. We don't know how difficult it is to prevent a WPA-style jobs program from degenerating into flaccid makework.

The third principle of reform, then, acknowledges the need to experiment and find out the answers. Those answers won't come from studying the mincing, incremental reforms that have been tried so far. They will come from the attempt to make various radical solutions work. The states play an obvious role here—but, as noted, there is no assurance that the governors, left to themselves, will undertake anything radical. If the federal government wants to test out various reform schemes, it will need to make sure they in fact get tested. Within the general work requirement, for example, Congress can induce (or require) at least one state to try Clinton's "work for wages" scheme. It can make sure another state tries the full replacement of welfare with WPA-style jobs available to all comers. Let one state (not ten) try the contract's idea of imposing a time limit on community service work. Let Congress provide enough money to give each of these schemes a chance—and let Congress then impose nationwide the plan that works the best.

Even those who do not accept the larger thesis of this book are likely to agree on the need for welfare reform. But those who embrace the idea of social equality, and the public sphere as a means of preserving it, will feel a special urgency. It may look now as if the hour of radical reform in welfare has come. But it's looked that way before (including when Clinton was elected in 1992), and not much has changed. The desire for ongoing experimentation is no excuse for once again postponing rigorous work-based reform. We need a national solution forceful enough to match the reality of the underclass.

IV.

President Clinton's character flaw, it's often said, is that he tries to be too many things at once. Is he a paleoliberal or neoliberal, an old Democrat or New Democrat? Well, we are told, he's both. The same applies to the categories of this book. Clinton has attempted to combine Money Liberalism with Civic Liberal attempts to expand the public sphere (through his small but significant national service initiative, for example).

The claim of this book remains that sooner or later liberals will have to choose between these two strategies. At some point, it will be obvious that the Democrats cannot succeed in reversing the inegalitarian economic trends. They will then either continue to tell Americans that their place on the income distribution tables is vitally important, in which case they are resigning themselves to failure. Or they will tell the voters that money is ultimately not the most important thing about America, in which case they will learn to live with income differences while preserving the possibility of a more profound equality.

The pursuit of that form of equality, I continue to believe, is one for which Democrats are better suited than today's Republicans. Beyond welfare reform, and perhaps the crusade against reverse racial discrimination, there is little in the Republicans' agenda that has much to do with preserving social equality. That task still takes more government than they can stomach. Given the growing divisions of money and merit, *not* to take vigorous government action is to abandon the social-egalitarian ideal.

I don't mean that those who call themselves conservatives are necessarily social inegalitarians, or that they may not one day join with today's liberals to support an affirmative program to build a democratic public life. The best commonsense definition of social equality I've heard remains that offered in the summer of 1992—not by a liberal, or even a Democrat, but by Ronald Reagan:

> Whether we come from poverty or wealth . . . we are all equal in the eyes of God. But as Americans that is not enough—we must be equal in the eyes of each other.

In many ways, little seems to have changed in the two and a half years since that summer (and, coincidentally, since the publication of this volume). Republicans may still believe that the equality Reagan invoked may be casually preserved. Democrats may still believe that nothing less than a reversal of the income trends that became evident during Reagan's term will rescue his appeal from hypocrisy. Convincing both groups otherwise—convincing them that preserving America's social equality is both more difficult and more possible than they may imagine—remains the job of this book.

Washington, D.C.
January 1995

THE END OF EQUALITY

CHAPTER I

From the Ground Up

I came to Washington, D.C., in the winter of 1977, a freshly minted leftish lawyer eager to work in the federal government. Those early months of the Jimmy Carter administration were something of a high-water mark of liberal activism. After two Republican presidents, the rightful Democratic order (or so it seemed at the time) had been restored. The consumer movement, the civil rights movement, the women's movement all appeared powerful and important. Washington was filled with young public-interest types, their hair still a bit long, with plants in their offices and Sister Mary Corita prints on their walls. My goal was simply to join them—to get a salary, a stapler, and a cause.

Three years later, I found myself among the crowd in the ballroom of a Washington hotel, waiting for Carter to arrive and concede his landslide defeat by Ronald Reagan. I'd lasted only nine months in government, having bailed out to work for a small political magazine. From there I had watched as the best minds of the Democratic party ran the liberal enterprise into the ground. They had put liberalism on the side of welfare rather than work. They funded housing projects that were among the most hellish places on earth. They defended absurd extensions of criminals' rights. They funneled billions to big-city mayors who gave the money to developers who built hideous, bankrupt downtown malls. They let the teachers' unions run the education department and the construction unions run the labor department. I hadn't wanted Reagan to win; I'd voted for Carter without hesitation. But as I waited for him to show up, and looked at the outgoing Democratic officials gathered on the stage, I realized there was not one of these people I wasn't happy to see go.

Since then, the Democrats, and the liberal tradition they represent, have been in deep trouble. Walter Mondale, Carter's vice president, was the liberal establishment's dream candidate, far more popular among that group than Carter himself had ever been. Mondale was buried in 1984. In 1988 the Democratic nominee spent most of the campaign denying he was a "liberal" at all, lest the epithet doom him.

Faced with public rejection, liberals were positively ingenious at thinking of ways to avoid rethinking. Each fresh defeat brought forth new varieties of denial—in the psychological sense of denial of reality. After Mondale's 1984 disaster, the favorite scapegoat was television. Mondale himself blamed the loss on his lack of affinity for the medium.[1] Outgoing party chairman Charles Manatt urged that future candidates take "professional training in television."[2] In 1988, the favorite excuse was the incompetence of the Dukakis organization. This time Manatt called for training a central cadre of fifty professionals to handle future campaigns.[3]

Others talked about more substantive issues. Veteran Democratic pol Frank Mankiewicz had a pithy explanation for liberalism's electoral failures: racism. "Liberalism is read as a code word for helping blacks," Mankiewicz said. "The battle over liberalism is a racist argument." It was depressing, but hardly liberals' fault, if they were the victims of mindless bigotry and selfishness.[4]

Denial was followed (in what may be a clinical progression) by a grasping at straw hopes. A succession of political saviors has been spotted on the horizon, each one transfixing the party elite and the press before melting away into thin air. The "gender gap" was going to save the Democrats.[5] Issues of "parental leave" and "elder care" were going to save the Democrats. The Hispanic vote would save the Democrats. The "kids issue"—whatever that is—would save the Democrats. Then the abortion issue was going to save the Democrats. An insider would save the Democrats. Or maybe an outsider. Finally, a recession! *That* would save the Democrats.[6]

One thing that would not save the Democrats was the ideology of liberalism itself. Political analyst William Schneider, seeking to reassure the party after Dukakis's defeat, declared "[n]o Democrat is going to win the presidency these days *because* he is a liberal. But with the right campaign, he can win *despite* being a liberal."[7] Yet, even if Democrats do manage to win elections, how much will those victories be worth if they are achieved despite liberalism rather than because of it—if liberalism remains (in Schneider's words) a "problem" that must "be overcome"?[8] Another Democratic presidency as confused as Carter's could cripple liberalism for good.

When liberals have admitted that perhaps they should change their *ideas*—as opposed to changing their tactics or changing the electorate—the results have been less than compelling. The most popular approach attempts to draw a sharp distinction between traditional Democratic ends and the means of achieving them. The "ends" are deemed eternal. The "means" are said to need work. Gary Hart hit upon this formula in his 1984 presidential campaign. Hart had been talking about "new ideas" and the "death of the New Deal" for years. Pressed to define the extent to which he would alter traditional liberalism, he typically responded: "What is changing are not principles, goals, aspirations, or ideals, but methods."[9]

By now this means-ends distinction has been programmed into the word processor of every Democratic speechwriter in the country. On the party's right, the Democratic Leadership Council has abandoned its former bland centrism for an agenda that stresses innovative "means" (educational choice, tenant management, national service) in the service of "enduring values."[10] On the party's left, even candidates who position themselves as defenders of the faith find the formula irresistible. Here is Mario Cuomo, speaking at Yale University in the mid-1980s:

> By saying I don't see the need for a new philosophy—that is for a new set of basic emphases and principles—I'm not implying we shouldn't be looking for new ways to apply our philosophy.... Ultimate objectives and commitments remain the same but their application to changing realities requires flexibility and adaptation ... with new programs and new ideas.[11]

Shortly thereafter, Sen. Edward Kennedy made it unanimous, jumping on the means-ends bandwagon in a speech at Hofstra:

We must offer new ideas.... Our truest commitment is not to time-worn views, but to timeless values which will never wear out.... [W]e must have the daring to try innovations—and the courage to discard them when they fail. For only then can we successfully stand against the Republican strategy of assailing ends as well as means....[12]

The appeal of the means-ends distinction is obvious. It avoids even implicitly condemning traditional Democrats—indeed it compliments them not only for their good intentions but for their "timeless values." Liberals simply failed to find the right tools to implement their noble goals. Or, even more excusable, they failed to adapt the tools that worked in the past to "changing realities" like the emergence of high-tech, the service economy, global trade, or the Information Age.[13]

I think this flattering self-portrait vastly understates the transformation necessary to revive American liberalism. The tip-off is the vague, banal quality of the "ends" that all the innovative new "means" are supposed to implement. Attempting to define his goals and principles, Hart talked about "concern for our families, our fellow citizens, and our fellow human beings; ... excellence, justice, and community."[14] Cuomo listed "compassion and common sense" to "promote new economic growth" and expand "opportunities for women and the disadvantaged."[15] Kennedy cited "shared progress, ... compassion, and equal rights."[16]

How many Americans would quarrel with those platitudes, or with the rest of the traditional rhetoric of liberalism: "fairness," "helping the helpless," "unlocking the doors for the locked out"? But these heart-warming sentiments do not add up to a political *ideology*, because they do not come close to answering the basic question that an ideology must answer—namely, what does it want our society to look like? What are the "locked out" to be let into? What sort of "community" does everyone have "equal rights" in? How will having "compassion" make anything different? What does that word "fairness" mean, anyway? Arthur Schlesinger, Jr., says liberals are liberals because they believe in "affirmative government." Fine. Count me in. But "affirmative government" for what?[17]

The unflattering truth is that American liberalism and the Democratic party have not provided an adequate response to these fairly fundamental questions. That is a failure of liberalism's past as well as its present, a failure in choosing *ends*, not just means—not so much that the ends chosen by liberals have been wrong as that they have remained ambiguous, incoherent, partial, or contradictory.

This book is an attempt to help end that confusion. Its thesis is that the house of liberalism needs more than repainting, remodeling, or even thorough renovation. We need to rip the house down and build it anew on a more secure foundation. The remaining eleven chapters try to begin laying that foundation, and to sketch out what the rest of the structure might look like.

Most of what follows, then, has to do with ideas and policies, not election strategies. My purpose isn't to advise liberals how to regain power or how to retain power. Rather, my initial working assumption is this: if liberals offer an appealing ideal of American society and a way to attain it, they will win elections, and they'll know what to do once in office. If they don't offer that ideal, it doesn't matter whether they win elections or not.[18]

I believe liberals have such an ideal available to them, an ideal the country badly needs to revive. Something unpleasant has happened in America in recent decades. It's not that the country has gotten poorer. It hasn't. It's not that the poor are poorer now than they were, say, when I was growing up in the 1960s. They aren't.[19] But the significance of money, the *role* of money has changed in ways that conflict with most Americans' image of their country.

We've always had rich and poor. But money is increasingly something that enables the rich, and even the merely prosperous, to live a life apart from the poor. And the rich and semi-rich increasingly seem to *want* to live a life apart, in part because they are increasingly terrified of the poor, in part because they increasingly seem to feel that they deserve such a life, that they are in some sense superior to those with less. An especially precious type of equality—equality not of money but in the way we treat each other and live our lives—seems to be disappearing.

This separation of ⋅ ⋅ica by class is not something today's Republicans are about to address. They are the party of the affluent; class division is not one of their historic concerns. They are also the party of laissez-faire. Overcoming the forces that are making our lives less democratic will take more government than they can stomach. Democrats, in contrast, have the right means—affirmative government—at their disposal. And, in their hearts, I think, they have the right purpose—the right *end*—as well. That is the second, more optimistic, meaning of this book's title.[20] If liberals can uncover their real goal, the real object of their efforts, they can come up with a plausible plan for achieving it. But that will be a very different strategy from the one they now so unsuccessfully pursue.

CHAPTER 2

What Do Liberals Want?

The automatic fulfillment of the American national Promise is to be abandoned, if at all, precisely because the traditional American confidence in individual freedom has resulted in a morally and socially undesirable distribution of wealth.
—Herbert Croly, *The Promise of American Life*, 1909

... as they have in the past, liberals once more favor bringing extremes of wealth, debt, and inequality under control through taxation and regulation.
—Kevin Phillips, *The Politics of Rich and Poor*, 1990

Rep. Morris Udall once described running in the Democratic presidential primaries as "political foreplay in which one must touch all the erogenous zones" of the liberal body politic.[1] Of all these zones, "equality" is probably the most often touched. But this veritable G-spot of liberal rhetoric is rarely defined or defended in public with any precision.

When it is, a common, traditional assumption is that equality has to do with money. It's virtually impossible to read a bit of modern liberal propaganda without coming upon a passage noting dolefully that "three-quarters of the country's total wealth is owned by one-fifth of the people" (that's from the 1976 Democratic platform), or that "the wealthiest 40 percent of families received 67.3 percent of the national income," or that "the proportion of all national income earned by the richest 1 percent of all families went from 8.7 percent in 1977 to 13.2 percent in 1990."[2] The better writers resort to clever metaphors to illustrate the "gross maldistribution" of our economic resources, likening the allocation of wealth to a parade of millions of dwarves followed by a few towering giants or to a banquet at which waiters keep bringing absurd quantities of food to the tables of the rich.[3] The sheer material inequality in these fables is supposed to shock us into agreement.[4]

During the Reagan-Bush years, Democrats found in their aversion to material disparity an especially comfortable base from which to mount easy attacks on the opposition. To condemn the Republicans, in this view, you need only trundle out tables showing that Reagan's tax and budget cuts benefitted the rich and lowered the incomes of the poor. By the early nineties, Democrats were being urged to explicitly rest their politics on opposition to the growth of income inequality during the previous decade. Kevin Phillips wrote his best-selling *The Politics of Rich and Poor* about how rising money inequality created a great opportunity for the party. Robert Reich, a prominent liberal analyst, advised Democrats to tell a "populist" story, in which "we advocate a progressive income tax, reining in Wall Street, and we talk about the wealthy getting wealthier and the poor getting poorer."[5]

Taking the advice, the party's leaders in Congress launched a campaign for "fairness" that keyed off the income-distribution charts. House Ways and Means Chairman Dan Rostenkowski began charging that "the richest 5 percent of the population enjoyed a real increase in their income of 46 percent [since 1977]."[6] Senate Majority Leader George Mitchell talked about the rising income share of the top 20 percent.[7] Democratic presidential candidate Bill Clinton complained of "the biggest imbalance in wealth" since "before the Great Depression." "[T]he rich are getting richer," echoed Clinton's Democratic rival Jerry Brown, adding that "government is there to reduce inequities." Significantly, such "populist" statements were almost invariably described in the press as expressions of the party's true liberal soul.[8]

Thomas Edsall, in his book *The New Politics of Inequality,* even gave a constitutional gloss to this modern consensus: "Inherent in the concept of equality, stressed by the country's founders, is the basic question of income and wealth distribution." Liberal Democrats, Edsall summarized, are the "proponents of redistribution," the stewards of "a fifty-year long tradition of tilting tax legislation toward those in the working and lower middle classes." They also favor "continuing expansion of benefits for those toward the bottom of the income distribution."[9] Or, as economist Robert Kuttner put it, more broadly, liberals want "greater equality than our society now generates"—equality meaning equality of money.[10]

There is an obvious problem facing the liberal pursuit of money equality: capitalism. Capitalism depends on money inequality as the spur to work—if you work more you get paid more. It depends on *vast* inequality as the spur to risk-taking—people will gamble their money on a project because they will get rich if it succeeds.

Capitalism is a *system,* after all; Marx was right about that. By "system" I mean it is a collection of institutions, economic and cultural, that work together. The system of capitalism runs on self-interest, on Adam Smith's argument that the pursuit of individual gain will result in the nation's gain. You cannot expect to change one part of this system without affecting the others, something the Eastern Europeans, Russians, and Chinese are in the process of discovering.

In particular, you cannot decide to keep all the nice parts of capitalism and get rid of all the nasty ones. You cannot have capitalism without "selfishness," or even "greed," because they are what make the system work. You can't have capitalism and material equality, because capitalism is constantly generating extremes of *in*equality as some individuals strike it rich—and then use their success as the basis for still further riches—while others fail and fall on hard times. Even if you are willing to settle for "equality of opportunity," you can't really have it under capitalism unless, as the philosopher Robert Nozick and others have pointed out, you're also prepared to get rid of the family. One of the motives that drives the system, after all, is the idea of giving one's children a better life—but if that is allowed, then the children of capitalism's "winners" start out their lives with an inevitable advantage in resources.[11]

Nor can you have capitalism without giving a large role to fate and luck. The great virtue of the system is that it plants a hundred flowers, a hundred entrepreneurial ideas, and then sees which one blooms in the marketplace. It's impossible to know beforehand which entrepreneur's brainchild will work (if it were, we could junk the system and let a board of experts decide). The heroic literature of commerce is filled with examples of individuals who went broke five times before striking it rich. The difference between those people and the hustler

whose sixth idea also fails (perhaps because a competitor got to it
first) is not quantifiable, and for all practical purposes is a question of
chance rather than "just deserts."[12] It is morally arbitrary. But that's
the system. It's a package deal.

This is not to say we must either pursue the full conservative program of laissez-faire, minimum-government, supply-side economics
or slide into a swamp of socialistic decay. Much of this book will consist of arguments that violate that proposition, which even most conservatives don't seem to really believe. It *is* to say that there are major
limits to the sort of tinkering with capitalism that can be done. We
can't make the system into something that it's not.

American liberals, unfortunately, have had difficulty coming to
terms with this fact of life. All too often they seem to be trying to
have it both ways, to accept the fruits of capitalism while somehow
outlawing its less pleasing aspects. Liberal energy has gone into criticizing those aspects of the free market of which liberals disapprove—
into railing against "greed" or "unconscionable profits" or "malefac-
tors of great wealth"—without equivalent effort at figuring out
whether those things can be changed within the limits imposed by
the system.

At times, faced with those limits, "progressive" liberals revert to a
half-socialist pose familiar to readers of *The Nation* magazine. In this
mode, the writer first chastises the government for the failure of this
or that liberal reform, but then intimates that true reform may be impossible without a "radical restructuring of society" in which the "un-
bridled profit motive" is replaced by "publicly framed investment decisions," in which "human needs" have priority over "greed."[13] Mention of this "restructuring" is typically confined to a crucial paragraph
near the end, so an excessively detailed discussion can be avoided.

Here is how one author danced this dance in 1972:

> [B]illions have already been poured into federal government pro-
> grams—programs like urban renewal, current welfare and aid to edu-
> cation, with meager results....
>   We can no longer rely on old systems of thought, the results of
> which were partially successful programs that were heralded as impor-
> tant social reforms in the past. It is time *now* to rethink and reorder the
> institutions of this country.... We must restructure the social, political
> and economic relationships throughout the entire society in order to
> ensure the equitable distribution of wealth and power.[14]

How tiresome those *Nation* writers are! Cancel my subscription.... Except that the above passage is not from the *Nation,* but from the Democratic Party platform of 1972.

Liberals might perfectly honorably choose to abandon capitalism. Socialism has its virtues, after all, and relative material equality may be one of them. I remember back in college listening to one of my radical teaching fellows, who had just returned from Cuba, describing an almost-finished housing block he had seen there. The apartments were on a hill, he said, with a spectacular view of the ocean on three sides. When finished, they would be occupied not by the rich, but by the ordinary laborers who had built them. He pointed out that this would not happen here in the capitalist United States, where the beautiful ocean views, along with most other desirable goods, go to those who can pay for them. He was right, of course. At least in its democratic forms socialism held out the possibility of a society where fraternity, community, and idealism would play a much larger role than they do now, and what George Orwell called the "grab-motive" would play a much smaller role. But there are consequences attached. The clearest consequence—now blindingly obvious—is that those who choose socialism must be prepared to give up the sort of material prosperity that only capitalist nations seem able to achieve.

The Berlin Wall's fall in 1989 put an end, for the moment, to most of the semi-socialist posturing. But if liberals have finally made their peace with capitalism, it's still true, as Rep. Barney Frank has pointed out, that they came to this acknowledgment reluctantly.[15] What remains is for them to confront the full consequences of their choice of economic systems, especially when it comes to pursuing things capitalism cannot provide, like money equality. True, smart money egalitarians now emphasize the compatibility of their proposed reforms with a market economy. They talk about the positive incentives created by progressive taxes and benefits.[16] They push worker-ownership and profit-sharing arrangements, arguing that if business enterprises distributed risks and responsibilities more democratically they would be more productive *and* generate more equal incomes.[17] But however sensible such reforms may be, they do not escape the reality that, at some point, greater money equality stops paying productive dividends and resumes its war with the natural dynamics of capitalism—a war the money egalitarians can never win.

• • •

No wonder modern liberalism has proved to be a less-than-exhilarating ideology. By telling Americans that "social justice" means material equality, it tells us we are doomed to live in an unjust society. Liberalism might be less depressing if it had a more attainable end—a goal short of money equality. But that's just the sort of end liberals have failed to clearly choose.

Here we encounter the second, more serious problem with the liberal Democratic pursuit of money equality: its incoherence. Liberal rhetoric is filled with the impulse to redistribute income from rich to poor. It's like a nervous tic. But there is no impulse that tells us when the redistribution ought to stop. At what point do egalitarians declare victory? What society do they *want?* My colleague Michael Kinsley declares that "the tax code should mitigate inequalities in income to some extent."[18] Perhaps some Democrats would find that a rousing slogan. But to *what* extent?

Liberals have developed a whole repertoire of rhetorical fudge-phrases to avoid this question: they want to "tilt the balance in favor of ordinary people"; they want "a good deal more equality than what we now have"; they believe "the strong owe a duty to the weak"; they favor—in FDR's early evasion—the "underprivileged" over the "overprivileged."[19] All these phrases leave the exact scope of the liberal enterprise conveniently open-ended. Surely you can't object to a little "tilt," a little help for the weak and underprivileged, a little "more equality"? But when do liberals stop demanding "more" and say "enough"?

That's a far more damaging question than they will admit. The most respected defenders of money equality deny they desire to go all the way, to pursue their goal until everybody makes the same amount and owns the same amount, et cetera.[20] The classic response is that of the great British historian and socialist R. H. Tawney, whose 1938 book *Equality* is often cited reverentially by today's money egalitarians.[21] Tawney ridiculed the idea that equality was to be arrived at "by the most assiduous working of sums in long division," a jibe echoed by contemporary egalitarians such as William Ryan, author of *Blaming the Victim.*[22] Those on the right who attributed such views to egalitarians were, according to Tawney, "bombarding a position which no one occupies." On the contrary, he asserted, "no one thinks it inequitable" that "exceptional responsibilities should be compensated by exceptional rewards, as a recognition of the service performed and an inducement to perform." Such forms of inequality were to be "regarded, not merely with tolerance, but with active approval."[23]

It was enough, Tawney said, that society be going in the right direction, toward greater equality: "What matters to the health of society is the objective towards which its face is set, and to suggest that it is immaterial in which direction it moves, because whatever the direction, the goal must always elude it, is not scientific, but irrational." The right analogy, he suggested, was with "crime and disease," maladies "which the most rigorous precautions cannot wholly overcome."[24]

But surely this is a terrible analogy. Inequality is not like crime and disease. We *want* to abolish crime and disease completely. We just haven't been able to do it. What the Tawneys and Ryans vehemently deny is precisely that they want complete, long-division, even-steven equality. All we want to do, they say, is head in that "direction." But why get in a car and head off in the direction of a place you don't want to reach?

There is something missing in the acceptance of the need for income inequality, on the one hand, and the righteous denunciation of "extremes" of inequality on the other. Why is an income range of "three or four to one" all right, as Ryan argues, while our current inequality is "excessive and intolerable, impossible to justify rationally and plain inhuman"?[25] Once we've failed to draw a line between equality and inequality, between 1 to 1 and 2 to 1, what's the basis for so self-confidently taking a stand at 8 to 1 or even 1,000 to 1?

Why do we care about money inequality anyway? If liberals aren't pursuing equality for its own sake, why *are* they pursuing it? There must be other, hidden desires sublimated within the general liberal urge to equalize incomes. Maybe if we bring those objectives out into the open, they will tell us how much money equality is enough.

In December 1936, George Orwell traveled to Barcelona "with some notion of writing newspaper articles" about the Spanish Civil War. Barcelona was in the control of Republican forces fighting against Franco. More precisely, it was in control of the city's largest political party, the Anarchists. They had carried out a far-reaching social revolution, which Orwell described in several famous passages:

> Waiters and shop-walkers looked you in the face and treated you as an equal. Servile and even ceremonial forms of speech had temporarily

disappeared.... Tipping had been forbidden by law since the time of Primo de Rivera; almost my first experience was receiving a lecture from an hotel manager for trying to tip a lift-boy.... In outward appearance it was a town in which the wealthy classes had practically ceased to exist. Except for a small number of women and foreigners there were no "well-dressed" people at all. Practically everyone wore rough working-class clothes, or blue overalls or some variant of the militia uniform.... Many of the normal motives of civilized life— snobbishness, money-grubbing, fear of the boss, etc.—had simply ceased to exist.... One had breathed the air of equality.[26]

Orwell found this "queer and moving.... [I]n some ways I did not even like it, but I recognized it immediately as a state of affairs worth fighting for."[27] He joined the Republican forces and was wounded at the front. On his return to Barcelona a few months later, he found a "startling" change:

Now things were returning to normal. The smart restaurants and hotels were full of rich people wolfing expensive meals.... Strangers seldom addressed you as *tu* and *camarada* nowadays; it was usually *señor* and *usted*.... The waiters were back in their boiled shirts and shopwalkers were cringing in the familiar manner.[28]

This account of revolutionary Spain, in *Homage to Catalonia*, must by now have supplied several generations of college students with their vision of what "equality" would actually look like. What is so appealing about this vision? Is it the idea of material equality per se? That was certainly what I assumed when I read Orwell in college. "A fat man eating quails while children are begging for bread is a disgusting sight ..." he wrote in another famous passage about Spain.[29] That image has always stuck with me (as it apparently stuck with Orwell) as about as fundamental and irrefutable a statement of egalitarianism as could be.

But if one thinks about these images more closely, their power comes from several distinct factors that have little or nothing to do with material equality as a goal in itself. I invite you to substitute for Orwell's Spain any similar incident or passage that has stuck with you—and see if your reaction doesn't boil down to some combination of these three concerns:

Minimum survival needs. A fat man eating quails while children are begging for bread *is* a disgusting sight. How about "a fat man eating quails while children are eating Bob's Big Boy hamburgers"? Doesn't quite pack the same wallop, does it?—although the amount of money *inequality* represented by the difference in price between a quail dinner and a hamburger may be very substantial. Equality isn't the gut issue here; starvation is—the availability of some basic minimum necessary to allow a person to participate in society. We can argue about what that minimum is. "Not to be able to afford a movie or a glass of beer," Dwight Macdonald argued, "is a kind of starvation—if everybody else can."[30] But it's still a minimum we're talking about.

Class immobility and privilege. Tawney, for one, conceded that "all forms of social organization are hierarchical in the sense that they imply gradations of responsibility and power," adding:

> But these gradations may be based on differences of function and office, may relate only to those aspects of life which are relevant to such differences, and may be compatible with the easy movement of individuals, according to their capacity, from one point on the scale to another. Or they may have their source in differences of birth, or wealth, or social position ... and may correspond to distinctions, not of capacity, but of circumstance and opportunity.[31]

It was the second type of society that got Tawney's goat—a society with class privilege, English style. Inequality of money and authority was one thing. It was another thing when this inequality was cemented into an immobile aristocratic structure, in which the rich went to different schools, spoke a different language, and had a monopoly on the good jobs in the government, banks, and military—in which people born into the lower classes stayed in the lower classes and people born upper class stayed upper class. "Do the English really prefer to be governed by old Etonians?" was a favorite Tawney query. Franklin Roosevelt touched this same anti-aristocratic nerve when he attacked, not rich people, but "economic royalists."[32]

Social equality. On close inspection, this is what Orwell really seems to have valued in revolutionary Spain. Waiters "looked you in the face and treated you as an equal." Servility and fawning disappeared. Money equality wasn't the issue. The waiters may have made less money than Orwell—the point was that they didn't let this affect their view of their own worth, and that judgment was reciprocated by the community. Everyone had equal pride as a citizen, human being, *camarada.*[33]

This sort of equality is apt to be confused with the abstract "equality before the law" enjoyed by citizens of Western democracies. But what Orwell is talking about is clearly something beyond formal legal equality, even beyond the basic freedoms of speech, association, and the ballot box. We can have all those things and still not live in a society in which everyone *feels* he is, at bottom, an equal member. That feeling is a species of equality that is quite substantive, not just procedural or formal. It is no less substantive because it concerns people's attitudes rather than their money.

Of these three goals, social equality turns out to be primary, because it subsumes the other two. Thus, social equality is impossible when some citizens are reduced to begging outside restaurants. The loss of dignity, as well as the loss of nutrients, was surely part of what upset Orwell. Likewise, social equality is probably impossible in a rigid class structure. You can't look somebody in the eye and treat them as an equal if you know you are doomed by circumstance of birth or other class association to an inferior position.

Others might express these "hidden" goals a bit differently—but, however they're expressed, I think they capture 95 percent, if not all, of what most of us really mean in our guts when we invoke the concept of "equality." They also capture the emotional core of the arguments of revered egalitarians like Tawney and Orwell. What is appealing about egalitarians is not really their egalitarianism, at least not their *money*-egalitarianism. The argument for money equality attracts us mainly when it borrows the cloak of these other, less mathematical values—when it promises a society where nobody starves or goes homeless, where everybody can get ahead without bumping up against arbitrary barriers, where nobody has to hang their heads or fawn or toady to anybody else.

CHAPTER 3

Two Strategies of Equality

What really bothers liberals about American society? Is it that William Gates, the 35-year-old founder of a computer software company, is worth four billion dollars and that some people drive new Mercedeses and Acuras while others drive Hyundais and used K-cars? Is it that "the wealthiest 40 percent of families received 67.3 percent of the national income"?[1]

Or is it that Orwell's experience of confronting degraded beggars is now a daily occurrence for Americans who live or work in our major cities? Is it that a whole class of Americans—mainly poor, black Americans—have become more or less totally isolated from the rest of society, and are acquiring the status of a despised foreign presence? Is it that the wealthiest 20 or 30 percent of Americans are "seceding," as Robert Reich puts it, into separate, often self-sufficient suburbs, where they rarely even meet members of non-wealthy classes, except in the latter's role as receptionists or repairmen? And is it the gnawing sense that, in *their* isolation, these richer Americans not only are passing on their advantages to their children, but are coming to think that those advantages are deserved, that they and their children are, at bottom, not just better off but better?

If I'm right, distaste for this second sort of inequality—social inequality—is at the core of liberal discontent. Yet the primacy of this value is only occasionally made explicit in our ordinary political conversations. It is "subliminal" in the sense that it forms the unacknowledged motive of liberal policies that are justified on more familiar rhetorical grounds. Specifically, liberals tell themselves they are for "more equality" of income and wealth when, if they asked themselves, I think they would probably discover they're actually after social equality, or one of the more specific sub-goals it entails.

These subliminal goals, brought into the open, could give the liberal attack on money inequality the clear, self-limiting purpose it otherwise lacks. Without seeking even-steven leveling, liberals might try to reduce inequality in order to assure those on the bottom the minimum necessary to participate in society. Even after that minimum was achieved, liberals could continue to pursue money equality to the extent that it was necessary to avoid the entrenchment of class privilege, or, more generally, the spread of social inequality—feelings of superiority among the rich, the onset of servile behavior among the nonrich. Here are reasons, in short, that might justify drawing a line between 3 to 1 and 800 to 1.

But once we recognize money equality as a *means* to these other, distinct ends, we are allowed to ask whether it is the best means. There is an alternative. Liberals have a choice between two plans, two overall strategies for achieving their real goal.

The first, familiar plan might be called Money Liberalism. It seeks to prevent income differences from corroding social equality by the simple expedient of reducing the income differences—or, more accurately, *suppressing* the income differences continually generated in a capitalist economy. This approach finds support in conventional Democratic politics, with its constant reference to the "disparity between rich and poor," its reflexive invocation of "fairness," its obsession with progression on all questions of taxes and spending, its faith in the healing and unifying power of cash benefits.[2]

The alternative, what I'll call Civic Liberalism, pursues social equality directly, through government action, rather than by manipulating the unequal distribution of income generated in the capitalist marketplace. Instead of trying to suppress inequality of money, this strategy would try to *restrict the sphere of life in which money matters*, and enlarge the sphere in which money *doesn't* matter. Unlike Money Liberalism, this approach avoids ongoing conflict with the requirements of a capitalist economy. It offers the best chance, I'll argue, of restoring the form of equality that liberals, at bottom, care about.[3]

The basic Money Liberal argument is simple and seemingly powerful: "gross disparities" of wealth inevitably strain the bonds of mutual self-respect between rich and poor in a way that lesser disparities don't. "A man with £3 a week and a man with £1,500 a year can feel themselves fellow creatures, which the Duke of Westminster and the sleepers on the Embankment benches cannot." That's Orwell again, arguing for his pet proposal of a 10-to-1 limit on the ratio of the highest to lowest after-tax incomes.[4]

But wait a minute. Orwell means to show that money inequality, by itself, leads to social inequality. Yet, first he admits that even a large (10-to-1) money differential need not undermine feelings of equal dignity. Then, in the comparison he uses to make his case against even greater inequality, he stacks the deck at both ends. The "sleepers on the Embankment," like the homeless of today, tug at our sympathies because they lack certain minimum survival needs. The Duke of Westminster drags in another evil: aristocratic privilege. Orwell apparently felt that a big money differential, in itself, wouldn't produce a convincing enough violation of social equality.

What if the sleepers on the Embankment all found cheap lodging while dukes were forced to compete with commoners in the job market? Would we still need the 10-to-1 limit? Can mere money inequality in itself undermine the dignity of free citizens, even if minimum needs are met and class barriers demolished? That is not such an easy case to make in a country where the relative absence of class distinctions had, long before the emergence of the mass middle class in the 1950s, produced a sense of social equality that was the envy of the world. In 1906, in *Why Is There No Socialism in the United States?*, German economist Werner Sombart offered an archetypal expression of admiration for America's success in this regard:

> In his appearance, in his demeanour, and in the manner of his conversation, the American worker also contrasts strongly with the European one. He carries his head high, walks with a lissom stride, and is as open and cheerful in his expression as any member of the middle class. There is nothing oppressed or submissive about him.[5]

Both Orwell and Tawney, in fact, recognized that they were pleading for money equality to overcome a virulent class snobbery that was peculiarly British.[6] America, Tawney noted, "is marked indeed by much economic inequality; but it is also marked by much social equality."[7]

Social equality, after all, is not a material concept, but a spiritual and (obviously) social one. What matters, ultimately, is not money disparity but what we make of it. We might all be living in Orwell's utopia, with its 10-to-1 income inequality ratio—but if it were a society in which income was considered *the* measure of social worth, the 10s could still lord it over the humiliated 1s. Money egalitarians are fond of pointing out that Japanese companies have much smaller salary differentials than their American counterparts. But in Japan those small differentials are often accompanied by bowing and scraping of the sort Americans would never tolerate. As long as people use money to measure status they will be able to latch onto whatever material gradations survive the redistributionist assault.

Of course, as long as people use money to measure status, it will also make at least some difference how much more of it some people have than others. Money Liberals are hardly crazy to think that "more" income equality would tend to translate into less class division—or (as we'll see in the next chapter) that growing money *in*equality has contributed to greater class division. The point is that money equality isn't the only variable in the equation that determines social equality, and it may not be the crucial variable. More important, perhaps, are those social attitudes and institutions that determine how important money inequality is—how much weight the money variable has.

But if that's true, why spend all our energies trying to twiddle the dial that produces greater or lesser money inequality? An equally promising approach, seemingly, would focus on changing the attitudes and institutions that translate money differences, however large or small, into invidious social differences.

That is the Civic Liberal alternative. Confronted with vast disparities of wealth, it attempts, not to redistribute wealth "progressively," but to circumscribe wealth's power, to prevent money inequality from translating into social inequality. The primary way it does this is through social institutions that create a second, non-economic sphere of life—a public, community sphere—where money doesn't "talk," where the principles of the marketplace (i.e., rich beats poor) are replaced by the principle of equality of citizenship. Just as the pre-1989 Eastern European champions of "civil society" tried to carve out a social space free of Communist domination, so Civic Liberals would carve out a space free of capitalist domination, of domination by wealth.

The foundation of this community sphere in the United States, of course, is the political institution of democracy. There the market-place stops, and the rule is not "one dollar, one vote" but "one citizen, one vote."[8] The same principle applies in other important components of our community life, such as the public schools, libraries, highways, parks and the military draft. Each of these institutions attempts to treat all citizens, rich and poor, with equal dignity. They are especially valuable parts of the public sphere because, in contrast with the rather formal and abstract equality of voting, they require rich and poor to actually rub shoulders with one another as equals. So do many other, less obvious but important institutions such as museums and post offices, even parades and softball leagues.

Now, you can argue that money "talks" in our democracy too, and that it talks even louder these days with the dependence of politicians on rich donors to fund their increasingly expensive campaigns. Meanwhile, the affluent and the poor no longer rub shoulders in the public schools of even small cities, as the middle class flees to its suburban enclaves or else abandons public schools entirely. In bigger cities, the everyday experience of public life in streets, parks, subways, and libraries has been ruined by crime, incivility, and neglect. The draft has been replaced by a volunteer army that the rich can simply avoid.

But these are precisely the sort of things with which Civic Liberalism concerns itself. Instead of worrying about distributing and redistributing income, it worries about rebuilding, preserving, and strengthening community institutions in which income is irrelevant, about preventing their corruption by the forces of the market. It tries to reduce the influence of money in politics, to revive the public schools as a common experience, to restore the draft. And it will search for new institutions that might extend the sphere of egalitarian community life.

Think, for a minute, of the liberating effect of choosing this less familiar alternative. No longer would liberals need to roam the economic countryside as prissy moralists, sniffing at the outcroppings of capitalist excess like parish priests who've discovered teenagers fornicating under a bush. Are some people motivated (shock!) by greed? Are there real estate salesmen who like to drive around in Bentleys? Will the success of new industry X create a whole new crop of moguls who will wear gold Rolexes and eat $200 meals? Well, so what! Let it all hang out! That's capitalism, the material sphere in which money and the things money can buy are made, lost, lusted after, and envied.

We can tolerate that sphere—no, "affirmatively approve" it (in Tawney's phrase) for the way it lets us dream and create—as long as we also maintain a sturdy community sphere that constantly reminds us that capitalist success is morally arbitrary, that the rich are no better than the poor, that we all share common obligations and status as citizens.

The idea at the heart of this strategy was first elaborated (as far as I know) by the contemporary philosopher Michael Walzer, in his book *Spheres of Justice.*[9] There's something proper, Walzer notes, in rewarding success at producing material wealth with material wealth. It's the obverse of "let the punishment fit the crime"—let the reward fit the virtue. "We owe different duties to different qualities," wrote the French philosopher Pascal in a passage Walzer cites. "[L]ove is the proper response to charm, fear to strength, and belief to learning." And money to productivity. Capitalism, as a system, makes us rich, and those who make it work merit riches more than anything else. Riches, that is, but not love, fear, belief, or servility.

Aspects of Walzer's idea can even be found in Tawney, whose writings are so often cited in defense of conventional money-egalitarianism. At one point in *Equality* Tawney writes:

> What is repulsive is not that one man should earn more than others, for where community of environment, and a common education and habit of life, have bred a common tradition of respect and consideration, these details of the counting-house are forgotten or ignored. It is that some classes should be excluded from the heritage of civilization which others enjoy, and that the fact of human fellowship, which is ultimate and profound, should be obscured by economic contrasts, which are trivial and superficial.[10]

In Tawneyan terms, today's Money Liberal Democrats, their Congressional Budget Office distributional charts spread before them, have elevated the "details of the counting-house" into the sine qua non of justice and "fairness." That may or may not make good politics (an issue we'll consider later on), but as a means of achieving social equality it hardly appears a necessary or natural choice. Indeed, in a society where income differences are inevitable, income might even seem a pretty foolish basis on which to try to make everybody feel like an equal.

• • •

In contemplating a struggle for social equality but not money equality, the Civic Liberal strategy makes a distinction that's not far from the center of America's national character, or at least what we like to think of as our national character. Americans are famously tolerant of the rich and protective of their own dreams of becoming rich themselves. This frustrates Money Liberals, the classic modern incident being the reception given George McGovern's 1972 plan to impose a confiscatory tax on inheritances of more than half a million dollars—$1 million for a couple. Senator Ernest Hollings likes to recount his discussion of this proposal with his South Carolina constituents. "What the hell, everybody gets a million, isn't that enough to inherit?" Hollings asks, before gesturing at an imaginary factory gate at which he might be campaigning. "You know those damn poor people comin' out of that mill gate over there bitched about that! They had no *chance* of making a million dollars but they didn't like that."[11] At least Huey Long, in his populist 1934 Share Our Wealth proposal, was shrewd enough to set his upper limit at $5 million—and that in the middle of the Depression, when $5 million was good money.[12]

Yet Americans also tend to react viciously when the rich and famous show signs of thinking that they're superior.[13] Carl Lewis won four gold medals and waved the flag all the way around the L.A. Coliseum track, but he couldn't sell a box of cereal when the American public got the impression he was stuck up. We prefer a millionaire like Bruce Springsteen, who had trouble getting into the "We Are the World" taping in Hollywood because he parked his own car on the street instead of being chauffeured through the studio gates in a limo.

Similarly, an imperious figure like France's Valéry Giscard d'Estaing could never get started in American politics. One of the secrets of Ronald Reagan's popularity was that he, personally, didn't seem to indulge in the money-centered elitism of his business backers, or of his own wife. Even George Bush attempts to project an unpretentious, pork-rind-chewing persona. Much of this is hypocrisy, of course, a show of allegiance to our semi-official social-egalitarian values. But hypocrisy, as they say, is the tribute vice pays to virtue. There *is* a virtue to pay tribute to, a value to build on. Money equality isn't what America is about. Social equality is.

But this only begins to make the case for a "public-sphere" strategy. Civic Liberalism also faces difficulties all its own. The market, after all, is an imperialistic institution. Declare that something can't be bought and the rich will try to find ways to buy it—and the less rich will find ways to sell it to them. Springsteen may ration tickets to his concerts through an egalitarian system of first come, first served, but scalpers will pay homeless people to stand in line, and the tickets will end up being sold to corporate lawyers. It's always difficult in our economy to draw a boundary and say, "Beyond this line, money doesn't count." An egalitarian public sphere, once established, will be under constant attack by the private, money economy.

Nor is it enough, really, to simply carve a public sphere out of a hostile money sphere. The goal is not to have two hermetically sealed areas of life. Rather, the idea is that human relations in all spheres, including the economic, will be the relations of dignified citizens. That is the point of Orwell's story about the waiters—their sense of equality had been carried over into their jobs. The public sphere would have to be big enough to have such a broad democratizing effect. That means Civic Liberalism will require an unfashionably large and somewhat intrusive government. It's an ambitious, even radical strategy—no less ambitious, perhaps, than a money-based approach.

Equally important, the case against Money Liberalism is hardly open and shut. As noted, money differences plainly have at least some effect on the "human fellowship" with which we are concerned. We could conclude, after reviewing the evidence, that this is a very large effect. It could also be true that liberals have a good chance to produce a dramatically different effect by sharply changing the distribution of income in a more-equal direction. If so, Money Liberalism would be a sensible social-egalitarian strategy.

The first test of Money Liberalism, then, is to answer the question: does money inequality necessarily have a large impact on social inequality? The alarming experience of recent decades provides an obvious natural experiment in this regard. There is little doubt that if there were a neat, numerical index of social differences, the way there are neat, numerical indices of money differences, the social inequality index would have gotten worse in recent years. Was this because of greater money inequality? Or were there other, more complicated forces working against social equality?

CHAPTER 4

Who Killed Social Equality?

The photograph shows three figures in a dry meadow. On the right is a tall woman, dressed very elegantly in a set of riding breeches and holding a saddle. She wears full lipstick and smiles like an ex-model who has eaten a few too many designer chocolates. On the left is a white pony with half-closed eyes. In the middle is a girl, about ten years old, with a smug, fat face. The girl is wearing a bowler hat and a large adult-sized mink coat, which is dragging on the straw. The caption, titled "Clotheshorsing Around," reads:

> Wife of award-winning jewelry designer Barry Kieselstein-Cord, CeCe Kieselstein-Cord is quintessentially country. From her early-eighteenth-century house in Millbrook, New York, the tall blonde Texan races out across rolling farmland on her favorite midnight rides. Her hacking gear is the finest—from M. J. Knoud, Madison Avenue—and her three horses, Basil, Bob, and Mo, "are much better dressed than I." Shown here with daughter Elisabeth Anne and the pony, Snowy, CeCe digs her spurs into good causes too: she's this year's honorary chairman for the New York City Ballet's School of American Ballet benefit on December 12.[1]

This is hardly an exceptional page of modern journalism. Repulsive perhaps (note especially the awesome double-reverse modesty of "the horses are much better dressed than I"), but not exceptional—quite the opposite. The month in 1987 when the above item appeared in *Vanity Fair*, I canvassed a few other magazines on my local newsstand. There was *Architectural Digest*, which contained an advertisement for a

$160,000 watch ("Genta—by the master, for the select") and a photo spread on the new St. James's Club in Paris, a refurbished former orphanage that now "draws an international clientele." ("[T]he challenge of having to turn an orphanage into a luxurious club wasn't altogether displeasing," said the designer, Andrée Putnam.)[2] In *Town and Country*, an editorial feature helped busy gift-givers select the ideal wristwatch and date book for Christmas. A cross-section of potential recipients was represented by a series of imagined diary entries, each paired with the correct timepiece. Sample entries: "Confirm 1 1/2 mil. reserve at Sotheby's.... Jackie O. needs rough draft soonest.... Reserve place for Young George, Princeton Class 2006.... Brioni fitting at 2:00...." And, inevitably: "Pick up mallets at Knoud."[3]

As noted earlier, it can't really be denied that in recent years America has become a more divided place in which the affluent and educated are seen not simply as objects for ordinary human envy, but as somehow a group apart—and in which the affluent and educated feel increasingly comfortable proclaiming that distinction ("for the select"). That's not to say we're as riven by class as, say, the English. It is to say that we've lost some of the egalitarian attitude that Englishmen such as Tawney and Orwell admired.

The American 1950s, in particular, now seem—apart from the evil of segregation—to have been a golden age of social equality. The mistake appears to have been assuming that the great egalitarian experience of World War II would continue to be reinforced by the mass prosperity that followed it. Hadn't the GI bill opened up the colleges to farmers' sons? Didn't almost everyone drive cars, watch "Leave It to Beaver," read *Life* and *The Saturday Evening Post?* In 1952, the editor and popular author Frederick Lewis Allen declared:

> What was striking about the social pattern of 1900, as we look back upon it today, was that in most communities it was much cleaner and simpler, the stratifications more generally recognized, and especially that they were generally taken much more seriously than they are today.... The rich man smokes the same sort of cigarettes as the poor man, shaves with the same sort of razor, uses the same sort of telephone, vacuum cleaner, radio and TV set, has the same sort of lighting and heating equipment in his house, and so on indefinitely.... Nor should we overlook the immense influence of mass circulation magazines, the movies, the radio, and television in imposing upon Americans of all in-

come levels the same patterns of emulation: in other words, making
them want to be the same sort of people.... In short, the social distance
between the extremes of American society is shrinking.[4]

What was striking about the American 1980s, in contrast, was not
that people with money affected superiority. People with money will
eventually make that attempt. The question is whether these affectations are rejected or affirmed by the larger society. In the eighties,
they were increasingly affirmed. The well-publicized airs of the ultra-
rich are only a small part of this story; Donald Trump, to pick an obvious example, was such a crude, arrogant money-snob he became a
national joke. But for every Trump there were a thousand CeCe
Kieselstein-Cords who *weren't* (and still aren't) regarded as jokes by a
vast segment of the American upper middle class. That's why, in the
mid-eighties, you could walk down to the newsstand and find racks
and racks of *Vanity Fair*–style magazines filled with fawning articles
about the merely wealthy, in which quintessentially country eigh-
teenth-century houses become the objects of subtle, degrading lust. I
say "degrading" because it's not rich people who buy these magazines,
not just people who can afford $160,000 watches (get serious). The
average *Vanity Fair* reader has an income of $46,000.[5] These are peo-
ple who once might have read *Life* and gotten thrills from the delivery
of their first color TV, who were supposed to be immune to snobbery
because they shaved with the same razors as grocery clerks. Now they
apparently need to know where to buy the finest in hacking gear.

Even this tendency of ordinary well-off Americans to look "up" the
social scale for their role models might not be so destructive were it
not accompanied by a tendency to look "down" with contempt. For
every thousand CeCe Kieselstein-Cords, for example, there are probably a hundred thousand classified ads searching for roommates or tenants or lovers and limiting the search to "professionals." No janitors
or drill press operators need apply. For social equality, the routine acceptance of "professionals" as a class apart is far more dangerous than
Trump or Robin Leach. The implication, of course, is that professionals are not just richer, but more civilized, better educated, wittier,
smarter, cleaner, prettier. A series of ads commissioned by *US* magazine in the late eighties to publicize the good taste of its young-pro-
fessional readership captured instead their smug contempt for the demographically inferior. "Definitely Not *US*," was the theme of the

ads, which (as described by journalist Jason DeParle) "display members of the *lumpenmiddleclass* in the most unflattering poses." These non-*US* readers "sit around the RV park ... wearing T-shirts and housecoats, looking dumb and vaguely menacing; a box of Ritz crackers is open on the table."[6] So much for Allen's common "patterns of emulation." It's hard to imagine the old *Life* basing an ad campaign on sneering at Americans who eat Ritz crackers.

Why did this happen? Why was the eighties zeitgeist less egalitarian than previous -geists? Who killed social equality? It's an interesting mystery, with several possible solutions. Money Liberals have their favorite plot line (not surprisingly, money is involved). Civic Liberals would tend to finger a second culprit. But there is at least one other suspect worth questioning. Perhaps, as in one of those annoying Agatha Christie novels in which "everybody did it," more than a single factor is at work. Still, identifying these factors will give us a picture of what determines whether our society has the democratic quality liberals prize—and what both the Money and Civic Liberal strategies are up against. Bring on the accused:

Suspect #1—Money Inequality

This is the favored villain of Money Liberals. Social relations became more inegalitarian, the argument goes, because the underlying distribution of income has become more inegalitarian—the heart of Money Liberalism being the belief that money differences almost automatically translate into social inequalities. Mark Kelman summarized the basic argument in a 1973 *Dissent* article: "Deferential behavior, and an associated dehumanization and loss of self-esteem, clearly arises from discrepancies in economic position rather than from a lack of goods or from poverty."[7]

Another familiar way of putting the argument is to blame social inequality on the "shrinking of the middle class."[8] It was America's "vast" middle class that followed the Cleavers and bought Chevrolets and read *Life* in the fifties. But now the middle class has split up, we're told, and Americans are bunching at the polar ends of the income scale. Wal-Mart and K-Mart serve the Ritz-eaters; Bloomingdale's and Nordstrom, the affluent. Stores like Sears, which once made money serving those in the middle, are finding fewer customers. In 1984, Walter Mondale told the Democratic convention that America's "middle class is standing on a trap door.... [T]he help wanted ads are full of listings for executives, and for dishwashers—but not much in between." It doesn't matter to this argument whether there are more people at the rich end or more at the poor end; it's the contrast between them that's important.[9]

Income inequality *has* been growing. The Congressional Budget Office's data is quite convincing on this score. In 1989, for example, Roberton Williams of the CBO, along with Wendell Primus of the House Ways and Means Committee, looked at Census Bureau data for 1973, 1979, and 1987, all peak years in the business cycle. The result was not shocking, but it was unambiguous. Between 1973 and 1987, the bottom fifth of the population saw its share of national income steadily drop from 5.6 to 4.3 percent. The next-to-bottom fifth's portion fell from 11.9 to 10.7 percent. The middle fifth also lost income share. Meanwhile, the share of the top two-fifths grew, with the top fifth's share moving up from 41.4 to 43.9 percent.[10] That's not even counting capital gains, a key source of wealth for the top tier during the stock market and real estate booms of the eighties. Subsequent surveys, which include realized capital gains, paint a more inegalitarian picture, with the share of the top ten percent alone jumping from 30.7 percent in 1977 to 36.5 percent in 1990.[11]

Not only are the rich getting relatively richer, but there are relatively fewer Americans clustered in the middle of the income distribution. Some studies show that more people left the middle because they joined the affluent than because their incomes went down.[12] Some studies show that more Americans went down than up.[13] Either way, it's inequality. How much did the middle shrink? In one Bureau of Labor Statistics survey, the "middle" was defined as between 68 and 190 percent of the median income ($20,000 to $55,999 in 1986 dollars). In 1969, about 60 percent of American families fell in this range; the percentage in the middle shrank steadily to 53 percent in 1986.[14]

Several things immediately need to be said about the money-inegalitarian trend. First, it began around 1970, so it's hard to blame on Ronald Reagan (who didn't become president until 1981). It's especially hard to blame on Reagan's tax cuts, since the data measure income *before* taxes. Second, the trend does not merely reflect the growth of the impoverished "underclass." Married couples with children are rarely underclass families, yet their incomes show a bipolar trend too. Most dramatically, money inequality appears to have grown among full-time workers.[15] Finally, the trend doesn't mean America is "on the verge of losing its middle class."[16] Most families are still in the $20,000 to $56,000 range. More *new* full-time jobs are still being added to the middle than to either extreme.[17] The "bell curve" of income is safely bell-shaped. But it's a flatter bell, with more people close to the edges.

The debate now is not over whether money inequality is increasing but why.[18] On the left, Barry Bluestone and Bennett Harrison, along with Robert Kuttner, advance their "bad jobs" thesis—the idea that the array of jobs offered by American capitalism has changed, with more jobs being low-wage and part-time.[19] The charge, however, can't be that too many jobs are now un*skilled*. As Kuttner notes, there is little skilled labor involved in traditional assembly-line auto production, yet auto jobs are exactly the sort of "good jobs" whose loss "bad jobs" theorists lament. The virtue of auto jobs is that they are low skilled but relatively high *paying*. Now, such jobs are scarce; low-skilled jobs tend uniformly to be *low* paying.[20]

Seen from this angle, the "bad jobs" idea is just a left-wing way of lamenting a trend economists of various ideologies acknowledge: the growing gap in pay between skilled and unskilled labor. For decades after World War II, guidance counselors told high-schoolers that without a college education they'd be sunk, and for decades the guidance counselors were wrong. In the sixties and early seventies, economist Frank Levy points out, the economic advantage of a college degree actually diminished. In 1973, 30-year-old men with four years of college made, on average, just 15 percent more than 30-year-old men who only had high-school degrees. But then the advantage of the college-educated grew rapidly until, by 1986, the gap in earnings had widened to 49 percent.[21] The world the guidance counselors warned us about has finally arrived. The ability of the skilled and educated to make relatively more money is one major source of inequality.

A second oft-cited source is demographic: the flood of relatively inexperienced "baby-boomers" into the labor market. Because young workers are typically in their low-earning years, the advent of the boomers produced a natural bulge (a "pig in the python") at the lower end of the wage scale. Worse, as these boomers competed with each other for entry-level work, they bid down entry-level wages—a phenomenon called "crowding."[22] Between 1973 and 1987, the real median incomes of full-time younger workers fell, while the incomes of older workers rose. Unskilled younger workers took an especially big hit.[23]

The demographic explanation is supposed to be reassuring, on the theory that income differences caused by the baby boom will cure themselves over time.[24] As boomers age and earn more, for example, the "pig" should slide into the middle of the income python. The effect of "crowding" should also dissipate as boomers compete up and down the income scale, not just at the lower end. The only problem with this reassuring scenario, as Gary Burtless of the Brookings Institution notes, is that it isn't happening. Boomers started hitting their mid-thirties in 1980. Age-wise, the pig is already near the middle of the python. If the maturing of the boom was going to reverse the trend toward inequality, that "should have begun happening at the beginning of the 80s," he says. Instead, "you actually see acceleration [of the trend toward inequality].... All the gaps have gone up."[25]

Several other factors are probably contributing to money inequality. One is the trend toward two-earners. Most families (about 60 percent) now get by on two incomes.[26] Those stuck with only one—unmarried mothers, divorced mothers, families with a disabled parent, families in which one parent must stay at home—are going to do relatively worse. To some extent, the new great divide is between the life one income can buy and the life two incomes can buy.

A second factor is the ominous trend known in the demographic business as "assortative mating." This is a fancy term for marrying someone in your own income class. Take two single men, one a lawyer making $60,000 and the other a clerk making $20,000. Suppose they both marry working women. If they choose their mates at random it probably won't increase the gap between their two double-earner families. That is because the vast majority of women work in jobs of modest pay.[27] If each of our two men marries a $20,000-per-year worker, their family incomes will be $80,000 and $40,000, respectively. But what if the $60,000 lawyer marries another $60,000 lawyer, and the $20,000 clerk marries a $20,000 clerk? Then the difference between their incomes suddenly becomes the difference between $120,00 and $40,000—and the $120,000 couple really leaves a $20,000 single-earner family in the dust. Although the trend is still masked in the income statistics by the low average wages of women, it's obvious to practically everyone, even the experts, that something like this is in fact happening. Male lawyers and executives used to marry their secretaries. Doctors used to marry nurses. Now, as Barbara Ehrenreich notes, a law partner would be faintly embarrassed to fool around with anyone lower than a junior associate.[28]

Third, there are trends that might affect the distribution of *wealth,* people's accumulated assets, more than the distribution of income. Less information is available about wealth, but we know it tends to be distributed much more unequally than income. It has undoubtedly become even more unevenly distributed, due in large part to that great disequalizer of the seventies and eighties, the real estate boom.[29] If you bought your house before, say, 1973, you paid a nice, low fixed mortgage and benefited from the average 121 percent increase in the value of the average home between 1973 and 1980. But someone who waited until 1981 got socked with high mortgage rates and missed the boat on appreciation. Two people might have the same identical incomes, but because of the timing of their home purchases they would wind up with very unequal wealth. This new inequality of wealth is, of course, then passed on from parent to child through inheritance.[30] In effect, the real estate boom (and, to a lesser extent, the stock market boom) created money inequality much the same way a stoplight strings out traffic along a highway. Two cars may be traveling along, one behind the other, but if the lead car makes the light and the second one doesn't, the lead car will eventually wind up blocks ahead.[31]

The Money Liberal explanation of social inequality, then, has an initial plausibility. Money inequality was rising at the same time class divisions were growing. Suspect #1 was present at the scene of the crime. And, again, when money inequality increases it must mean something in a society that pays as much attention to money as ours does. (Of course, if we paid less attention ...) But it doesn't necessarily follow—and if it does follow, it doesn't follow in any simple way—that the increase in money inequality *caused* the increase in social inequality.

A bit of perspective is in order. It's true that income inequality, as Democrats frequently point out, is at its highest level since World War II. Still, Levy notes, "the most obvious feature of the postwar family income distribution was its stability."[32] At the beginning of

the eighties, James Tobin, the Nobel prize–winning economist, justified "inequality-mitigating policies" with the complaint that inequality hadn't fallen very far "in the last thirty to thirty-five years."[33]
Well, if it hadn't fallen very far since World War II, then it didn't rise
very far to get back to the level of World War II. And if we're only
now back to where we were in the forties, that means the level of inequality in the middle of the inegalitarian eighties had only gotten
back to about the level of the 1950s and early 1960s.[34] But the latter
weren't bad years for social equality. They're the "Wonder Years" we
now look back on nostalgically.

Obviously, there can't be any mechanical, linear relationship between the level of money equality and social equality. Money Liberals
will have to argue that the *trend* of money equality is what counts. If
money is getting less equal, maybe people somehow feel less equal
and treat each other less equally, even if the trend is starting from a
base of relative equality.[35] That's the rough outline of one theory presented in Barbara Ehrenreich's book *Fear of Falling*. But Ehrenreich,
to her credit, doesn't stop there. She tries to figure out why a money-
inegalitarian trend would have this insidious effect.

It turns out to be more complicated than you might think. A crude
theory would be that the rich, having more and more money, simply
start to show it off. Faced with CeCe Kieselstein-Cord's well-dressed
horses, average Americans just begin to feel increasingly inferior. The
trouble with this theory, Ehrenreich realizes, is that the Kieselstein-
Cords don't control American culture. The middle class—or rather
what Ehrenreich calls the "professional" middle class—controls
American culture. Kieselstein-Cord isn't in *Vanity Fair* because she
wants to be in *Vanity Fair* and has paid good money for it. She is in
Vanity Fair because *Vanity Fair*'s readers want her to be in *Vanity Fair*
and will pay good money for it. What about the middle class during
the eighties caused it to react to the ostentation of the wealthy not
with contempt but with fascination, respect, envy, and pathetic attempts at imitation? ("At last, chewing gum for the rich" was one
mid-eighties ad campaign.)

Ehrenreich's basic answer is that in the eighties rising money inequality made the middle class more anxious. "The extremes of
wealth and poverty moved further apart, and, as if stretched beyond
the limit of safety, the ground in the middle began to tremble and
crack," she writes. Even those who didn't lose ground were worried

they might fall. Anxiety, in this equation, breeds a hypertrophied status consciousness, in which Americans try to reassure themselves of their position by acquiring and consuming in ways that validate their superiority, usually by buying things that attest to their good taste. ("I have a Cuisinart, so I'm OK.")[36]

Ehrenreich's theory resonates. Nobody who has read an issue of *New York* magazine or *Esquire*—instruction manuals for status-anxious middle-class snobs—can doubt that something like this is at work. The problem is that once you accept "middle-class anxiety" as the engine of social inequality, you open the door to a whole slew of other reasons why that anxiety might increase, reasons that have nothing to do with money equality.

Take a look, for example, at Figure 4.1, which shows the U.S. family income distribution (adjusted for inflation) for the years 1947, 1973, and 1984. Note that the income curve isn't quite an exact "bell" curve. It's asymmetrical, with a tail of rich people drifting off to the right. As the economy grows (between 1947 and 1973, for example) and more people make more money, the whole curve shifts down and to the right, with the tail of richer people growing much fatter and the "spike" of average earners spreading out into a more modest hump.

So, looking at this chart, which curve would you predict would produce more social inequality? You might say 1973. In 1947, after all, most families were in the big cluster making about $12,000. They enjoyed the safety and security of numbers, and there were relatively few $50,000 families to sneer down at them. The $12,000 families were so numerous that they might have been able to dominate national culture (Ritz crackers, *Life*).[37] By 1973, in contrast, there were quite a few $50,000 families for the remaining $12,000 families to look up to. Enough, perhaps, for anxious $12,000 to $20,000 households to wonder why they weren't in the $50,000 bracket; enough for the $50,000 families to achieve a sort of "critical mass" of self-consciousness; enough for marketers to develop specialized products to sell to them, so that if you watched TV and read the papers and visited the malls it began to seem as if making $50,000 was somehow a prerequisite for a comfortable life.

But by all of the economists' standard measures—the measures cited by today's Money Liberal Democrats, and a few paragraphs ago by me—the 1973 curve is *more* "equal" than the 1947 curve. In 1947, there were a few very rich people and a lot of pretty poor people. Be-

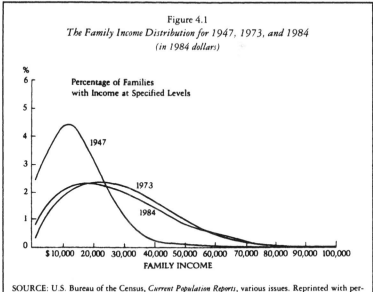

Figure 4.1
The Family Income Distribution for 1947, 1973, and 1984
(in 1984 dollars)

SOURCE: U.S. Bureau of the Census, *Current Population Reports*, various issues. Reprinted with permission from Frank Levy, *Dollars and Dreams: The Changing American Income Distribution* (New York: Russell Sage Foundation, 1987), 19.

cause the vast majority of people were near the bottom, those in the middle and bottom of the population didn't take home much of the total national income; the rich took home a large share. But by 1973, after 24 years of growth, so many people had become, not rich, but reasonably prosperous, that they took home proportionately more of the national income; the rich, proportionately less. The year of 1973 is in fact near the peak of modern money equality.[38] The rise in post-war equality, again, wasn't that big, and it isn't immediately obvious just looking at the two curves. But that's the point. The money egalitarians' measures of inequality don't capture the major change reflected by this chart.

What the chart shows, rather, is that between 1947 and 1973 economic growth itself, quite apart from any increase or decrease in inequality, created a spreading-out effect in which "the extremes of wealth and poverty moved further apart." And this "growth effect" might, all by itself, produce class division—and Ehrenreich's middle-class anxiety—as those near the center of the curve see more and more people who are a lot richer than them. Yet, according to the Money

Liberal explanation of social equality, the obvious, gross difference between the 1947 and 1973 curves didn't matter—but the almost imperceptible shift in shape from 1973 to 1984 (which reflects greater money inequality) made all the difference in the world![39]

There were plenty of other potential sources of anxiety, according to Ehrenreich. In the fifties, she says, the middle class feared that too much affluence would make it go soft. In the seventies the middle class feared it wasn't getting affluent enough. During the turmoil of the sixties, the middle class worried about losing its values (those hippies had no respect). When the turmoil of the sixties stopped, the middle class worried about losing its values (those stockbrokers were so materialistic). "The anxious middle class was obsessed with not only how much they ate but also what they ate," Ehrenreich reports. Indeed, it's hard to think of something that *didn't* make the middle class anxious. Even the brief "voluntary simplicity" movement of the early seventies, Ehrenreich notes, led to middle-class snobbery—revulsion against tacky working-class types who bought ornate furniture and drove flashy gas-guzzlers.[40]

At bottom, Ehrenreich argues, the middle class is anxious because its success is based on skill and knowledge (or "at least on credentials imputing skill and knowledge"), a form of capital that is dangerously insecure because it "must be renewed in each individual through fresh effort and commitment."[41] That's a good explanation too, but it also has nothing to do with money inequality. Instead, Ehrenreich is close to joining commentators such as Nicholas Lemann and George Gilder in noting that any mobile capitalist society will produce status anxiety, because one's "place" is uncertain and subject to change.[42] In short, given what can only be called the status-anxious predisposition of the middle class, pinning the blame for social inequality on changes in the income distribution seems a bit like blaming the ticking clock that keeps awake an insomniac.[43]

Early in her book, in fact, Ehrenreich points to a particular moment in American politics that suggests money inequality may not have had much to do with rising social inequality after all. The moment (and it came as a revelation at the time) was when the presidential campaign of Alabama Gov. George Wallace began to catch on in the North. Ehrenreich cites a study showing that blue-collar Wallace supporters in Indiana most vehemently resented, not blacks, but the white-collar, professional middle class. Or, as Wallace delicately put it, "the over-educated ivory-tower folks with pointed heads looking down their noses at us."[44] Here was the social gulf, in all its yawning splendor, as seen from the bottom. But the year was 1968. Long before the "growing gap between rich and poor," over a decade before the "regressive" Reagan years, fifteen years before Gordon Gekko and yuppies and personal trainers. The trend for decades had been one of growing money *equality.*[45] Suspect #1 was nowhere to be seen. Yet *something* was dividing Americans; something had destroyed the vaunted "classlessness" of the 1950s. What? Perhaps it's time to question the other suspects.

Suspect #2—Meritocracy

Maybe something in the ordinary workings of the economy was producing social inequality even when incomes were growing more equal.[46] This villain would be a change in *how* people attain affluence, not how *many* are affluent or how affluent they are. Specifically, the advent of "meritocratic" criteria for advancement may have altered the very meaning of success in a way that encourages invidious distinctions between the successful and unsuccessful. Here is a factor both the Money and Civic Liberal strategies will have to contend with.

Most obviously, if education and training are increasingly necessary to get ahead, as they apparently are, that fact in itself could produce social inequality even if it were not accompanied by greater income inequality. It's one thing to have an unequal distribution of income. It's another to have that same distribution of income rigorously based on schooling and skills. In the latter situation, those with more money will be able to claim not just that they have more money, but that they have something else, knowledge, that makes them more valuable. The pay-for-skills trend lends all income differences, small or large, a nasty meritocratic bite.

Worse, the *range* of skills valued by the economy seems to be shrinking, with physical talents worth less and brain-skills worth more. This is an old worry; the presumption has usually been that technology would be the culprit. Kurt Vonnegut's 1952 novel *Player Piano* depicts the relevant dystopia, in which automatically controlled machines have reduced the bulk of the population to a state of uselessness. A cadre of skilled managers and engineers (living in separate, elite suburbs) remains necessary to rejigger the machines, while the masses are kept busy staging ceremonial parades or filling potholes.[47] Fear of this sort of "automation" fueled a respectable labor-economics debate when, during World War II, it looked as if the arsenal of democracy could run with much of its work force absent. But after the war, machines didn't put people out of work. Most economists stopped worrying.

Where technology failed, however, free trade may be succeeding. Robert Reich (among others) argues that global economic competition is creating a milder form of Vonnegut's anti-paradise in the U.S.[48] Unskilled physical labor is still technically necessary. But international trade increasingly enables it to be performed anywhere in the world. These days it can be done most cheaply in Asia or Mexico; soon it may be done in Africa or India or Eastern Europe. For an American auto worker, a strong back was once a valuable attribute. Increasingly, it's not, as "routine production" jobs (Reich's term) move overseas. Meanwhile, American brainworkers—"symbolic analysts," Reich calls them—are still competitive. They include the usual suspects: "lawyers, investment bankers, commercial bankers, management consultants, research scientists, academics, public-relations executives ... architects, writers and editors, musicians, and television and film producers." When it comes to "the manipulation of information," America is still number one, at least for the moment.[49]

What becomes of American production workers, if they lack the necessary skills to become "symbolic analysts"? They are forced to compete for the remaining non-intellectual jobs that can't be shipped overseas because they involve personal services that have to be performed locally. They work as store clerks, restaurant workers, nurses, cabdrivers, custodians, and security guards. Unfortunately, these service workers don't get paid very well, in part because they are now competing against all the people who would otherwise be production workers.

On one level, Reich's trade scenario is simply a good explanation for the rising relative pay of those with skills, one of the basic causes of growing American income inequality. But it also adds a threat to social equality that is not easily neutralized: the permanent prospect of an economy in which good jobs are available only to those with good brains.[50]

Surely an intuitive fear of the Reichian scenario underlay the press's fascination, in the early eighties, with the poignant stories of auto workers who had been laid off and were unable to find other jobs. It's why the 1989 film *Roger & Me* struck a nerve by contrasting unemployed GM assemblers with partying yuppies. The point was not just that the autoworkers were hard up. It wasn't even that they were at the bottom of a growing income divide. The suggestion was that what they had to offer may simply not be needed anymore, that the only talents that count now are mind-talents.[51] Yuppies, with their unpronounceable cheeses, foreign films, and other complicated tastes, weren't resented merely because they had money.[52] The problem, as journalist James Fallows argues, was that their "money came from 'intelligent' professional work, by people who'd done well in school."[53]

This social-inegalitarian threat, too, is quite independent of the trend in money inequality. Suppose Americans react to the premium paid for brain-skills by going out and developing them, by getting more education and training. If millions of unskilled, low-paid Americans do that, many economists argue, it could replenish the middle class, producing a more equal income distribution.[54] Whether this hoped-for money equality would actually materialize is a question that will be considered in the next chapter. But even if it did, it wouldn't alter the unpleasant implications of the Reich scenario. The millions who succeeded in the new brain-based order would still be tempted to think not just that they had more money than those who remained poor, or even that they had more "skills," but that they were smarter.

Three factors compound this divisive tendency. By far the most significant, historically, is the peculiar mechanism America has come to use to select who gets what sort of training. Fallows calls the system Confucianism, but a better name might be Phony Meritocracy. It attempts to identify in each of us the mysterious presence of "merit," most obviously through the dubious offices of the Educational Testing Service, the organization that administers the Scholastic Aptitude Test. Those thus selected—on the basis of *predicted* success in life—acquire generalized college training and perhaps a professional degree. Only after being sorted on the basis of potential and then anointed with one or two degrees do the "meritorious" actually confront "the real world."[55]

In this familiar system, college and graduate-school admissions (based in large part on test scores) are the crucial, nail-biting "meritocratic moment" at which the fate of much of the American middle class is determined. "Face it, one exam can change your whole future," as the ads for Stanley H. Kaplan's SAT cram courses subtly put it. Will it be Yale or Towson State? In theory, it's possible to be a bum from Yale or a doctor from Towson. But of course the whole point of our "meritocracy" is to make this difficult, by channeling those with higher "aptitude" into the higher occupations while avoiding the waste of scarce educational resources on those better suited for the lower ranks.

There are a number of reasons why this system is especially noxious to social egalitarians. It selects and labels individuals on the basis of traits that are tested and recorded at an early age. Scores on SATs appear to be used by college gatekeepers as rough proxies for a whole host of desirable attributes. In this context, who can blame people for treating the tests as if they measure, not what cynics say they measure (how well you do on tests), or what they're supposed to measure (how well you'll perform in college), but something more, something closer to innate personal worth—Merit! [56] Nobody believes this more deeply and guiltily than those who score well on the tests and then learn to scoff at their significance. These invidious effects are enhanced when "merit" is measured on a single scale—one reason egalitarians of various stripes have spent so much energy debunking the idea that IQ or "scholastic aptitude" is a unitary "thing" like height or weight.[57] Measuring people for all their various narrow abilities would be cumbersome. It might be difficult to tell at a glance who was superior. Our "meritocracy" makes it easy.

The test-driven, credential-bound idea of "merit" is not just the snobbery of the well-educated. If it were, it would be relatively harmless. As Ehrenreich observes, educational credentials have always been a way the American upper middle class has distinguished itself not just from the poor but more importantly from the rich.[58] "Confucianism" means something more. It means the marriage of the education sphere and the money sphere. It seeks a world, not where those with credentials can look down on those with money, but where those with credentials *are* those with money.

To all this, Fallows says we must add another, more controversial fact: the "ability" measured by the tests (he charges) is intergenerationally transmitted.[59] Fallows isn't clear on what the mechanism of inheritance is. Is it cultural (reflecting different home environments and upper-class bias on the tests)? Or is it genetic? Either way, "merit"—originally conceived as a way to break the grip of class on college admissions—becomes the basis for a new, more durable class system, in which success is passed on from generation to generation, English style. This was the wound probed by George Wallace with his 1968 attacks on "over-educated ivory-tower folks with pointed heads." Wallace's crusade may have predated the playing out of the Reich scenario, just as it predated the rise in income inequality. But the Educational Testing Service and its meritocratic machinery had been at work for decades.[60]

Of course, if all the tests and credentials really do measure how much people will contribute to society, social egalitarians might have to live with them. Fallows's argument is that we don't: the traits all the tests and graduate degrees measure are largely irrelevant to actual performance in the jobs to which they assign people. Today's meritocracy is phony, first, when it measures theoretical potential, "ability," rather than "competence," which Fallows defines as "what you can actually do today." People who get good grades in college probably have the potential, on average, to become better doctors and lawyers than those who get mediocre grades. But there's a lot that goes into being a good doctor or a good lawyer that can only be tested on the job.[61]

Second, the current system attempts to come up with a general ranking ("yes, you're smart enough to be a doctor and treat anything") when a multiplicity of narrower judgments would give a more accurate picture ("you're dextrous enough to set broken bones," or "you're good at diagnosing diseases"). Finally, even this too-broad evaluation typically stops once someone enters a profession—the precise moment when evaluation becomes most practical. Out of 615,000 American doctors, for example, only 456 lost their licenses in 1990.[62]

Fallows doesn't propose to get rid of evaluations and let anyone who wants call himself a doctor or air traffic controller, et cetera. He isn't anti-merit. On the contrary, he seeks to replace irrelevant judgments with relevant judgments, to supplant Phony Meritocracy with True Meritocracy. He has two models here. One is apprenticeship, where individuals learn skills and move up to progressively more difficult jobs step by step, starting at the bottom. Secretaries, for example, were once apprentices who were expected to move up the chain of executive responsibility as they learned on the job.[63] The second model is sports, where results are too clear-cut for coaches to rely on credentials. Sports, Fallows argues (with some exaggeration), "is the single area of American life in which *performance* matters more than anything else."[64]

A Fallowsian True Meritocracy would replace our current all-purpose, go-anywhere, Eurailpass-style educational credentials with a graduated, open system of more discrete and frequent judgments of a given person's actual performance at a given job.[65] In medicine, for example, sociologist Randall Collins has proposed beginning all medical careers with a position as orderly. These orderlies could then move up the ladder, through various levels of nursing, as they acquired specific competencies and performed well on the job. When necessary, they could go to school to acquire any academic learning necessary to move up to the next level. Eventually, they would qualify as physicians. Nobody would know, in advance, who was going to end up a doctor and whose career would peak at nursing. This idea produces an intense discomfort, I've found, among liberal Ivy League graduates, one sure sign of its revolutionary nature.[66]

The point would not be to avoid judgments, but in each case to make them on the basis most relevant to the job that actually has to be done. Let the doctors be those who actually show skill at diagnosing and healing. Let the lawyers be those who show skill at questioning witnesses. Let the hitters be those who get hits and the pitchers be those who get outs.[67] The neoconservative Irving Kristol likes to talk of the "tyranny of the bell-shaped curve"—the hard truth that human talents are distributed unequally. But there is no single bell curve of "merit." There are many different curves corresponding to the different skills necessary for human progress. The True Meritocratic idea, as Walzer puts it, "is that many bells should ring."[68]

There's little doubt that True Meritocracy would be good for social equality. Nobody would be branded semi-permanently by tests taken early in life. If you didn't rise very far in one profession, you could start from the bottom in another. It would be far more difficult for Americans to impute a permanence to their present place in the academic or economic hierarchy. As for the specific skills rewarded by the economy, they would be harder to confuse with generalized "merit." One woman might succeed as a surgeon because she is good at cutting people open. She is not "better" in any all-round sense than I am. She's just good at cutting people open. Similarly, a man who makes good blintzes would just be a man who makes good blintzes. Something like Fallows's scheme may be what Tawney had in mind when he argued that "gradations" in income might be compatible with social equality because they "may be based on differences of function and office, may relate only to those aspects of life which are relevant to such differences...."[69]

Alas, even a radical True Meritocracy might not be enough to undo the implications of two other long-term changes in the basis of American mobility. Suppose we enacted the Fallows program. We'd have a more freewheeling capitalist society where everyone could take maximum economic advantage of his or her peculiar bundle of discrete skills. Yet skills would exist. The SATs may often measure traits irrelevant to performance on any particular job, but some traits will be relevant to job performance—not generalized "intelligence" perhaps, but specific physical, mental, and moral abilities. These discrete traits—let's call them "relevant factors," or "R-factors" for short—don't have to be the same for each job. They can be "task-specific." But in each case some people would have them and some wouldn't.[70] Some people would find their skills were "specific" to tasks that are worth a lot of money.

One possibility is that some of these discrete traits (the R-factors) would indeed be, at least in part, genetically inherited. In a famous 1971 *Atlantic Monthly* article, Harvard psychologist Richard Herrnstein used this possibility as the basis for the following disturbing syllogism:

1. If differences in mental abilities are inherited, and
2. If success requires those abilities, and
3. If earnings and prestige depend on success,
4. Then social standing (which reflects earnings and prestige) will be based to some extent on inherited differences among people.[71]

There are two strongly held opinions about Herrnstein's thesis. The first is that he is, of course, wrong. The second, privately held by many of the same people who espouse the first view in public, is that he is, of course, right but since nothing good would come from acknowledging that he's right we should act as if he's wrong.[72] The

taboo on confronting his syllogism is easy to maintain because Herrnstein himself is vulnerable to criticism as a defender of IQ tests who
seems to believe not only that they predict who would do best in a
broad range of society's "more consequential" jobs, but that they account for who has those jobs now.[73]

All this gives Herrnstein's enemies a variety of targets to bom-
bard—so many that it's easy to forget, as his turrets and conning tow-
ers are being blown off, that his ship still floats. Quite simply, you
don't have to believe that our current social structure reflects func-
tional wisdom, that rich people are smart, that intelligence can be
measured on a single scale, that IQ tests have predictive value or any
significant meaning at all—or even that "mental abilities" are especially valuable—to recognize the ominous implications of inherited
talent for social equality. All you have to accept is that there are *some*
traits, the R-factors, that are relevant to success in each human endeavor. Again, these traits don't have to be the same for each activity.
They don't have to be intellectual talents, as opposed to physical abilities or habits of personality. You can buy the whole Fallowsian package, but if you concede that these discrete R-factors exist, then Herrnstein has you.

Because whatever the R-factors are, it is likely that they'll be inherited "to some extent" (to invoke Herrnstein's elastic clause).[74] Sure,
discrete, specific talents might not correlate with success and social
standing in the dramatic, straightforward manner that Herrnstein and
others claim unitary "IQ" does. But they'll still be heritable, and at
least *some* R-factors—verbal facility, for example—are likely to be relevant to a wide variety of jobs. It helps to be articulate, whether
you're working at The Gap or teaching Comparative Literature at
Harvard. Even Fallows admits "some people are generally smarter
than others...." Well?[75]

It's obvious why Herrnstein's syllogism, rightly, alarms social egalitarians. To the extent that differences in R-factors are hereditary, there
presumably are limits to meritocratic mobility (what Fallows calls our
"sense of possibility"). We might not be able to discover all these limits early in life (in a True Meritocratic regime, remember, many hundreds of skills would have to be measured), but the limits are there all
the same. The invidious conclusion that more successful people are in
some respects superior people becomes, if not ineluctable, a bit harder
to resist. The nerd down the street is a better computer programmer

than you. True, that's only one skill of many, but you can probably never be as good at it as he is.[76]

Worse, a class system becomes hard to avoid. Sons and daughters of successful people would be genetically more likely to be successful than the sons and daughters of unsuccessful people. That might not be such a problem if people married at random, but unfortunately they don't. They tend to marry in their class. This is the scariest implication of the "assortative mating" trend noted earlier: not that it will amplify income differences (which it will), but that it will amplify genetic differences.[77]

Take Fallows's favorite model, sports. Suppose athletics were all our society really cared about and rewarded. The only way you could get rich was through success in sports. But in keeping with strict Fallowsian principles, society recognized that athletic ability shouldn't be measured and rewarded along a single scale. Instead, each sport or event selected its major leaguers and champions by True Meritocratic methods. As Fallows notes, this wouldn't require much change from current practice. Hundreds of different physical talents (strength, short-distance speed, reach, endurance, quickness, spring, coordination, balance, metabolism, et cetera) would be relevant to hundreds of events. Relief pitchers would indeed need a peculiar mix of "R-factors"; football linemen would need others, bobsledders still others.

Now add in assortative mating—that is, the most successful athletes marry the most successful athletes, the least successful the least successful, and so on. "Success" needn't be in the same sport. A champion figure skater might marry an All-American tackle. But despite that randomizing factor, does anyone doubt that after enough generations of assortative mating, the offspring of the successful athletes would tend to be noticeably more successful than the offspring of the unsuccessful athletes? If that happens with the wide variety of athletic R-factors, why not (to a lesser, but still significant extent) with the admittedly wider variety of R-factors that are relevant to economic success in a modern economy?[78]

Now, I'm not saying the Herrnstein Nightmare of genetically determined classes is even close to being with us. Most obviously, success in America is now determined by (*a*) luck, (*b*) acts of will, and (*c*) social, cultural and environmental influences as well as by inborn talents.[79] Even where R-factors are passed on from generation to generation, the extent to which this is currently genetic, as opposed to cultural, may be low. To pick the most obvious case, the explanation for relatively low black average achievement is surely not genetic but social. A clear goal of social egalitarians is to eliminate these gross environmental differences through civil rights laws, education and training, better nutrition, and the breakup of underclass culture (see Chapters 7 and 8). But even success in these attempts to "equalize" environments won't equalize all the particularized *non*-genetic forces that combine to produce the R-factors. Some fathers and mothers (of all races and classes) will still be domineering, some permissive, some optimistic, some embittered; some will encourage book-reading, some music, some nothing at all. Some families will split up.[80]

Yet these weak spots in Herrnstein's syllogism don't disarm it, for our purposes. We're trying to explain the increase in social inequality. The question is not whether success (and social class) is now primarily passed genetically from generation to generation—I assume it isn't—but whether it's passed genetically from generation to generation *more now than it used to be.* Perversely, recognizing the traditional importance of class and culture is precisely what seems to compel a gloomy answer. Because (and this is Herrnstein's big point) the more we minimize gross environmental differences and eliminate class biases, the less success and failure will be influenced by environment and class, and the more they will be influenced by heredity.[81] Fallows's True Meritocracy, by eliminating some barriers (arbitrary credentials) that now hold back talented Americans, would in this sense be another step in the direction of Herrnstein's syllogism.

It doesn't do any good to respond by pointing, as Fallows does, to the GI bill, to the story of how farm boys who were thought to be incapable of higher learning went to college and did spectacularly well.[82] Neither does it help to cite the success of the Eastern European and Southern European immigrants who early hereditarians worried were polluting our genetic stock. These are wonderful examples of the idiocy of class and race prejudice. They are also examples that seem to confirm Herrnstein's thesis. After all, immigrants and GIs weren't held back by lack of innate ability. They were held back by *anti*-meritocratic social barriers. But now the meritocracy has been busy sucking the best and the brightest out of these pools of previously untapped talent. Who's left on the bottom? Herrnstein suggests, not implausibly, a sort of centrifuge effect. As each new group gets processed by the meritocracy, the most talented tend to rise to the top, the least talented fall to the bottom ("precipitated out of the mass of humanity," he says).[83]

The only reason this isn't obvious, perhaps, is that new groups—Vietnamese, Salvadorans, and other new immigrants, and previously isolated African Americans—keep getting sucked into the system, which keeps egalitarians supplied with heartwarming stories of the talented poor rising to the top. At some point, however, we may run out of new groups to run through the centrifuge. And at that point, the dramatic success stories will slow to a trickle; the ongoing process of genetic stratification will stabilize and clarify.

I don't like this argument, believe me. But I find it hard to deny that something along these lines has been at work, augmenting the trend to social inequality. Even if the actual Hereditary State is a long way off, and even if it will never be reached, social equality might still suffer if everybody thinks it's the direction in which we're headed. Some unspoken intimation of the Herrnstein scenario surely reinforces what Fallows identifies as the vicious core of yuppie pride—not just "I'm smarter than you," but also "My children will be smarter than yours. (So don't expect me to send them to the same school.)"

Finally, even if Herrnstein's scenario doesn't apply, there is a more fundamental difficulty with any Fallowsian attempt to defuse the inegalitarian implications of meritocracy. Call it the Loser Problem. The Loser Problem is the possibility that, in any money hierarchy—even a flexible, impermanent, True Meritocratic money hierarchy—those on the bottom, the losers, will feel they somehow deserve to be on the bottom. The bottom, after all, is where some people will wind up. If they feel therefore inferior, that's likely to be bad for social equality. It's bad whether the degree of money equality is 3 to 1 or 300 to 1. It's bad if the losers fail due to lack of brains or lack of brawn, due to their genes or to their environment. It's bad even if they fail as a result of their own free will—worse, maybe, since then they have nobody to blame.

Indeed, in a True Meritocratic society, with its bouquet of opportunities to demonstrate specific talents, its lack of arbitrary barriers, its constant, continuing judgments about performance, people are likely to feel that the implicit decision rendered by their success in the marketplace is all the more valid. Here we come to a great nasty irony that inflames the Loser Problem, an irony that might be called the Fairness Trap: *The more the economy's implicit judgments are seen as being fair and based on true "merit" (and "equal opportunity"), the more the losers will tend to feel they deserve to lose, the easier it will be to equate economic success with individual worth, and the greater the threat to social equality.* Conversely, the more arbitrary and random the economy's judgments, the more they are perceived as the result of luck or qualities widely recognized as otherwise valueless or trivial, the less likely it is that individuals will ascribe larger significance to economic success or failure, and the less likely it is that money inequality will translate into social inequality.[84]

In 1987, at the height of the "good jobs/bad jobs" debate, *Newsweek* economic columnist Robert Samuelson attempted to make the case that America's "job creation process ... on the whole, has been a success." Yes, many full-time workers were losing their jobs. Of the 5.1 million workers displaced between January 1979 and January 1984, nearly a fifth had taken a pay cut of 20 percent or more. But a third had earnings *gains* of 20 percent or more. More workers had increases than decreases. For the downwardly mobile minority, the suffering was "undeniable," Samuelson argued, but it was the price we paid in a flexible economy for continued prosperity overall.[85]

If all you cared about was overall prosperity, or even money equality, Samuelson's numbers were vaguely reassuring. Most of the displaced workers were holding their own or moving up. But if you cared about social equality, Samuelson's statistics missed the point, because they didn't answer the question of *who* was moving up and *why*. The diverging fortunes of displaced industrial workers might simply reflect the Brownian motion of the market. But they could also reflect invidious meritocratic judgments. Were the fifth who wound up with lower pay penalized because they didn't have the right skills? The right degrees or professional credentials? Were they held back by lack of intellectual talent? *Inherited* talent? Even if two Americans were getting richer for every one American getting poorer, that would still be bad news for social equality if (to pick the worst case) all the Americans getting richer were getting richer because they were smart, and all the Americans getting poorer were failing because they were stupid. For social egalitarians, there was nothing reassuring about Samuelson's statistics at all.

Suspect #3—The Decline of the Public Sphere

There is, however, a final possible explanation for the decline of social equality—the Civic Liberal explanation. The subtle innuendoes of meritocracy may well encourage the translation of increasingly unequal economic fortunes into feelings of superiority or inferiority. But what of the institutions designed to block that translation, the institutions of an egalitarian public sphere? They constitute our immune system against these social toxins. If we've contracted the disease, it could be because the toxins have become more virulent. But it could also be because our immune system has broken down.

Let's briefly look at what has happened to three significant components of our common life: the draft, the schools, and public spaces.

In the summer of 1943, 26-year-old John F. Kennedy was a well-known author, a graduate of Choate and Harvard, and the son of one of the richest men in America. Serving with him on a small PT boat in the South Pacific (as recounted by Robert J. Donovan) were:

- Andrew Kirksey, 25, a high-school dropout who before the war had been working as a refrigeration engineer in Macon, Georgia;
- Leonard Thom, the left tackle on the Ohio State football team of 1939 and 1940;
- Leon Drawdy, 30, a machinist from Chicago;
- Maurice Kowal, 21, son of Polish immigrants, who had been working in a factory that built engines for Victory ships;
- John E. Maguire, 26, from Dobbs Ferry, New York, who had quit his job at Anaconda Wire & Cable;
- George Henry Robertson Ross, 25, another Ivy Leaguer (Princeton, Class of '41);
- Raymond Starkey, 29, a former commercial fisherman who had been working in the oil fields of California;
- Charles "Buck" Harris, 20, from Watertown, outside of Boston, who had taken a job at Hood Rubber after high school;
- Gerard Zinser, 25, a career Navy man from Illinois; during the Depression he had joined the Civilian Conservation Corps;
- Edmund Drewitch, 30, a jazz pianist who had worked as a steel inspector at Jones & Laughlin and attended law school at night;

- Harold Marney, 19, who had finished tenth grade at a trade school and enlisted in the Navy at 17;
- William Johnston, 33, who had driven a trailer for Gulf Oil;
- Patrick MacMahon, 37, a mechanic for the Detroit Street Railway Company.[86]

You get the point. During World War II, Kennedys and other wealthy types served with a broad cross section of ordinary Americans. Part of the reason was that they had little choice. The World War II draft was notably democratic; the need for soldiers overwhelmed any impulse to carve out exemptions for the rich. Between 1941 and 1946, ten million Americans were inducted into the armed forces and six million more volunteered (many, of course, with the knowledge that if they didn't they would be drafted). Student deferments were sharply restricted to those studying engineering, science, or medicine. By war's end, 70 percent of all able-bodied males from age 18 to 38 had served.[87]

Is it just because we won that so many Americans seem to feel that this war, despite all the death and dislocation, provided some of the best years of their lives? I don't think Charles Peters is far off when he suggests that it was World War II itself, and the draft, that as much as anything cemented America's mid-century sense of social equality and consensus (embodied in the "massive middle class" notion).[88]

The draft also provided the social background for the egalitarian fifties.[89] In 1951 Congress passed the Universal Military Training and Service Act, which extended conscription beyond the end of the Korean War. The need for military manpower was relatively low, compared with World War II. But so (thanks to low Depression-era birthrates) was the cohort of draft-age men. The result was that even during the peaceful, Cold War years of the late fifties, young men of all classes could expect to get called. Fully 64 percent of the eligible age group wound up serving. An additional 24 percent were declared unfit. Only 12 percent escaped both the draft or some form of military service.[90] They even drafted Elvis.

Now compare that draft, and Kennedy's World War II experience, with the diary entries of William Broyles, who served as a second lieutenant in Vietnam (and later recounted the experience in his book, *Brothers in Arms*):

I have fifty-eight men. Only twenty have high school diplomas. About ten of them are over twenty-one. Reading through their record books almost made me cry. Over and over they read—address of father: unknown; education: one or two years of high school; occupation: laborer, pecan sheller, gas station attendant, Job Corps. Kids with no place to go. No place but here.[91]

Meanwhile, their more affluent contemporaries, myself included, were doing their best to avoid wartime service, and succeeding.[92] Through undergraduate and graduate-school deferments, including a grotesque "College Qualification Test" (nicknamed "score high or die"), the Johnson administration made sure that the sons of people rich and powerful enough to raise a stink about the war weren't drafted. All told, 57 percent of draft-age men were somehow excused or exempted. Those who went to Southeast Asia, a famous 1971 Harris Poll reported, were seen as "suckers." Gordon Dillow, an Army sergeant in Vietnam and later a newspaper columnist, remembers it this way: "[W]e were losers in the great American pastime: avoiding Vietnam.... By 1971, anybody who was smart or wealthy or educated, and who couldn't manage to beat the draft in one way or another, simply wasn't trying very hard."[93]

No wonder the "suckers" tended to be the less affluent and educated.[94] In the working-class neighborhood of South Boston, of 2,000 draft-age men, 25 died in Vietnam. In contrast, James Fallows surveyed his Harvard Class and found only 2 of 1,200 classmates who had even served in Vietnam. A northern Wisconsin Congressman surveyed one hundred inductees from his district, and not one came from a family with an annual income of over $5,000, Broyles reports.[95]

In 1973, the Vietnam-era draft was replaced with the current All Volunteer Force (AVF). It would be crude to say that this simply legalized the exemption of the rich. The pre-1973 draft forcibly inducted those who couldn't escape it; the AVF doesn't coerce either rich or poor. And it hardly approaches the depravity of the Civil War draft, where the wealthy could literally buy their way out by hiring a substitute or paying a "commutation fee" of $300 (then almost a year's salary for a working man).[96] But the effect of the AVF has been to abandon military service as a class-mixing institution. It's not that the volunteer forces are so "disproportionately" poor—they are mainly lower middle and middle class. It's that they're almost zero-proportionately rich. Of Army recruits in 1988, for example, only 1.6 percent reported that their parents owned houses worth more than $200,000. It's a close call whether today's upper classes are receiving a bigger share of the income distribution than they did during World War II. But there is no doubt that, in the distribution of the risk of defending the nation, their share has shrunk radically.[97]

American public schools were never as successful as the World War II draft at mixing rich and poor. We did achieve universal education (at least for whites) before the English and Europeans. But as Ira Katznelson and Margaret Weir point out in their book *Schooling for All,* common access to schooling isn't the same thing as access to common schooling.[98] Common schools, ideally, are places where children of all incomes actually meet under conditions of equal dignity. They curse the same teachers, play on the same football fields, chase after the same dates for the prom.

In rural areas and smaller cities, American public schools appear to have come pretty close to this Civic Liberal ideal. Charles Peters grew up in Charleston, West Virginia, in the early 1940s:

> Except that it was lily-white, Charleston High was very close to a perfect democracy. All social classes—at least all that there were in Charleston—were represented. A very few of the wealthy sent their children away to private school, but seldom before the eleventh grade. Students were not judged on the basis of social position. Popularity was determined by physical attractiveness, athletic skill, and—unlike those attributes or money or social position, all of which you were born with—by something called "personality," which you could develop on your own.[99]

But big cities have been another story. As Katznelson and Weir point out, urban centers were originally much like small towns: the various classes lived close together because they all had to live near where they worked. Unfortunately, "primary schools for all white children were founded just at the moment when this pattern was beginning to be transformed." This suspicious coincidence of trends occurred in the decades following the Civil War. "Firms grew too large to house their workers. Factories required space to expand. The population grew too rapidly ... transportation technology improved."[100] It became feasible to separate living areas from working areas, to build neighborhoods that were exclusively residential. The rich built houses on what was then the "periphery" of cities—the Upper East Side in New York, Evanston and Highland Park in Chicago. The working class had tenements built for them on the Lower East Side in New York, the West Side in Chicago, the South End in Boston.

Did the rich move out in part to avoid attending schools with the masses? Good question. Either way, because schools were "neighborhood" schools and different classes tended to live in different neighborhoods, different classes tended to wind up at different schools.[101] Yet geographic segregation was never perfect. The typical urban district might incorporate a wealthy neighborhood plus a group of children from "the other side of the tracks." And at least until roughly World War II, the upper middle, middle, and working classes were all in the same school system. They shared the same curriculum, the same budget, the same board of education. They played each other in sports.

Even this attenuated form of cross-class community started to disappear with the suburbanization that followed World War II. The affluent classes now moved outside city boundaries completely, walling themselves off with restrictive zoning, setting up their own, independent school districts. The middle classes, likewise liberated by the auto, moved to their own distinct suburbs. At the end of World War II, Katznelson and Weir note, the majority of Americans who did not live on farms lived in cities—not suburbs. As late as 1960, urban incomes were higher than suburban incomes. Today, almost twice as many people live in suburbs as live in the cities they surround. The median suburban income is approximately $42,000—$10,000 higher than the median urban income.[102]

When it comes to explaining recent social inequality, it's worth noting that even since 1965 there has been a large increase in the percentage of Americans who live in suburbs—from 31 percent in 1970 to 48 percent in 1990. Middle-class blacks, especially, joined the exodus during these years.[103] As affluent taxpayers left, urban tax bases shriveled, which meant there was less money available for central city schools to educate their increasingly intractable student populations, which in turn caused more taxpaying parents to leave. Meanwhile, the percentage of Americans in rural towns, the traditional bastions of educational democracy, has continued to shrink—from 36 percent in 1950 to 30 percent in 1960 to 26 percent in 1980.[104]

The ongoing migration to the suburbs appears to have been accompanied by continuing increases in segregation by income. Paul Jargowsky of the University of Texas at Dallas has constructed a "sorting index" to measure the extent to which households are grouped into isolated neighborhoods by income. For the nation as a whole, Jargowsky's index shows a slight rise between 1970 and 1980. But the rise in the North has been substantial, masked by a decrease of class separation in the racially desegregating South and the West. Similarly, demographers Douglas Massey and Mitchell Eggers found that affluent white families were significantly less likely to live near poor *white* families in New York, Chicago, Miami, Detroit, Philadelphia, and (to a smaller degree) Los Angeles.[105] Keep in mind that these figures are for the seventies; Massey and Jargowsky both expect that when census statistics for the inegalitarian eighties become available they will show a pronounced class-separation trend.

Throughout this period, busing (to achieve racial integration) had the clear effect of accelerating the flight of middle-class whites from urban public schools. It made urban school districts, with their large underclass populations, unacceptable to ambitious parents, since even living in a "good" neighborhood no longer offered assurance of avoiding an underclass presence at your child's school. Simultaneously, because the Supreme Court refused to extend busing beyond municipal boundaries, the suburbs were established as a safe haven. In Boston, busing left a public school system only 21 percent white out of a metropolitan-area school population 87 percent white. Almost 40 percent of the children in the Boston public schools now come from welfare families. In Seattle, public schools have lost a third of their students since busing began in 1978, cutting enrollment to half of what it was in the early seventies. In a city 79 percent white, whites are now only 46 percent of the public school population.[106] In Los Angeles, the number of whites in the public schools dropped by 25 percent between the initial talk of mandatory busing in 1976 and its implementation two years later.[107]

Many middle-class parents, rather than simply moving to the suburbs, have been bailing out of public education entirely. Enrollments in non-Catholic private schools have been increasing at about 8.2 percent a year, a striking trend masked in the statistics by the equally striking decline of Catholic private schools (which were often quite effective at class-mixing). Overall, private schools still enroll only about

12 percent of the nation's elementary and high-school students.[108] But the trend is there.

Public school defenders can argue, in education historian David Labaree's words, that schools "still provide students with an environment that is more democratic [and] less conducive to the reproduction of inequality than any institutional setting they are likely to experience in later life."[109] But that's partly a comment on the demise of the public institutions of later life (such as the draft). Certainly the schools are providing a less democratic experience than they used to.

That's even more true, perhaps, of our parks and public spaces. Ideally, public spaces are important venues for socializing where we trust each other to obey the same rules of civility. Sometimes they still are. But increasingly they aren't. Where citizens do mingle comfortably they are less and less likely to be citizens of different classes.

Many factors contributed to the general decline of public spaces. As Walzer notes, "the process is overdetermined."[110] Television and VCRs allowed in-home entertainment to replace public spectacles. The automobile allowed developers to replace shopping districts, with their inherently public sidewalks, with get-in-buy-get-out shopping strips. Zoning laws often exacerbate the uni-dimensional, dead feeling of public spaces by discouraging a mixture of residential and commercial buildings.[111]

But two familiar, intertwined causes appear dominant: suburbanization, and the greater presence of people who make public spaces unpleasant and dangerous—mainly criminals and the homeless. In many of our major cities, the latter groups have all but ruined the enjoyment of communal facilities for the rest of society. A stroll through a park, at a time or in a neighborhood where there are not hordes of other strollers, has become an act of courage. Public restrooms quickly become centers for drug-dealing or other crimes and are closed down. Landlords remove public phones from building lobbies (because dealers tend to use them). Libraries find their books stolen or vandalized. If they try to keep out foul-smelling vagrants, the ACLU sues them (to protect "alternative lifestyles").[112] In Los Angeles's West Side, public parks have been removing their basketball hoops. It seems that undesirables tended to congregate at off-hours basketball games. Drugs were dealt, neighbors robbed and assaulted. Many of the basketball nets that remain have strange-looking metal locks on them, which are opened only during business hours.

When the public sphere is degraded, people do two things: they move out of town, to ever more exclusive suburbs that keep out strangers with gates and armed security guards if necessary.[113] Or they take refuge in the private sphere. They rent extra videocassettes instead of going to the movies. They join private health clubs instead of using the public pools, parks, and basketball courts. They take their kids to franchised private "pay-per-use" play centers. ("[Public] playgrounds are dirty," the owner of one such franchise explained to *Time* magazine.)[114] They shop at suburban malls that are privately policed to keep out much of urban life. They use private university libraries instead of public libraries. They avoid large public urban celebrations—like the 1983 Diana Ross concert in New York's Central Park or the infamous 1975 "Human Kindness Day" on the Mall in Washington, both of which were accompanied by widespread muggings and assaults.

A vicious cycle begins, similar to the one that undermines the public schools. The less the middle class uses the public spaces, the more they come to be dominated by undesirables, making them even less attractive to the middle class. The affluent become even more reluctant to pay the taxes necessary to cover the (now increasing) costs of keeping the spaces clean, policing them, repairing them. Eventually they are abandoned, or privatized.[115]

Private spaces don't necessarily segregate the classes. As sociologist Ray Oldenburg notes, cheap, casual gathering places—taverns, cafes, coffee shops, and beauty parlors—are often treasured precisely for the refuge they provide from the status rankings of the outside world. But these sorts of private institutions have also been disappearing in the years since World War II, the victims, again, of suburbanization, fear of crime, zoning laws, and the attempt by purveyors of entertainment to precisely target various demographic groups. Oldenburg claims "we've probably lost half of the casual gathering places that existed at midcentury."[116] Today, when different classes do mingle in malls, restaurants, and theaters, it's more likely to be a relationship of busboy to diner or clerk to customer than citizen to citizen.

The deterioration of such class-mixing institutions was, of course, aided and abetted by money inequality, and probably also by the divisive effects of meritocracy. When affluent people have relatively more money they are more able to "buy their way out" of the public sphere.

If they think their kids have more "merit" than the kids from across town, they might want to segregate their kids in a school for the "gifted." Prosperity itself, even if it were shared perfectly equally, might allow consumers to choose privacy over community—to purchase cellular phones and Walkmen instead of using public phones and attending outdoor concerts, to bypass public institutions like schools or the Post Office when they become inefficient.[117]

But the decline of the three public institutions discussed here—the draft, the schools, and public spaces—was not inevitable, or simply a product of the other "suspects." It proceeded apace during periods of growing money equality (like the sixties, when democratic conscription collapsed) and growing money inequality. Neither money nor "merit" required Congress to design the Vietnam-era draft or switch to an All Volunteer Force. They didn't mandate school busing or exclusionary zoning. They didn't require cities to allow the homeless to camp in parks and sleep in libraries. They didn't force states to create a welfare system that (I'll argue in Chapter 7) sustains the destructive urban underclass. The public sphere's decline seems largely an independent, preventable event.

If the civic institutions that had once embodied and enforced an egalitarian attitude have deteriorated or collapsed, do we really have to talk about a rise from .361 to .385 in the "Gini index," the economists' measure of overall income inequality, in order to explain the rise in social inequality? The public sphere's decline certainly helps resolve the mystery of the "Middle American" rebellion in the 1968 Wallace and Nixon campaigns. The blue-collar workers who were rebelling, as noted earlier, were already on the wrong side of the great meritocratic divide. When you add that they had seen their sons drafted to die in Vietnam while the sons of the more affluent were exempted, seen their public schools deteriorate while those who could afford to leave moved away, and seen the public spaces of their cities destroyed by criminals (while, again, the affluent escaped to the suburbs), need we invoke incipient changes in the income distribution to explain why they might have been a little angry?

CHAPTER 5

Money Liberalism's Lost Battle

Money inequality, the previous chapter suggests, is hardly the sole cause—maybe not even the leading cause—of the inegalitarian atmosphere of recent years. It can't have helped. But the other suspects look to be just as guilty, if not more so. The increasing stratification of society by smarts and skills might give even small income differences a harsh, meritocratic meaning. And the public sphere has declined precipitously in several areas where it used to perform a tangible democratizing function.

What's a social egalitarian to do? At this point, the two liberal strategies outlined earlier offer sharply different prescriptions, each geared to a suspected cause of class division. Money Liberalism says reverse the rise in money inequality. Civic Liberalism says reverse the decline of the public sphere.

What about "reversing" the middle suspect, meritocracy? That seems hopeless. We can eliminate the arbitrary credential-based barriers critics such as Fallows complain about—but, as noted, that doesn't eliminate meritocracy or the invidious cast it gives to success. On the contrary, it leads right into the Fairness Trap. It hardly makes sense to try to avoid that trap by preserving arbitrary barriers to success that are themselves violations of social equality. Instead, we're going to have to learn to live with some form of meritocracy, complete with its ugly Herrnsteinian baggage. It's a divisive factor both the Money and Civic Liberal strategies will have to somehow counteract, one that complicates the process of figuring out which of those two strategies holds more promise.

That comparison is the job of the next several chapters. Identifying the potential causes of class division is only its starting point. After all, even if rising money inequality is a major cause of social inequality, it doesn't necessarily follow that the best way to restore social equality is to try and produce money equality. In the 1988 presidential campaign, Jesse Jackson liked to argue that the way to solve a social problem was to "back out the same way you got in." But sometimes you can't back out. Perhaps we can't expect to reverse the income inequality trend, in which case a strategy based on doing so would be doomed to failure. That is in fact the case. There are no proposed Money Liberal policies that can reliably restore the American income distribution to its previous shape. And some money-equalizing strategies will actually aggravate the meritocratic threat to social equality.[1]

When it comes to reequalizing incomes—or, rather, reestablishing their old levels of inequality—no single, simple "cure" dominates Money Liberal discussion. Rather there are a number of suggestions, embraced in quick succession rather like miracle diets. Liberal physicians who would lower society's unhealthy money-inequality level prescribe, alternatively, the Tax and Transfer Cure, the Training Cure, the Union Cure, protectionism, and two more speculative, appealing strategies, "flexible production" and profit-sharing. That's a crowded medicine chest. Let's take them one at a time, starting with the current favorite.

The Tax and Transfer Cure.   Christopher Jencks has written: "If we want to redistribute income, the most effective strategy is probably still to redistribute income."[2] Are some people making too much money? Why not just tax it away from them and send the cash ("transfer payments," in economists' language) to those who are making less? For example, Democrats and liberal editorialists routinely endorse expanding the Earned Income Tax Credit (a transfer payment to poor working families) not just as a good way to end poverty, which it is, but as a way to "help reverse the trend toward greater income inequality that has arisen in recent years."[3]

Such transfers "help" reverse the trend toward greater income inequality, just as by filling my bathtub I "help" lower the rise in the world's oceans. Every bit helps. Actually reversing the trend is something else. Money Liberals like to give the impression that it's a matter of undoing Reagan's regressive tax cuts and flipping a few other switches at Progression Control. It isn't. The income distribution, remember, is becoming more unequal *before* taxes are taken into account. The size of this underlying shift far outweighed the impact of the Reagan-era changes that let the affluent keep more of their rising incomes. Between 1980 and 1990, for example, the richest 10 percent of American families dramatically increased their share of the nation's total after-tax income, but less than 20 percent of that increase came from tax and benefit changes, according to a study by Edward Gramlich of the University of Michigan and Richard Kasten and Frank Sammartino of the Congressional Budget Office. The rest of the increase came from the changes in the before-tax income distribution.[4]

Even relatively modest shifts in something as big as the American income structure are probably too big to be easily negated by making the tax code more progressive. The problem isn't the expense of boosting the earnings of the poor, or at least the earnings of the poor who work. It wouldn't take that much money, for example, to bring all working families up to the poverty line.[5] The problem, the place where large sums would have to be moved, is higher on the income ladder, where large sums are being generated.

Suppose, for example, we wanted to tax the richest one percent enough to counteract the effect of the recent rise in income inequality. Specifically, we'd like to tax them so their share of after-tax income would be equal to what it was, say, in 1977. In 1977 their share after federal taxes was 7.3 percent. By 1990 it was about 12.6 percent. Do a little arithmetic, and you realize that to lower the share back to 7.3 percent, these richest Americans would have to lose about 42 percent of the income they now have left over after federal taxes. The effective federal tax rate on this group (as of 1990) was about 27 percent, leaving 73 percent left over. We'd have to tax away 42 percent of that 73 percent, which works out to an extra tax of about 30 percent of their entire pre-tax income. In short, the total effective tax rate on the rich would have to be more than doubled, to around 57 percent (the current 27 percent rate plus 30 percent).[6]

The U.S. has never had an effective tax rate on the rich of even close to 57 percent, except perhaps during World War II (and probably not even then, though data are sketchy).[7] Sure, we've had high "marginal" rates, the marginal rate being the tax paid on the last dollar someone earns in a given year. But "effective" rates, the percentage of *all* dollars someone earns that gets paid in taxes, are invariably lower than marginal rates. One reason is that even if the rich pay high-bracket rates on the last dollars they earn, they usually pay lower rates on a lot of their earlier dollars. Another reason is that the rich invariably find legal ways to avoid actually paying the high marginal rates on any of their income. In 1966, for example, the top marginal income tax rate was 70 percent. The effective income tax rate on the richest one percent was 16.4 percent.[8] Money Liberals tend to naively assume (or cynically pretend) that impressively high marginal rates mean the rich are getting socked.[9] The rich know better.

Among our industrial competitors, only Sweden has had an effective income tax rate in the range that would be required for the Tax and Transfer Cure.[10] But the Swedes are the world's champions at taxation. Asking Americans to out-tax Sweden is like asking us to play cricket better than the English or cook pasta better than the Italians. It would require transforming the United States not into what it was in some more liberal era, but into something it has never been. During the 1990 budget deal, after a great deal of huffing and puffing about "fairness," Democrats managed to raise the effective rate on the rich from 27 percent to about 29 percent. Nice try. Even going back to 1977, the high-point of tax progressivity before all those nasty Reagan-era cuts, will only produce an effective rate on the richest one percent of about 35 percent.[11] To get to a 57 percent rate you'd need a "tax revolution," as Henry Aaron of the Brookings Institution puts it.

In fact, there is a tax revolt. Unfortunately for Money Liberals, it's in Sweden. Marginal income taxes for the rich are being cut from more than 80 percent to 51 percent.[12] There are limits, Swedes have discovered, to how much you can counteract the market's inequality through the tax system. Set taxes high enough, and many otherwise honest people will be tempted to cheat, especially small businessmen who can easily hide their income. Even resolutely honest citizens will find it pays to spend hours on household tasks rather than in their normal occupations. (A great architect may be a lousy mechanic, but if he works on his own car he gets to keep 100 percent of his work product.) Before the Swedish tax revolt, some economists put the size of Sweden's untaxed "gray market," which includes both cheating and untaxed home work, at 25 percent of the country's gross domestic product.[13] Finally, high tax rates make it worthwhile for the rich to exploit loopholes that can't be easily closed. They will, for example, invest in assets that appreciate untaxed (e.g., art) rather than income-producing assets. The only way to completely counter this move would be to appraise everyone's assets each year and then tax any increase as if it were income, an overwhelming administrative task no developed nation attempts.[14]

Even if it were technically feasible to tax the rich sufficiently, we might not want to. Many Democrats scoff, sensibly, at the Republican argument that marginal rates of 38 percent would stifle initiative. But what about the marginal rates of 70 or 80 percent that would be needed to produce an effective rate in the 50s? Economist Lester Thurow thinks high taxes restricted to the top 1 percent or so "wouldn't hurt their work effort," because at that level people "work for reasons other than money." I suspect Thurow severely underestimates the allure of added cash even to the top 1 percent (which, in 1989, included all taxpayers reporting more than about $163,000).[15] It's hard to believe that extremely high tax rates wouldn't have at least some perverse economic effects, even on the rich.[16] Nor is it clear that we want to encourage the rich to be motivated by "reasons other than money." Many of those reasons (snobbery, megalomania) are motives and impulses social egalitarians are trying to suppress. Money is a relatively benign incentive, given these alternatives. Better an entrepreneur inspired by the desire to drive a Lotus than the desire to impress a maître d'.

In sum, the Tax and Transfer Cure is probably both undesirable and technically unworkable. Politically, it's highly unlikely. It violates what might be called the Take Away Principle, the idea that it's far harder to take something away from someone than it is to prevent them from getting it. Most of the taking, it's true, would come from a small minority: the rich. But, as the CBO's figures on rising income inequality suggest, the trend Money Liberals are trying to counteract involves something like the top 10 to 30 percent of the income scale.[17] And what if the underlying inequality of income kept on increasing? Tax rates would have to be raised even further to compensate. Politicians who really believe in the Tax and Transfer Cure must be ready to dial taxes ever upward should the market keep generating new inequality.[18]

You don't have to be ideologically opposed to tax increases to realize this isn't going to happen. Even Thurow concedes that "[r]egardless of what one thinks about the role of taxes and transfers in limiting inequality, they are clearly not the appropriate means for counteracting the current surge in inequality."[19] Money Liberals may well win what they will regard as tremendous victories—increases in the top marginal income tax rate to 38 or even 50 percent. The press will hail the Democrats' populist success in fighting "rising income inequality." But in fact the Democrats won't come close to actually negating the rise in income inequality. Instead of trying to tax away what the affluent are making in the marketplace, maybe Money Liberals should instead try to prevent people from earning such unequal incomes in the first place.[20]

The Training Cure. If money tends to follow skills, why not make the distribution of income more equal, before transfers and taxes, by making the distribution of skills more equal? Better schools, more college loans, ambitious training programs for the "forgotten half" of the population that doesn't go to college—this is everybody's preferred cure for money inequality. Thurow, Reich, and countless Democratic study groups endorse it. In the 1992 presidential campaign, it formed the core of Bill Clinton's plan to "build the middle class back."[21]

It's hard to argue against training. Highly skilled workers make America more prosperous in a world where a nation's "comparative advantage" comes not so much from natural resources as from the resources people carry around inside their heads. Democrats, rightly, say that much of the investment in this "human capital" needs to be made by the government. Private companies don't have enough financial incentive to train workers who might then take their new skills and go work for somebody else.[22]

When it comes to reversing the surge in income inequality, as noted earlier, advocates of training evoke an especially appealing picture: today's unemployed steelworkers and $5-an-hour oil-changers, newly schooled as computer programmers and accountants, stepping up into a swelling middle class. If mass education reduced the supply of unskilled workers, it might even force employers to raise *their* wages a bit. But, as Reich says, there's no economic reason why, in a global economy, Americans can't all be "symbolic analysts."[23]

Yet an economy full of well-trained Americans might not be as egalitarian a place as you might think. To understand why, we have to look a bit more closely at the two acknowledged causes of money inequality: demographics (mainly wage-competition among baby-boomers) and the rising value of skills (reflected in the growing pay gap between high-school and college graduates).[24] Because it turns out that neither the demographic explanation nor differences in skills—at least formal skills—account for all the growing disparity in income. Income inequality isn't just increasing between young and old, or between those with only a high-school diploma and those with a college degree. It's increasing *within* the ranks of 40-year-old men with four years of college. In 1967, if you made $54,844, you were in the richest 10 percent of this well-trained group, according to data compiled by Brookings's Gary Burtless. By 1987, the income necessary for making the "top 10 percent" club had jumped to $70,531 (adjusted for inflation). Over the same two decades, inflation-adjusted incomes in the bottom 20 percent of this group actually dropped.[25]

"There must be a third factor," concludes Frank Levy. What that third factor is remains something of a mystery. But one candidate is this: *as skills become more important and are rewarded financially, differences in performance between individuals with the same formal "skills" or training also become more important, and are rewarded financially.* The more significant training becomes, the greater the money inequality among those with the same training.

The ideal type here is Hollywood. Suppose we gave one hundred people extensive training as actors (a species of "symbolic analyst") and set them loose at Sunset and Vine to seek their fortunes. What would we see if we came back ten years later? An equal distribution curve? Hardly. We'd see some actors waiting on tables, some working in commercials, and others, the Eddie Murphys of the world, commanding astronomical salaries. All this would make some economic sense. Eddie Murphy is worth millions to the film industry, because he performs well enough—or was lucky enough to catch on at just the right time—so that his films make much more money than the films of equally well-schooled actors who nevertheless don't have what Murphy has. In economic terms, Murphy's "marginal product" is simply a whole lot greater.[26]

So it is in the rest of the economy, on a less dramatic scale. When the middle class consisted of workers tightening bolts on the assembly line, the difference between a superlative bolt-tightener and a merely competent bolt-tightener wasn't much, economically. As long as the bolts didn't come loose, management had no compelling reason not to pay both workers the same. But train those workers as computer repairmen, and the picture changes. The differences between a good repairman and a mediocre repairman are probably substantial, and worth rewarding. Train workers as computer *programmers,* and the picture changes even more. The difference between a really good programmer and a merely adequate programmer can be enormous, and management will be strongly tempted to recognize this enormous difference with an enormous difference in pay. The more skilled the job, the greater these differences and the greater that temptation.

The other part of this "Hollywood Effect" is the collapse, under pressure from the market, of various mechanisms that once prevented the most talented members of a skilled trade or profession from extracting the full measure of their worth from their employers. Unions were the most obvious of these mechanisms.[27] But other, often informal, practices were more important in the upper ranges. When big law firms were a cozy bunch, aggressive young associates simply didn't leave after only one or two years. Who would hire them? In general, it was considered an act of disloyalty for executives to desert their employers for a rival firm. If your résumé showed a new job every two or three years, prospective employers were apt to assume you were an alcoholic. Today, if you don't switch employers every few years you run the risk of being branded a "tree-hugger." Professional "headhunters" dismember old firms by bidding away hot talent. Baseball free agents negotiate $7-million-a-year contracts. Brokerage houses have ceased to be WASP clubs, and top brokers routinely take home more than a million.[28] The studio system is dead, and Jack Nicholson makes $50 million for a single movie.

Only a hopeless credentialist would think that the earning power of these people is related in a linear fashion to "skills" that can be imparted through "training" courses or college degrees as part of some government industrial policy. Remember Reich's list of "symbolic analysts"—"lawyers, investment bankers,... research scientists,... advertising and marketing specialists, art directors, design engineers, architects, writers and editors, musicians,... television and film producers." All of these professions require some, often a lot of, training. But they are also all professions in which there is a big difference between being merely competent and being really good, between being worth a decent salary and an enormous salary. How do you train somebody to be Tom Wolfe?

One problem with the Training Cure, then, is this: the more government policy pushes Americans into Reich's "symbolic-analytical" pursuits, the more it pushes them into lines of work subject to the Hollywood Effect. It is "symbolic analysts," after all, who form the "richest one percent" that money egalitarians stay up nights worrying about. If everyone were a lawyer or architect, mediocre lawyers and architects might become the new proletarians, bidding down salaries dramatically. But the bigger America's "analytical" industries get, the bigger will be the salaries of the superstar lawyers, architects, et cetera who rise to the top of them.[29]

The impact of this unequalizing effect might well be outweighed by the egalitarian impact of moving low-wage unskilled workers into the skilled category. But even if it were, there is a *social*-egalitarian price to pay. Some of the more ominous tendencies of meritocracy would be reinforced if—thanks to training—every individual had the chance to maximize his skills and earning power.

First, there's the touchy issue of whether everybody can be trained to perform even competently at skilled jobs. If training is universally available, those who don't make it will, increasingly, be those who somehow don't have what it takes to develop a skill—usually an intellectual, "symbolic analytical" skill. Some people just aren't smart enough to be computer programmers no matter how much they're trained. Worse, at least some aspects of that smart quality are probably inherited. If you offer everyone training, you offer everyone the chance to discover the inherent limits of his or her talent. Herrnstein's centrifuge will be running full speed.

But forget about inherited talent. If you're offered all the training in the world and you still can't climb into the middle class, what does that make you? Universal training opportunities will spring the Fairness Trap, as the losers in the scramble for skills and money face the invidious implication that they are, well, losers.[30]

The Union Cure.   One Money Liberal who has at times been skeptical of the Training Cure is Robert Kuttner. Kuttner resists the new link between pay and skill. All the talk of skills, he has argued, turns the problem on its head: "Since the real problem is the supply of good jobs rather than the supply of good workers, emphasis on education and training will make the work force even more frustrated than it is now."[31]

As noted, by "good jobs" Kuttner doesn't mean skilled jobs. The old "good" industrial jobs he misses weren't very skilled at all. "There is nothing intrinsic in assembling cars, mining coal, or pouring molten steel that requires high wages," Kuttner admits. "These jobs *do* pay well mainly because of the efforts of strong unions." The solution to income inequality seems to follow: "The simplest way to promote relatively equal wage scales is to encourage trade unionism." Left-liberal economists like Bennett Harrison and Barry Bluestone also endorse the Union Cure.[32]

You can't blame liberals for wanting unskilled workers to be able to live comfortable middle-class lives, especially given the implications of an income scale linked rigidly to knowledge and ability. Much nostalgia for the days of mighty unions, I suspect, comes not simply from the belief that they produced a better income distribution, but from the intuition that by securing high wages for low-skilled work they avoided the ominous social-inegalitarian side-effects of meritocracy. Better a society in which virtually anyone can earn a nice living for a full day of physical labor.

But it's hard to see how a union comeback is going to solve the money egalitarians' problems. Can American unionism take $6-an-hour supermarket check-out clerks and get them $20-an-hour UAW-level salaries? Perhaps, if the clerks had a union with the bargaining leverage of the UAW. But that's like saying that all firms could make money if they had the market power of IBM. There are reasons, after all, why many unions don't have that power.

Under the Wagner Act, the 1935 law that provides the basic framework for American collective bargaining, unionism doesn't uniformly improve the lot of underpaid workers. It improves the lot, first, of those who have the most leverage in a strike. Unionists who work in a few easy-to-shut-down locations in an industry vulnerable to disruption (for example, Boeing's machinists) have power and win big wage increases. Unions have less leverage when their members are geographically dispersed (like check-out clerks), or when they operate automated facilities that can run a long time with skeleton managerial crews (as in much of the petrochemical industry).[33] American unions also have leverage when they can negotiate with a few big firms to set uniform wage increases across an entire industry, a practice known as "pattern bargaining." When everyone knows that no competitor will come along and steal business by cutting labor costs, all can relax and pass the increased cost of higher wages on to the public. The UAW did well when the auto industry was an oligopoly of four U.S. companies.[34] Once foreign competitors entered the market, the UAW's power began to erode.

Unfortunately for money egalitarians, some unions have never been blessed with any particular leverage. The late Sol Chaikin, president of the International Ladies Garment Workers Union, often referred to the "two-tier labor force" in the United States. He was complaining about a differential within the ranks of organized labor—because his union didn't have any of the advantages others had. While auto- and steelworkers made $20 an hour in the early eighties, Chaikin's seamstresses made an average of $6 an hour—and they got to pay for the UAW's raises whenever they bought a car. American unionism didn't produce much money equality.[35]

Kuttner, for one, recognizes this, which is why he doesn't really want a resurgence of American unionism. He wants Swedish unionism.[36] Swedish unions are not just bigger than American unions, though they are that: over 80 percent of the Swedish labor force is organized, including white-collar professionals. The difference is also qualitative. American unions are primarily organized industry-by-industry, the better to pursue "pattern bargaining." In Sweden all blue-collar workers are part of a single big nationwide labor organization, the LO, or Landsorganisationen. White-collar workers are organized into just four unions (one for private-sector workers, one for professionals, and two covering government workers).

These big Swedish unions are free to behave very differently from their American counterparts. Bargaining with the national employers' federation, they can agree to a single, nationwide wage increase, knowing that no other union will get more. More important to Money Liberals, Sweden's huge blue-collar labor union has been able to pursue a "solidaristic" wage policy that intentionally narrows wage gaps, paying more to those whom the market would tend to slight, and holding down the wages of those who might be able to demand more in individual bargaining.[37]

Did it work? At the very bottom of the income scale, the "solidarity" policy does seem to have enforced a minimum wage (Sweden has no minimum wage law). Above that level, though, its impact appears to have been largely chimerical. Most of the equality the unions enforced in national bargaining was undone in the period between contract talks, as employers rewarded skilled employees with increases at the local level. By 1984, this inegalitarian "wage drift" accounted for between 40 and 50 percent of the earnings increases of Swedish blue-collar workers. According to one economist, "drift" undid fully two-thirds of the equalizing effect of the "solidarity" policy on the wage structure. When you consider that skilled individuals could also boost their incomes by moving to better and better slots within this more egalitarian structure, you wonder whether the "solidarity" policy did much equalizing at all, in the end.[38] In the late seventies, Swedish unions began to back away from it.[39]

Worse, for Money Liberals, a "solidarity" wage policy can't be expected to control the increases at the affluent end of the distribution that are the distinctive feature of today's growing inequality. Even the Swedish employer's federation, in a 1986 pamphlet that attempted to dramatize the "distortions" of the solidarity wage, had to admit that wage dispersion remained "quite substantial among higher salaried employees."[40] And "solidarity" hasn't stopped the Swedish income distribution from growing more unequal over the past decade, due to increases at the top.[41]

It's obvious why unionism might have a hard time reining in the incomes of high earners, most of whom work as skilled professionals or entrepreneurs in industries where they are unlikely to be organized, especially in the U.S. Why should they join a big, egalitarian organization? They have no interest in decreasing their relatively high pay. On the contrary, if they organized at all, they'd probably want to form an industry-only guild to try to boost their pay even higher. The American Medical Association comes to mind.[42]

Unions might at least try to suppress inequality within industries, as they've done within blue-collar occupations.[43] But, again, that's a lot easier to do in occupations that aren't subject to the Hollywood Effect, where performance differences, and the incentives for management to reward them, are small (good vs. mediocre bolt-tighteners) rather than large (good vs. mediocre software writers). Are militant investment bankers going to impose a uniform salary scale on Wall Street? Are lawyers going to go on strike to hold down the income of Melvin Belli and Gerry Spence? Don't hold your breath. In Hollywood itself, where actors and screenwriters *are* organized, periodic strikes have done nothing to reduce salaries at the top.[44]

It's just as likely that high-wage professional unions would try to increase their distance, in status as well as salary, from their supposed inferiors. In Hollywood, the unionized writers are forever trying to seize power and prestige from the unionized directors. In health care, nurses try to seize status from doctors while dumping less dignified tasks onto the lower ranks. "[N]urses are a scarce resource and should not be used to fill in for orderlies, bookkeepers, and dietitians," sniffs Peri Rosenfeld of the National League of Nursing.[45] In "egalitarian" Sweden (where Ph.D.'s routinely list their titles in the phone book) status anxieties clearly lay behind the 1981 strikes by white-collar unions, which were designed to restore traditional wage differentials. Whatever its effect on money equality, all this professional rank-pulling and self-pity can't be good for social equality. It seems more like a social egalitarian's nightmare.[46]

Protectionism. If international trade underlies the inegalitarian pay-for-skills trend—as Reich, for one, says it does—one way to halt the trend would be to halt our international trade. Semi-protectionist half-measures wouldn't do; they'd only slow the Reich scenario down. But there's no doubt that by flat-out stopping imports of automobiles and steel we could preserve the middle-class jobs of American autoworkers and steelworkers. Critics of this strategy typically point out that the economic cost of preserving those jobs—higher prices for automobiles, retaliation against our exports—is higher than what it would cost to let imports in and simply send the autoworkers and steelworkers checks in the amount of their former salaries. But that misses the guts of the protectionist argument, which is not an appeal to efficiency but to social equality.

Sure, the nation as a whole would be richer if it adapted to international trade. But that means increasing emphasis on skills. For Money Liberals, there's the likelihood that the income distribution of this new, richer nation will be less equal than the old income distribution. Even non-Money Liberals might value protectionism, however, not for the number of jobs it would save but for the *type* of jobs it would save, namely well-paying unskilled jobs. As noted, these jobs are precious because they confound the invidious correlation of skill with income (and with it the Herrnstein Nightmare and the Loser Problem).

Meanwhile, protectionism would harm precisely those Americans who have what the world wants to buy from us: skills. If protectionism hurts two software engineers for every unskilled autoworker it helps, that might not seem such a bad bargain to social egalitarians.

They not only get to enrich a worker at the bottom of the meritocracy, they also get to punish two educated yuppie "symbolic analysts." So much the better!

But the dispositive objection to this bargain remains: in the long run protectionism would make us far poorer as a nation. An autarchic, fortress-America economy might generate a "bell curve" that was more equal, with more unskilled workers clustered in its fat middle, but the whole curve will be drastically lower than it otherwise would be. Ask Argentina. Before World War I, it was one of the world's more prosperous countries, with a per capita income equal to Germany's and higher than Sweden's. Even on the eve of World War II, Argentina was richer than Italy and Austria, had more cars than Britain and more physicians per capita than any European country except Switzerland and Hungary. Then, after a military coup in 1943, Argentina began protecting its domestic industries. By 1982, its per capita domestic product was a third of Italy's, a fourth of Austria's, and a fifth of Sweden's.[47]

Perhaps there are Money Liberals so concerned about the shape of the income distribution that they would forego prosperity in their quest. Civic Liberals have a far easier time rejecting this course, because they don't rely on the income distribution to produce their social equality in the first place.[48] But protectionism isn't the answer for either group.

"Flexible" production.   Sophisticated Money Liberals reject protectionism. But they also know that global trade is producing greater money inequality for Americans. They know that taxes and unions won't do the job of reversing the inequality trend, and they're honest enough to be skeptical of training as a money-egalitarian fix. Like Marxists confronting the spread of capitalism, they must entertain the sullen suspicion that the freight train of history just isn't going their way. They need a happier ending.

Robert Reich (for whom this dilemma must be especially acute) has proposed a happy ending of the sort Marxists would find familiar, involving as it does a propitious shift in the "mode of production." Not the end of capitalism, in this case, but a shift within capitalism to a new form of production that (it just so happens) will generate more equal incomes:

In the era of human capital, an era that all industrialized nations are entering, high-volume, standardized production will to a great extent be replaced by flexible-system production, in which integrated teams of workers identify and solve problems. *This new organization of work necessarily will be more collaborative, participatory, and egalitarian* than is high-volume, standardized production, for the simple reason that initiative, responsibility, and discretion must be so much more widely exercised within it [emphasis added].[49]

Reich's new form of production seems to combine two different trends. The first is what Michael Piore and Charles Sabel, in their book *The Second Industrial Divide,* call "flexible specialization"—enterprises that turn out a variety of products in small batches to serve rapidly changing markets. An example would be textile firms that survive against mass-producers of cheap fabrics by creating and staying ahead of fashion trends. Because the boss must be able to talk with the designer and the artisans who will quickly produce the products, unnecessary (and inequality-producing) layers of hierarchy must be eliminated.[50]

The second trend is the direct effect of computer automation on productive enterprises, whether they are specialized or not, whether they produce goods in large batches or small. What is new about computers, says Harvard Business School professor Shoshana Zuboff, is not just that they help automate things, but that they make unprecedented amounts of information instantly available to everyone in a firm. Taking advantage of this potential requires a new "informated" type of organization, one that lets the low-level operators who have their hands on the computer alter and improve a production process that is "flexible" in that it's constantly evolving. These newly empowered operators are paid more, and paid for their capabilities rather than their seniority or rank. Meanwhile, layers of middle management simply become obsolete.[51]

Neither type of flexible production pretends to preserve unskilled jobs. On the contrary, the "flexible" firm is the kingdom of the skilled. Who else is going to reprogram machine tools to produce some designer's fantasy, or tinker with the software at a pulp mill? If the work ever stopped changing and became routine, then it might be organized so that unskilled workers could perform it—but then it would move overseas.[52] Flexible-production thus presupposes training.[53] Zuboff, for example, describes an automated pulp mill, where the workers—most not college graduates—had to be taught "the basics of math, physics, and chemistry in addition to specific material on the pulping process."[54] What "flexible production" adds to the Training Cure, for Money Liberals, is the claim that all this training will be for jobs in companies with hierarchies considerably flatter than we're now used to.

Will flatter hierarchies lead to more equal salaries and wages?[55] Within the firm, there will be fewer levels—but people won't be paid according to their level anymore, Zuboff says. They'll be paid according to their skill and knowledge. That means flexible firms are likely to be case studies of the Hollywood Effect. As Reich puts it, "[i]n flexible-system production the quality of work is often more important than quantity ... workers' skill, judgment, and initiative become the determinants of the flexible-system enterprise's competitive success." Isn't it likely that workers with more of these qualities will be paid more—a lot more?[56]

If wage disparities within flexible firms do shrink, it will largely be because the unskilled don't have jobs there anymore. Zuboff happened to examine a pulp mill where an existing, pre-automation work force of non-college grads was moved into new, "informated" jobs. At a second pulp mill observed by Zuboff, a new group of workers was selected and trained especially for the new jobs, and they proved to be much more productive. But even they weren't knowledgeable enough to take full advantage of the computer technology.[57] "In order to use the data, not just read the data, people need huge amounts of education," says one designer of computerized-production systems. "Informated" firms may simply learn to hire only extremely well-educated people.[58]

But if you need skills to work in a "flexible" firm, and flexible firms come to dominate the economy, then the unskilled are in for an especially rough time. "Flexibility" may mean more money equality within each firm, but it hardly means money equality between different firms, or between different sorts of employment. Sabel, for one, admits that if "flexible specialization" takes hold, "you could get a lot of new segmentation with the unskilled being pushed out."[59]

Put these money-inegalitarian possibilities together and you have ... well, you may have something like the high-tech economy of Massachusetts in the late eighties, which Piore and Sabel cite as the closest thing in the U.S. to a "flexibly specialized" regional economy. Is it an accident that Massachusetts is also the region Harrison and Bluestone claim "dramatically" illustrates the "tendency toward polarization" of jobs and incomes?[60] Money Liberals can't count on flexible production to close the growing pay gap based on skill. It's part of what will *cause* that gap.

What liberals can count on is that the hypertrophied demand for skills and smarts in such an economy will inflame the socially-inegalitarian effect of money differences. Zuboff actually refers to her "informated" organization as "smart people around the machine."[61] She reports that in these organizations "Formal intelligence is up; experiential know-how is down." In support of the latter point, she cites employees (presumably managers) who say things like "A low-IQ operator will not accept a computer on the job." Managers talk about needing a "higher, more advanced type of person" with "a high level of intelligence." Zuboff notes that "these intellective skills are unlikely to be equally distributed, and the variation in their distribution can become a new source of hierarchical distinctions within even the most fluid organizations."[62] It sure can. It can also become a source of hierarchical distinctions within society as a whole. Losers in the economy will know they weren't "intellective" enough to be allowed near the "data interface."

The Herrnsteinian implications of all this are pretty grim. In Piore and Sabel's world there appears to be room for artisanal as well as abstract intellectual skills. In Zuboff's computerized future, however, the variety of "R-factors" has narrowed drastically. "The computer screen takes more mental skills, and we reward those skills," as one manager puts it.[63] In keeping with the taboo on hereditarian fears, Zuboff studiously avoids confronting the disturbing potential of her findings. She asserts simply that in her flexible, "informated" organizations individuals will "elect to align themselves with the jobs best suited to their sensibilities or talents."[64] That sounds nice, but the talents of some individuals will allow a lot more aligning than the talents of others. And the more the relevant talents are confined to peculiar intellectual abilities, the greater the chance that success in the "informated" future will be inherited.

Profit-sharing and worker-ownership.   OK, forget "flexibility." Why not spread profits more equally among the workers of all enterprises, flexible or not, through profit-sharing or actual worker-ownership?

That wouldn't necessarily require any fancy changes in the technology or product mix of a firm. The Ford Motor Company has profit-sharing, but Ford still mass-produces cars on assembly lines.[65]

Basically, profit-sharing takes whatever economic return accrues to the function of "owner" and, to some extent, disperses it among the work force instead of concentrating it in the hands of a few capitalists or investors.[66] Instead of Victor Kiam (the Remington razor king) making $1 million, say, a thousand workers may make $1,000. That's an egalitarian effect. Of course, the risks of capitalism will be spread around along with the rewards. But in modern America, the rewards tend to outweigh the risks, in part because losses are limited by the bankruptcy laws.

Among the worker-owners themselves, a new form of *in*equality would crop up. Some groups of workers would profit mightily. Some who own losing firms will lose a lot more than if they had been mere employees—as did the workers at the Rath meatpacking company, who lost not only their jobs but most of their pensions when their company failed. This disparity between winning groups of workers and losing groups presumably wouldn't cancel out the egalitarian effect of spreading the winnings around instead of letting them accrue to a few owners. But it has been enough to prompt Sweden's "solidaristic" unions to oppose profit-sharing within individual firms.[67]

The main point about profit-sharing, however, is that it is usually combined with "participatory" schemes to unlock the energy and knowledge of shop-floor employees. Both rewards and *power* are redistributed, and what's more, they are redistributed to the unskilled as well as the skilled. Japan is the model here, as in so much else. Japanese firms pay their workers about a third of their compensation in the form of variable bonuses, a de facto system of profit-sharing.[68] Big Japanese firms also involve shop-floor workers in all sorts of "quality circles" and decision-making teams. Pay differentials between managers and workers are low, and at each level pay is linked to seniority rather than individual performance (in the interest of group "cohesiveness"). As a result, overall pay differences within Japanese companies are from one-half to one-third those in American firms.[69]

The problem, as usual when emulating Japan, is figuring out how to get from here to there, how to act Japanese without somehow magically adopting all of Japanese culture. It's not easy to explain the Japanese system in strict economists' terms. If Toyota has "compressed wage differentials," for example, why doesn't some other firm spring up and hire away Toyota's "star" employees by paying them more? David Levine and Laura d'Andrea Tyson ask this question in a recent Brookings paper, but they don't come up with much more of an explanation than "a cultural element that discourages job changing" in Japan.[70] Over there, it's just not done. Over here, of course, it's done all the time, now more than ever.

The prospect of turning American business culture around when it's going full speed in the opposite direction might reasonably strike liberals as remote. Just as likely is the possibility that Japan will become more like us. Maybe Japanese firms have been able to hold on to their "stars" only because since World War II they've been continuously growing, which made room for promotions. Let the Japanese economy "mature" and stagnate, and the headhunting will begin.[71]

In the long run, profit-sharing—especially in the extreme form of worker-ownership—could simply flop. If each worker gets to share profits equally, a firm's existing workers may want to underhire (to avoiding having to cut new employees in on the profits) and over-mechanize.[72] Worker-shareholders might be reluctant to take efficiency-enhancing steps (such as moving to another state in search of cheap raw materials) that ruthless entrepreneurs would take.[73]

We don't know. Of all the schemes designed to equalize incomes before taxes and transfers, profit-sharing would seem to hold the most promise for Money Liberals. But even if it survives in the American marketplace and succeeds in compressing income scales a bit, there's no guarantee it will come close to canceling out the broad inegalitarian trend of higher-pay-for-skills. A good computer programmer will be able to demand more from a worker-owned firm, just as he or she would extract more from an investor-owned firm. The Hollywood Effect would continue apace. If we're at a stage of economic evolution in which "symbolic-analytical" skills (and superstar performance) are rewarded, then they'll have to be rewarded. Another country where income inequality is rising is Japan.

Money Liberals might still argue that, even if none of these strategies alone can reverse the money-inequality trend, pursuing all of them at once might have the desired effect. There are several problems with this Chinese menu approach. First, some of the strategies are flat-out losers. Protectionism is simply too costly to be included in any package. Flexible-production seems more likely to increase income inequality (by magnifying the skills effect) than to decrease it.

Second, some of the remaining approaches are incompatible. Liberals can't pursue them all. In particular, a unions-based strategy seems unlikely to coexist peacefully with a profit-sharing approach. As noted, the sorts of unions that enact "solidaristic" incomes policies (huge Swedish-style unions) also tend to oppose Japan-style profit-sharing. Some American unions, such as the Machinists, vigorously oppose Japan-style employee "participation," fearing it gives workers a grievance mechanism outside the union.[74] Japan itself practices neither American nor Swedish unionism, but rather a docile company-union form of collective bargaining.

That leaves the possibility of combining a few of the least unpromising Money Liberal approaches—say, pursuing a progressive tax and transfer system while encouraging profit-sharing and undertaking a large training program. That seems to be the intelligent Money Liberal's agenda. If enacted it would presumably have a bigger effect on the income distribution than would any of its components if they were enacted by themselves. Even so, the distributional gains from training would come at some social-egalitarian cost in the form of greater meritocratic division.

More important, could Money Liberals say with any degree of confidence that this package would have *enough* of an effect? I doubt it. Keep in mind that none of the Money Liberal approaches, by themselves, comes even close to reliably reversing the money-inegalitarian drift. In pursuing them, Democrats would be making a dramatic political commitment, in effect telling voters: "The rich are getting richer. But if we make these wrenching changes we'll stop it, and that's how we'll have social equality." It's a wager of expectations, goodwill, and resources, with a highly uncertain result. Is the precarious prospect of reequalizing incomes really the horse on which we want to place liberal hopes for a democratic society? There are better bets.

CHAPTER 6

The Public Sphere

A durable liberal strategy would be able to achieve social equality whether the rich were getting richer or not, whether skills were becoming more or less valuable, whether the Herrnstein Nightmare was approaching or receding. Instead of struggling against money-inegalitarian tides in the world economy over which American liberals have little control, it would make the most of a factor the government does have control over, namely the public sphere.

The Civic Liberal idea is to use this public sphere to incubate and spread an egalitarian culture. Cultures don't fall from the sky. They come from institutions. The institutions of the private sphere, left unencumbered, will create their own culture, a culture in which money is likely to the dominant, if not monolithic, determinant of status. We can keep reminding ourselves that there is an ineradicable element of chance in an entrepreneurial economy, that the Fairness Trap will never completely close, and that we have not and will not achieve the meritocratic equilibrium in which material reward corresponds perfectly to applied talent.[1] But when money is the only game in town, it's hard not to follow the score.

What's needed is another area of life with a different method of scoring. In the money sphere, after all, not *everyone* can succeed. But everyone, even the economy's losers, should be able to pass the test necessary for equal dignity in the public sphere. The institutions of that sphere would drive home the point of social equality—and the ultimate moral arbitrariness of capitalist success—through the crude expedient of treating all citizens equally and the more subtle tactic of providing a part of daily life actually enjoyed by various economic classes on this equal basis.

The next several chapters suggest possible components of such a public sphere, and of the Civic Liberal strategy. Many are democratic institutions—such as schools, public spaces, and the draft—that have been in decline. But, just as the money inequality trend may be impossible to reverse, some aspects of the public sphere's decline probably can't be reversed. We can't, for example, easily undo the process of suburbanization. To compensate, Civic Liberals will have to create new public institutions, as well as rebuild old ones. Ultimately, they'll also have to engage in longer-term strategies to mix classes in the suburbs, and solve the underclass problem that lies at the root of the class segregation and deterioration of our cities.

In the shorter term, however, as the necessary first stage of Civic Liberalism, there *are* important egalitarian institutions that could be built or rebuilt quite expeditiously—within, say, the next five years. Some of these institutions would consume many billions of dollars. Some would probably save money. Others require simply the passage and enforcement of a law. All are reforms that can reliably be accomplished, but they don't all have to be accomplished to achieve Civic Liberalism's objective. What is important is not that any particular institution be included in the public sphere. It is that those which are included absorb enough of our lives to condition our attitude toward our fellows in the portion that remains.

Let's start with the institution that has (as noted in Chapter 4) deteriorated most dramatically.

The draft. There are perfectly good military reasons for replacing the current all-volunteer force (AVF). Some of these reasons are related to social equality. The Persian Gulf war showed that the egalitarian objections to an AVF tend to become loud at the worst possible time, just as the prospect of combat and death looms. At the very moment when we were trying to intimidate Saddam Hussein in the winter of 1990–91, the country was split by a debate over whether the rich would bear their fair share of the fighting. The only reason the controversy wasn't crippling in that instance may be that the battle turned out to be short, with few casualties on our side.

There are other, more technical problems with the AVF that have less to do with egalitarianism. As Senators Nunn and Hollings have long pointed out, the pool of young men from which we must buy our volunteers is shrinking (from 8.6 million men aged 18 to 21 in 1981 to an estimated 6.6 million in 1995). True, the military has been downsized. But so has the military's budget. We may one day need a deep recession, or budget-bursting pay levels, in order to make the armed forces an appealing enough career alternative.[2]

But the main justification for a draft remains moral. Volunteer-army advocates rely on the logic of the private sphere, in which everything, even soldiers' lives, is convertible into cash. If some young Americans are freely willing to go into battle for $25,000 a year—well, it's a deal. ("You took the money, now shut up and die," as former Navy Secretary James Webb caricatured the argument during the Iraq crisis.) But it is one thing for society to pay people to pick up garbage and drive buses. It's another to pay people to risk their necks in battle. If dying in combat isn't outside the economic sphere, it's hard to see what is.[3] The draft is the most natural, and—again, because it involves the risk of death—most potent, arena of democratic experience. It doesn't break down class barriers for only a couple of years; it breaks them down for life, in part by giving all who serve a network of military acquaintances that cuts across class lines. Even Henry Kissinger used to hang out with his old Army buddies.[4]

A democratic draft is hardly a bold, idealistic step into the future. It's something America has done before. All we need to achieve its social-egalitarian benefit is a change in the law. We don't need to restructure capitalism. We don't need a miraculous surge of European trade unionism. We don't need to out-tax Sweden. We don't even need a Democrat in the White House, or a Republican for that matter.

For class-mixing purposes, the main problem with the draft is that by 1995, thanks to communism's collapse, the military will need only about 11 percent of America's draft-age men.[5] Not even social equality is important enough to justify doing what it takes to have a draft with the impact of World War II's. (What it takes is World War III.) But however modest the manpower needs of the military, a draft is the most socially egalitarian way of meeting them. Even if only 11 percent of men in the upper, middle, and lower classes served—and all the others had to think about serving—it would do more to promote social equality than all the "transfer payments" liberals might conceivably legislate.

Yet it would be even more effective to involve more than 11 percent, and more than just men—to make the military part of a broader scheme of national service, including civilian service. Here is an idea that separates Civic Liberals from those who have other priorities.

National service. "At the age of 18, you should be focusing on your dreams and ambitions, not picking up cans in Yellowstone," sniffs Republican Jack Kemp. For social egalitarians, however, national service is valuable precisely because it would force Americans to pause in their disparate career trajectories and immerse themselves in a common, public enterprise. It is the draft in a weaker dose, more widely dispensed.[6]

National service was an idea whose time came in the eighties—to no apparent effect. Universal service was endorsed by Gary Hart, who predicted it "might be the biggest issue" of the decade. Senator Nunn and Congressman McCurdy of the Democratic Leadership Council introduced legislation that would have made federal student aid contingent on one or two years of service. (The Nunn-McCurdy Bill went nowhere when the education establishment realized it would supplant existing loan programs.) William F. Buckley distinguished himself from most on the right by calling for a service scheme that would enroll 80 percent of America's youth by means of various "inducements" and "sanctions." Buckley's proposal, too, went nowhere.[7]

Part of what afflicts the national service idea is confusion about its purpose. It's been sold as the Veg-A-Matic of domestic policy, able to accomplish at least five important goals with one institutional device. They are:

1. To build character; in particular, to counteract the perceived selfishness of youth.[8]
2. To repay a social debt. Buckley calls service a "formal attempt of requital" for benefits inherited from previous generations.
3. To "salvage impoverished youths" by giving them work experience, training, and opportunities for social integration.
4. To provide needed services—caring for the sick, cleaning up the environment, et cetera.
5. To mix the classes in a common endeavor.

For Civic Liberals the overriding goal, of course, is number 5, class-mixing. That helps to clarify the sort of national service program we're talking about. For example, it excludes Job Corps–type programs designed to help salvage underclass kids through elaborate vocational training regimens. The more national service "targets" the poor, the less it will be seen as a duty for all the classes. Salvaging the underclass will require a separate program (see Chapter 8). Nor is the Civic Liberal test of success whether national service participants become less selfish. It's simply whether a large cross-section of the population winds up serving together under conditions of equality.[9]

Purely voluntary programs fail to meet this test; the ambitious sons and daughters of upper-class families just don't sign up.[10] Some national service advocates nevertheless hope that "incentives" of various sorts might subtly "induce" participation by the rich. But such financial inducements can still be easily ignored by people who don't need the money. The most well-known national service scheme, the Nunn-McCurdy Bill (based largely on the ideas of Northwestern University sociologist Charles Moskos) promises national servers a $10,000 voucher, good for a scholarship or a first home purchase, in addition to a subsistence "stipend" of $100 a week plus health benefits. That's an attractive package for poor and even lower middle-class teenagers—the equivalent of an $8-per-hour job. But Moskos admits that it's not enough to lure the children of the affluent, who can finance their own education and homes.[11] Even a 5 percent lifelong tax surcharge (suggested by Richard Danzig and Peter Szanton) might not be enough to persuade affluent kids to sacrifice a year's income, or a year's lead in the career race.[12]

The only way to guarantee class-mixing is to make national service mandatory. That means a penalty harsh enough to be coercive. It could be jail. It could also be a heavy money penalty that judges could tailor to fit the financial circumstances of any refuseniks—though it would have to be a potential fine of hundreds of thousands, perhaps even millions, of dollars if it were going to guarantee the participation of the truly wealthy.[13]

A mandatory service scheme would enlist a lot of people—3 to 4 million a year, assuming the plan targeted young men and women of draft age.[14] What would they be doing? Here again, it matters that social equality is the main goal. If we see national service mainly as an antidote to the "culture of selfishness," then the grungier the work, the better. Cleaning up mud slides is just the thing to teach incipient yuppies a thing or two. But the Civic Liberal imperative is to mix the classes, not to beat the selfishness out of them. National service jobs could be enjoyable, even career-enhancing. What's important is that they have a heterogeneous, communal aspect.

There are plenty of worthy tasks that fit this bill. Care for the infirm elderly is probably the most pressing need. Buckley notes that between 125,000 and 300,000 old people now living in nursing homes could move back into the "normal community" if there were enough workers to assist them with their daily chores. Those who are incapable of leaving nursing homes may need a different kind of assistance. They often lead lives of brutal loneliness, and the occasional visits of relatives can't possibly compensate. But the cost of professional attendants is too great for the vast majority of Americans to bear. Seventy percent of single elderly Americans are impoverished after just 13 weeks in a nursing home, even at the current inadequate level of care.[15]

In strict economists' terms, national service is almost surely an inefficient way to help these lonely, old, and ill Americans. It would be cheaper—once you count the "opportunity costs" of forgoing all the productive things servers could be doing with their time—to raise taxes to pay for a lot of nurses and hand-holders. Of course, taxpayers show no sign of willingness to foot this enormous bill. But even if they did, even if we could meet the needs of the elderly through other means, we could still reasonably *choose* to meet them through national service.[16] National service allows us to do something in addition to providing services. It allows us to carve out a part of life where the market is negated, where the common, non-market values that even conservatives like Buckley invoke—fellowship, solidarity, and social equality—can flourish.[17]

Almost three-quarters of a million people could be fruitfully employed caring for the elderly or infirm, according to Danzig and Szanton (who are not unskeptical of claims made by national service advocates).[18] There are other needs almost as critical: tutoring the illiterate and semi-literate, helping maintain or patrol public spaces, perhaps assisting in the care of pre-school children in day care. As long as the tasks are class-mixing and valuable, the national service should be free to do whatever work the market, for one reason or another, cannot do—whether that work is grungy or exhilarating, whether or not the government could do it more cheaply some other way.

Unfortunately, an emphasis on the most useful work puts national service on a collision course with public employee unions, who see young draftees as a threat to their jobs (the same reason, as we'll see, that they also fear a New Deal–style guaranteed jobs program). The more useful the job, the greater the chance some union member might already be doing it. Even the Democratic Leadership Council, which routinely attacks the influence of unions on the party, wilted when faced with the prospect of opposition to its service scheme from public employee organizations. The DLC's plan attempted to placate the unions by shunting national service workers into a variety of less important, less threatening, tasks (for example, "installing smoke detectors in homes for senior citizens").[19] The other lazy way to avoid a labor confrontation is to farm work out to the nonprofit sector.[20] This, too, is a recipe for trouble. What nonprofit group is going to turn down the chance to get a free worker? The farmed-out youths are likely to pursue their various tasks in isolation—answering phones at nonprofit dance troupes, leading walking tours of historic riverfront warehouses—without any contact with co-workers from other classes.[21]

Better to override union objections while restricting the national service to a few concrete tasks of proven utility and practicality. "There are four or five jobs we clearly know how to train kids to do," says Kathleen Kennedy Townsend, who runs a student service organization for the state of Maryland. Her list: teachers' aides, police aides, nurses' aides, a rural "conservation corps" to clean up the environment, plus a similar corps to repair and maintain urban public spaces. Put those together and you probably have enough jobs to keep several million young people usefully employed at a time.[22]

The final question facing any mandatory national service scheme is how to integrate it with the military. That's trickier than you might think. The armed forces, as noted, need only a small fraction of those eligible to serve. What's more, they require stints of service lasting at least two years (otherwise training costs become too high). Requiring two years of civilian service seems a bit much. But one year of civilian service could hardly be treated as the equivalent of two years in the army.

Clearly military service should count as the fulfillment of any service requirement. Beyond that, we could attempt to give young Americans a choice of military or civilian service—but the military's wages would have to be set much higher to compensate for the greater risks and longer tour of duty. Since the rich would be less tempted by such financial incentives than the non-rich, the result would probably be a class division, with the military disproportionately poor and the affluent opting to avoid the perils of potential combat.

The better approach, for social egalitarians, would combine universal service with conscription. Teenagers would first be subject to a military draft, with no civilian alternative. If they escaped in the draft lottery, they'd have to do a year of civilian service.[23] This hybrid draft/service setup might well be perceived as fairer than any attempt to allow more freedom of choice at the expense of universal exposure to military risks. Rich and poor teenagers would take their chances in the draft together; if they were chosen, they would serve together for two years. If they weren't chosen, they would still serve together as civilians for one year.[24]

This sort of service scheme is the most intrusive institution in the Civic Liberal arsenal. It would interrupt the lives of all Americans. But precisely because it is intrusive, it holds out the possibility of doing for everyone what Joseph Epstein, editor of *The American Scholar*, remembers the peacetime draft did for him: "... it jerked me free, if only for a few years, from the social class in which I have otherwise spent nearly all my days. It jerked everyone free...."[25]

The ballot. Not all components of the public sphere have deteriorated as drastically as the draft. The jury system, for example, still brings disparate members of the community together, if only occasionally, in a way that usually seems to convince those who serve that common sense isn't a function of income or race. More generally, the courts still treat a Michael Milken or Leona Helmsley with an inspiring lack of deference. And the basic mechanism of electoral democracy remains intact. But it, quite evidently, *has* been compromised over the past two decades. Here is another large egalitarian institution that Civic Liberals could repair fairly expeditiously.

It may be difficult, today, to conceive of the ballot as the basis for social equality. American elections (unlike, say, Russian elections) no longer provide much in the way of a democratic thrill. How can going to the polls once every few years, in separate suburbs, offer rich and poor the same equalizing experience as attending common schools, or sharing common foxholes? From a modern perspective, someone like the American socialist Eugene Debs, who saw in the ballot the substance of "manhood," looks (as his biographer Nick Salvatore notes) not a little naive.[26]

But political equality is still the necessary, if insufficient, condition for social equality. It still provides an area of life grounded not in the power of dollars but in the principle, enforced in America with almost mathematical purity, of one person, one vote.[27] The actual ritual of voting may produce only a fleeting experience of equality, but the need of politicians to appeal to all classes—and the need of citizens, homeowners, and associations from all classes to talk and bargain with each other as equals—provide more frequent occasions for egalitarian behavior.

If we've grown cynical about the social-egalitarian effects of the ballot, it may be because over the past several decades, the inequality of the money sphere has steadily and visibly leached into politics. Things aren't as bad as they were in, say, 1896, when (journalist Walter Shapiro reminds us) Boies Penrose spent $500,000 in bribes to "win" a Pennsylvania Senate seat. Compared to that, the recent practice of paying Congressmen $2,000 for a speech was petty commerce.[28]

The threat today isn't direct bribery, but the more insidious, reform-resistant role of money in financing campaigns. Twenty-five years ago, a former party chair and cabinet official who calls himself "Mr. Democrat" would not have boasted to a reporter that "there hasn't been anybody who can reach the rich people the way I can."[29] Congressmen of both parties didn't spend most of their waking hours trying to milk contributions from special interest groups, and lobbyists didn't spend their time delivering Congressmen $5,000 checks. Candidates for president were not dismissed by the press before the first primary simply because they'd failed to raise enough money from the affluent. These are examples of what Walzer would call money exercising power outside its sphere, of dollars being converted into the currency of democracy.

Preventing this conversion has always been difficult, because Americans have been reluctant to adopt what is the simplest response when confronted with an invasion of the public sphere by the money sphere, namely outlawing the threat. We could say that money is not speech, and erect a legal wall between the economic and political spheres. Limit the amount a candidate can spend to a reasonably small sum and ban all other spending on his behalf by anybody—that's the

British system. In part because the U.S. Supreme Court has said money *is* speech, Americans have tended to rely on a more complicated strategy that attempts to play off moneyed factions against each other.[30] Yet this strategy worked for several decades in the middle of the century due to a peculiar set of conditions: the "threshold" amount of money that a candidate needed to have a chance of winning was fairly low, and spending more beyond that amount produced diminishing returns in terms of votes.

But then money became more important. Everyone knows why: the decline of the party organizations, which used to publicize the names of likely candidates for free; the disappearance of the stay-at-home housewife and unemployed student, two erstwhile sources of free volunteer labor; the invention of television and of the maverick candidate who uses it to run against the party regulars; technological advances that make feasible "phone banks" and complicated direct-mail appeals; and finally, the rise of expensive consultants who know how to use the new technologies to best advantage. In 1948, Shapiro points out, a 35-year-old lawyer named Gerald Ford could defeat an incumbent congressman, in a typical campaign, with a budget of $7,400—$42,100 in today's currency. In 1984, Shapiro asked political consultants what it would cost to run for a contested seat in Ford's old district. He was told it would take a minimum of $250,000 to even stand a chance.[31] "I get almost-rich men in here all the time who say they've got $50,000 or $75,000 of their own money to run for Congress," consultant Matt Reese told Shapiro. "And I have to be the one to tell them that isn't enough."

In 1974, Congress attempted a reform that only seemed to make things worse. Individual campaign contributions were limited to $1,000 per election per candidate.[32] This made it more difficult for prospective candidates to raise the minimum amount of money necessary to have a chance. Instead of convincing one multimillionaire to give $250,000, they now had to convince 250 millionaires to give $1,000. Meanwhile, Congress approved far more generous donations funneled through the now-infamous "political action committees," or PACs. Some PACs are motivated by ideology, but most are looking to purchase votes on behalf of a single, private, economic interest.[33]

Reforms that might actually end this money influence get complicated, but they aren't as complicated as politicians, angling to preserve personal and partisan advantages, tend to make them. True, limiting individual campaign contributions does seem a dead end. You might think that if the limit were set low enough—say, only $25 to each candidate from each citizen—the result couldn't help but be democratic. But the effect of such a strict limit would be to transfer power to the sleazy direct-mail fundraisers who know how to tap the wallets of the middle class. Meanwhile, candidates who are rich themselves wouldn't have to struggle to raise small donations, thanks to a loophole carved out by the Supreme Court. According to the Court, it violates the First Amendment to restrict the amount a candidate may spend on his *own* campaign.[34]

A more promising approach is public financing. This is already the system used in presidential general elections, where it works reasonably well. Presidential nominees, once chosen, spend their time campaigning rather than fundraising.[35] The same effect could be achieved in congressional and lesser races. In essence, the taxpayers would offer each party's nominee something above the threshold amount required to get his basic message across—say $300,000 for a typical House race.[36] But the candidate would accept the government money on the condition that he not supplement it with his own wealth or with individual donations, a bit of arm-twisting that doesn't seem to upset the Supreme Court. That wouldn't stop well-funded candidates from refusing government money and financing their own campaigns, but if they did their opponents could be allowed to bust the limit as well.[37]

The main problem with public financing is that it's difficult to apply to primary elections, when there might be dozens of candidates who need to "get their message across." If we promise each entrant $300,000 in public funds, everyone will run for office. But some combination of "threshold" fundraising requirements and matching funds would ensure the ability of diverse candidates to reach voters, while ending the advantage of champion fundraisers. For example, we could raise the individual contribution limit to something like $50,000 per candidate, per primary election—but candidates could raise only $100,000 or so this way, and only on the condition that they agree to overall spending limits. Once a primary candidate raised a given amount of "seed money" ($50,000 again seems reasonable) public financing would kick in. Legislation now before Congress would create a similar system, though without relaxed contribution limits for "seed money."[38]

A second necessary reform would ban the PACs of corporations from soliciting corporate employees, and require that all PAC contributions be charged (on a pro-rated basis) against the individual PAC donor's campaign contribution limits. This would effectively eliminate the PAC advantage, and probably most of the PACs.[39]

Third, we could reduce the underlying need for campaign expenditures by, in effect, expanding the public sphere. Instead of prohibiting TV advertising, we could lower the amount of money candidates need to reach voters by providing free mailing privileges, plus free radio and television time. What if, for the two weeks before an election, the evening drive time on radio plus a half hour following the evening news on television were reserved for debates and free political speeches by the candidates? Ratings would decline, in all probability.[40] But elections would be public rituals far more absorbing than they are now—in no small part because it would be much easier to mount challenges to incumbents.

Changes along the above lines would visibly alter the culture of modern campaigns, and of government itself. Lobbyists would have to spend their time trying to organize grass-roots letter-writing campaigns instead of putting $5,000 checks in envelopes. Legislators would stop sponsoring "juice bills"—the professional slang for proposals designed mainly to provoke monied interests into frenzies of contribution. Politicians would be judged more on their speeches and less on their fundraisers' Rolodexes. The core of public life would again be firmly grounded in the egalitarian distribution of ballots.

Health care.   Given the continuing threats to social equality, Civic Liberals can hardly be satisfied with restoring the public sphere where it has deteriorated. They need to seize on new possibilities to expand it. Of all the potential new egalitarian institutions on the horizon, the biggest one involves the provision of health care.

Health isn't a good like other goods. If someone can't afford a car, we're willing to say well, he doesn't have a car. But if a man who can't afford medical care is bleeding on the sidewalk, we are going to provide him with it one way or another, at public expense if necessary. As with the draft, the issue is life or death. The impulse to remove at least some health care decisions from the marketplace is almost primordial. We can debate how to pay for those who can't afford care.

But no respectable American politician would leave the man on the sidewalk.

Of course, saying health care should be available to everyone doesn't necessarily mean it must be available in equal measure, or that the experience of getting it will necessarily be one that mixes classes. But the goal of universal coverage offers a solid base for building a potent democratic institution. We know it cements social equality to have Americans attend the same schools and serve in the same army. What effect would it have if they used the same doctors? The experience might not be as intense as school or service, but it would be repeated throughout a person's life.

Certainly health care seems to play a major socially equalizing role in Western Europe, where every country has some sort of universal national health plan. In most of them, the plan's egalitarianism is a matter of fierce national pride, "part of the cement that binds a people together as a nation."[41] When everyone uses the same system, it not only reinforces "solidarity," it also helps ensure the quality of the treatment. The upper middle class will not tolerate bad service for very long (just as it wouldn't have tolerated the Vietnam War if its sons had been drafted).[42]

European social democrats look on American health care with horror. We have a patchwork system that, rather than putting everyone in the same boat, puts different groups in different boats and lets some fall in between. At the bottom, Medicaid covers only about 42 percent of the poor, mainly those on welfare or other mothers with young children.[43] At the top, the revenue code heavily subsidizes generous employer-paid health plans by not counting them as income (a $40-billion tax break).[44] Falling between boats are those who are unemployed, self-employed, or whose employers don't have a company plan. They are left to fend for themselves, to buy private insurance (with after-tax dollars). Between 31 and 37 million people aren't insured at all, and that number has been growing. But if Americans reach the magic age of 65, they can relax. They qualify for Medicare, which will cover most of their bills.[45]

Now, these are just different ways of paying for health care. Conceivably they could all wind up financing the same actual care for everyone. And it's true that there's more class-mixing in the health system than in, say, the restaurant system. The best hospitals serve people from all classes. If you have a car crash, you go to the same emergency room as everyone else.[46] A doctor friend of mine who worked at a New York hospital remembers a corporate CEO who had symptoms of a mild heart attack and had to wait for treatment behind more serious cases. He couldn't believe his money and status couldn't get him a place at the front of the line.

But in important ways health care is in fact segregated according to the method of financing. A quarter of American doctors don't take Medicaid patients, in large part because the program pays so little—roughly two-thirds what Medi*care* pays. In New York, Medicaid will reimburse a physician only $11 for an office visit.[47] Meanwhile, Americans without health insurance tend not to see doctors at all for routine treatments; then when they get sick they wind up in hospital emergency rooms. Hospitals used to try to "dump" such uninsured patients. Now by law they must treat them until their condition "stabilizes," at which point they typically transfer them to public hospitals, which can't refuse them. At Washington, D.C.'s General Hospital, for example, 60 percent of the patients are now uninsured.[48] Meanwhile, high-end health consumers seldom go near an emergency room. They routinely visit the best doctors, whose offices are uncrowded by Medicaid cases or the uninsured.

This medical system is often called "private" (even though the government foots 41 percent of the bill) because it retains significant free market features.[49] Doctors and hospitals are typically paid for each service performed. If you have more money, you can buy more and better services, or more and better health insurance. Doctors and many hospitals (as well as the industries that supply them with drugs and technology) are free to follow the logic of the market and make as much money as they can.

What's unusual isn't that this market system is inegalitarian, but that it also seems to be quite inefficient. Several well-known factors conspire to prevent the health care market from working. First, conditions of informed consumer choice appear to be absent. Most people shop for health care when they are ill, and they aren't about to question a doctor's opinion of what treatment they need. Doctors tend to order up expensive tests and procedures because that's how they make money, and because they're scared of malpractice suits. Since most people are insured, they don't care that much about the cost. Those who *are* paying (employers, insurance companies, and the government) have found it difficult, if not impossible, to force doctors and patients to economize on treatment when neither has much of an interest in doing so.

Second, as noted, we won't *let* the health care market operate like other markets. We aren't going to let the uninsured who come into an emergency room go untreated, and it happens that emergency room care is exceptionally expensive. If society had to pay Cadillac prices to buy a car for everyone who couldn't afford a Chevy in the market, our "automobile delivery system" might not be so efficient either.

A health care system in which competing insurers pay for every service doctors can think of ordering up is, economist Uwe Reinhardt points out, an efficient way of doing one thing: transferring the maximum share of GNP to doctors and hospitals.[50] By the late eighties, it had become clear that insurance companies and employers weren't getting anywhere controlling costs on their own. America was paying 12 percent of its GNP for health care, while Canada was paying 8.8 percent, West Germany 8.1 percent, and Japan 6.8 percent.[51] Americans didn't even seem to be getting better care for their extra money. Business leaders, faced with higher health bills than their foreign competitors, turned against capitalism in the health sector. Bipartisan commissions sprouted to consider national health plans.[52]

We're probably going to get some such plan in the not-too-distant future. The candidates are:

- The socialized British model, in which everyone is eligible for care in a national health service run by the government. Doctors are employed by that health service for a salary, rather than being paid for every operation or exam they perform.[53]
- The Canadian system, which in theory socializes the financing of health care but not its provision. Basically, everyone gets free government insurance. Doctors remain "private"—they aren't government employees. Patients choose the doctor they prefer. But the doctor has to accept the government's insurance payment. (No "extra billing.") As the only buyer of health services, the government then uses its leverage to bargain down the price doctors and hospitals charge. In practice, it also winds up rationing some expensive procedures by maintaining waiting lists.[54]
- The German system, in which most citizens are assigned to one of several insurance pools. They pay premiums according to their incomes. The government in effect negotiates for all the pools, bargaining down prices as in Canada.[55]

- Medicaid "buy-in" plans. Under this scheme, everyone could buy a basic, Medicaid-like government insurance policy for a variable premium that reflected their ability to pay. The big government subsidy for low-income purchasers would have to be funded somehow, and costs would have to be controlled somehow. Individuals could actually be *required* to obtain some minimum insurance package, much as they are required by many states to have auto insurance. No more relying on unpaid emergency room care.[56]
- Subsidizing insurance in a competitive marketplace. The idea, as proposed by the conservative Heritage Foundation, is to break the link between insurance and employment by ending the tax break for employee health benefits. Instead, the government would provide tax credits or vouchers that varied with an individual's income and medical needs. In theory, people would take these credits and bargain with insurers. In practice, health insurance for the poor would have to be almost 100 percent subsidized to keep it affordable, and some of the poor might still be served by Medicaid. President Bush endorsed a voucher approach in 1992.[57]
- Plugging holes in the current patchwork. Employers would be required to either offer health insurance to their workers or else pay a tax to the government. This "play or pay" approach reinforces, rather than breaks, the link between insurance and employment. It has been promoted most conspicuously by congressional Democrats, including Sen. Edward Kennedy, Sen. Jay Rockefeller, and Rep. Henry Waxman. In this plan, too, the government would need to operate some sort of residual scheme that offered insurance to the uninsured (including the unemployed).[58]

The important thing for Civic Liberalism isn't which of these systems is more "socialistic," which is more "redistributive," or even which is most efficient in controlling costs.[59] Certainly efficiency is important (it's the inefficiency of a pure market approach that makes health care a candidate for inclusion in the public sphere). But Civic Liberalism is concerned with social equality. It would demand that whichever system we choose be one that the vast majority of Americans, rich and poor, use on an equal basis. In short, what matters is that everybody wait in the same waiting rooms.

It's not necessarily true that the more "socialized" a system is, the better it meets this social-egalitarian requirement. The British, German, and Canadian systems all currently meet the goal. The "socialized" British system allows those with money to purchase private insurance, but that doesn't undermine class-mixing because most of the private insurance merely supplements the national health system, which is where the most advanced, high-tech medicine is still practiced. Only about 10 percent of the population uses the private system (though that percentage is growing).

Germany also manages to include about 90 percent of its population in a single system. The Germans do this by the simple expedient of requiring 75 percent of the population to join one of several "statutory sickness funds." Those Germans with incomes above a certain threshold can opt out, but once they opt out, they can never opt back in.[60] Not surprisingly, most remain with their assigned funds. The system's motto might be, "We have ways of making you stay." Canada pursues an even simpler and more effective strategy. It flat out makes it illegal to buy private basic health insurance—and Canada's waiting rooms mix virtually 100 percent of the population.[61]

But less sweeping plans are less likely to achieve this objective. Senator Kennedy's patchwork employer-based scheme, in particular, looks like a loser for social equality. Medicaid and Medicare would still exist, probably with differential standards of care. Some employers would still provide lavish, fee-for-service insurance; some would consign their employees to spartan HMOs. Taxpayers (most of whom would be already covered, one way or another) probably wouldn't want to pay for much in the way of gap-filling last-resort insurance. We'd still have a system in which different classes report to different waiting rooms.[62]

It's at least conceivable that a broader subsidized-insurance scheme would do better, especially if (by ending the tax break for health benefits) it cut the tie between the insured and their employers. The government could, for example, so heavily underwrite a standardized, basic insurance policy that the vast majority of citizens would want to take advantage of it. In practice, however, this is unlikely to happen. Subsidies are expensive (roughly $1 billion to provide even inadequate Medicaid-level insurance for each million people).[63] Upper middle-class taxpayers might still not want to finance, for everyone, health insurance that is also good enough for upper middle-class taxpayers.[64] And if, as in the Heritage plan, Americans are encouraged to buy all the fancy medical services they can afford, there's no reason to think the health care system wouldn't be as segmented by income as other markets.

Even under the most promising plans, the crunch (for Civic Liberalism) will come when attempts to control the overall cost of health care force some method of rationing ever-more-expensive medical procedures. What happens when affluent Americans—*increasingly* affluent Americans, remember—are faced with this rationing? They will not calmly take their place in the queue for CAT scanners or proton-beam accelerators or artificial hearts. They will try to go outside the "universal" system and pay more money to get the expensive technology they want.[65]

⌐he temptation will be to let them, with the result of producing a two-tier system of elaborate care for the affluent and basic care for everyone else. A Civic Liberal strategy could not afford to be so accommodating. It would have to impose regulations, such as those in Germany, making it unappealing to opt out of the "universal" system. At the very least a heavy tax disincentive will be required. The goal would only be to make enough (say, 90 percent) of the populace use the public sphere's waiting rooms. It's one thing, Civic Liberals could argue, for the rich to be able to buy the nicest cars, or the houses with the nicest views. It's another thing to make it easy for money to buy life itself.[66]

Day Ca   lealth care isn't the only new public sphere possibility.[67] Day care is another service with impressive growth potential. The debate over day care has been between those (mainly Democrats) who want to encourage communal day-care centers, and those (such as President Bush) who would simply give cash to parents with preschool kids and let the parents decide whether to use the money to buy day care. Civic Liberals would tend to favor communal centers. Indeed, as a public-sphere institution day care offers a rare opportunity to escape the tyranny of suburban class-segregation. Unlike schools, day-care centers can be conveniently located near places of work rather than near homes. And poor preschool children aren't nearly as threatening to upper middle-class parents as, say, poor adolescents. Locate the d⋯ ⸱re centers near work, and let the toddlers of secretaries mix with ⸱ ⸱dlers of bank presidents. Let their parents worry together and visit together.[68]

These major Civic Liberal initiatives don't exhaust the possibilities for creating an expansive public sphere. Take the transportation system, for example. Highways are the urban public spaces that have been degraded the least, perhaps because they are what makes possible the avoidance of all the other public spaces. But the car is not solely the insidious engine of privatization that communitarian planners like Lewis Mumford inveigh against. It is an egalitarian public-sphere institution in its own right. The rules of the highway do not respect money; a Rolls-Royce can't buy the right to go through stop signs. And where roads are well-maintained, experiencing this automotive democracy is generally pleasant. That, I think, is one of the reasons that Southern California has yet to achieve the day-to-day class stratification of New York City. True, the rich in Los Angeles are different—they drive better cars. But they can only enjoy those cars under the egalitarian constraints of the public highways. In New York, nobody drives and the difference between being poor and rich is the difference between riding the fetid subway or summoning a radio-call taxi.

The Civic Liberal issue, when it comes to transportation, isn't whether to have mass transit or rely on private cars. What counts is less the mode of transportation than whether it is a universal and satisfying experience. Mass transit systems can be wonderful. But if they are allowed to deteriorate so that only the poor (who have little choice) use them, they become an instrument of class segregation. If they are sufficiently safe, clean, and efficient so that virtually everybody uses them (as is the case in Washington, D.C., despite its underclass problem), they can be a powerful egalitarian device, one that affirms rather than negates the ability of everyone to get along without class distinctions.

A whole range of other government institutions—museums, post offices, libraries—at least potentially enforce social equality by providing services to all citizens. There is an important distinction to be made here, habitually ignored by American admirers of European social democracies, between provision of such common *services* and the provision of *cash* favored by Money Liberalism. With "in-kind, universal" services, Robert Kuttner notes, people of all classes actually meet and interact with each other and with those doing the servicing. They wait together, flirt, swap sob stories and advice, save each other's place in line, keep an eye on each other's kids. The "middle class is ... reminded that poor people are human," Kuttner writes.[69] This is the stuff of social equality. But virtually none of these virtues are evident when all the government does is distribute cash benefits—even if, as Money Liberals typically recommend, benefits go to the middle class and rich as well as the poor. Recipients receive their benefit checks in isolation. The cash is spent, and is intended to be spent, in the private, money sphere. No communal experience is involved. On the contrary, the recipient's attention is focused more intensely on the importance of money and what it can buy. How much solidarity is there in cashing a check? Rich and poor don't even cash them in the same places.[70]

Yet American social democrats (including Kuttner) tend to lump cash payments—family allowances, income subsidies, old-age pensions—with libraries, health care, and other services as noble "citizen entitlements" that "reinforce a sense of community and solidarity."[71] This idea that "universal" cash transfer programs somehow produce social equality is another reflection of the Money Liberal faith that social equality can be grounded in the distribution and redistribution of money.[72] Civic Liberals would reject it. "Services for all, not checks for all" is the motto they would squeeze onto their bumper stickers. Social equality requires more than a community of check cashers.[73] It requires a part of *life* in which prosperous and non-prosperous Americans actually do things on an equal footing.

The problem confronting Civic Liberals is that government seems to provide services so damn inefficiently. But here, perversely, liberals mainly have themselves to blame. A variety of misguided liberal policies, all largely correctable, virtually guarantee government ineptitude. One example: liberal Democrats, at the behest of the AFL-CIO, tenaciously defend a law called the Davis-Bacon Act that requires government builders to pay inflated union wage scales even when workers might be willing to work for less. In Boston, in 1981, the Act required the federal government to hire carpenters at $19 an hour when private contractors were paying only $13.34.[74] Bush's housing secretary, Jack Kemp, had to beg the AFL-CIO just to exempt a few tenant-run housing projects. Something called the Service Contract Act extends similar rules to government contractors (such as window-washers and garbage collectors) outside the construction trade.

Why should the government have to pay more, when it decides to provide a service, than what it would take to attract willing, qualified workers? Even without Davis-Bacon–style rigging, the tendency of liberals to support the wage demands of government employees almost always leads to a deterioration in service.[75] In 1977, Alex Heard reports, the District of Columbia library system had 555 employees and branches were open seventy-two hours a week. By 1981, after years of steady raises, librarians were making $20,000 to $30,000 a year—but the system had only 384 employees, local branches were open forty hours a week, and the number of librarians actually serving the public was cut from twelve per branch to six.[76]

Then there is the civil service. As Charles Peters points out, when the Post Office was run as part of a political patronage system, it worked relatively well. The postmaster might be your Congressman's uncle, but he'd have to deliver the mail or you could vote both your Congressman (and him) out of office. In this sense, patronage is to government what the profit motive is to private enterprise: the only reliable incentive for performance. Yet liberals, in part at the behest of their public-employee "constituency," have tended to promote the near-complete replacement of patronage with civil service protection. Today, out of about 2,200,000 federal workers, a grand total of 3,227, or 0.15 percent, are political (that is, patronage) appointees. Civil service rules, coupled with liberal judicial decisions granting public workers "property rights" in their jobs, make it virtually impossible for a manager to fire an incompetent worker who wants to fight his dismissal through the courts. In 1990, in the whole federal government, only 403 civil servants were fired for poor performance.[77]

The net effect of all of these progressive liberal reforms is to ensure that anything the government does it will do less well than private enterprise. That includes building parks, theaters, and sewage treatment plants, or issuing drivers' licenses, stocking libraries, cleaning the sidewalks, and caring for the bedridden. No wonder people use Federal Express, UPS, and Mailboxes U.S.A. instead of the Postal Service—that wherever possible they abandon the public for the private sphere.

Even if all the misguided liberal policies of the past were repealed, of course, government services such as the Post Office would probably still be less efficient than UPS. That's a price Civic Liberals would be willing to pay to preserve these institutions as centers of egalitarian community life. But now the price is so high that only the poor, who have no alternative, must pay it. In big cities, post offices increasingly resemble Third World institutions, filled with immigrants mailing complicated packages to Nicaragua. The lines are interminable, the clerks often jaded and unhelpful. Middle-class patrons take one look and head for the door. The government institution remains, but it is no longer an institution that mixes the classes, except in the most abstract sense that both rich and poor still get letters with stamps on them.

Civic Liberalism would also recognize and protect the social-egalitarian power of class-mixing institutions that are technically in the "private sector." Some of these have already been mentioned: casual hangouts like taverns, coffee houses, and drug stores. Ray Oldenburg calls these "third places" because they offer an alternative to the other two main sites of our lives, home and work. One essential characteristic of a good third place is that it is accessible to people of all income levels, that, as Oldenburg puts it, "worldly status claims must be checked at the door in order that all within remain equals."[78] In the mid-seventeenth century, he points out, coffee houses were actually called "levelers" because they mixed the various classes in a way unheard of in the old feudal order.[79] It's easy to underestimate the significance of such unpretentious institutions. But they embody much of what Americans feel they've lost since the move from small towns— the general store, the pharmacy soda fountain of *It's a Wonderful Life*, the neighborhood bar romanticized in "Cheers."

The decline of those "private" democratic places is bound up in the process of suburbanization. Zoning changes that allow coffee shops, stores, and taverns to locate near residences, instead of in single-purpose commercial strips, would help.[80] Still, it would be hard for even a nearby neighborhood tavern to mix classes in a neighborhood that is itself segregated by class.[81] Fully restoring third places as class-mixing institutions will have to await the success of longer-term strategies to integrate the suburbs by income, as well as by race.

But some privately operated enterprises that are part of our public life don't rely on class-mixing at the neighborhood level. Organized professional sports are an obvious example. Going to a major league baseball game remains one of the few enjoyable experiences shared at the same time, in the same place, by people of various classes—one reason it's considered so precious. But even the democratic aspects of spectator sports are threatened by a number of recent developments. Attending a ball game has become a distinctly less egalitarian experience, for example, with the unfortunate invention of the tax-deductible corporate "skybox." Team owners now routinely demand stadium renovations that enable them to maximize the square-footage devoted to the rich.[82] Another inegalitarian development is cable television, which allows broadcasters to restrict spectatorship to those who can afford to subscribe. In 1987, most New York Yankee home games were available only on cable. The result was a tremendous protest and a threat of congressional action, in part because large sections of New York—the poorer sections—weren't even wired for cable.[83]

In general, the decline of network broadcasting (and the advent of demographically targeted "narrowcasting" on cable) should disturb social-egalitarians. Network TV is often awful, but it once had the virtue of giving all Americans a common, classless set of cultural experiences. As the network audience share declines (it's fallen from 92 percent to 64 percent), that is increasingly no longer true. Instead of everybody watching Milton Berle, young professionals watch the Arts & Entertainment network while the less cultured watch "Married...With Children."[84]

Once the egalitarian importance of these private institutions was acknowledged, Civic Liberals could take some simple steps to halt their deterioration. The tax deduction for tickets to sporting events (stadium skyboxes and season tickets) could be completely eliminated, for example—not on economic grounds, but on social-egalitarian grounds.[85] Television coverage of sporting events could be strictly regulated to keep it universal, preventing cable companies from buying the rights and then broadcasting only to the cable-ready affluent. If necessary, sports franchises themselves could be regulated, or purchased by municipalities, or even seized by eminent domain.[86] If the TV networks collapse completely, the government could establish a BBC-style network, less snooty than the current Public Broadcasting System, with a preferred spot on the broadcast spectrum nationwide. These may seem like relatively small things, compared with the draft or national health care. But they matter.

Holidays constitute a final, easily overlooked public-sphere institution that might be revived. Holidays were once typically days of actual common celebration, of parades, ceremonies, feasts, songs, speeches, and marches. Today, most of this has been replaced by the public holiday's private competitor, the vacation. "Holidays are a more egalitarian distribution of leisure than vacations," Walzer argues, "because they can't be purchased: they are one more thing money can't buy. They are enjoined for everyone, enjoyed by everyone."[87] In contrast, private vacations are frequently spent flaunting the inequalities of the money sphere at expensive resorts.

The vacation is a relatively recent innovation, the product of bourgeois prosperity. The idea that wage earners could take paid vacations is an even more recent development; it only became widespread after World War I.[88] It's fair to say that even in the 1930s and 1940s ordinary workers spent much more of their leisure time attending parades, carnivals, funerals, executions, and other communal events than they do today, and a good deal less time checking into motels. Today even solemn public holidays—holidays with as much contemporary meaning as Martin Luther King's birthday—are widely seen as simply more private leisure time, which is why we routinely fiddle with their dates to create three-day weekends.

It's not that vacations are bad while holidays are good. On any given Sunday, I'd probably rather be lying on the beach in Florida than watching a parade. But parades are valuable too. Civic Liberals could take some minimal steps to restore the integrity of holidays. They could be returned to their original dates, interrupting the week if necessary. Communal observance of at least the most solemn holidays could be restored, even if it were tailored to fit the time constraints of modern life. What if, on Memorial Day, the whole nation—cars and buses, factories and TV stations, lawyers and mailmen—stopped for a minute, in silence, to memorialize the dead? With a draft in place, the democracy of the commemoration would echo the risk of being commemorated.

After the Persian Gulf War in 1991, there were what seemed like three months of victory parades. Even the troops got sick of it. Others objected to the corporate-sponsored, Super-Bowl pomposity of some of the events, the maudlin yellow-ribbon imagery. All of these objections were valid. But when I went down to the Mall in Washington to see the capital's parade for myself, the objections also dropped away. Mostly I saw a bunch of soldiers, both young and middle-aged, being cheered by a well-behaved crowd of their fellow citizens. Blacks and whites, crackers and yuppies mingled without any of the submerged tension that is so often evident in Washington, D.C. Rich and poor mingled too, though it was difficult to tell who was which, since practically everyone in the crowd was wearing sports shirts or sweatshirts. Here, in this tacky, militaristic setting, was something the left-wing radicals of the sixties had been trying to achieve, something I'd almost given up thinking our society could provide. It wasn't Orwell's Barcelona, I don't doubt. But it was as close as I'd seen in decades.

The point isn't that the Civic Liberal reforms suggested above would ensure social equality. That, as the next chapter argues, will require something more. The point is that once we set out to rebuild the public sphere, we can make fairly large improvements fairly expeditiously. It requires nothing we haven't done ourselves in the past— or that we can't copy, with appropriate modifications, from other democratic capitalist nations. We can have a health care system that almost everyone uses on an equal basis. Canada has one. Britain has one. Germany has one. We can minimize the role of money in our democracy and maximize the time we spend in egalitarian political dialogue. We can frame our obligations so that rich and poor Americans serve the nation together. We did that in World War II. We did it in the 1950s. We can have a society in which the various classes use the same subways and drop off their kids at the same day-care centers and run into each other at the post office. We don't have to repeal capitalism or abandon meritocracy to do these things. We don't have to equalize incomes or make incomes "more equal" or even stop incomes from getting more *un*equal to do these things. We just have to do them.

CHAPTER 7

Welfare and the
Underclass Threat

Not every part of the public sphere is readily revived, however. In particular, nothing I've suggested so far would change where people live or with whom their children go to school. Nor would it encourage them to use urban public spaces that have been abandoned for fear of crime. Without class-mixing in such places, can a Civic Liberal strategy hope to counter the inegalitarian forces of money and merit? Maybe not. Imagine a well-to-do American who is drafted at age 18, or who serves in a "teacher's corps." He votes in publicly financed, PAC-less elections, visits a doctor who also serves the poor. As time passes he may check into a public hospital or take his preschool children to a class-mixed day-care center. But he still lives in an exclusive suburb, still sends his school-age kids to classes with other affluent kids, still avoids the parks at dusk. Contact with members of other classes, as equals, is not necessarily a major part of his daily routine.

Why are neighborhoods, schools, and public spaces so difficult to make part of a class-mixing public sphere? There are reasons peculiar to each institution, as we'll see. But there is one factor common to all: fear of the "ghetto poor" underclass. The very existence of an underclass, of course, represents a profound violation of social equality. Americans in our ghetto communities are not only frequently too poor to lead dignified lives. They are isolated from the rest of their fellow citizens, isolated physically and culturally—isolated by, if nothing else, the antipathy of the larger society. For them, social equality is an impossibility.

But it is also the underclass that most obviously sets in motion the vicious circle in which the degradation of public life in cities encourages the flight to the suburbs (which drains cities of the tax money with which to maintain the public sphere, et cetera). This might not be such a problem for social egalitarians if the suburbs mixed all the various *non*-underclasses. But of course suburbs tend to be class-segregated.[1] That means the opportunities for face-to-face mingling of rich and poor are (quite intentionally) restricted, even when suburbs themselves maintain extensive public facilities. Beverly Hills, California, has a beautiful Post Office and a very nice library. But they are venues of socializing mainly for the affluent who live nearby. Every institution of daily leisure and commerce, every "third place," every grocery store, coffee shop, tavern, YMCA, florist, or newsstand that would be an instrument of social equality in an income-integrated neighborhood is lost to Civic Liberalism when those institutions flee to stratified suburbs. Even in a Canada-style national health insurance system, many doctors' offices might remain class-segregated if the neighborhoods in which they're located are not class-mixed.

Unless we can reverse the vicious circle provoked by the underclass, the public sphere will remain fatally incomplete. This is a quantitative problem facing the Civic Liberal strategy. There is also a qualitative problem. If my version of Civic Liberalism is susceptible to a generic delusion, it's the idea that we can create social equality by the facile exertion of public authority, by simply forcing the classes together in subways, in hospitals, in national service outposts. But will those experiences by themselves add up to a culture of equality? Without a basis in common, cross-class *values,* almost certainly not. Lacking these values, the communal exercises of public life might be numerous but meaningless. At worst, they will be resented and resisted.

My argument is that these two problems, quantitative and qualitative, have the same solution. Specifically, if it's the underclass that destroys the possibility of a sufficiently capacious civic sphere, it's the *solution* to the underclass problem that offers the normative foundation for a culture of equality. We're looking for a value, shared by rich and poor alike, on which to build an egalitarian life. It seems to me there is only one real candidate: work. And work, not coincidentally, is the value that is in danger of disappearing in the culture of the underclass. Bringing the isolated ghetto poor back into the mainstream society requires enforcing the work ethic—in the process, firmly establishing (or reestablishing) work as a unifying civic virtue. This will take another sharp break with Money Liberalism, as well as another stage of Civic Liberal activism.

Karl Marx, in his early writings, confessed his need to find a class whose aspirations would establish universal values, a class with "radical chains." He found that class in the proletariat, the liberation of which was supposed to end the domination of man by man.[2] The underclass plays a similar role for Civic Liberalism, but in reverse fashion, as villain rather than hero. It is a class whose values are so inimical to America's potential universal culture that its negation, and transformation, will allow those universal values to flower.

What do I mean by "underclass"? Like "middle class" or "upper class," "underclass" has no single, precise definition. The term has acquired lurid connotations, suggesting something monstrous and even subhuman, as if, once caught in this "under" group, people can never escape. That's obviously untrue. Americans escape the underclass all the time.

But that doesn't mean "underclass" fails to usefully describe something. The sociologist William Julius Wilson talks mainly of urban residents with a "weak attachment to the labor force." Others emphasize additional types of impoverishing behavior—out-of-wedlock births, single-parent families, school truancy, crime, and welfare dependence. The key point is that, when concentrated in ghetto neighborhoods, all these problems reinforce each other in a way that frustrates the power of even a robust economy to pull people out of poverty. Certainly the private economy, by itself, will not transform "communities" where 80 percent of the children are born into fatherless families, where over 60 percent of the population is on welfare, where the work ethic has decayed and the entrepreneurial drive is channeled into gangs and drug-pushing, where "getting paid" is slang for mugging somebody.[3]

How big is the underclass? In 1980, in America's one hundred largest cities, there were about 1.8 million poor people living in "extreme poverty areas"—that is, neighborhoods with poverty rates of more than 40 percent. There were about 2.5 million people living in neighborhoods with a high incidence of social problems (female-headed families; welfare receipt; low male participation in the labor force; school dropouts). Obviously, not everyone living in those neighborhoods is a member of the "underclass."[4] Even if you counted them all, the underclass would embrace only a fraction of the approximately 31 million poor Americans.

Is the underclass black? Certainly most blacks aren't in it. Two-thirds of African Americans currently live above the poverty line.[5] And it has become fashionable among some conservatives to downplay the significance of race in the poverty culture, the better to lay the blame squarely on liberal welfare policies. "The focus on blacks cripples progress," wrote Charles Murray, the most prominent conservative underclass theorist, in 1986. He claimed to have found a poor town in Ohio where white mothers were producing illegitimate babies at the same levels (25 percent of all births) that, among blacks in 1965, had prompted Daniel Patrick Moynihan to produce his famous report on the decline of the black family.[6]

But it's simply stupid to pretend that the underclass is not mainly black.[7] A large ongoing survey at the University of Michigan shows that although African Americans compose only 12 percent of the population, they make up 55 percent of those who stay poor for a long time, and over 60 percent of those on welfare for a long time.[8] In this respect the old stereotype that most of the poor are black is accurate. In 1980, of the 1.8 million poor people in "extreme poverty" neighborhoods in America's one hundred largest cities, some 68 percent were black (21 percent were Hispanic; only 10 percent were white). Blacks constituted 58 percent of those living in neighborhoods with extreme social problems (high dropout rates, female-headed families, et cetera). Whites made up 21 percent, Hispanics 19 percent.[9]

So yes, the problem we are talking about is the culture of our largely black (and largely urban) ghettos.[10] It is only a part of the problem facing black Americans, although all blacks are unfairly stigmatized by the behavior of the underclass minority. It is only part of the broader problem of poverty, although it is the most intractable part. But it is the part that poses the greatest threat to the public sphere and social equality.

Much, though by no means all, of the fear provoked by the underclass has to do with crime. I'm not saying that most people who live in ghetto areas are lawbreakers; they're more likely to be victims of lawbreakers. I am saying what every urban resident knows to be true, and what the statistics show to be true, which is that underclass areas are awful environments that produce a large subculture of criminality, often violent criminality. Economist Kip Viscusi has estimated that about a quarter of the income of young ghetto men comes from crime.[11] That's less than many stereotypes would have it. But it's still a very high percentage, compared with criminal activity among other segments of society. It's enough to represent a significant chunk of what crime there is in our cities. Several studies document a connection between welfare and criminal activity, even after other variables have been accounted for.[12] In New York City in the mid-seventies, according to one series of studies, half of the juvenile delinquents and young drug users were from welfare families.[13]

New York can spend all the money it wants—$2.5 billion is the current figure—rebuilding Times Square. But if tourists continue to be murdered by roving "wolfpacks," Times Square will never be a place where most ordinary New Yorkers go unless they have to, and even then they'll hurry through looking over their shoulder and avoiding all possible human contact.[14] Safe public restrooms will be an impossibility, so people will have an excuse for urinating on the street. The affluent will seek the pleasure of crowds in private spaces—restaurants, galleries, corporate functions, privately policed malls—with members of their own class.

Again, New York is only the most prominent example of public-sphere deterioration. The same process is at work in most major metropolitan areas. In late June 1991, Detroit tried to alter its image as a dying ghetto town by staging an International Freedom Festival. An evening fireworks display drew an estimated 700,000 people to the city. Later, videotapes surfaced showing roving crowds of teenagers, mainly black women, punching and kicking at least six white women in two separate incidents. According to the victims, the attackers had yelled "Get the white bitch," and the police had paid little attention until the videotape appeared. The immediate reaction of the Detroit city council was to criticize the police for assigning only 863 officers to the event. But who wants to go near a city if a massive police presence is necessary to contain the hostility and criminality on the streets?[15] Detroit, in fact, lost a fifth of its population in the eighties, and almost *half* its population in the three decades before 1990. Portions of its depopulated core are now returning to nature, as the municipal government can't afford the tractors required to cut the tall grass growing in vacant lots.[16]

When it comes to the schools, fear of the underclass magnifies an exclusionary impulse that is always present. As an upper middle-class American, I'd have few qualms about sending my child to the same doctor as a teenage welfare mother's child, or even to the same daycare center. It's another thing to send my child to a school populated with welfare children. The point of schools is to transmit culture, and nobody (in the black middle class, especially) wants his kids immersed in a culture of poverty.

Even without the underclass, of course, the schools would be subject to powerful stratifying forces, because education is a peculiar good. It is, for one thing, a "competitive" good. What counts isn't only how much of it you have "bought," but whether you have bought more of it than others. I can enjoy listening to an expensive stereo system even though all my neighbors also have one. But a big part of the reason I would pay to send my kid to Exeter is precisely that my neighbors' kids won't get that advantage.[17] Likewise, I might move to an expensive suburb with good schools to give my children a leg up over those who can't afford to live there.

Worse, education is not like other goods, even other "competitive" goods, because its worth, in some sense, varies with the qualities of the other people consuming it. Health care would be hard to distribute on an egalitarian basis if the care I got depended on how healthy my fellow patients were. Absent contagion, it doesn't (in fact, hospitals with a lot of really sick people in them are often the best hospitals, in part because they get the most practice). But my kid's education obviously depends, to some degree, on the attitudes and actions of the other children he goes to school with. He will learn from them as well as from his teachers.

Parents, therefore, tend to choose schools precisely because they have the "right" kind of people in them—perhaps smart people, perhaps people from the class or ethnic group with which they wish their kids to identify. That means parents also want schools that exclude the "wrong" kind of people. A lot of this is snobbery, some of it is racism, but the point is it's not just snobbery and racism. To at least some extent, kids will learn more math and speak clearer English if they're surrounded by kids who care about learning math and who speak clear English.[18]

Turning the schools into class-mixers, then, would be difficult even if the underclass didn't exist. The Civic Liberal strategies that might be attempted in that situation are considered in Chapter 10. But, for now, the reality is that the underclass does exist, and it is the underclass that transforms the suburbs' natural exclusionary impulse into a primordial demand. All it takes is a single drive-by shooting, or the sight of metal-detectors in school hallways, to make the virtues of class-mixing seem fairly theoretical. It will be one thing for social egalitarians to ask a $150,000-a-year lawyer to risk sending his child to school with the children of $15,000-a-year working-class families. It's another thing to ask him to send his kids to a school where they might be stabbed by crackheads. The Civic Liberal ideal of class-mixing in the classroom is quite hopeless as long as the underclass is one of the classes to be mixed.

How did the underclass happen? There are many places to start, but a good one is President Franklin Roosevelt's State of the Union address in the winter of 1935, the middle of the Depression. FDR had assumed office in 1933, and since then his government had spent billions attempting to help the poor back on their feet. The Federal Emergency Relief Administration was handing out money to the states, most of which chose to spend it on "direct relief"—a cash dole—or thinly disguised "makework." But the relief rolls were rising. Twenty million were receiving public assistance, including a third of the state of South Dakota. Roosevelt was now convinced that any form of handout sapped the morale and spirit of the unemployed.[19] He told Congress:

> [C]ontinued dependence upon relief induces a spiritual and moral disintegration fundamentally destructive to the national fibre. To dole out relief in this way is to administer a narcotic, a subtle destroyer of the human spirit.... I am not willing that the vitality of our people be further sapped by the giving of cash, of market baskets, of a few hours of weekly work cutting grass, raking leaves, or picking up papers in the public parks. We must preserve not only the bodies of the unemployed from destitution but also their self-respect, their self-reliance and courage and determination.[20]

To take the place of "direct" relief, Roosevelt proposed a large new public works program, the Works Progress Administration, to employ over 3 million jobless.[21] Unlike makework, WPA work would be "useful in the sense that it affords permanent improvements in living conditions or that it creates future new wealth for the nation." FDR mentioned slum clearance, housing construction, rural electrification, highway construction. Those who weren't expected to work (the aged, the blind) would still get cash relief. Workers might also earn the right to collect unemployment compensation if they lost their jobs. But aside from those temporary benefits, there would be no cash aid for Americans who were considered capable of joining the labor force. "Work must be found for the able-bodied but destitute," Roosevelt declared. "The Federal Government must and shall quit this business of relief."[22]

Roosevelt's 1935 State of the Union is the founding document of our "welfare state." Social Security pensions, as well as unemployment compensation and assistance to the aged and disabled—they all date from this speech. It's ironic, then, that the word "welfare" has come to mean the very thing FDR denounced in his address: cash "relief" to the able-bodied. It's ironic, too, that the defenders of such cash relief for the past several decades have been liberal Democrats. Worse, today's liberals are unable to shake conservative charges that the "relief" programs they've come to support have actually financed the proliferation of single-parent families in the underclass.

How did FDR's decision come unravelled? In one important respect, it didn't. Our "welfare state" still doesn't offer much cash (mainly food stamps and stingy state "general assistance" money) to able-bodied men and women, married or single, *if they have no children.* But if you are a poor single parent (almost always a mother) responsible for taking care of a child, you qualify for Aid to Families with Dependent Children (AFDC).[23] This is the program most people mean by "welfare." It's also the program that is most often blamed, by Charles Murray and others, for the growth of the underclass.[24]

FDR, it turns out, didn't quite nail down his "no dole" choice.[25] His 1935 plan included aid for families in which the breadwinner was "dead, disabled, or *absent*" (emphasis added). At the time, this was considered one of the least significant New Deal programs. Also, at the time, the idea of giving money to unattached mothers had a lot to recommend it. It's easy to tell an able-bodied man or woman with no family responsibilities to "go get a job." It's not as easy to tell a single mother. She already has at least one job, raising her children. Society has an interest in having this job done well. In those pre-feminist days, even women who didn't have children weren't necessarily expected to work. Fewer than 10 percent of married women were in the labor force.[26] Well before the New Deal (starting in 1911) many states had set up programs of "Mother's Aid" to simply pay single mothers for mothering.[27]

The obvious danger was described as early as 1914 by Homer Folks, an early Mother's Aid advocate: "[T]o pension desertion or illegitimacy would, undoubtedly, have the effect of a premium upon these crimes against society."[28] Most states guarded against this possibility by restricting Mother's Aid to "suitable homes," a vague term inherited from social workers that basically meant aid was reserved for widows, not broken families.[29] In 1931, on the eve of the New Deal, only eleven states even allowed the possibility that illegitimate children might receive Mother's Aid, and 82 percent of the families in the nation receiving it were headed by widows. Two years after the law was passed, only 3.5 percent of all children receiving Aid to Dependent Children (the program's original name) were illegitimate.[30]

From these fatefully obscure beginnings, without much help from Congress or the voters, ADC developed into a program that not only "pensioned" the "crimes against society" Folks had warned against, but that, de facto, was almost solely directed at supporting the children of desertion, illegitimacy, and divorce. The initial impetus came from the federal bureaucrats administering the program, who saw state "suitable home" policies as paternalistic and irrational—as if children of deserted mothers were any less needy![31] Congress, meanwhile, considered widows so deserving that it amended the law to bring them (and wives of disabled breadwinners) under the far more generous provisions of old age insurance, what we call "Social Security." Perversely, as Social Security siphoned off the "deserving" elements of the single mother population, it had the effect of leaving on welfare mainly mothers who had been divorced, deserted, or who had never married.[32] By 1960, 64 percent of families on welfare (now AFDC) were "absent father" cases; only 8 percent were widows.[33]

Panicky states tried to reassert "suitable home"–type restrictions, especially when the number of Americans on welfare started rising rapidly. In 1935 there had been only 300,000 children receiving

"Mothers' Aid." In 1960, there were 3 million people on AFDC and it was the largest federal assistance program.[34] States staged "midnight raids" to catch welfare mothers in the act of receiving "male callers," enforcing the notorious "man-in-the-house rule." In part because these raids seemed directed against blacks, removing the barriers to AFDC became a cause of the civil rights movement.[35] A few thousand regulations, lawsuits, and court decisions later, it was clear that any poor single mother with a child was entitled to aid, whether she had married the father of the child, been deserted by the father of the child, or had no idea who the father of the child was. She could even live with a man, as long as he hadn't been legally found responsible for any of her children—the "man in the house" rule having been struck down by the Supreme Court in 1968.[36]

In the early 1960s, liberals worried about AFDC along with everybody else. Because AFDC was available to mothers in broken homes but not to poor families that stayed together, the clear message to poor women seemed to be "leave your man, or have an illegitimate baby, and the government will take care of you." To poor fathers, the message was "desert your family so they can get on welfare."[37] The preferred liberal solution, however, was not to deny benefits to broken families but to extend them to intact ones.

Thus began a decades-long process in which liberals tried to eliminate the perverse incentives of welfare by broadening its coverage. Unfortunately, each extension of welfare created new problems, which in turn could seemingly be solved only by extending welfare still further. If the problem was that unemployed fathers were deserting their families, then (liberals argued) you should offer welfare to poor families with unemployed fathers who *hadn't* deserted.[38] But that created an incentive for fathers to become unemployed. To eliminate that incentive, you had to extend aid to families with fathers who *were* employed but were nevertheless poor, which created another perverse incentive for the family to split up if the husband began earning enough to move out of poverty ... et cetera ... et cetera.... This train of thought rolled through Washington between 1960 and 1978. It was quite obvious where it was heading—namely, towards expanding cash welfare so that it would cover everybody, or at least everybody who was poor.[39]

The idea of a "guaranteed income" had a terrific appeal to welfare technocrats of the right as well as the left. One of its originators was conservative economist Milton Friedman. Government was going to try help the poor anyway, reasoned Friedman. It might as well do so efficiently. What the government could do efficiently was one, simple thing: mail checks.[40] Democratic anti-poverty crusaders found this vision equally appealing, having by the mid-sixties turned against what they called the "vested interests" of a "welfare establishment" that was more interested in employing itself (as provider of "services") than in ending the reason for its employment (by giving the poor money).[41]

Like one-stop shopping, the guaranteed income promised to solve numerous problems with a single visit to Congress. It would reach "all the nooks and crannies where other programs have not reached," Sargent Shriver (head of the War on Poverty) wrote to President Lyndon Johnson in 1965. Call it the Thomas's English Muffin theory of poverty-fighting. If you ladled cash benefits like butter over the entire population, you could be sure they would plug up every hole.[42] Of course, if you gave benefits to everybody whether they worked or not, you would also be violating popular ideas about the work ethic. But, increasingly, liberals dismissed such concerns as archaic.[43]

In essence, liberals had confronted anew the "relief" question FDR faced (and probably thought he'd settled) back in 1935. But they came up with a very different answer, a Money Liberal answer. What is the best way to satisfy the minimum income needs of Americans? Well, they reasoned, if the problem is a maldistribution of money, the solution is a redistribution of money in a "more equal" direction. The poor need cash. Give them cash. Money, after all, is what matters to Money Liberals.[44]

Johnson himself never bought the English Muffin theory. His War on Poverty, in conception, was neither a cash nor a jobs program. Its theme was "a hand up, not a handout."[45] The emphasis was on training, education, and legal aid—grease for the machinery of equal opportunity—plus "empowerment" through the vague idea of "community action."[46] At the initial bill-signing ceremony in 1964, LBJ actually announced, "The days of the dole in this country are numbered."

But when the early War on Poverty seemed to falter, liberals other than Johnson himself gravitated quickly to the pure Money Liberal, give-them-cash solution. In 1966, a White House conference panel headed by industrialist Benjamin Heineman (in a report signed by Martin Luther King, Jr.) had proposed an FDR-like two-prong plan

of "'last resort employment' to those willing and able to work" and
cash welfare for those "unable to seek employment."[47] Just two years
later, 1,300 economists from 150 institutions, led by ex-Kennedy ad-
visers James Tobin of Yale and John Kenneth Galbraith of Harvard,
presented Congress with a petition urging a "national system of income guarantees." The 1968 Democratic Platform also appeared to
endorse the guaranteed income idea.[48] By 1969, Heineman was chair-
ing another blue-ribbon White House commission that explicitly rejected the distinction between able- and non-able-bodied Americans.
Declaring that government jobs were "not fundamental alternatives
to income supplement proposals," Heineman's second panel recommended a "universal income supplement" paying cash to "all members of the population with income needs" without regard to whether
an individual was "deemed employable by some official."[49]

A set of powerful new pro-dole ideas *had* come to the fore within
the Democratic party's policy elite.[50] Unfortunately, these ideas also
appear to have had a profound effect on at least one segment of the
population at large.

By the early 1960s, as noted, the gradual, steady increase in the
welfare rolls was already alarming Northern Democrats and angering
Southern ones. They hadn't seen anything yet. Starting around 1964,
coincident with the War on Poverty and the emergence of the give-
them-cash consensus, welfare caseloads began a period of truly spectacular growth. The number of Americans on public assistance went
from 7.1 million in 1960 to 7.8 million in 1965, and then soared to
11.1 million in 1969 and 14.4 million in 1974, at which point it lev-
eled off. "All of this growth," James Patterson points out, "came in
the numbers on AFDC," which more than tripled, "from 3.1 million
in 1960 to 4.3 million in 1965 to 6.1 million in 1969 to 10.8 million
by 1974."[51]

Why the explosion? The economy was booming. The eligible welfare population was increasing, but only gradually. Patterson notes
that "the absolute number of female-headed families that were poor
remained stable throughout the period of explosive growth in the
rolls."[52] The big change, it turns out, was in the percentage of eligible
families that actually applied for and received welfare. There was "a
fantastic jump in the participation of eligible families in AFDC, from
perhaps 33 percent in the early 1960s to more than 90 percent in
1971."[53]

Quite simply, at some point in the mid-sixties it seems to have become much more acceptable to go on welfare. The give-them-cash consensus had been embraced, not by the electorate at large (among whom the National Welfare Rights Organization remained about as popular as the National Man-Boy Love Association) but by enough people in enough institutions to produce a minor social revolution. It had been embraced by legal scholars and judges, who decided cases in favor of government poverty lawyers when they attacked restrictions on welfare.[54] It had been embraced by federal bureaucrats, who had always pushed for more liberal welfare rules, and by local bureaucrats, who typically hadn't.[55] Now New York City's welfare commissioner lectured caseworkers on closed-circuit television about the need to sign up those who were eligible for welfare but not receiving it.[56]

Most important, the new attitude appears to have been embraced by many of the poor themselves. Previously, their own sense of dignity, reinforced by the condescension or hostility of local social workers, might have prevented them from seeking government aid. But now all sorts of officials and "community action" activists assured them welfare was an "entitlement" like Social Security, not a shameful handout.[57] The attractions of this entitlement, moreover, increased dramatically in 1966 when free medical care (Medicaid) became part of the welfare package. By the millions, poor families decided they might as well take advantage of the dole.

Many Money Liberals found AFDC's expansion a heartening step toward "universal cash coverage." Patterson describes it in terms normally reserved by historians for the storming of the Bastille: "Despite the hostility of the middle classes to increases in welfare, poor Americans refused at last to be cowed from applying for aid.... [T]hey stood firm in their determination to stay on the rolls as long as they were in need."[58] Only some of the poor—mainly those in broken homes and eligible for AFDC—had the opportunity to demonstrate such resolve, however. In the grand Money Liberal scheme, AFDC (with its nasty anti-family incentive) was supposed to be superseded by the more benign universal guaranteed income. But this part of the plan did not come off on schedule. In fact, it never came off. Twice Washington welfare experts seemed to have the guaranteed income within reach, and twice they came up empty-handed.[59] Instead of "universal cash coverage," the most tangible legacy of the Money Liberals' efforts was tumorous growth of the very program they once hoped to render obsolete, AFDC.

• • •

Now, just because the welfare rolls exploded doesn't mean AFDC caused today's underclass problem. But the contentious debate on this subject, in the wake of Murray's 1984 book *Losing Ground,* has oddly tended to obscure welfare's almost indisputable, indispensable role. In part, that's because the argument is typically presented, somewhat misleadingly, as a confrontation between William Julius Wilson's underclass story and Murray's underclass story. In part, it's because Murray tells not one story, but two.

Wilson's story goes something like this: When Southern blacks migrated to the North, they settled (thanks to segregation) in the African-American ghettos. Poor blacks, middle-class blacks, and rich blacks all lived together in Harlem, on Chicago's South Side, or in other bustling neighborhoods in the North's big cities. Then two things happened. First, unskilled jobs—especially good unskilled manufacturing jobs—started leaving the cities. Here Wilson relies on the research of John Kasarda of the University of North Carolina, who blames changing manufacturing and transportation technology for the job flight.[60] Second, middle- and upper-class blacks, aided by civil rights and fair housing laws, started leaving the inner city too. This out-migration left the poorest elements of black society behind, now isolated, concentrated, and freed from the restraints the black middle class had quite self-consciously imposed on them.[61] Without jobs, without role models and socializing institutions, the men left behind in the inner city drifted out of the legal labor market. Without enough "marriageable" employed men around, single-parent families multiplied.[62]

Wilson's account doesn't seem to give welfare much of a role to play, and hence it tends to be championed by Money Liberals whose enthusiasm for cash solutions has (somewhat pathetically) been reduced to a defense of AFDC. Wilson himself contrasts his theory with Murray's welfare-causationism.[63] But there is more than one way that welfare might have contributed to the underclass—as Murray's writings themselves demonstrate.

One possibility is the familiar charge that AFDC offers an incentive to break up families, with mothers and fathers influenced directly by its economic blandishments much as if by bribes. A mother might have a baby "to go on welfare." A father might leave his wife or girlfriend so she qualifies for the program. The bribe theory is the basis for Murray's notorious "Harold and Phyllis" story, which compares in minute detail the financial prospects of a fictitious ghetto couple on and off welfare. Murray concluded that between 1960 and 1970 benefit increases and eased eligibility rules had tipped the balance and made non-marriage and welfare rather than marriage and work an appealing option.[64]

Liberals used to worry about perverse incentives, too, when they thought a guaranteed income was what would eliminate them. And such incentives can't have *helped*. But as an explanation of the underclass, the bribe theory of welfare doesn't hold up that well. First, as Nicholas Lemann points out, it doesn't account for black exceptionalism. Welfare certainly couldn't have caused the black family patterns that W. E. B. Du Bois noted in Philadelphia in 1899, thirty-six years before welfare existed.[65] Second, the impact of marginal Harold-and-Phyllis–style calculations on the decision of women to have a child out of wedlock does not appear to be that great. The illegitimacy problem got worse in the mid-to-late 1970s, even though AFDC benefits were falling in real terms. And, in a much-cited study, David Ellwood and Mary Jo Bane of Harvard compared family structures in states with varying benefit levels, concluding that higher benefits had no measurable effect on the decision to have a baby.[66]

Ghetto teenagers don't have children to go on welfare, these experts tell us. They have babies to increase their self-esteem, to give themselves "something to love" in a world where delayed gratification seems pointless. Teenage men seek to prove their masculinity, while girls, as Leon Dash describes it, are often ridiculed by other girls if they remain virgins too long into their teens. ("I *drowned* him," boasts one 14-year-old girl on the phone immediately after luring her 15-year-old boyfriend into having sex.)[67]

But there is a second, more plausible, theory that implicates welfare in this cultural catastrophe. It holds that although cash welfare might not cause the underclass, it nevertheless sustains the underclass. With AFDC in place, young girls look around them and recognize, perhaps unconsciously, that other girls in their neighborhood who have had babies on their own are surviving, however uncomfortably. (But who lives comfortably in the ghetto?) Welfare, as the umbilical cord through which the mainstream society sustains the isolated ghetto society, enables the expansion of this single-parent culture. It is its economic life support system.

Certainly there is a significant population of single mothers who stay on welfare for a long time. Some liberals still argue righteously that these long-term recipients comprise only a "tiny minority" of welfare's beneficiaries.[68] That's a lie. A substantial group of mothers on AFDC—about 30 percent of those who ever use the program—are on welfare for eight years or more. They account for *more than 65 per-cent* of those on the welfare rolls at any one time, according to a study by David Ellwood. Indeed, they stay on for so long that (even counting the many mothers who go off welfare quickly) the average welfare stay, for those on the rolls at any given moment, is 11.6 years.[69]

The "enabling" theory, unlike the bribe theory, doesn't talk of families being directly "pulled apart" by welfare, but of families that are never formed in the culture welfare subsidizes. Once AFDC benefits reach a certain threshold that allows poor single mothers to survive—a threshold achieved, even in stingy Southern states, after the 1965 introduction and subsequent expansion of federal food stamps—the culture of the underclass can start growing as women have babies for all the various non-welfare reasons they have them.[70] Indeed, precisely because nobody has babies *in order* to go on welfare, marginally lowering welfare benefits (that is, reducing the "bribe") won't have a dramatic effect.

If the bribe theory is the basis for Murray's "Harold and Phyllis" story, the "enabling" theory underlies his equally notorious "thought experiment."[71] What would happen, he asks, if there were no welfare at all? Answer: things would have to change. "You want to cut illegitimate births among poor people? ... I know how to do that," Murray told Ken Auletta in a *Washington Monthly* interview. "You just rip away every kind of government support there is. What happens then? You're going to have lots of parents talking differently to daughters, and you're going to have lots of daughters talking differently to their boyfriends...." If the daughters didn't, their plight trying to raise kids without welfare would serve as an example to their neighbors.[72]

Murray's prescription is so harsh ("you just rip away ...") that it's understandable liberals would set him up as a foil for the compassionate, social-democratic Wilson. Lemann, for example, says that Murray's "explanation for the underclass [is] entirely at odds with Wilson's."[73] That's not really true even of Murray's "bribe" theory—presumably AFDC may have induced some single women to have babies even if it wasn't the main cause of black family breakdown.[74] But it's certainly not true that there's a contradiction between Wilson's story and Murray's second, "enabling" theory. In fact, the two accounts complement each other perfectly.

After all, Southern blacks moved North to work and get ahead. Most did just that. Then, according to Wilson, the jobs moved to the suburbs. Why didn't the migrants (and their descendants) follow the jobs? Again, many did. But what enabled some of them, a lower-class remnant, to stay behind in the ghetto? And what then allowed them to survive in the absence of legitimate sources of income? Certainly it's not enough to note, with Lemann, that many of the migrants were sharecroppers, who had formed the lower class of black society in the rural South. Sharecroppers worked hard, often from sunup to sunset under unpleasant conditions.[75] What allowed these hard-working people, who'd uprooted themselves and moved hundreds of miles in search of better paychecks, to stop moving and stop working, in defiance of the pattern of every other migrant peasant group?

This isn't a question that only a Charles Murray would ask. It's a question that John Kasarda, on whose job-disappearance research Wilson relies, asks:

> What continues to attract or hold minority and other disadvantaged persons in central cities undergoing severe blue-collar employment decline? How are economically displaced inner-city residents able to survive? What, in brief, is the economic substitute for traditional blue-collar jobs?[76]

Kasarda has an answer too: "welfare programs." *Welfare* is what subsidized and sustained a demoralizing lower-class culture in the ghettos. Kasarda notes that by 1982 some 40 percent of black males unemployed or not in the labor force were receiving either public or subsidized housing, food stamps, or AFDC. And that's just the men (who don't typically qualify for AFDC). Among black women, in the cities of the Northeast and North Central region, there were by 1982 "more black female household heads who are unemployed or not in the labor force than who are employed." And 73 percent of those unemployed black single mothers were on some form of welfare; fully 83 percent of the far larger group of black single mothers who had dropped out of the labor market entirely were on welfare.[77]

Without welfare, these people would have had to move to where the jobs were, as they'd done in the past. It's not as if the jobs didn't exist—Kasarda notes that "contrary to conventional wisdom" there were "massive increases in entry-level jobs nationwide." It's just that this job growth had occurred "almost exclusively in the suburbs, exurbs, and nonmetroplitan areas...."[78] Without welfare, the lower-class ghetto subculture might have dissolved into the working and middle class outside the downtowns.[79] Instead, Kasarda argues, the creation of "urban welfare economies" allowed "a large minority underclass" to become "anchored" in the isolated urban cores where there were no jobs, where the subculture only intensified. Welfare, in effect, paid the least motivated ghetto residents to stay put when everyone else around them was getting out and getting on with their lives.[80]

A similar point can be made with respect to family patterns. Sure, as Lemann notes, the family structures of Southern blacks, especially sharecroppers, were larger, looser, and more turbulent than the structures of white families long before AFDC appeared on the scene.[81] But if AFDC *hadn't* appeared on the scene, wouldn't those black family structures have had to change? Wouldn't the ordinary economic incentives to settle down in a stable two-parent home, sharing the work of childrearing and breadwinning, have asserted themselves? Instead, a group whose families were already disproportionately matriarchal was, tragically, exposed to a cash welfare system that subsidized single-motherhood. Is it really surprising that single-parent households, instead of fading away, exploded in number, until they constituted a majority of black families?[82]

CHAPTER 8

The Cure for the Culture of Poverty

Welfare may not have been a sufficient condition for the growth of the underclass, but it's hard to see how contemporary liberals can deny that it was a necessary condition. As Murray (at least Murray II) might say, AFDC's "give them cash" solution enabled an underclass to form, just as FDR might have predicted. Which raises the obvious question: could altering this necessary ingredient somehow "de-enable" the underclass?

Certainly, if we're looking for a political handle on underclass culture, there is none bigger than the benefit programs that constitute the economic basis—the "mode of production," a Marxist might say—of the ghetto. In the average "extreme social problem" neighborhood, 34 percent of the households are on welfare.[1] According to the Congressional Budget Office, cash welfare (mainly AFDC) is some 65 percent of the above-ground income of single mothers in the bottom fifth of the income distribution—up from 45 percent in 1970.[2] A second, hidden chunk of ghetto GNP is illegal income, including income from the sale of drugs. But after interviewing urban welfare mothers in confidence about where they really get their money, Christopher Jencks and Kathryn Edin report that AFDC and food stamps account for 57 percent of their incomes. Work accounts for 12 percent, crime only 9 percent.[3] Even assuming crime is a bigger factor than that (especially for young ghetto men), it's not a factor the larger society has been able to control. Welfare is something society *can* control.

The alternative approaches certainly are not very promising. They include:

Black self-help. This strategy accords with both the hesitancy of liberal whites to tell blacks how to behave, and the interest of bootstrapping black neoconservatives in shifting the focus away from government. "Only blacks can effectively provide moral leadership for their people," says Glenn Loury of Boston University, a prominent self-help advocate. More successful blacks, especially, "are strategically situated to undertake" this task, he says. Even Loury's liberal black critics, such as Roger Wilkins, accept the assumption that "only black people can do this."[4]

When you get to just how the black community itself is going to achieve what Wilkins calls a "massive cultural turnaround," however, things get vague. Loury talks about "discussion of values." Wilkins says that the "local Urban League" could "assemble a roster of role models and present them as a package of assembly speakers for inner-city schools." Good luck to such efforts, but let's be realistic: today's underclass infants will be great-great-grandparents before these limited schemes begin to accomplish their goal. Is it even fair to expect middle-class blacks to bear the load of reshaping the underclass simply because they share the same skin color?[5]

Tight labor markets. The high-paying unskilled jobs that lured black migrants North are, increasingly, gone. As we saw in Chapter 5, they aren't about to come back. The jobs available to the unskilled ghetto poor in the Reichian future will not be $20-an-hour autoworker jobs, but $5- and (if we're lucky) $7-an-hour retail and service jobs. William Julius Wilson argues that, even so, a tight job market will give ghetto men and women a chance to start climbing the ladder. The evidence bears him out—up to a point. In the 1980s, in the hottest metropolitan economies, unemployment among disadvantaged young black men *who were looking for work* fell sharply, from 40.5 percent to 7 percent, according to economist Richard Freeman.[6] In Boston, with what was at the time probably the tightest labor market in the nation, the overall black poverty rate dropped by a third, from 36.8 to 22.3 percent (using a poverty line 25 percent above normal).[7]

But as Murray points out, the percentage of young black men who *weren't* looking for work at all—the core of the underclass—wasn't much affected by economic growth. In cities with extremely hot economies (an unemployment rate of 4 percent) 21 percent of disadvantaged young black men remained out of the labor force in 1987, down from 28 percent in 1984. In slightly less hot economies, though, the black male "labor force non-participation rate" barely budged, and when the unemployment rate hit 5 to 6 percent (still not bad, by recent standards) the percentage of black men not looking for work actually rose.[8] Similarly, in Boston, after half a decade of spectacular growth, the percent of black families headed by a single woman dropped only slightly, from 57 percent to 55 percent.[9] Remember, it's highly unlikely the entire U.S. could sustain a boom economy like Boston's for an extended period.

Acculturation programs. The lowest-common-denominator liberal approach to the ghettos is to fund a variety of "interventions" that would attempt to change underclass culture for the better. Lemann lists most of them: "Programs offering education, counseling, and birth control devices in high school.... Programs that send nurses and social workers to the homes of expectant mothers to provide prenatal care or food ... Head Start...."[10] There's nothing wrong with these relatively inexpensive programs. They just won't solve the problem.

Take everybody's favorite, Head Start. Head Start offers preschool education, with lots of parent involvement, to disadvantaged kids. The study most frequently cited to support it compares poor black children enrolled in the Perry Preschool Program in Ypsilanti, Michigan—which is not a Head Start program, but a more elaborate and expensive effort—with a control group of kids who got no preschool training. Fully 40 percent of the control group flunked a year of school. The Perry graduates did better—but 35 percent still flunked. By adulthood, 22 percent of the controls were serious criminals. "Only" 19 percent of the Perry kids were serious criminals. Instead of the controls' 56 percent rate of welfare receipt at age 19, the Perry kids had a 45 percent rate.[11] You get the picture. Programs like preschool education can make a significant, measurable difference. But even if they are "fully funded" they won't come close to overcoming the multiple pathologies of the underclass. They pass the test of cost-efficiency, but fail the test of sufficiency.

"Empowerment." This is the so-called "new paradigm" of poverty-fighting. The idea is to empower ghetto residents by giving them the

tools to succeed and then having the government get out of the way. New-paradigmy initiatives include enterprise zones and Jack Kemp's plan to sell public housing tenants their apartments. Lemann notes the disturbing similarity between these programs and the disastrous "community development" strategies of the War on Poverty, which failed because the black ghettos are singularly inauspicious sites for economic development.[12] Ghetto residents make it by getting out of the ghetto, not by developing it. Why direct the opportunities for black enterprise to the nation's poorest communities? "Empowerment," to the extent it tempts the underclass to stay put, might have the perverse effect of "anchoring" it even more firmly in the ghetto. Some tenant-ownership plans actually require the poor to stay in their apartments for six years.[13] And does it make such a difference that a single mother owns her own apartment if she pays her subsidized mortgage with AFDC money? At tenant-managed Cochran Gardens in St. Louis, a showpiece of Kemp's antipoverty strategy, 40 percent of the household heads are on welfare. Only 27 percent work. At tenant-managed Bromley-Heath in Boston—another "empowerment" success story—the unemployment rate is 81 percent.[14]

Changing welfare, by contrast, offers a chance to transform the economic role of the ghetto poor without tying them to their dying neighborhoods. Instead of attempting to somehow teach mainstream culture to people who spend most of their day immersed in ghetto culture, we could make ghetto culture economically unsustainable.

In this respect, the implications of the "enabling" theory of welfare are far more radical, and perhaps nastier, than those of the "bribe" version. For decades, Money Liberal reformers have assumed that if you extended welfare to two-parent families, then AFDC's "bribes" (or "incentives") would no longer pull families apart. The poor would never willingly have illegitimate babies and go on welfare if they could get married and go on welfare.

But if the "enabling" theory is correct, the culture of poverty is now so entrenched that young girls will keep on having illegitimate babies and going on welfare even if they could form two-parent families and still get their checks. If that's true, it isn't enough to extend benefits to intact families (which indeed has had little effect on the underclass in the states where it's been tried).[15] You have to somehow *deny* benefits to one-parent families, unplug the underclass culture's life support system.[16] In short, you have to re-make FDR's 1935 choice—this time applying it to able-bodied single parents along with everyone else.

That means something like this: replacing AFDC and all other cash-like welfare programs that assist the able-bodied poor (including "general relief" and food stamps) with a single, simple offer from the government—an offer of employment for every American citizen over eighteen who wants it, in a useful public job at a wage slightly below the minimum wage for private sector work.[17] The government would supplement the wages of all low-wage jobs, both public and private, to ensure that every American who works full-time has enough money to raise a normal-sized family with dignity, out of poverty.

In this system, if you could work and needed money, the government would not give you a check (welfare). It wouldn't give you a check and then try to cajole, instruct, and threaten you into working it off ("workfare") or "training it off." It would give you the location of several government job sites. If you showed up and worked, you would be paid for your work. If you don't show up, you don't get paid. Simple.

Unlike welfare, these public, WPA-style jobs would be available to everybody, men as well as women, single or married, mothers and fathers alike. No perverse "anti-family" incentives. It wouldn't even be necessary to limit the public jobs to the poor. If Donald Trump showed up, he could work too. But he wouldn't. Most Americans wouldn't. There'd be no need to "target" the program to the needy. The low wage itself would guarantee that those who took the jobs would be those who needed them, while preserving the incentive to look for better work in the private sector.

Perhaps most important for Civic Liberals (as for FDR), such work-relief wouldn't carry the stigma of a cash dole. Those who worked in the neo-WPA jobs would be earning their money. They could hold their heads up. They would also have something most unemployed underclass members desperately need: a supervisor they could give as a job reference to other employers. Although some WPA workers could be promoted to higher-paying public service positions, for most of them movement into the private sector would take care of itself. If you have to work anyway, why do it for $4 an hour? The whole problem of "work incentives" that obsesses current welfare policy dwindles into insignificance when what you're offering is work itself, rather than a dole that people have to then be "incentivized" (that is, bribed) into leaving.[18]

Those who didn't take advantage of the neo-WPA jobs, however, would be on their own as far as income assistance went. No cash doles. Mothers included. The key welfare question left unresolved by the New Deal—do we expect single mothers with children to work?— would be resolved cleanly and clearly in favor of work. The government would announce that after a certain date able-bodied single women who bear children would no longer qualify for cash payments.[19] Young women contemplating single motherhood couldn't count on AFDC to sustain them. As mothers, they would have to work like everyone else. The prospect of juggling motherhood and a not-very-lucrative public job would make them think twice, just as with Murray's cold-turkey solution. But the public jobs would (unlike Murray's plan) also offer both mothers and non-mothers a way out of poverty.

Most American mothers, 67 percent, now work. Most single mothers work.[20] Today's liberals are eager to acknowledge these facts of modern life when it suits their purposes—when arguing for parental leave, or deriding Phyllis Schlafly's "Ozzie and Harriet" vision of the ideal family. But they can't have it both ways. If mothers are expected to work, they're expected to work.[21]

If poor mothers are to work, of course, day care must be provided for their children whenever it's needed, funded by the government if necessary. To avoid creating a day-care ghetto for low-income kids, this service will have to be integrated into the larger system of child care for other American families. That will be expensive. But it won't necessarily be as expensive as you might think. When free day care has been offered to welfare mothers who work, demand has fallen below predictions. "It is never utilized to the extent people thought it would be," says Barbara Goldman of the Manpower Demonstration Research Corporation (MDRC). Most welfare mothers, it seems, prefer to make their own arrangements.[22] (Whether those arrangements are any good is another question. The government might want to take steps to actually encourage day care, as part of an "acculturation" campaign to get underclass kids out of the home and into classrooms at an early age.)

What happens if a poor single mother is offered decent day care, and a WPA-style job, and she refuses them? The short answer is that nothing happens. There's no penalty. Also no check. Perhaps she will discover some other, better way of feeding herself and her family. If, on the other hand, her children are subsequently discovered living in squalor and filth, then she has neglected a basic task of parenthood. She is subject to the laws that already provide for removal of a child from an unfit home. The long answer, then, is that society will also have to construct new institutions, such as orphanages, to care for the children whose parents so fail them.[23]

This is not a new idea. Similar proposals have been advanced, in recent decades, by Sen. Russell Long of Louisiana and (of all people) the straitlaced Republican economist Arthur Burns.[24] It's an obvious idea, even, combining as it does the ancient Democratic dream of a guaranteed job with traditional antipathy to the dole. Somehow, our politics has conspired to preclude this conspicuous synthesis. Today, liberals who righteously invoke FDR's "compassionate" legacy tend to forget his anti-dole decision of 1935, or else pass it off as a quaint bit of residual conservatism. Meanwhile, Presidents Reagan and Bush both gleefully repeated Roosevelt's description of the dole as "a narcotic," somehow failing to mention that Roosevelt said this in the speech where he proposed the largest government jobs program in the nation's history. In fact, FDR's anti-dole and pro-WPA opinions were of a piece, a Civic Liberal decision in favor of work-welfare and against cash-welfare.

But Roosevelt's WPA was designed to combat general unemployment at a time when most of those needing "relief" were veteran workers. Our goal, in contrast, is to break the culture of poverty by providing jobs for ghetto men and women who may have little work history and few work habits—at the same time as we end the option of a life on welfare for single mothers. More broadly, the idea is the transformation of the welfare state into the Work Ethic State, in which status, dignity, and government benefits flow only to those who work, but in which the government steps in to make sure work is available to all. There are a number of obvious objections to so obvious a notion:

How could a low-wage "WPA" job ever support a family? The poverty line for a family of three was $10,857 in 1991. A full-time, minimum wage job brings in only $8,840, and the government jobs proposed here would pay less than that. The government would, as noted, have to step in and supplement the incomes of *all* low-wage workers—in the WPA and the private sector. There are several ways to do this, but the easiest is to expand the current Earned Income Tax Credit, or "work bonus," as Russell Long called it. The EITC currently pays about $1,300 to workers with family incomes of $7,000 to $11,000.[25] The credit applies only to breadwinners with dependent children, and it still isn't enough to take all poor working families out of poverty. But both those defects could be easily, if not cheaply, fixed.[26]

Because the supplement would boost the incomes of all low-wage workers, there would be no unfairness to those slogging it out in lousy private sector jobs. And, since those private jobs would be supplemented too, they'd still pay more than the guaranteed public jobs (though not quite as much more). In effect, we'd have a guaranteed income *for those who work.*

Will people be allowed to starve?   The state's basic obligation, in this scheme, is to provide decent work for all who are able and a decent income for the disabled. There will be able-bodied people—not only mothers—who need money but who don't take advantage of the WPA jobs.[27] Many ghetto men, at least initially, may prefer the world of crime, hustle, and odd jobs to working for "chump change." (One advantage of the Work Ethic State would be that criminals could be treated as criminals, without residual guilt about the availability of employment.) Others will simply fail at working.

The first underclass generation *off* welfare will be the roughest. Those people who fail at work will be thrown into the world of austere public in-kind guarantees—homeless shelters, soup kitchens—and of charitable organizations. This aid will be stigmatizing (as it must be if work is to be honored). It will be frankly paternalistic. But it could also be compassionate.[28] Nobody would starve. The government could (and should) offer to subsidize all the counseling, therapy, and job training it could afford, in order to help people back on their feet. The one thing it would not offer them is cash.[29]

What if women take the jobs but still don't form two-parent families? Suppose the work-for-welfare swap goes well. A life on welfare becomes impossible. Young women who would previously have had children and gone on welfare now go to work, have children, and put them in day care. But has the underclass culture really been transformed if these women don't form stable two-parent families? After all, as Lemann reminds us, many of the black family patterns we lament today were in evidence before AFDC, when black women and men had little economic alternative to working.[30]

There are three answers to this question. The first is that, yes, the ghetto-poor culture would be transformed. A working matriarchy is very different from a non-working matriarchy. If poor women who work to feed themselves and their children prefer to stay unmarried—supporting their children without help from a stable working partner—that's their choice. At least they are out of the welfare culture; they will be able to participate in the larger working society with dignity.

The second answer, which naturally follows from the first, is that many working mothers will not want to make that choice. Certainly it's doubtful that they'll be willing to share their hard-earned paychecks with non-working men the way they might have been willing to share their welfare checks. Once work is the norm, and the subsidy of AFDC has been removed, the natural incentives toward the formation of two-parent families will reassert themselves. Why go crazy trying to raise a kid on $10,000 a year when you can marry another worker and live on $20,000 a year? It makes no sense. Soon enough ghetto women will be demanding and expecting that the men in their lives offer them stable economic support.

Finally, the next generation off welfare—men as well as women, even men growing up in single-mother homes—will be better prepared not only to find jobs but to get the skills that will let them find "good jobs." That's because they will have grown up in a home where work, not welfare, is the norm, where the rhythms and discipline of obligation pervade daily life. A growing body of evidence shows that one of the most important factors in determining success at school is whether a child comes from a working home.[31] Simply put, if a mother has to set her alarm clock, she's likely to teach her children to set their alarm clocks as well.

Eventually, replacing welfare with work *can* be expected to transform the entire culture of poverty. It won't happen in one generation, necessarily, or even two. But it will happen. Underclass culture can't survive the end of welfare any more than feudal culture could survive the advent of capitalism.

What about mothers with very young children, two years and under?
A destitute mother with a newborn infant presents the basic AFDC
dilemma in its starkest form. Children need the most mothering in
their earliest years. Yet more than half of American mothers with kids
under three already work, most of them full-time.[32]

One alternative is to allow temporary cash welfare—for, say, two
years—when a mother has her first child. Once that time was up,
young mothers would be offered only a WPA-style job and day care.
The two-year limit would be non-renewable; mothers wouldn't be allowed to get more cash by having another baby.[33] And a two-year free
ride on welfare would be vastly different than the 18 years on welfare
single mothers can now obtain with every birth. The economy of the
ghetto, and the expectations of its residents, would change substantially. Potential single mothers would realize welfare wasn't going to
sustain them for long; they'd probably know someone with a two-
year-old who's run out of benefits.[34]

But no free ride at all (except for in-kind nutritional assistance to
avoid health problems) would clearly have stronger impact. Even a
two-year dole might encourage some young women who would otherwise work or marry to have a baby first, get the check, and worry
about working later.[35] If we want to end the underclass, remember,
the issue is not so much whether working or getting two years of cash
will best help Betsy Smith, teenage high-school dropout, acquire the
skills to get a good private sector job *after* she's become a single
mother.[36] It is whether the prospect of having to work will deter
Betsy Smith from having an out-of-wedlock child in the first place—
or, failing that, whether the sight of Betsy Smith trying to work and
raise a child without a husband will discourage her younger sisters
and neighbors from doing as she did. The way to make the true costs
of bearing a child out of wedlock clear is to let them be felt when they
are incurred—namely, at the child's birth. If would-be single mothers
were faced with the prospect of immediately supporting themselves,
most would choose a different and better course for their lives.[37]

Hasn't welfare already been reformed?   In 1988 Congress passed a "welfare reform" bill. Senator Moynihan, the bill's chief sponsor, declared it
would "turn the welfare program upside down." Of course, it did nothing
of the sort. The Family Support Act, as the law is called, didn't really an-

swer the crucial question of whether (or when) the able-bodied recipients of AFDC should work; rather, it formalized official ambivalence on the issue. The 1988 law did furnish a few billion dollars to induce states to provide day care and ask a bit more of welfare mothers. But it still allows states to exempt mothers with a child under the age of three, which excludes about half the current caseload. When the child reaches three, the mother remains exempt if she has another one.[38]

Of the remaining half of their caseloads, states need only get 20 percent up and "participating" in some activity. "Participating" is much more likely to mean part-time remedial education or training than actual labor. In 1991, 75 percent of those listed as participating were in some kind of education program (including "self-esteem" classes). Only 4 percent of those participating—less than half a percent of the entire welfare caseload—were in an actual "work setting."[39] Sophisticated supporters of the 1988 law, such as the MDRC's Judith Gueron, estimate that at best it will reduce the welfare caseload by "several percentage points."[40] That won't solve the underclass problem, Gueron admits, explaining, "I'm not a person who seeks solutions to things. I seek to make systems work better...."

What about the fathers? Shouldn't they be made to bear some responsibility?   Sure. If potential fathers knew they'd have to support an illegitimate child, they'd be less likely to produce one. Tougher measures at enforcing the male parental obligation—withholding child support from paychecks like taxes, for example—are all to the good.[41] But there's little reason to expect enforcing child support, by itself, to alter underclass culture. Even if underclass fathers can be identified and located, many have no legitimate income. Unless the government is prepared to throw them in jail if they don't go to work and fork over their wages, a support obligation may be relatively ineffective as a deterrent.[42]

That's especially true when all the parties know that if the husband doesn't support the mother, the government will. Columbia University's Irwin Garfinkel, for example, proposes not only that states assume responsibility for collecting child support, but that they guarantee minimum payments (of $1,000 to $3,000 per child per year) to a single mother even if they can't extract the money from the father.[43] Garfinkel's plan was endorsed in the heavily promoted report of the National Commission on Children, chaired by Sen. Jay Rockefeller.[44]

But if the child support is guaranteed, it is not much different, in it's "enabling" effect, from welfare—single mothers still can stay at home and get a check from the government.[45]

On the other hand, if single mothers know there will be no checks (without work), then extracting support from fathers will take on real urgency. Potential fathers will know that if they don't send their child support check it won't simply be made up by the government—and that the mother, faced with the prospect of working to make up the missing money, is likely to really come after them, not just satisfy bureaucratic formalities.

Will there be enough jobs these people can do?   The objection can't be that there aren't enough worthwhile jobs to be done. The crumbling "infrastructure" that so recently preoccupied Washington hasn't been patched up overnight. All around the country governments have stopped doing, for financial reasons, things they once thought worthwhile, like opening libraries on Saturday and picking up trash twice a week. Why not do them again?

The more plausible doubt is whether those who would need public service employment are suited to doing all these worthwhile jobs. One objection has to do with women and physical labor. Are we really going to have teenage girls repairing potholes and painting bridges?[46] One response is, why not? Women can fill potholes and paint bridges (and water lawns and pick up garbage) just as women can be telephone repairpersons and sailors. Anyway, there are also many non-arduous jobs that need doing: nurse's aides, Xerox operators, receptionists, clerks, and cooks.[47]

A second objection has to do with competence. Can an illiterate, immature, high-school dropout be trusted to work in a hospital as a nurse's aide, or in a public office as a clerk? Maybe not. But who can't sweep a floor? The liberals who make this objection often seem to have an opinion of underclass capability that makes William Shockley look generous. In fact, the supervisors of welfare recipients working in "workfare" programs rated them as highly as regular entry-level workers, according to an MDRC survey.[48] For people with severe limitations—well, even a leaf-raking job rakes leaves. If that's all someone's capable of doing, does that mean she shouldn't be paid for doing it? The alternative, remember, is to pay her to stay home and raise children.[49]

A third objection is that any program will inevitably degenerate into makework. Exhibit A here is not the WPA, which after an initial period of confusion and inefficiency managed to leave a legacy of valuable public works.[50] Even the occasional conservative politician has been known to get misty-eyed about FDR's program:

> WPA—some people have called it boondoggle and everything else—but, having lived through that era and seen it—no, it was probably one of the social programs that was most practical in those New Deal Days.[51]

Unfortunately, Ronald Reagan got hold of himself before he could follow through on this line of thought.

No, exhibit A in the "makework" case isn't the WPA, it's CETA, a Nixon-Ford-Carter program. CETA (the Comprehensive Employment and Training Act) was a disaster for a variety of reasons, but one big reason was that doing anything useful would have offended labor unions. Construction unions insisted on restrictions that basically prevented CETA workers from building anything. The American Federation of State, County, and Municipal Employees (AFSCME) was on guard lest CETA provide any valuable service that might be performed by local civil servants. WPA workers had been precluded from competing with private industry. CETA workers were precluded from competing with government too. So we wound up with CETA workers in experimental film workshops and mime troupes. In California they decided to take a dog and cat census.

It's not as if government unions are wrong to think a guaranteed job program will hurt them. It will. It's not as if the unions can be easily "bought off." I once asked AFSCME lobbyist Al Russo if there was anything—any bribe, compromise or protective language that would allow his union to sign off on the idea of low-wage public service jobs. He had a ready answer: "No." At some point, if we are serious about breaking the poverty culture, we must ask why well-paid government workers should be shielded from the competitive labor market at the expense of the poorest segment of society?[52] Suppose the worst happened, from the unions' point of view, and current government workers were thrown out into the street, displaced by cheaper neo-WPA workers who would otherwise be on welfare. The truth is it would still be a net plus for society. The WPA workers would be lifted from the culture of welfare into the culture of work. The erstwhile civil servants, meanwhile, are already in the world of work. They would find other jobs.[53] The net result would be an expansion of the working culture.

In the real world, pragmatism, as well as fairness, requires that no current government workers be laid off. But as those workers leave through natural attrition, the government should be free to replace them with guaranteed jobholders not subject to "prevailing wage" requirements.[54] WPA-style projects could then be chosen on the basis of how useful they are, not whether a union objects to them. Wherever possible, they would be designed to produce a visible, tangible benefit—collected garbage, a clean subway station, a basketball hoop with a new net. If the jobs took "ghetto poor" workers outside the ghetto, so much the better.[55]

Yes, public works jobs would be relatively inefficient compared with their private sector counterparts. Even when the original WPA was operating at its peak level in New York City, completing a building every three days, its administrator estimated it was only 60 percent as efficient as an equivalent private enterprise.[56] A neo-WPA would have to learn to work with the dregs of the labor market. Parts of the program would have to be relatively authoritarian, even a bit militaristic. Boondoggles would happen. But at least the public would be getting *something* for its money. Precisely because middle-class taxpayers could see what they were getting, they would begin to demand the most efficient operation possible. ("Why hasn't my subway stop been cleaned yet?")[57]

Won't it cost a fortune?   The WPA, at its peak, employed 3.3 million people full-time; CETA, at its peak, 750,000. At the pit of the 1982–83 recession, there were 11.4 million unemployed, 4.6 million for more than 15 weeks. What fraction of them would want subminimum wage jobs—and how many of those not in the labor force would come out of the woodwork to claim those jobs—is anybody's guess. It's usually more expensive, in the short run, to give people jobs than it is to give people cash welfare. Jobs require materials and expensive supervisors. A reasonable estimate, based on previous programs, is at least $10,000 per job. That's $10 billion for every million jobs. Pretty soon you're talking real money. Meanwhile, the benefit of the work done would show up in the government's budget only if it was work the government would be doing anyway. Add to this the cost of an expanded Earned Income Tax credit, the cost of day care, and the cost of caring for those who fail to work and require compassionate assistance.

The best estimate I've been able to come up with (after consulting with people who know more about the numbers than I do) puts the total bill at between $43 and $59 billion a year more than we're spending now.[58] That's *not* counting the value of any of the public service work performed by the neo-WPA workers. Still, it's expensive. So? This isn't a cost-cutting program. It's a solution to the underclass problem. In the long run, if the welfare culture is absorbed into the working, taxpaying culture, the budgetary payoff will be enormous—not to mention the payoff for social equality.

CHAPTER 9

The "Work Test"

Work—honest work—is not degrading. The man who by honest toil earns an honest living is a peer of the realm. He is not a mendicant. Equal to the richest and proudest before the law. Equal to any man in all rights and prerogatives of citizenship, with every avenue of advancement open to him, he spurns the idea of "upper" and "lower" class, and says "we, the people."   —Eugene V. Debs, 1885

Confronted with the problem of degrading poverty, Money Liberals have characteristically fixated on their preferred means—the distribution of cash—instead of the ultimate non-economic goal of dignified lives. But giving people money only gives people money. The measure of liberal progress isn't the number of Americans who, thanks to government payments, have been raised above the poverty line.[1] The single mother pushed over that line when her Section 101 rent supplement is added to her AFDC and food stamps grant is no great welfare state triumph if she doesn't work, can't find a husband, if her son disdains school and spends part of her check on PCP while her teenage daughter assumes she'll soon have a child and get a check of her own—if they all live in a demoralized and dangerous neighborhood where they are held in contempt by the mainstream community surrounding them. A mother cannot, in that situation, feel she is a full citizen, even if (to turn Dwight Macdonald's example on its head) she can "afford a movie or a glass of beer."

Or, for that matter, if her check were increased so she could afford a VCR.

Replacing cash welfare with work would over time end this indignity. It would, as a first step, end the disgrace visited on the underclass by welfare itself. Money Liberal reformers thought the prejudice against cash benefits was obsolete, that (as James Patterson put it) "demoralization came mainly from being unemployed and poor, not from accepting relief." Surely if benefits were billed as a "right" and delivered in a dignified setting, the stigma of receiving them would be erased.[2] But it turned out that welfare is not stigmatizing because it's administered by a callous bureaucracy.[3] Welfare is stigmatizing because it's "welfare"—because it goes to able-bodied people who haven't necessarily worked and who aren't necessarily working. However appealing individual recipients may be, the indelible taint of the "undeserving" pervades the program. The ghetto poor who rely on welfare will be scorned by the larger culture as long as they rely on welfare. By offering work to each able-bodied citizen, the plan sketched in the previous chapter takes away any excuse for non-work—but by the same offer of work, it guarantees all the chance to join the community of workers, a community in which their earned dignity will not be undermined by penury.

Absorption of the underclass into the mainstream working culture also supplies the missing ingredient of the Civic Liberal strategy to rebuild public institutions. The biggest cost of the underclass, after all, isn't the dollars spent on welfare, or the dollars spent to prosecute criminals. It is the pervasive degradation of public life. A WPA-like jobs program would, quite literally, set the underclass and anyone else who needed a job to work rebuilding the public sphere rather than destroying it—planting trees, if you will, rather than lurking behind them. City parks would be more pleasant for the poor and the rich. Eventually you might even be able to walk in them at dusk. Since above-poverty jobs would be available to all, panhandling could humanely be proscribed. An unashamedly paternalistic program would shelter, feed, and counsel the destitute able-bodied who failed to work, including many of those who today constitute "the homeless."[4] With a neo-WPA maintaining highways, schools, playgrounds, and subways, with libraries open every evening and city streets cleaned twice a day, we would have a common life more people would find worth reclaiming.

I don't mean to pretend that without an underclass all the other classes will mix freely in every aspect of their lives. Assimilating the ghetto poor won't by itself produce integration of neighborhoods and schools, where the affluent may wish to avoid not just the underclass but the working class as well. That issue is discussed in Chapter 10. The point is only that a substantial additional part of public life would be opened up, the part that requires only the restoration of minimum levels of civility. I don't have to want to send my kid to school with someone before I'll be content to use the same post office he does, or walk in the same park, or eat at the same sidewalk sandwich stand. As long as neither of us disrupts the other, we can easily treat each other as equals within these public institutions. The improvement in civic life that comes almost automatically with the assimilation of the underclass constitutes the second stage of public sphere reconstruction.

The process works both ways: Just as assimilating the underclass would remove the most acute threat to the public sphere, reestablishing the public sphere would, in turn, accelerate assimilation. For one thing, it will instantly make the ghetto poor less poor. Poor people always depend heavily on public facilities because they have little choice. Public goods can substitute for a lot of private goods. Even under the current system, Mark Lilla has pointed out, "If a frightened welfare mother locked in her apartment received less AFDC but could take her children down safe streets to a well-maintained park, she would be better off. She would have a new backyard."⁵

By creating public-sphere goods to supplement minimal private incomes, a Civic Liberal strategy would enable what today seems like an increasingly remote possibility: an enjoyable but non-affluent life. A $5-an-hour short-order cook would still get only $5 an hour from his employer. He still wouldn't have a glamorous job. But he would qualify for enough of a wage subsidy to raise a family out of poverty. He would get decent medical care through the same system used by virtually everybody else. Along with everybody else, he would enjoy safer streets and parks and plazas. He would have the tangible honor society reserves for workers.

Politicians, teachers, and parents would have a new story to tell kids growing up in the ghetto. What, after all, can we honestly tell them now? That if they go to school and work hard they can be lawyers, doctors, and executives? Yes, many can, but many also realize that even if their schools dramatically improved, they'd have little hope of becoming lawyers and doctors. Maybe in the old unionized industrial economy we could tell them they could take an unskilled blue-collar job, stick with it, and enjoy a comfortable middle-class life. But not in today's pay-for-skills world. If we make money their goal they may quite rationally conclude that drugs and crime are their best chance to get it, if only for a short period of time.

No, we can't tell them they'll be rich, or even comfortably well-off. But we can offer them at least a material minimum, and a good shot at climbing up the ladder. And we can promise them *respect*.[6] This is the way to subvert the "adversary culture" of the ghetto—not by parading a few spectacular success stories (who may only make anything short of spectacular success seem loserish) but by creating hundreds of thousands of unspectacular respect stories.[7] Only respect for work itself will undermine the ghetto pathology of "rich or nothing," in which low-wage workers are scorned as chumps and suckers, in which the only mainstream life worth living seems to take more money than can be legitimately earned.

Money Liberals (and some "empowerment"-style conservatives) will charge that what I've proposed is a "work test," similar to that advocated by nineteenth-century philanthropists.[8] So it is. The nineteenth-century philanthropists had a point. Today, when any liberal calling for an increase in the food stamp budget fancies himself a "populist," it's worth remembering the slogan of the actual Populists, back in 1892: "If any will not work, neither will he eat." Not a Money Liberal motto. A half century later, Orwell, like many socialists, vigorously attacked the "class of mere owners who live not by virtue of anything they produce but by the possession of title deeds and share certificates." In a socialized economy, he proclaimed, "nobody shall live without working."[9] Surely that sentiment goes for the poor as well as the rich. Indeed, that it goes for the poor as well as the rich is the source of much of its appeal.

The object of Civic Liberalism's second stage, then, would be to do more than replace welfare and assimilate the underclass. It would make the work test the clear basis for the entire American "welfare state," including those parts that help the middle class. All government cash benefit programs, in this view, gain legitimacy when they assist only workers (or those who aren't expected to work). By making that requirement explicit, liberals would, in effect, make work the prerequisite for full citizenship. That's a very egalitarian notion, as Lawrence Mead has pointed out, since work is one of the few tests in our society that may be as easily passed by poor and rich alike.[10] The work ethic could assume its place as the basis of a unifying, egalitarian culture, in which the affluent as well as the poor judge themselves, not by how much money they make but by whether or not they are pulling their weight. If this requires an attitude adjustment on the part of the rich as well as the "underclass," that, again, doesn't detract from its appeal.[11]

In fact, it's no accident that the vast majority of our current cash "welfare state" benefits are *already* work-tested, which is why they (unlike AFDC and food stamps) are generally popular and non-stigmatizing. Unemployment compensation, for example, only goes to Americans who have worked for a certain period of time—and even then they don't get it if they've quit their jobs or been fired for cause.[12] Workers' compensation, by definition, covers only workers.

Most important, Social Security, the biggest cash benefits program, is already work-tested. Actually, it's *double* work-tested. First, Social Security sends checks only to people who are either old, retired (after age 62), or disabled—or to their survivors. We don't expect the elderly or the disabled to work. Second, Social Security distinguishes, even among the elderly and disabled, between those who have worked and those who haven't. It does this by paying benefits only to those who earn them by contributing payroll taxes for a sufficient length of time—for a prescribed number of "quarters"—and by paying benefits that are related to past earnings.[13] Whatever else it does, this "contributory" requirement functions as a crude test of work history.[14] The wealthy heir who clips coupons all his life doesn't qualify for Social Security any more than the lifelong AFDC mother. Old and disabled people who are poor but haven't met the "quarters" requirement are relegated to a separate (and inevitably less respectable) program called Supplemental Security Income, or SSI.[15]

Unfortunately, Money Liberals have spent much of the past three decades trying to obscure the obvious importance of the work test to the legitimacy of government benefits. Even the phrase "welfare state" seems calculated to promote confusion on this point. To Money Liberals, the popularity of programs like Social Security is a miraculous political achievement attributable, not to the common value of work, but to the enlightening effects of cash. The not-so-secret Money Liberal hope, of course, is that if the legitimacy of benefits can be divorced from work, then cash-dispensing programs might be freely expanded to cover poor non-workers.[16]

The Money Liberal argument boils down to two claims. First, cash benefit programs are popular not when they are restricted to workers, but rather when they spread around benefits, like so many military bases or water projects, to the bulk of the population. Income assistance programs simply aren't "sustainable," sociologist Theda Skocpol argues, if middle-class voters see "no gain for them."[17] What's important, in this view, is that benefit programs be "universal." Charles Peters calls this the "More the Merrier Principle."[18] As noted in Chapter 6, the more romantic Money Liberals go so far as to assert that universal cash benefits are not only popular—they are themselves a basis for social equality.[19]

Conversely, Money Liberals argue, programs like AFDC aren't stigmatizing because they are not work-tested, but rather because they are not "universal"—they are restricted to the poor. In policy parlance, they are "means-tested" (limited to those of insufficient means). The public doesn't scorn welfare mothers because they're not supporting themselves, according to this theory. Rather, the means test itself is what "inevitably leads to unacceptable invasions of privacy and hence an undermining of ... dignity and self-respect," in the words of Elizabeth Wickenden, a veteran liberal social worker and activist. By restricting aid to the poor, Wickenden charges, means-tests divide the community into two groups, "those who pay and those who receive.... The paying group looks with suspicion on the beneficiaries and inevitably ... an element of judgmentalism among the former toward the latter manifests itself in an effort to control behavior and thus expenditures. Why don't they work?"[20]

Well, why don't they? Why isn't that a good question to ask? Maybe they *aren't* working when they could be. Without a work test, the public can't be sure, can it? This is not (as the growth of the underclass attests) merely an irrational worry born of middle-class resentment at being cut out of the action. The attempt to avoid acknowledging the centrality of the work test would be more convincing if Money Liberals could point to a single popular government cash benefit that has *not* been work-tested. They can't. Skocpol's big examples are cash veterans benefits after the Civil War and modern Social

Security. But veterans benefits were linked to work of a particularly risky sort—service in the Union Army.[21] Social Security, as we've seen, is rigorously conditioned on work history, and anyway the elderly aren't expected to work. In contrast, Civic Liberals can point to cash programs, such as the Earned Income Tax Credit (or regulations like the minimum wage law) that are overwhelmingly popular and non-stigmatizing despite the fact that they are "means-tested"—that is, restricted to the poor. Have resentful middle-class taxpayers imposed degrading, privacy-invading requirements on those who get the EITC? No. The taxpayers' elected representatives have practically fallen all over themselves to heap more benefits on the working poor.[22]

It should be relatively easy, then—once a neo-WPA is in place—to build a "work ethic state" that promotes social equality based on labor by distributing benefits based on labor. The popular distinction between the deserving and undeserving already forms the basis of the structure Roosevelt set out in 1935, a structure that largely survives. The problem is mainly that this distinction wasn't implemented ruthlessly enough, that AFDC and food stamps were allowed to emerge as dole-like exceptions to the New Deal regime. Eliminate those exceptions, and the benefits of the American "welfare" state will be thoroughly work-tested. Provide the work, through a guaranteed-jobs program, and those benefits will be available to all.

Proclaiming work the general prerequisite for cash benefits would have an additional, practical payoff for liberals: it would allow them to escape the budget straitjacket that currently restrains activist government. The accepted euphemism for this budgetary problem is the "uncontrolled cost of entitlement programs." What that means mainly is the expense of Social Security. Because the Social Security system pays benefits to rich, middle-class, and poor retired workers, it is very expensive.[23] The payroll taxes that fund it total 12.4 percent of earnings below $55,500—or about $326 billion in 1991 (compared with, say, the $24 billion that goes for AFDC).[24] Despite this huge revenue stream, Social Security may well still go broke—if not soon, then when the baby boomers need to collect their checks shortly after the turn of the century. One example: the current projections for the system assume that the unemployment rate will drop to 6 percent and stay there, even though in the 1980s it averaged 7.2 percent.[25]

Is sending retirement checks to affluent Americans the highest and best use of 12.4 percent of our earnings? A Civic Liberal agenda would seem to have more effective ways to spend the money, including on a national health system and on the jobs program necessary to end welfare and assimilate the underclass. And there is a simple, obvious reform of Social Security that would save enough money to finance a neo-WPA, without imposing any new tax burdens on workers, and without hurting any impoverished retirees.

That obvious reform is, yes, "means-testing." Cut the benefits of recipients who have plenty of income anyway. Even a little means test—taking away half the benefits of couples with incomes of more than $32,000 a year—would generate savings on the order of an extra $25 to $30 billion a year immediately. A more vigorous means-test, one that would pay back affluent recipients' payroll tax contributions but no more, could easily bring in $60 billion a year.[26] Applying the same principle to the Medicare benefits of the affluent would save still more (helping finance health care for those now uninsured).

The rub, of course, is that means-testing violates Money Liberal dogma about the importance of "universal" cash benefit programs. Combine this with the Take Away principle—the natural hesitancy of politicians to cut anyone's check—and the result is vehement liberal opposition to means-testing of "entitlements." When Paul Kirk, then chairman of the Democratic National Committee, suggested in 1985 that Congress might consider shaving the benefits of rich recipients, he was forced to eat his words within hours. Sen. Ted Kennedy, in a 1985 speech calling for (what else) "new ideas," felt compelled to blast this particular idea as nothing less than an attempt to "repeal the New Deal and the New Frontier." In the late eighties, most Democratic politicians dared not even denounce means-testing publicly, lest by doing so they admit to having actually possessed the idea for an instant within their skulls.[27]

The Money Liberal opposition to means-testing Social Security appears perverse, in that means-testing, by denying benefits to the elderly rich, would make Social Security more "progressive" and redistributive. In other contexts, Money Liberals have been compelled by fiscal reality to endorse means-tested benefits—the guaranteed annual income plans of the sixties and seventies were about the biggest means-tested programs you could imagine.[28] But Social Security is seen as a delicate bargain with a touchy middle class. The deal, for

Money Liberals, goes something like this: They will swallow financing the system with a regressive payroll tax ("I don't justify this method of taxation," conceded Wilbur Cohen, President Johnson's Secretary of Health, Education, and Welfare).[29] Money Liberals will also consent to a retirement scheme that pays higher earners higher benefits. The payoff is that these affluent workers don't get benefits as high as their salaries might justify in a private pension plan. The Social Security benefit formula is "carefully devised to weight benefits in favor of low earners," as a pamphlet prepared by the liberal Study Group on Social Security puts it. For example, a $9,000-a-year janitor might receive a monthly benefit of $461 while a $54,000-a-year Teamster would receive $1,022 a month—still more than twice as much, but relatively low compared with the six-fold difference in their paychecks.[30]

This moderate "skew" in benefits might not seem like much to connoisseurs of progressivity.[31] Yet liberals cling to it as if it were the formula for Coke Classic, to be defended against all changes that might threaten it. And threatened it constantly is, in their view, by the possibility that the middle class might pack up its payroll contributions and go home. Here is Wilbur Cohen justifying the system in a debate with Milton Friedman in 1972:

> ... Mr. Friedman attacks the idea that Social Security is primarily a system of redistribution of income to middle income people. Actually I think he is probably right about that. But that is part of the system's political sagacity ... let me emphasize that the reason why the [War on Poverty's] Office of Economic Opportunity and other such programs don't get the appropriations, don't get support from the taxpayer, is that they do not appeal to the middle-class, middle income person.[32]

What assures middle-class support for the system, in the Money Liberal view, is simple: money. It's certainly Social Security's porkbarreling feature that impresses Cohen with its "political sagacity." The More the Merrier. Bribe everyone—except to Money Liberals it isn't just a bribe, but something more profound, an expression of their belief in the communitarian power of cash benefits. Meanwhile, we're told, means-testing will stigmatize: if Social Security is means-tested it will become "just another welfare program," as unpopular as AFDC.[33]

But even if we concede that, perhaps, a poor, lonely widow feels a twinge of self-respect when she goes to the mailbox because she knows that the check she receives is the same type of check David Rockefeller is getting, what is the source of that pride? Is it knowing Rockefeller is getting a check, or knowing that she (along with Rockefeller) has earned her check by satisfying society's expectations of labor? *That* link between rich and poor isn't threatened by a means test.

What the Money Liberal opposition to the means-testing of Social Security ignores, of course, is the program's work requirement. Means-testing wouldn't threaten Social Security's legitimacy, a Civic Liberal could argue, because Social Security's legitimacy is based not on the absence of a means test but on the presence of a work test.[34] *Means-testing can never turn Social Security into welfare, because after means-testing Social Security will still pay benefits only to workers.* Recipients won't feel as if they're on a dole because they won't be on a dole.

A means-test would make Social Security less like a pension and more like "insurance against poverty in retirement." But it would be earned insurance, unlike AFDC or even the SSI program. You couldn't get it, when you needed it, if you hadn't worked for enough "quarters." The rich would still benefit—even in extreme forms of means-testing, Social Security would be there to protect them if they fell on hard times (if they'd earned that protection). No way this system could be characterized as "welfare."[35]

Australia has put a means-test on its Social Security system, without stigmatizing recipients or prompting a middle-class revolt. As a result, Australia's system cost only 5.49 percent of total national earnings in 1981, compared with 9.15 percent for the U.S. system in 1983.[36] The extent to which the Western European social democracies have avoided means-testing is also vastly overstated by Money Liberals.[37] Universal check-cashing doesn't seem necessary for either legitimacy or solidarity. The work question is the key. Our "welfare state" will find enough universality in posing a work-test that all may pass.[38]

Civic Liberalism doesn't *require* the means-testing of Social Security. Why should there be something inherently wrong with a socialized pension system that pays benefits to rich and poor, any more than there is something inherently wrong with the economic system that

makes the rich rich in the first place? Means-testing is just a way to
save a lot of money. But there are at least two changes that Civic Liberals would need to make in the current system, since some of its features clearly violate the goals of assuring dignity to all who work or
are excused from work.

First, benefits under the SSI program—the one that gives a minimum income to the elderly and disabled who don't qualify for Social
Security—are too low, especially for single men and women living
alone. The maximum federal SSI and food stamp benefit for an individual with no income and no Social Security coverage was about
$5,800 a year in 1991.[39] The poverty line for aged individuals was
$6,532. About half the states supplement federal SSI benefits, but
only five bring benefits up to the poverty line.[40] The elderly on SSI
haven't necessarily worked in the past, but many have, and in any case
they can't be expected to work any more. Their benefits should be
raised to bring them out of poverty.[41]

Second, and more scandalously, the Social Security system doesn't
even guarantee a decent minimum income for elderly Americans
who've worked and contributed all their lives. A cook who worked at
the minimum wage for 40 years could retire in 1991 and get a pension of approximately $460 a month—only about 85 percent of the
poverty line.[42]

It's hard not to be cynical about why these minimum benefits are
so low. I mean, here we have total Social Security benefits rising 34
percent in real terms since 1967, pushed ever upward by the most
powerful lobby in the nation, with payroll taxes soaring and the Treasury sinking into permanent debt to pay for them, and those hundreds of billions of dollars have somehow not taken care of the most
deserving retired contributors.[43] Would the middle class really desert
the system if benefits were raised to protect former low-wage workers? Or is the problem that if there were no deserving impoverished
ex-workers, scraping to get by on $460 a month, then the American
Association of Retired Persons wouldn't have any heart-rending tales
to tell when campaigning to preserve the higher benefits that go
mainly to its affluent middle-class constituency? ("460 dollars a
month. How can anyone live on that these days?")[44]

A Civic Liberal program would want to do more than merely guarantee lifelong workers a poverty-line retirement, especially if they
could get almost that much from SSI without working at all. We

want people who work all their lives to get a chunk more in retirement than what non-workers get—another "work bonus," if you will. I suggest increasing the minimum pension to $600 a month for someone who retires after working full-time for 30 years.

Among its intended side effects, a souped-up minimum pension would send an immediate message into the ghettoes, restoring a bit of lost status to the elderly men and women who've played by the rules, sticking it out in jobs that paid what their grandchildren now deride as "chump change." If the old ex-garage attendant down the street suddenly bought a new television, or a car, that wouldn't hurt; it might even have a subtle, subconscious effect on his teenage neighbors. It will be hard to expect single mothers with toddlers to work for $4 or $5 an hour, or to refute the idea that only "good jobs" are worth keeping, if we allow those who take low-wage jobs anything other than a respectable retirement.

Together, these two reforms shouldn't cost over $10 billion a year.[45] But if they were more expensive, it wouldn't be a disaster. In a "work ethic state" there would be no ideological objection to generous benefits, as long as they were rigorously conditioned upon work. Indeed, the public would be far more likely to support decent benefits precisely because they would be conditioned upon work.

In his 1982 book *The Underclass*, Ken Auletta interviewed Michael "Junior" Antonetty, a 37-year-old Puerto Rican who lived in a Brooklyn housing project. Antonetty worked as a janitor. "I have friends," he complained. "They're strong. Yet they're not going to work. No way. They get rent. They get food stamps. They get welfare checks. They say to me, 'What are you going to work for?' They're supposed to work like I do. I go to work at five o'clock in the morning. The guys don't seek.... Right now I could send my wife over there and she could tell welfare, 'Junior left me.' She would get a check. I won't do it."[46]

It's fair to say we will never achieve (through Money Liberal cash-redistribution or any other means) the economic equality that would enable a janitor like Junior Antonetty and a banker with a stock option plan to afford the same level of housing, clothing, education, or general comfort. That's capitalism. But we might be able to achieve a society where a Junior Antonetty—even if he only makes a barely adequate living—feels, is felt by others to be, and by and large is treated as just as good as a banker because he works just as hard. In a "work

ethic state," labor would be the ticket of admission to Civic Liberalism's egalitarian public sphere, the common denominator that allowed waiters and WPA-workers to "look you in the face and treat
you as an equal." How foolish of liberals to discard this egalitarian,
unifying measure of social membership, to abandon Roosevelt's and
Orwell's distinction between work and non-work, to instead try to
build equality of citizenship on the universal receipt of government
checks.

CHAPTER 10

An Ecology of Equality

The second stage of Civic Liberalism takes us a long way toward realizing the goal of social equality. Work becomes the conspicuous qualification for government income assistance, the common test of full citizenship. Underclass culture can no longer sustain itself once welfare is replaced with a system of guaranteed jobs and day care. As women who would otherwise have been welfare mothers go to work—some settling for modest wages, some succeeding beyond their wildest dreams—the "ghetto poor" culture is gradually absorbed into the mainstream working culture. Middle-class resentment of the underclass, and its attendant racial prejudice, subsides, as does the adversarial response of the ghettos.

Eventually, as the underclass is assimilated (and the "homeless" of today are either assimilated or supervised), crime decreases. The cycle of urban decay starts to reverse. City sidewalks and parks become safe. Middle-class taxpayers start to enjoy them again, and become willing to invest in rebuilding them and keeping them clean. In downtowns, as well as rural areas, richer and poorer Americans bump into each other as equals with increasing frequency—in the post office, the corner coffee shop, and the public library. These refurbished public institutions would be added to the egalitarian institutions of Civic Liberalism's first stage: the draft, day-care centers, national service, a national health care system, and a democratized political process. Is there any doubt that if all this happened—and it's all well within the realm of political possibility—the country would in an important sense be transformed? It would be a more socially egalitarian place than Money Liberals could ever hope to create by trying to rearrange incomes.

Yet, it must be admitted, this society would still fall short of the liberal ideal of social equality. Most conspicuously, rich and non-rich Americans might remain relatively isolated from each other in two of the institutions identified in Chapter 7 as being especially hard to integrate by class: neighborhoods and schools. If the underclass disappeared, would postmen, plumbers, and our hypothetical $5-an-hour short-order cook be able to live in the same neighborhood as a successful lawyer? Would their sons and daughters attend class together?

The hope, of course, is that as the peculiarly threatening culture of poverty evaporates, parents of all income levels might freely live near each other, and send their kids to common schools without a second thought. It's hard to overestimate the impact of the underclass in discouraging such class-mixing, but the precise extent to which ghetto poverty and the traumas it causes are to blame is something we won't know until those problems abate. In effect, ending the underclass threat would alter the ecology of the entire society. What would then happen to the composition of cities and suburbs can't be predicted in advance. But if Civic Liberals can alter the ecology of daily life by transforming the underclass, maybe they can alter it in other ways too.

The struggle to democratize suburbs and schools represents a third, final, and frankly more speculative stage of Civic Liberal activism. Instituting a draft, creating a health care system, and absorbing the underclass would require a huge government exertion and the sustained application of political will. The third stage of Civic Liberalism requires something more, namely a wager on the direction of the American character. I think Civic Liberals could shape that direction and win their bet, creating a society in which our social-egalitarian self-image is fully reflected in the events of our everyday lives. But that will come only as the end result of a long, complicated effort to change the social environment of our metropolitan areas—an effort that would cultivate egalitarian civic life institution-by-institution, suburb-by-suburb, much as one might green a desert by planting the more precious, less hardy species in the shade of the earlier, more rugged plantings. An ecology of equality.[1]

• • •

Even were the underclass completely assimilated, and crime reduced to the levels of the 1950s, affluent suburbanites wouldn't necessarily be overcome with a mingling spirit. The gaps within "mainstream" society—including the gap between affluent professionals and the working class—aren't about to disappear overnight, especially if they are reinforced by the divisive tendencies of a brain-based meritocracy. People may not be scared of Ralph Kramden the way they're scared of Willie Horton, but not everyone wants Ralph as a neighbor. Suburbs and restrictive zoning laws were invented, in large part, to enable the affluent to avoid that fate.

In particular, it's possible to identify at least four social dynamics that might promote suburban segregation even in the absence of an underclass.[2] The first is psychological. As noted earlier, George Gilder defends class segregation by tracing it to a status anxiety that surfaces whenever moorings of blood and breeding are ripped away: "In a society of rapid social mobility, all but the most supremely rich know they can plummet down.... In order to escape such tensions, economic classes will seek out their own kind, whenever possible, and send their children to schools dominated by their own economic class...."[3]

Actually, if you read Gilder's book, *Wealth and Poverty,* it's quite apparent (and revealing) that he's mainly talking about the desire to avoid the non-working underclass. But the insecurity he describes could produce a desire to avoid other non-affluent classes—a theory echoed by Ehrenreich, Gilder's political opposite. Middle-class snobbery, remember, is wildly overdetermined in Ehrenreich's schema, one reason her Money Liberal attempt to pin the rap on growing income inequality is unpersuasive. At least since the fifties, she shows, affluent American professionals have been groping for taste distinctions and status purchases (hardwood floors, Volvos) to distinguish themselves from working-class schlubs.[4] This snob principle permeates the patter of real estate brokers, the unacknowledged legislators of housing patterns. Every now and then it breaks into the open when some insecure suburb passes a law to prevent plumbers and electricians from parking their vans in front of their houses.

But there are less abstract forces at work than the desire to accommodate middle-class insecurities (though snobbery, once embodied in property values, is not abstract at all to homeowners). The least of these other factors is architectural: a nice house is simply nicer, and therefore worth more, when it's surrounded by other nice, well-maintained houses. It's also nicer when surrounded by fewer houses on bigger lots, since that usually translates into less noise and traffic. People who can afford nice, large homes, and who can afford to keep them in top condition have a non-snobbish aesthetic reason to surround themselves with similar people—and the value of doing so will be reflected in the price of their homes.

A third, particularly stubborn dynamic is the familiar stratification impulse in education. Absorbing the underclass would drastically diminish this impulse, but not eliminate it. If my upper middle-class child will learn more if he's surrounded by other upper middle-class children, then it's in the interest of us upper middle-class parents to control access to our neighborhoods in order to control access to the local schools.[5]

Finally, there is a more vulgar economic motive for the affluent to retreat into exclusive suburbs: the desire to cut taxes. It's a hard mathematical truth that if the rich people from a community can somehow form their own little suburb, with their own schools and services, they can tax themselves at a lower rate and still finance the same per capita expenditures, since then they don't have to pay for the children of poor people who don't have as much property or income to tax.[6]

Something like this crude, tax-minimizing scenario has in fact been played out across the nation, where state authorities have allowed it. New Jersey, broken up into 611 small school districts, is one of the worst examples. The well-to-do citizens of Princeton Township pay a property tax of only 1.59 percent, but that generates school spending of $8,659 per pupil. The residents of nearby working-class Trenton must pay property taxes at a 3.09 percent rate, but that only generates $6,881 per pupil.[7] Building lower-cost housing in a suburb like Princeton would threaten this upper middle-class tax racket by bringing in people who aren't rich enough to be taxed but who still use government services.[8]

Of course, whatever the psychological, architectural, educational, or tax advantages of living in an exclusive suburb may be, they are likely to be capitalized and reflected in home prices. That means most people who live in exclusive suburbs today *aren't* financial beneficiaries of class segregation—they paid for the benefits when they bought their houses. It also means they will be extremely angry if anyone tries to take away the advantages they've already paid for. And it means further class-segregation eventually becomes almost inevitable, since only the affluent can afford to "buy into" such an expensive community.

But Civic Liberalism is not without responses to these stratifying impulses. The first response is to lower expectations. The goal need not be to make all the various non-underclasses love each other. A certain proportion of rich people will always prefer to associate with other rich people (just as some ethnic Americans, given the choice, prefer to spend time in ethnic communities). Some smart people will always want to associate only with others they deem smart. We don't have to stop yuppies from ridiculing the taste of people with wall-to-wall carpeting (just as we don't have to stop others from laughing at overpriced Saabs). Social equality can accommodate a pluralism of tastes and associational preferences.

What Civic Liberals want is a civic life pervasive enough so that, in their public lives and their Sunday morning selves, the vast majority of Americans wouldn't pretend to any fundamental superiority (or, even subconsciously, concede inferiority). We can argue about what, precisely, that requires. But surely it doesn't require mixing classes house-by-house, rich-poor-rich-poor. It doesn't mean that lawyers must live next door to grocery checkout clerks (though that would be nice). It probably does mean that lawyers and their families can't be completely isolated from the families of checkout clerks, and can't separate themselves out when it comes to important, life-determining institutions such as the schools. In short, it means getting the classes to mock each other's tastes from a few blocks away, rather than from across town—or from within the same school district rather than from separate, homogeneous jurisdictions.

It will take a political struggle to complete the public sphere in this fashion, once the struggle to assimilate the underclass has been waged and won. The upper middle class, with its impulses toward self-segregation, will have to be bought off or beaten down—or else its impulses will have to be overcome by an appeal to the compensating virtues of social equality. The political effort required is all the greater because the issue probably can't be settled easily by majority vote in a national election (the way, say, the issue of federal trade policy can be settled). A big part of the problem is that suburbs are autonomous jurisdictions, and we're trying to get them to do something they might democratically not want to do.[9]

Buying off the suburbs isn't as crazy as it sounds. Civic Liberals, unlike Money Liberals, have a big chip they can bargain away—namely, the program of Money Liberalism. The Money Liberal response to the class segregation of suburbs, after all, remains the approach New Jersey's Democratic Governor Jim Florio took in 1990. He doubled New Jersey's top state income tax rate, reduced state aid to wealthy school districts and redirected it to poor districts. Affluent homeowners suddenly were faced, not only with higher state taxes, but with the prospect of raising their local property taxes to make up for the cutoff of state funding.[10] The result was a grassroots rebellion, in which Democrats not only lost control over both houses of the state legislature, but lost them by veto-proof margins. Even were Florio-style reform to succeed, of course, it wouldn't mean rich and poor attend the same schools. It would just mean their schools are comparably funded, a class version of separate-but-equal.[11]

A direct class-mixing strategy might actually be more successful, once the underclass is no longer one of the classes to be mixed. Suppose a governor offered his state's affluent suburbanites this deal: a big cut in top state income tax rates in exchange for zoning changes and new municipal boundaries designed to integrate schools and suburbs by class. The revenue lost by cutting income tax rates for the affluent could be made up by increasing levies that fall less heavily on the rich, including regressive taxes like sales taxes.

For Money Liberals, this deal is anathema. What about Progressivity! For Civic Liberals, it's a big winner: state income taxes make a negligible contribution to income equality, and a virtually undetectable contribution to social equality. Instead of desperately reshuffling tax money while leaving class-segregated institutions essentially intact, why not trade away the Money Liberal gestures for real public sphere improvements? Democratize life instead of the tax tables.

Would affluent suburbanites buy it? Maybe not. They'd be trading away their precious isolation (with its own tax advantages) for lower income taxes. But they might not have much choice.[12] Suburbs are not sovereignties, after all. States retain the right to redraw the boundaries of their subdivisions, or even to eliminate them altogether. Rich suburban homeowners would know that, if they appeared too selfish, they might get rolled in the state legislature.[13] Legislatures in

Oregon, Washington, California, and Florida are already beginning to pressure exclusive suburbs into zoning changes that allow higher-density, more affordable housing. In Massachusetts a state-level committee has been empowered to overrule restrictive local zoning.[14] A tax cut is simply one way to lessen the suburbs' resistance—to induce them to go along with a general rezoning or boundary-realignment by neutralizing their natural impulse to "secede" in order to reduce taxes.

There are other techniques Civic Liberals might use to weaken that resistance, techniques corresponding to the stratifying impulses outlined earlier. The architectural objection, for example, can surely be overcome in part by better design and traffic controls. Would a doctor with a big yard really find his aesthetic bliss destroyed if a neat row of small townhomes was constructed nearby? In planned communities like Reston, Virginia, and Columbia, Maryland, this sort of integration has been pulled off quite well.

Another possibility is "microzoning." Zoning laws might still mandate big, expensive houses in some areas and restrict small, high-density houses to other areas. The catch is that these areas would be small. Instead of having a big rich suburb miles away from a big poor suburb, zoning rules would carve out a few blocks of estates, then a few blocks of medium-sized lots, then a few blocks of cheaper units. Our doctor, should he choose, could still sit in his back yard and see nothing but other back yards. But he would be part of the same basic community as the less affluent living nearby.

Of course, this means the doctors will worry about the public schools. That is a more difficult fear to neutralize. One possibility—offered by the current trend to school "choice"—is that the whole link between neighborhoods and schools might be broken.

There are innumerable versions of "choice." The most radical are so-called "pure" choice plans, which would in effect give students tuition vouchers they could use at public or private schools. Our hypothetical doctor wouldn't worry about his neighbors because his kids wouldn't necessarily be going to school with his neighbors' kids. Private-school choice shouldn't faze a Civic Liberal just because it's private—again, there's nothing that says the public sphere must consist only of state-run enterprises. Many private schools in fact mix classes quite well. But an unfettered system of pure choice (whatever its educational merits) would almost certainly be a social-egalitarian disaster.

Take the relatively undiluted choice plan proposed with great fan-fare in 1990 by John Chubb of the Brookings Institution and Terry Moe of Stanford.[15] In the Chubb-Moe regime, each student in a given district would get a "scholarship" of a fixed amount. Students could then take these scholarships to any school, whether run by state and local governments or organized privately. The key, with this and all choice plans, is the method these schools would use in picking students. The Chubb-Moe method is clear: "Schools will make their own admissions decisions, subject only to nondiscrimination requirements."[16] If a school wants to take only students from the surrounding neighborhood, or students with IQs over 130, it can.

Ask defenders of pure choice about the dangers of class division, and they'll typically ask what system could be more inegalitarian than the system we have now?[17] It's not easy to devise one—but Chubb and Moe have done it. True, they would prohibit parents from supplementing the scholarships with private "add-on" funds.[18] That might prevent the rich from immediately setting up exclusive elementary schools charging $10,000 a year. But Chubb and Moe would allow the geographic exclusivity of the public schools to persist, while on top of that they would add a layer of exclusivity based on merit.

When Lamar Alexander, Education Secretary under President Bush, boasts that under choice elementary and high schools would "end up like our system of colleges and universities" he confirms this inegalitarian forecast. Our system of colleges and universities viciously stratifies by merit and money. Does anyone really doubt that, under the Chubb-Moe plan, elementary schools and high schools would be as academically selective as they could, quickly sorting themselves out in a hierarchy of prestige and student quality, just as colleges do now? Each city would have its little mini-Harvards and Yales that all parent-fearing middle-class children would try to get into. If they weren't accepted there, they'd settle for a second tier of high schools, and so forth down the hierarchy.[19] From kindergarten through adulthood, smarter and richer kids would go through life without meeting as fellow students kids who were poorer or not-so-smart.

More promising for social egalitarians are choice schemes that attempt to curb the tyranny of the admissions office—so called "controlled choice." The most obvious method of control would be to replace both "merit" and "neighborhood" admissions with random admissions, a lottery. Some of the educational benefits of choice would go out the window, because students would have less incentive to compete to get into schools (good grades wouldn't help them). But schools would still have to compete for students. The worst schools would attract no "entrants" into their lotteries. The best schools would be oversubscribed. No school could get to be "best," however, simply by picking the best applicants.[20]

Today, lotteries are mainly used in admissions to "magnet" public schools. There the lesson seems to be that, despite the lottery, if "choice" is optional (in that if you don't choose, your kids are simply assigned to their regular neighborhood school) the result is class strat-ification. It tends to be the more upwardly mobile, middle-class par-ents who figure out how to play the lottery system.[21] Once the kids from these striving families are skimmed off by the best "magnets," the kids from less motivated families, who don't make a choice at all, are left in the neighborhood schools. "Those schools become absolute dumps," says Charles Glenn, a Boston school official and controlled-choice advocate. In the eighteen non-magnet neighborhood high schools in low-income areas of Chicago, only 4 percent of students in the Class of 1984 both graduated and were able to read at the national average.[22]

But we might *require* every parent to make a choice. This could en-courage even unmotivated parents to investigate the possibilities. If you have to choose a school, why not pick the best one? Make parents pick, let them pick any school in a district, use a lottery, and you'll see some class-mixing, say "controlled choice" proponents such as Glenn. They point to Cambridge, Massachusetts, where such a scheme has been operating in the public schools since 1982.[23] But the statistics from Cambridge aren't all that encouraging. The town's "choice" scheme has totally desegregated the schools by race (the program's of-ficial goal). But Cambridge schools remain relatively segregated by class, with poorer children, both black and white, concentrated in the two elementary schools that previously served them. This may be be-cause poorer kids are subtly encouraged to pick non-rich schools. It may be because kids who live within half a mile of the better, richer schools still get priority.[24] In Montclair, New Jersey, a "choice" system that gives no preference to people who live next door to a school seems to have had a bit more success mixing low- and high-income children.[25]

Of course, the rich don't have to subject themselves to the vagaries of a lottery at all. "If you are an upper middle-class parent, you don't even bother with this," says Christine Rossell of Boston University, who has studied the Cambridge choice system. Rossell herself thought about buying a home in Cambridge, but found that "when we looked for a house ... everyone told us that if you move into Cambridge you will have to put your kids in private school." There is evidence that, without the guarantee of access to a neighborhood school, upper middle-class families with school-age kids simply don't move to Cambridge at all anymore.[26]

The problem, then, is that the sort of choice system that might mix classes within a public school district isn't likely to encourage affluent parents to want to live in that school district.[27] Why would our hypothetical doctor be content to have his children admitted to schools by lot?[28] He is probably quite happy with the existing, non-random way his kids are assigned to their "neighborhood" public schools, and he will still resist any attempt to make the neighborhood more heterogeneous.

Faced with such resistance, Civic Liberals could adopt a pure choice approach, sacrificing democracy in the schools for democracy in the neighborhoods. That is, if our doctor knew he could "choose" a good, exclusive public or private school no matter where he lived, much of his motive for insisting on geographic segregation would disappear.[29] Given the potential egalitarian power of class-integrated schools, however, this is an unappealing tradeoff.

The alternative is to take other steps to reduce the threat posed by class-integrated schools. The institution of "tracking"—the division of students into separate classes on the basis of ability—plays a double-edged role here. Tracking would seem toxic for social equality, and surely it is in its extreme forms, when students are sorted out at an early age and subjected to entirely different curricula (including "vocational" and "academic" tracks) based on their presumed ability. Critics of tracking such as Jeannie Oakes point out that it was adopted, shortly after the turn of the century, because middle-class Anglos wanted to create separate tracks for themselves and for immigrant, "lower"-class children.[30]

What these critics tend to ignore is that, even if tracking did reflect class prejudice, it was only necessary because the various classes were attending the same high schools in the first place. Where schools are totally segregated by class, after all, the educated middle class doesn't need to worry about undesirable intermingling. In fact, according to Oakes, the original 1918 endorsement of tracking by the National Education Association specifically saw it as a package deal that included class-mixing—academic subjects would be tracked, but "unification" would be accomplished through the "social mingling of pupils" and extracurricular activities in "comprehensive" high schools.[31]

This suggests that a relatively common, mild form of tracking might reassure the affluent and ambitious while keeping kids of all types in the same public school, sharing a variety of classes (as well as their extracurricular social life). I have in mind a "Fallowsian" True Meritocratic system that attempts to distinguish the wide variety of talents children of all classes can display. This system wouldn't separate kids for life, starting in kindergarten. But, around the ninth or tenth grade it would let the kids who are good in math get advanced math classes, and let the kids who are good in history get more challenging history classes. These will mostly be the same kids, but not entirely. Some students would mix with one group in one subject and another in another subject. No upper middle-class parents, looking at this relatively benign form of tracking, could have legitimate worries that their "gifted and talented" child would be held back by his proximity to the children of the working class. To the extent little Jeremy was good at math, he would get accelerated schooling in math.

True, the prosperous parents of Adam, who is not so talented, might lose the advantage they now get in an exclusive suburb, where the unprecocious but well-born benefit by being surrounded by kids more academically inclined than they. The point isn't that True Meritocratic tracking can remove all forms of affluent resistance to class integration. The point is that, as with the architectural and the economic objections to heterogeneity, the educational objection can be diluted, and resistance by the affluent weakened.

That leaves the snob-objection. Civic Liberals would need to blunt, if not totally repress, the Ehrenreichian insecurities of the middle class, and build on a contrary impulse that prizes social equality for its own sake. Changing the culture of the affluent, in this respect, may be almost as important to social egalitarians as ending the culture of poverty. The Civic Liberal bet is that it can be done: that well-to-do Americans aren't irredeemable snobs, that they aren't eager to impoverish their lives by limiting their associations to people of their own income level—that ultimately they are only unwilling to share their neighborhoods with people who reject a few basic values.

This is obviously the most uncertain terrain. When Orwell, in *Wigan Pier*, confronted the "class difficulty"—the problem of getting the upper classes not just to cooperate with the working class, but to drop their feelings of superiority—he basically threw up his hands. Even enforcing the work ethic, through a work test for government benefits, would not by itself establish a single cross-class culture. In theory, after all, it is far more likely that the poor will adopt work as an overriding value than that the rich will. The rich have another potential value on which to rely, namely money. When we ask Americans to treat anyone who works as the social equal of anyone else who works, whatever their income, we are asking the affluent to abandon a game in which they hold a winning hand.

Yet these are Americans we're talking about, not Orwell's British. Surely whatever anti–working-class antagonism afflicts today's affluent suburbanites doesn't approach in viciousness either the current anti-underclass prejudices ("face it, they're animals") or the sort of British middle-class prejudice ("the lower classes smell") confronted by Orwell.[32] At least not yet. Classlessness still figures prominently in how we see ourselves. Even in the 1980s, the infamous decade of greed, for every snob ad on the television ("'So who was the first to be Vice-President?' ... 'And last with the corner office'"—Apple Computer) there were probably five spots attempting to tap the national sense of social equality, usually featuring guys of various races sitting around on a stoop after a game of basketball, drinking beer. During the 1990s, the non-snob to snob ratio has visibly increased ("Because the rich guys shouldn't have all the fun."—Nissan).[33]

Again, much of this is hypocrisy, given how rich Americans actually live their lives, but at least we're hypocrites. And we may be better than that. This is the perversely optimistic lesson to be drawn from the impulse toward residential segregation. The desire for protected, homogeneous neighborhoods can be seen as an expression of snobbism, but it is also something else. *Within* even the most exclusive suburb, the forms of social equality tend to be maintained—and not just the form. With neighborhood schooling, most suburban kids at least go to school as equals with the kids who live near them. Adults mingle with their neighbors in the PTA, the supermarket, the drug store, without affectation or deference. The egalitarian texture of daily life is maintained.

In a sense, then, suburban isolation is a sort of backwards tribute to social equality. We don't like to act superior to people we actually come into contact with in daily life, so we set things up so we don't have to come into contact with the people who might provoke such feelings. That way we can continue to relate in an egalitarian manner with the people we do meet (our neighbors). Real inegalitarians— Englishmen living with their manservants, Boers bossing around blacks in South Africa—are usually all too happy to mingle with their inferiors and treat them as such. One reason Americans must stratify themselves is that they aren't such natural snobs at all.[34]

The opportunity is there, once the peculiar threat of the underclass is removed, to build on these underlying sentiments. The initial extensions of the public sphere, in the earlier stages of Civic Liberalism, would set the scene for a gradual cultural evolution, in which the relatively mild downward-looking prejudices of affluent Americans would be neutralized as they are revealed in everyday life to be either false or trivial.

Civic Liberals would readily concede, after all, that in a society dominated entirely by private commerce, money will logically be the dominant measure of social standing. Texas oil men even refer to it as "how they keep score." But in a society with a civic sphere, even an incomplete one, the second scorecard exists where each citizen's worth is judged not by his bank balance or SAT score but by "the content of his character": Does he work? Is he polite? Does he fulfill his other obligations? Grading on this scorecard tends to be pass-fail. Either somebody is a good citizen or he's not. If he is, he can hold his head up.

The more we have the opportunity to judge people according to these alternative public sphere standards, the harder it will be to break the habit. In *Wigan*, Orwell put off the day of class reconciliation until the proletariat and the middle class could fight side by side in a socialist revolution. The war that soon came did indeed have that effect, on Americans at least. Under Civic Liberalism's draft, a war would have that effect again. But can't the cumulative daily struggles of civilian life in the public sphere be as potent a method of reconciliation in the long run?

Tawney's aphorism went: "If men are to respect each other for what they are, they must cease to respect each other for what they own."[35] That's right. But his point has different implications than he may have imagined. For one thing, it's not such an insurrectionary concept. It doesn't require socialism. It doesn't require money equality or "more" money equality (or even more tax progressivity). If men cease to respect each other for their money, what does it matter how much they have?[36]

The idea is not to have so many different spheres, each with its own scoreboard, that in effect nobody knows what the score is and everybody gives up making comparisons. That sometimes seems to be Walzer's notion, but it suffers from the same problem as his "100 bells" idea—namely that some people will score high in a great many spheres while others will only pass the minimal work test.[37] Nor, as noted earlier, is the goal to have two separate areas of life, one where all workers have equal dignity and the other where their worth depends on their bank statements. The riddle of social equality under capitalism isn't solved by achieving a "balance" between two contradictory cultures, or by simply slapping them together. (Thesis, antithesis, sandwich.) The idea, rather, is that the public sphere will eventually have the sort of primacy to which religions have aspired. The egalitarian community must be strong enough to contain large economic differences and condition their effect on social relations across the board.

The larger the public sphere is, the more likely it is to have this conditioning effect, which will in turn make possible further public-sphere expansion, which will have an even greater conditioning effect, and so on. Eventually—slowly, perhaps quietly—social equality will extend into the forbidden zones of housing and schooling, which means the public sphere expands by a decisive order of magnitude. Class-mixing in neighborhoods and schools will never be perfect, or even close; but it doesn't have to be. It need only be sufficient to sustain Tawney's "common tradition of respect." Once a neighborhood is sufficiently integrated, virtually every local institution—every gas station, drug store, tennis court, and supermarket—becomes a formidable social equalizer, and victory for Civic Liberalism is assured.

• • •

To help speed up the class-mixing process, Civic Liberals might remind suburbanites that as long as they live in a society where people are judged mainly by how much money they have, Americans—even rich, isolated, comfortable Americans—will always live to some degree in the state of uncertainty that Barbara Ehrenreich describes. Are they making enough? Have their careers topped out? What if they lose what they have? Just as you can't have capitalism without money inequality, you can't have it without this uncertainty. But it cuts deeper when the money game is the only one being played, when the affluent live only in the sphere of the market.

In a social-egalitarian world, well-off Americans will still be able to worry about going soft, about losing their edge, about money, about their children. But they would also have a sense of worth grounded in civic life and its respect for work. Fear of falling, yes, but not so far. Given this bit of security, they might enjoy their money all the more. With social equality, they have nothing to lose but their anxiety. (And maybe valet parking.)

There is another sense—also ecological—in which social equality is in the enlightened self-interest of all Americans, especially the affluent. The central political fact confronting America's rich, after all, is that they live in a democracy. One man, one vote. Reich's symbol-analysts may be tempted to think they're better because they have more brain-skills or because they can afford a Lexus. That those sentiments are also arguments against democracy doesn't necessarily make them unappealing to everyone. But the arguments against democracy are not about to prevail. The affluent are going to have to learn to live comfortably with people who may not use the same parks and schools as they do, but who, given the right set of circumstances, might outvote them.

Once the underclass is gone and the bottom class is the working class, the rich and the working poor will have lost their unifying enemy. Who knows how Americans will react as the income gap between the skilled and unskilled widens—as it comes to be perceived, not just as a difference in income or skills, but increasingly as a difference in "merit" (the Fairness Trap) or even inherited ability (the Herrnstein Nightmare)?[38] When the reality of these trends begins to sink in, American society will be subject to terrific strains. Only a strong civic culture will be able to contain the potential insecurities, prejudices, and outright animosities. And nothing, certainly not money inequality itself, will produce more animosity than the seeming assertion by the successful of a money- or "merit"-based superiority. If well-off Americans keep trying to isolate themselves in suburban neighborhoods and schools even after the underclass threat recedes, it won't take long for the stench of snobbery to reach the noses of the excluded.

In the end, rich and poor Americans won't build a culture of social equality simply because it's right, though it is, or because it's the natural outgrowth of an expanding public sphere, though it's that too. They will also do it because it is the only way our democracy can expect to hold together.

CHAPTER 11

Winning

Finally, could Civic Liberals get elected?

When political analysts talk of reviving American liberalism, winning elections is usually the *first* thing on their minds. Polls are consulted. Focus groups are convened. Key "constituencies" are identified. And the conclusion pops out. The Democratic party must mobilize its natural "base" among blacks and the poor. Or the party must recapture disaffected working-class whites, or baby boomers, or non–college graduates aged 24 to 35, or whomever.

This gets it backwards. The idea isn't to design policies to please a focus group, the way you might decide to market a product if it tests well at a consumer "clinic." Politics isn't selling products. People sell products to make money; if the product doesn't move, they'll bring out a different one. Politics is about what we think our lives together should be like. First we figure that out. Then we try to sell it. Again, how much of a victory is it if Democrats, even "liberal Democrats," win presidential elections if nobody knows what being a liberal or Democrat stands for, or if what they stand for is wrong?

Liberals, I've argued, haven't really known what they stand for. On the whole range of issues surrounding the central topic of equality, liberalism as practiced has been inchoate, failing to choose a clear end (money equality or social equality?) and a clear strategy for achieving that end. Faced with the growing class division of America, liberals have been effectively paralyzed. Civic Liberalism is an attempt to end the paralysis. It would have liberals embrace a clear goal (social equal-ity) and a plausible strategy for achieving that goal (the three stages of public sphere expansion and reform). That's not a complete domestic political agenda—there's nothing about abortion, gun control, the environment, or industrial policy—but it is the heart of one.[1] By unearthing and expressing liberalism's underlying social-egalitarian concern, it addresses the wrenching undemocratic changes in American life in the decades since World War II.

The Civic Liberal agenda is certainly not conservative, or Republican, at least as the modern Republican party has defined itself. It's not that Republicans are necessarily social inegalitarians. The party has both a country-club streak and a populist streak. It's simply that the Republican agenda—or rather, the agendas of its various factions—have little to do with social equality. The GOP's cliques have other concerns: low taxes or isolationism or laissez-faire economic theory or opposition to abortion. But given the ominous trends of money and merit, and the breakdown of the public sphere, *not* to take vigorous countervailing government action is in effect to give up on social equality, to consign America to a stratified future where even the affluent lead half-lives of demographically pristine isolation.

To avoid that future, Civic Liberalism would ask a lot of the voters. They are to accept the risks of a draft and the impositions of national service. They are to foot the bill for other new public sphere institutions—most expensively for a guaranteed jobs-program, but also for public services such as day care, for publicly financed elections, for parks and libraries. It's true that national health insurance, another large new public institution, should actually save the voters money, with the taxes that finance it being more than repaid in the form of vanished medical bills. But those taxes would still have to be imposed somehow, on somebody.[2] In the short run, the Civic Liberal package could easily require voters to finance (through taxes, benefit cuts, defense cuts, or other savings) budget additions of $150 billion a year *before* the budget costs of national health insurance are counted. It would amount to a transformation of near New-Dealish proportions. Trickiest of all, as discussed in Chapter 10, Americans are to be asked eventually to give up the security of class-segregated suburban havens.

The first thing to emphasize, then, when we ask whether the voters would buy such a plan, is that they might not. A Civic Liberal agenda could be a practical strategy for achieving social equality but a poor way to win elections. Money Liberalism, conversely, could be a good way to get elected and reelected ad infinitum without ever doing much about the trend toward class division. The only way to really find out whether Civic Liberalism makes good politics is to go out and make the argument that social equality is worth a new and expensive round of affirmative government. If the attempt is made, and Civic Liberalism loses, then it loses. That's what standing for something means. Americans will have decided they want a different sort of society.

But I don't think Civic Liberalism would lose. It certainly has a far better chance of winning than Money Liberalism or some promiscuous blend of both liberal strategies. A Money Liberal campaign might have more immediate appeal to the pocketbooks of various core Democratic "constituencies." But it's not clear that appealing to Democratic constituencies wins elections anymore.[3] Has Money Liberalism been so wildly successful over the past two decades that we shouldn't tamper with the formula? If Plan A doesn't work, why not try Plan B? Even on pocketbook issues, I'll argue, the potential appeal of a relatively pure form of Civic Liberalism is far broader. When it comes to the larger issues on which elections are often decided—"values," noneconomic notions of self-interest—there's no contest.

Civic Liberalism's enemy is not really the electorate, which time and time again has shown that it embraces Civic Liberal notions. Its enemy isn't necessarily even the Republicans, whose natural elitist streak (coupled with a tendency to oppose all expensive and ambitious federal endeavors) would provide the best foil Civic Liberals could hope for. The biggest hurdle for Civic Liberal politics will be overcoming the ingrained habits of the Democratic party.

The case *against* Civic Liberal politics is simple. First, the self-interest of powerful "constituencies." The Civic Liberal agenda has something to offend many of them. Unions—or at least construction and public employee unions—won't like the employment of WPA workers at a subminimum wage. Many black leaders will object to confronting potential welfare recipients with the need to work, though the schemes that have been branded "slavefare" in the past haven't offered above-poverty jobs to both men and childless women.[4] The affluent elderly will surely object to having their Social Security checks "means-tested," and even the non-affluent elderly might be effectively mobilized by a demagogic scare campaign. Well-off suburbanites may not want to see the carefully protected trajectories of their sons and daughters interrupted with a period of national service (though the current popularity of community-service programs in suburban schools tends to refute this).[5] The affluent will surely resist the prospect of class-mixing in the suburbs and schools, at least initially. Everybody would be faced with the prospect of some sort of tax increase.

Of course, Civic Liberalism has something to attract each of these groups as well. Unions would see the realization of a full employment economy that would put a wage floor under all workers. The majority of blacks who aren't in the welfare culture would cease to be stigmatized by the minority who are. Those who depend heavily on the public sphere (the poor, the elderly) would have the immediate possibility of a richer existence. Many would also, for the first time, have the eventual prospect of entry into the comfortable public life of the suburbs from which they are now excluded. Everybody could stop worrying about doctors' bills, just as everybody would eventually be freed from worrying about the economic and social wounds inflicted by the underclass.

The constituencies for and against Civic Liberalism, in other words, are often the same people. Most of us would lose something; most of us would gain something more. Such a complicated distribution of benefit and loss frustrates the most common notion of how Democrats should get elected, which is not by presenting 95 percent of the population with an interesting and difficult choice, involving large sacrifices and rewards, that makes them think about where their real self-interest lies. The favored strategy is, rather, to hammer together a bare majority coalition of groups through an uncomplicated appeal to their unalloyed, unexamined self-interest. Nail down the votes of the elderly, of blacks, of the unions, and above all of the poorer who want to get more at the expense of the richer. Get these groups 100 percent behind you. Don't do anything that might give them second thoughts.

In this view, most forcefully expressed by Robert Kuttner, it makes no sense for liberals to abandon their redistributive impulses. That is "politically innocent" because it might cost the Democrats the votes of those who would be on the redistribution's receiving end. Redistribution also offers a way to deflect self-interested opposition to the large tax increases needed to fund the public sphere—liberals can simply impose the increases on the rich minority who aren't part of the liberal coalition anyway. Even if liberals might not need Money Liberalism to achieve social equality, the argument goes, they need it to assemble their electoral majority. Money and Civic Liberal initiatives aren't in conflict; they are at least politically "interdependent."[6]

In fact, Money and Civic Liberal notions currently coexist in varying proportions in the brains of most Democrats, though the redistributive lobes seem dominant among those on the party's left. One day Democrats will propose a progressive tax cut, or an increase in welfare or food stamps or union power, and justify it mainly on income-equalizing grounds. The next day they propose campaign finance reform or civil rights legislation and justify it mainly on social-egalitarian grounds. The day after that they support national health insurance and justify it on both grounds. Why should they give up one of their arguments?

Yet, even if we concede for a moment that American elections are won and lost on the basis of hard economic self-interest, is there really no advantage for liberals in breaking with their tradition of open-ended income-rearranging? When Kuttner asks, "How does abandoning greater equality of wealth and income produce more votes for day care or health insurance?" the question practically answers itself.[7] If Democrats renounced their money-egalitarian ambitions, they would get more votes from those who are threatened by the attempt, namely voters with money. The party would be telling the affluent that, once reforms such as guaranteed jobs and day care and health insurance had been financed, they weren't going to be the targets of a continuous program of redistribution. Taxes might be raised to build parks, roads, hospitals, and schools, but not to reshape the upper deciles of the income charts. Democrats would be able to steal away voters from the Republicans' affluent "base."[8] Even a hard-bitten "constituency" pol should appreciate the value of that.

Civic Liberals could pay for their program in a way that maintained their ability to appeal up as well as down the income ladder. Suppose the Civic Liberal agenda really did require raising $150 billion in new revenues. Other things being equal, the money might as well be raised "progressively." There is, after all, a perfectly plausible Civic Liberal justification for tax progressivity: it offers a way to equally share, on an "ability-to-pay" basis, the sacrifices of funding government.[9] Progressive taxes, in this sense, express social equality the way a draft expresses social equality. This "equal sacrifice" rationale has nothing to do with the pursuit of money equality—even after the sacrifices are evenly shared, incomes might still be wildly unequal.[10]

But progressive taxes are pretty weak social-egalitarian medicine compared with the public sphere institutions they can finance. Writing a tax check doesn't produce much more in the way of civic fellowship than cashing a Social Security check. Drafting Donald Trump's son (and daughter) would make the social-egalitarian point a lot more forcefully than raising his taxes. That means Civic Liberals are free—in a way Money Liberals or hybrid Money–Civic Liberals are not free—to trade away the mild virtues of tax progressivity in pursuit of a bigger public sphere (as the previous chapter suggested they might do in the context of integrating the suburbs).

What if the prospect of $150 billion in progressive tax increases were enough to scare the affluent—already covered by corporate health plans, already insulated from the underclass—away from the Civic Liberal agenda? What if the price for enacting that agenda were an agreement to fund it through a regressive value-added tax? A hybrid Money–Civic Liberal would undoubtedly balk. "To levy a regressive tax in order to finance progressive government makes no sense," the *Washington Post* editorial page has declared.[11] A pure Civic Liberal wouldn't balk. Rather, the tax burden could be adjusted to suit the political requirements of appealing across class lines. Far from being an indispensable complement to Civic Liberalism's pursuit of a majority, Money Liberalism sharply narrows the political options. Civic Liberals might even accept a flat-rate income tax if that were the price of gaining support for a public-sphere agenda. Money is not that important to them.

Which brings up a significant point: abandonment of the Money Liberal appeal would not only be politically liberating, it would in itself reinforce social equality. The ultimate goal of Civic Liberalism is to create a sphere of life in which money is devalued, to prevent those who have more money from concluding they are superior. But if money is so damned unimportant, why do today's liberal Democrats spend so much time and energy trying to redistribute it? Obviously, they think money is very important indeed. The very pursuit of redistribution can undermine the social-egalitarian cause, because it carries the message that wealth, rather than membership in a democratic public sphere, is what is crucial to worth. Likewise, the very act of selling the Civic Liberal agenda to both poor and affluent Americans will reinforce the social egalitarian message. It will demonstrate that Democrats expect the underclass, the middle class, and the rich to live, and vote, by the same principles.

There is a familiar response among Democrats to anyone who suggests an attempt to capture part of the Republicans' affluent "base." It goes like this: "The Democrats must stand up and be Democrats." "Throw away the 'search for the center.'" "If there's one thing America doesn't need it's two Republican parties." "Given a choice between an imitation and the real thing the voters will choose the real thing every time." John Kenneth Galbraith ridicules political consultants whose "genius consists entirely in a mastery of elementary arithmetic—you seek to subtract votes from the opposition by being as much like it as possible...."[12] All this makes good sense if, like Galbraith, you think money equality is what the country needs. Given those views, why abandon or dilute your essential prescription in a vain attempt to lure those for whom it is inevitably anathema, at the risk of losing those for whom it might be a prime motivator?

But that's not what Civic Liberals think the country needs. They seek social equality, and don't believe they need money equality to get it. And if you don't particularly want money equalizing for its own sake, surely it's perverse not to notice that there are a lot of Americans who are potential Civic Liberal voters but who are repelled by Money Liberalism. Are the affluent necessarily opposed to a large public sphere? How would we know? Sure, they're likely to be dead set against our current hybrid Money–Civic Liberalism, which would be continually after their money. But many are not dead set against a strong government that recognizes the common worth of rich and poor. They are at least potential social egalitarians. Some are Republicans, in fact, precisely because they revel in the civic equality of military service, or because they feel that the current version of liberalism, by endorsing welfare programs, has failed to uphold the equal dignity of working Americans.[13] We're constantly reminded by distraught liberals that the affluent hold disproportionate political power, in part because they register and vote in disproportionate numbers. So why write off their votes simply because they're on the wrong end of a futile distributional war? At least that doesn't seem an obviously plausible way to win elections.

• • •

Nor is it clear that the liberals *gain* all that much politically by chasing after money equality. The idea that redistribution equals re-election—because the poorest 51 percent can always outvote the richest 49 percent—does have a certain pristine mathematical plausibility. Democratic politicians usually enhance their margin of error by attempting to mobilize, say, the bottom 80 percent against the top 20 percent. Most of the "populist" Democratic tax initiatives of the early 1990s were clinical examples of this reasoning.[14] In 1990 for example, congressional Democrats led by Senator Al Gore and Congressman Tom Downey pushed for a rejiggering of tax rates and credits, pointing out in their first press release that their plan would reduce taxes for the bottom 80 percent of Americans while raising them for 15 million Americans "in the top 10 percent of the income distribution." Other variations followed—a $300-per-child tax credit, a $350-per-child refundable credit, a $200-per-worker credit—all hailed as attempts to win back the "forgotten middle class," usually at the expense of the rich.[15] Here was money-egalitarianism quite openly packaged as interest-group politics, with your interest group being defined as your decile on the income charts.

Two obvious problems with this redistributive "populism" are pointed out by Thomas and Mary Edsall.[16] First, the underclass. The Money Liberal task of building a "bottom up" coalition will be difficult as long as those on the bottom with whom liberals are asking middle-income voters to identify include the despised and feared ghetto poor.[17] The second problem is that the redistribution-equals-reelection equation runs equally well in both distributive directions. If the bottom 80 percent can outvote the top 20 percent, the top 80 percent can also outvote the bottom 20 percent.[18] Actually, since the rich tend to vote more regularly, the top 50 percent can usually beat the bottom 50 percent. Something like this is part of what happened when Reagan sold his tax and spending cuts in the early 1980s. It's easy to imagine it happening again on various Republican tax breaks, with the majority who have *some* prospect of, say, a capital gain ganging up on the poorer minority.

Live by the majority's bank balance, die by the majority's bank balance. Appeals to narrow economic self-interest are a particularly inauspicious basis for redistributive politics at a time when there are increasing numbers of affluent and semi-rich Americans who fall way above the middle on the distributional chart. "We latch onto the us-versus-them rhetoric," Bruce Babbitt, the Democratic ex-governor of Arizona, has observed. "The problem is, something's changed. There used to be more of 'us'; now there's more of 'them.' "[19]

You get the sense that today's Money Liberal populists recognize redistribution's limited long-term political potential. After all, suppose Democrats win this year's tax cuts for the "middle class" and tax increases for the rich. What do they do next year for an encore? At some point (well below the point necessary to restore relative income equality, much less social equality), the electorate will almost surely conclude that the tax code is redistributive enough. That may be why current Money Liberal proposals often have a salami-slicing quality— a $200 tax cut this year, $200 more next year, keeping the "fairness" issue alive by pursuing reforms small enough so that there is always room for one more reform.[20] But, what happens if, after a decade of "populist" redistribution, the voters realize the rich are *still* getting richer?

In sum, when they are appealing to voters' concrete economic self-interests, Money Liberalism and Civic Liberalism would pursue dramatically different strategies. Money Liberals (or attempted Money-Civic hybrids) try to make a clean, hard pitch to a coalition of groups on the bottom end of the income distribution.[21] Civic Liberals would make a more complicated, diffuse pitch to a far larger group of voters all over the income distribution. Call it a draw.

The bigger problem with Money Liberalism's "pocketbook populism" is that Americans don't necessarily vote their concrete economic self-interests. It's hard to think of two issues having less to do with voters' pocketbooks than the Pledge of Allegiance and prison furloughs, the pivot points of George Bush's victory in 1988. When Bush raised the issue of furloughed killer Willie Horton, it was widely condemned as a racial ploy, which it undoubtedly was in part. But it was also a powerful synecdoche, the argument being that Michael Dukakis's value structure tended to invert the importance of law-abiding citizens and criminals (an inference Dukakis himself did little to dispel).

Even when they consider economics, political scientist Jean Bethke Elshtain notes, Americans tend quite patriotically to make an overall assessment of the health of the nation and vote accordingly.[22] Can you imagine FDR babbling self-consciously about the needs of the "middle class"? He talked about "the people." Why can't today's liberals make a similar appeal to Americans' common self-interest as Americans?

If Money Liberalism's individualized, economistic obsession isn't reciprocated by the electorate, it's actually good news for Democrats. The reason, again, is the underclass. It's one thing to sell voters tax increases that will immediately redound to their benefit in the form of public services and amenities. It's another thing to get them to accept tax increases to clean up the underclass mess. In the short term, any underclass solution (even the ones that won't work) will cost money—for training, for "early intervention," for day care, for public-service jobs—without delivering an immediate payoff to the middle class. Democrats simply can't sell a program to save the ghetto poor with an appeal to the majority's narrow economic self-interest.[23] Certainly nothing they can say would have the direct wallet-impact of "no new taxes."

That the party's leaders know this is demonstrated by a curious phenomenon. When the topic turns to helping the poor (of whom the underclass is the most visible sub-group), even cynical Democrats stop pandering to the hard self-interest of various "constituencies" and start making gooey appeals that ignore, even denigrate self-interest itself—framing the issue as one of "compassion" versus "selfishness."[24] If voters can't be bribed with "middle class tax cuts," the thinking seems to go, they'll have to be guilt-tripped.

But compassion is a miserable basis for Democratic politics and a fatal basis for Civic Liberal politics. In the dictionary and in Democratic usage, it carries the unmistakable implication of charity, of dependence and piteousness on the part of those on the receiving end of the sentiment. It subtly but decisively subverts social equality. The intimation of moral superiority is no less palpable in the typical liberal defense of the school lunch program than at one of Nancy Reagan's charity balls.[25]

What's missing from Democratic rhetoric is something between the checkbook and charity, between economism and altruism—a more encompassing (economic and non-economic) notion of self-interest. It would be a type of self-interest that incorporates the importance of public morality in our daily lives, replacing the question, "Are you better off today than you were four years ago?" with the question, "What sort of society do you want to live in?" But it's not simply an appeal to morality or values. I may want to live in a society where there is no alienated race and no racism, where I need not feel uncomfortable walking down the street because I'm white. That's a form of self-interest. I may want (as much as any Christian fundamentalist) to live in a community with a moral order, where you can treat a bum like a bum and a thug like a thug. But on a less moralistic level, I'd simply like to live in a society where the sheer volume of interactions between myself and my fellow citizens was vastly greater and more pleasurable than now. There is nothing necessarily virtuous or theoretical about this interest in satisfying reciprocal interactions among members of a community. If these are social, interpersonal goods, they are no less real for it.[26]

Let the Democrats cultivate these *public* self-interests, the interests of everyone in a sphere of joint activity where money doesn't talk, where we can confront each other simply as citizens. Let them appeal to the selfishness of those who want to walk in the parks, use the library, enjoy clean streets, sit in a sidewalk cafe, hear a concert, leave their car unlocked, who want to rediscover the aesthetics of democracy. Let Democrats recognize, before the pollsters' "focus groups" tell them, that without this communal sphere, Americans—even middle-class Americans pocketing populist tax cuts, senior citizens with full cost-of-living allowances, fathers enjoying "parental leave," and doctors tracking their IRA investments—will lead an increasingly stunted existence filled with merely private pleasures.

But it's when Civic Liberalism appeals to the most moralistic bases of decision—"values"—that it obtains a decisive advantage. What values does it invoke? Social equality, most obviously. Here the polls only confirm what Sombart and Tawney observed: Americans tend to be steadfast social egalitarians but unreliable money egalitarians.[27] Where is the political advantage in going against their nature?

A Civic Liberal approach, in this sense, is not Plan B but Plan A; it is the traditional first resort of American politicians. When our candidates want to win votes, they instinctively invoke social-egalitarian symbols—driving tractors, mingling at church picnics. Where liberals take their stand, not against wealth but against the translation of wealth into differential status, they get the votes of everyone who admires Steve Jobs or Warren Buffett but dislikes Leona Helmsley and thinks Zsa Zsa Gabor shouldn't get away with slapping cops. Social egalitarians are not less "populist" than money egalitarians. Theirs is just a more popular populism.

Another American value is work. When Jesse Jackson wants to move a national audience, he doesn't talk about race or poverty or "kids" or the "middle-class squeeze" or the other issues liberal political consultants recommend. He talks about maids and janitors who "work every day." The values of work and social equality are not, need I add, unrelated. Ask most Americans why they feel they're as good as anyone else and the answer will be that their family works to pay its bills. This ethic isn't abstract. It is how the vast majority of voters themselves survive and try to prosper.

Money Liberals don't merely conflate the work ethic with other, more esoteric values (the way they conflate social equality with money equality). They positively offend the work ethic, especially in their give-'em-cash mode. The pathetic attempts of pro-welfare liberals to persuade voters that AFDC doesn't violate the work ethic are familiar by now. First, liberals try to pretend welfare mothers can't work.[28] When it becomes clear most are able-bodied, liberals tell us, "Of course they want to work! There are just no jobs." Propose creating the jobs and then requiring that welfare mothers take them, and many of the same liberals pop up to say, in effect, "You don't really expect those people to work, do you?"[29] Lawyers call this "pleading in the alternative." When Democrats defend cash payments to AFDC mothers, 93 percent of whom say they do no work at all—when Democrats argue, oh, the issue is very complex, these women "don't get much by being assigned to some work site to act as a clerk," maybe they need training, they need "social skills," they need $20-an-hour jobs—then Democrats needn't look much further to explain why they lose the public's confidence.[30]

How did Ronald Reagan get elected governor and then president? By telling anecdotes about welfare. How did David Duke attract votes from ordinary, respectable Louisianians, despite being burdened with a wacko Nazi background? By talking about welfare and the underclass. When welfare became an issue in the 1991 and 1992 campaigns, Money Liberals had an explanation ready: "The cry about welfare is about people's own frustration with declining living standards!" said Democratic strategist Stanley Greenberg. Why isn't the cry about welfare a cry about welfare?[31]

Everywhere politicians talk about making welfare recipients work, they pick up support. Everywhere proposals to actually replace welfare with work get on the ballot (as one did in Oregon), they win.[32] It's that simple. There's no need for focus groups or subtle demographic analysis. Liberals have only maintained AFDC in the face of public anger by pretending, through various "welfare reform" initiatives, that they are putting welfare mothers to work when really they aren't. As the voters find out how weak the 1988 federal welfare reform really was, the anger will become palpable.[33]

Faced with Republican attempts to exploit popular disgust with AFDC, liberal Democrats have taken to lecturing voters about how welfare takes up less of the government's budget than they think it does. With an air of righteous expertise, Mario Cuomo explains that *"AFDC* is less than 1 percent of the *federal* budget. Throw in food stamps and you're up to 3 percent. *AFDC* represented only *3.4* percent of expenditures of all states in 1991." Theodore Marmor, Jerry Mashaw, and Philip Harvey argue that America's welfare state is "misunderstood" because what the public considers "welfare" is "fiscally trivial."[34] But what does that prove? Mainly, it proves that through a relatively small expenditure, Money Liberals have managed to poison voters against government spending in general. Quite an accomplishment.

The apparent attitude of the public—that we can't let the liberals spend money because they'll spend it on welfare—may be fiscally ignorant, but it also contains a good bit of sense. Welfare spending, though small in comparison with the overall budget, does perpetuate the underclass and frustrate the egalitarian potential of the work ethic. If liberals are willing to spend even a small amount to put mothers on the dole, what other disastrous, value-flouting expenditures are they willing to undertake? Welfare is, yes, another Willie Horton, a synecdoche, a test of values. Money Liberals flunk it. The Civic Liberal hope, and calculation, is that this reasoning will work in reverse: if voters are faced with a Democrat who wants to spend money to end welfare, they will open up their wallets—both for ending welfare and for other government projects.

The standard rhetorical tricks Democrats use to get on the "right side" of the work question won't produce this shift.[35] It's not enough for Democrats to proclaim that they "stand with America's working families." The question is whether they will keep subsidizing America's non-working non-families. It's not enough for Democrats to pledge stern measures to root out welfare cheats. The problem isn't the people who get welfare illegally, but the people who get welfare legally. It's not enough for a candidate to say she plans to "encourage" work or "require" work or create "incentives" for work. Voters know Democrats have been promising that (and spending on that) for decades to no effect. Certainly the electorate isn't going to fall for the perennial Democratic ploy that disguises welfare as a program to benefit "kids" or "children at risk." Voters know the checks go to the mothers, not the kids.

To regain the taxpayers' confidence, and with it access to their pocketbooks, Democrats must be ruthless in drawing the work/nonwork distinction. This is the ultimate answer to Kuttner's gibe about whether abandoning Money Liberalism is going to "produce more votes for day care or health insurance." Money Liberalism's disparaging of the work ethic has in fact cost tens of millions of votes for almost all government programs. Renouncing the give-them-cash solution—declaring that government benefit programs, whether "universal" or "targeted," will only help working families or those who can't work—will gain back those millions. It neatly solves the political dilemma Edsall and others say the Democrats face: how to help the poor without seeming to underwrite the underclass.

If I'm correct, Democrats don't really need to win some intellectual debate about the role of the state or the proper size of the federal budget. They don't even necessarily need to convince voters that liberal "investments" in the future are "cost-effective," or that they will "work" in the sense of, say, assimilating the underclass. That would certainly help. But it's mainly a question of persuading voters the money will be spent in accordance with their values.

In effect, Civic Liberals would be making another bet, a bet that the vast majority of American voters aren't instinctively antigovernment. They are not just trying to reduce the hit they take on April 15. They are not racists. They are willing to spend more money *if it will be spent differently*. As political wagers go, this one seems a lock. "Billions for workers, not a penny for welfare." I think the politician who credibly makes this his or her slogan will sweep the nation.

CHAPTER 12

Conclusion

With the global ascendance of capitalism, some argue, our politics are doomed to be unideological, uninteresting, and even unimportant.[1] But if the trends described in this book are in fact underway, American politics is now more significant, perhaps more ideologically charged, than at any time since World War II. Our main domestic debate, after all, has always taken place between two democratic capitalist parties. It's been an argument over what sort of market society we want to have. That the rest of the world has come to focus on the same question hardly makes it less essential. And there are consequences of having a market society that are only now becoming evident.

Choosing capitalism obviously means we will have richer and poorer Americans. But it also seems to mean, at this stage in our economic evolution, that the rich will get relatively richer, and that they are likely to keep getting richer. It also means (assuming we remain part of the world market) that those Americans who get rich will increasingly do it by exploiting skills and talents that are mainly mental.

These are trends capable of transforming American society into something very different from what it has been for most of our lives. They are trends Americans are going to have to cope with, one way or another. But they're trends we have only recently begun to confront. The key political responses will come in the next one or two decades. Are we to be a society of equals or not? It's hard to think of anything similarly fundamental at stake in, say, the Kennedy-Nixon election of 1960. What will be effectively decided in our next several political contests is nothing less than the issue—social equality—that lies at the core of liberalism.

What do Democrats have to say in this coming debate? What do they offer to counter the divisive tendencies of money inequality and meritocracy? $350 tax breaks? Get serious. A 10 percent surtax on a few thousand Americans with incomes over a million?[2] Not even close. Even universal health coverage won't do much to reverse the class division of American society if it doesn't mean people of different classes wind up using the same doctors and hospitals.

American liberalism has failed to rise to the moment, I've argued, because liberals have been distracted by an unnecessary and unrewarding obsession with the very thing they should be trying to render less significant, namely money. Money Liberalism has produced the Democrats' endless appetite for tinkering with the income distribution, manifested in their recent progressivity fetish. Why must every policy and subpolicy, every benefit or subsidy, every cigarette tax, gas tax, Social Security cut, VAT, or tariff be judged in terms of its effect on the income charts? Money Liberal thinking underlies the increasingly unaffordable Democratic faith in programs, such as Social Security, that seek "community" and "solidarity" by simply mailing checks to as many people as possible. Most destructively, Money Liberals have relied on a check-mailing solution to end poverty—and have wound up sustaining, if not creating, the urban underclass whose existence precludes social equality.

I think most liberals are liberals for the same reason most Americans are glad to be Americans: they dislike assertions and affectations of class superiority. But if we are going to preserve this American virtue in the face of the inegalitarian forces now arraying against it, we will have to act quickly. Americans may be social egalitarians today. But give the affluent two more decades to grow comfortable in their gated suburbs, two more decades to revile the underclass and avoid the cities as if they were a dangerous foreign country, two decades to isolate their "gifted" children from their supposed inferiors, two decades of "symbolic analysis" and assortative mating, and we might wake up to discover that Americans aren't such egalitarians at all any more. Then politics really would be dispiriting.

Affirmative government—the liberal's weapon—can prevent that day from coming. I've tried to suggest over the preceding eleven chapters how this might be accomplished. There are ample grounds for optimism. It's true that "meritocracy" has sinister implications, and the fairer the meritocracy the more sinister those implications may be. But no amount of "merit" or "fairness" is going to eliminate the ultimate arbitrariness of affluence, because there is no way to stamp out the role of sheer luck in capitalism. Yes, money is growing less evenly distributed. But the ideal of social equality makes no rigid arithmetic demands. Money is still only money; it will always be only money. What matters will always be what society makes of it. We could all drive government-issue Ford Tauruses in a Money Liberal paradise, but if only some people could afford the LX edition we might soon be craning our necks to spot those two letters on every car that passed. By the same token, if people valued money as a means of making life more enjoyable, but considered it no more related to essential human worth than the ability to curl your tongue, the dignity of all Americans could survive even in the face of inegalitarian income trends far more pronounced than the ones we now must contemplate.

Much of today's social inequality, I've argued, derives from neither money differences nor "merit" differences, but from the breakdown of public sphere institutions (like the draft and schools) that once discouraged the translation of those differences into inegalitarian attitudes. This is the most solid ground for optimism. It suggests that restoring those institutions, or inventing their modern equivalents, will restore social equality even in the face of rising money inequality.

It would be *easier* to build social equality if we lived in an age when incomes were growing more equal. It would be easier if, thanks to centuries of oppression, meritocracy were still mainly a mechanism for overturning old elites rather than entrenching new ones. The challenge for liberals today, however, is to build social equality when neither of those advantageous conditions exists. Is this really impossible?

Of course not. We can have the egalitarian society we want whether the top quintile controls 43.9 percent of the nation's income or 49.9 percent. We can have that society even when the inherent chanciness of life is all that prevents talent and "merit" from correlating with material success. We can have it, that is, if we build a public sphere sturdy enough to cabin wealth's power—a sphere with (to quote Tocqueville) enough of the "pleasures of equality" so that "in order to taste them, nothing is required but to live." This is the great unfinished business of liberalism: not to equalize money, but to put money in its place.

ACKNOWLEDGMENTS

Lu Haas of Los Angeles first suggested I write this book when we were both working on a doomed campaign against California's state lottery in 1984. I shopped the idea around, and Steve Wasserman, then of New Republic Books, showed genuine enthusiasm. In 1985, I also went to work as *The New Republic*'s West Coast correspondent.

Martin Peretz of *The New Republic* subsequently gave me continuing support, encouragement, and editorial advice. In early 1986, when we were driving on Sunset Boulevard, Marty suggested that I come to Washington to make a long article out of the chapters on replacing welfare with work. Marty also wrote the only funny line in that extremely sober piece. Friends still quote it back to me, much to my annoyance.

I worked for *Newsweek* during the 1988 campaign, then returned to *The New Republic*, where Hendrik Hertzberg and Dorothy Wickenden elegantly edited and published an earlier version of this book's basic thesis in 1990. Rick also gave me a number of valuable suggestions, particularly regarding the importance to the public sphere of informal "third places" such as coffee shops, movie theaters, and sidewalk cafes. Andrew Sullivan, *TNR*'s current editor, has helped me resolve several difficult issues.

I'm especially indebted to two people with (and for) whom I've worked for most of my adult life: Michael Kinsley, my friend since law school and my editor at both *Harper's* and *The New Republic*, and Charles Peters, editor-in-chief of *The Washington Monthly*. As an editor,

Charlie is fated to see others appropriate ideas that originate with him, and that's the case here (even though he probably doesn't agree with the book's criticism of money-egalitarians). His influence is so pervasive it is impossible to credit fairly. The same goes for Mike, who, in addition to editing several articles incorporated here, also read the entire manuscript and offered his usual authoritative advice.

Robert Wright of *The New Republic* undertook the even less enviable task of reading and criticizing a longer, earlier draft of the manuscript. I relied on his sharp editorial judgments. Nicholas Lemann read a very early draft of the first few chapters, and unselfishly shared his ideas about the underclass. Timothy Noah persuaded me to revise my views on national service.

Bill Newlin and Peter Bejger of New Republic Books nursed this project through its various mid-life crises. Peter Edidin got stuck with the job of actually editing the final manuscript, which he did with intelligence and good humor. Bryan Ryan skillfully copyedited the manuscript. Matthew Levie provided indispensable research assistance. Amit Shah and Michael Mueller of Basic Books did what wasn't supposed to be possible by producing this book quickly despite my tardiness at virtually every stage. My agent, Amanda Urban, ably served my interests and tirelessly batted down my stupider ideas.

I also need to thank the various scholars, government officials, journalists, and friends who let me pick their brains or who otherwise offered generous advice and assistance. They include: Henry Aaron, Jodie Allen, Jonathan Alter, Robert Ball, Harry Ballantyne, Mary Battiata, Rikki Baum, Fred Barnes, Blanche Bernstein, Sidney Blumenthal, Donna Bojarsky, Patricia Bradbury, Bill Bradley, Peter Brown, Dominique Browning, Gary Burtless, Margaret Carlson, Deborah Colton, Sheldon Danziger, Jason DeParle, Greg Duncan, Deirdre Duzor, David Ellwood, James Fallows, Howard Fineman, Geoffrey Garin, Thomas Geoghegan, Edward Gramlich, Josh Gotbaum, Judith Gueron, Margaret Hamburg, William Hammett, Helen Hershkoff, Ann Hulbert, Walter Isaacson, Christopher Jencks, Mary Jordan, Rick Kasten, Karlyn Keene, Joe Klein, Morton Kondracke, Marvin Kosters, Charles Krauthammer, Ellen Ladowsky, Karen Lehrman, Frank Levy, Laura Lippman, Theodore Marmor, Charles Moskos, Sara Mosle, Charles Murray, Robert Myers, David Osborne, James Pinkerton, Wendell Primus, Robert Reischauer, Christine Rossell, Charles Sabel, Walter Shapiro, Reuben Snipper, Abigail Thernstrom, Evan Thomas, Kathleen Kennedy Townsend, Jason Turner, Jacob Weisberg, David Whitman, Leon Wieseltier, Roberton Williams, Edward Young, and Jonathan Zasloff.

This book was made possible by a series of grants from Peggy and Otto Kaus. As a source of funding for political books, parents have much to recommend them. There are no committees to flatter and few ideological strings attached. My brother Stephen also provided steady support and encouragement. My grandmother Gina Kaus offered kind, writerly advice at the right moments.

Finally, I note my debt to Dorothy Huttenback, my maternal grandmother and an inspirational figure.

* * *

This book is dedicated to Carol Trueblood.

NOTES

Chapter 1
From the Ground Up

1. See, for example, Dudley Clendinen, "Mondale and TV," *New York Times*, Friday, 9 November 1984, A22.

2. Keith Love, "Manatt Urges TV Training for Nominee," *Los Angeles Times*, 13 November 1984, 5. The excuses of Mondale and Manatt correspond to the third of the "four stages of political defeat" identified by columnist Mark Shields. The stages are: 1.) Blame the candidate; 2.) Blame the customer; 3.) Find the gimmick; and 4.) Get me a winner. See Mark Shields, "The Four Stages of Political Defeat," *Washington Post*, 14 April 1986, A13.

3. "Democrats Urging More Professionals for Campaign Team," *Washington Post*, 12 March 1989, A14. See also Mark Shields, "Lame Excuses," *Washington Post*, 27 March 1989, A15.

4. Mankiewicz is quoted in Andrew Jaffe, "Democrats at the Crossroads: Is the Old Liberalism Dead?" *Los Angeles Herald-Examiner*, 11 November 1984, A1.

5. The gender gap: See "Closing the Gender Gap," *Newsweek*, 24 October 1988, 22, cited in Jean Bethke Elshtain, "Issues and Themes in the 1988 Campaign," *The Elections of 1988*, ed. Michael Nelson (Washington, D.C.: CQ Press, 1989), 116. Parental leave and elder care: See Roger Craver and Jeffrey Hallett, "The Online Crystal Ball," *Campaigns and Elections* (March/April 1988), 49, cited in Elshtain, "Issues and Themes," 113.

6. The "kids issue": See Mickey Kaus, "Playing Politics with Children," *Newsweek*, 13 June 1988, 26–27. Abortion: See Robin Toner, "Democrats Take Offensive on Abortion and Flag," *New York Times*, 23 October 1989, A16. An insider: See Tom Wicker, "Why Democrats Lose," *New York Times*, 6 February 1991, A21, discussing two proposals for returning power to party insiders in order to avoid untested nominees. An outsider: See Pat Caddell, "A Party Afraid of the Truth," *The Mainstream Democrat*, December 1990, 7–9. See also Sidney Blumenthal, "Flatliners," *The New Republic*, 20 May 1991, 18.

7. William Schneider, "Tough Liberals Win, Weak Liberals Lose," *The New Republic,* 5 December 1988, 15. Emphasis in original.

8. Ibid. See also Mary McGrory, "A Chance to Truly Help Poland," *Washington Post,* 12 September 1989, A2.

9. See Richard Reeves, "Old Wine in New Skins," *New York Times,* 29 July 1984, sec. 7, 12. I confess to having embraced Hart's means-end distinction myself. See Mickey Kaus, "Should This Man Be President?" *Washington Monthly,* October 1981, 32.

10. The slogan "New Directions, Enduring Values" was in fact printed on the bottom of the DLC's bimonthly magazine, *The Mainstream Democrat.*

Interestingly, the means-ends distinction is also a feature of the "New Paradigm" outlined by Bush White House aide James Pinkerton: "So now the argument shifts away from *goals*—which we all agree upon—to *means.*" See Pinkerton, "The New Paradigm," remarks to the World Future Society, 8 February 1990.

11. Mario Cuomo, "E Pur Si Muove," Chubb Fellowship Lecture, Yale University, 15 February 1985.

12. Sen. Edward M. Kennedy, remarks at the John F. Kennedy Presidential Conference, Hofstra University, New York, 29 March 1985.

13. See Arkansas Gov. Bill Clinton's keynote address to the DLC in Cleveland, Ohio, 6 May 1991, in which he argues that the "Information Age" has rendered government bureaucracies inefficient. See also Al From, "The New Politics," *The Mainstream Democrat,* March 1991, 4: "Just as in the 1930s, new conditions are imposing new requirements on government and those who conduct it." The less convenient truth, I'd like to suggest, is that the causes of liberalism's crisis are largely internal. The seeds were there from the beginning—in questions about *ends* that the New Deal didn't quite answer.

14. See Gary Hart, "Toward True Patriotism: A New Course for the 1980s," speech delivered 4 February 1985; see also Hart, "Foundation for an American Renewal," speech delivered 23 April 1985.

15. Cuomo, "E Pur Si Muove," 15 February 1985.

16. Kennedy, remarks, 29 March 1985.

17. Schlesinger thus differs from the Democrats who would distinguish enduring Democratic "ends" from transitory "means." He seems to define liberalism largely by its means—"affirmative government." See Schlesinger, "The Liberal Opportunity," 14, 16; also "For Democrats, Me-Too Reaganism Will Spell Disaster."

18. The question of whether this working assumption holds—whether the liberal strategy outlined in this book can win elections—is discussed in Chapter 11.

19. In fact, the family income of the poorest fifth of the population grew about 55 percent between 1960 and 1980. (See House Committee on Ways and Means, *1990 Green Book,* 5 June 1990, Table 69, 1146.) In the 1980s, this group either gained or lost about 5 percent, depending on whether you believe Census or Congressional Budget Office statistics. (Compare *1990 Green Book,* Table 94, 1194, with *Money Income of Households, Families and Persons in the United States, 1990* [Washington, D.C.: Bureau of the Census, August 1991] and Current Population Reports, Series P-60, No. 174, Table B-13, 216.)

20. This dual meaning was of course suggested by the "deliberately ambiguous"

title of Theodore J. Lowi's classic, *The End of Liberalism,* 2nd ed. (New York: Norton, [1969] 1979). See especially xv.

Chapter 2
What Do Liberals Want?

1. Quoted in Martin Tolchin, "Here Come the Democrats," *New York Times,* 13 March 1983, sec. 6, 45.

2. "The wealthiest 40 percent ...": See "Smaller Slices of the Pie: The Growing Economic Vulnerability of Poor and Moderate Income Americans," Center on Budget and Policy Priorities, Washington, D.C., November 1985, 3. "The proportion of all national income ...": See "Lip Flop," Editorial, *The New Republic,* 23 July 1990, 8. For similar expressions, see, for example, Thomas Byrne Edsall, *The New Politics of Inequality* (New York: Norton, 1984), 221 ("the top fifth of the population receives 40.6 percent of total income while the bottom fifth receives 4.9 percent"); Robert Kuttner, *The Economic Illusion* (Boston: Houghton Mifflin, 1984), 6; William Ryan, *Equality* (New York: Pantheon, 1981), 14; Robert Reich, "A More Perfect State of the Union Address," *Wall Street Journal,* 30 January 1991, A10 ("The top fifth of income earners now brings home more than the bottom 80 percent put together—the highest portion in 40 years—and the gap continues to widen"); Paul Starr, "The American Eighties: Disaster or Triumph?" *Commentary,* September 1990, 32 ("Between 1980 and 1988, America's upper 20 percent of households increased their share ...").

3. See Kuttner, *Economic Illusion,* 1. The dwarves metaphor is that of Dutch economist Jan Pen, quoted by Kuttner in ibid., 260. The banquet metaphor is in Ryan, *Equality,* 12.

4. "Would that ordinary people might simply grow indignant at the gross inequalities of American society and organize for progressive change...." Kuttner, *Economic Illusion,* 277.

5. See "What's Wrong with the Democrats," *Harper's,* January 1990, 50.

6. Opening Statement by Chairman Rostenkowski on the Administration's Budget, Hearings before the Ways and Means Committee, 6 February 1990.

7. Mitchell is quoted in David Broder, "Who's the Fairest of Them All?" *Washington Post,* 13 February 1991, A19. See also the statement of House Majority Leader Richard Gephardt before the House Ways and Means Committee on 6 December 1991. ("[T]he rich are getting richer.... The nation's longest peacetime expansion was certainly that—if you are talking about the incomes of our most fortunate citizens.")

Congressional Democrats talking about "fairness" typically conflate two distinct issues: the distribution of income and the distribution of the tax burden. When Congressman Gephardt demands "fairness," is he saying that taxes have grown less progressive since 1977 (as they have) and that "equality of sacrifice" should be restored? Or is he saying the equality of income has eroded since 1977 (as it has) and that progressive taxes should be imposed in order to change the income distribution back to where it was? It seems fair to say that Gephardt uses the word "fairness" in part precisely because he doesn't want to pick too clearly between these two answers.

In general, tax progressivity can be justified on both money-egalitarian and the "equal sacrifice" grounds. See the classic discussion in Walter J. Blum and Harry Kalven, Jr., *The Uneasy Case for Progressive Taxation* (Chicago: University of Chicago Press, 1953). One tax scholar of the 1920s summarized the disingenuous relationship between progressivity and redistribution by cracking, "We have all heard that it is wrong to marry for money, but quite praiseworthy to marry where money happens to be." Ibid., 73. See also Mickey Kaus, "For a New Equality," *The New Republic*, 7 May 1990, 18.

8. See Gwen Ifill, "Clinton's Standard Campaign Speech: A Call for Responsibility," *New York Times*, 26 April 1992, sec. 1, 24; Cathleen Decker, "Jerry Brown of Old Ardently Seeks New Audience," *Los Angeles Times*, 29 October 1990, A3. During one debate, Clinton flatly declared, "What we want is more income equality." See Thomas B. Edsall, "Tsongas Message Called Strongest in TV Debate," *Washington Post*, 2 February 1992, A13.

For press views of money-egalitarianism, see, for example: Sidney Blumenthal, "Chapped Lips," *The New Republic*, 30 July and 6 August 1990, 21 ("the issue of the distribution of post-Reagan wealth will not vanish"); George Will, "A Party Starting to Get Interesting," *Washington Post*, 29 March 1990, A27; E. J. Dionne, Jr., "Loss of Faith in Egalitarianism Alters U.S. Social Vision," *Washington Post*, 30 April 1990, A1. See also the recent novel by economist John Kenneth Galbraith, in which the hero, also an economist, declares his desire to make a "small contribution to the liberal agenda. Peace ... greater equality in income distribution...." *A Tenured Professor* (Boston: Houghton Mifflin, 1990), 38.

9. Edsall, *New Politics of Inequality*, 18, 233, 17, 14–15.

10. Robert Kuttner, "The Poverty of Neoliberalism," *The American Prospect* (Summer 1990): 7.

11. This would be true even if inheritance were abolished—as long as parents could use their money to assist their children while they were alive.

Nozick is quoted in "If Inequality Is Inevitable, What Can Be Done About It?" *New York Times*, 3 January 1982, sec. 4, 5. See also Blum and Kalven, *Uneasy Case*, 90; Christopher Jencks, *Inequality* (New York: Harper & Row, 1972), 4.

12. George Gilder, in one of his more lucid moments, frankly acknowledges the ineradicable role of luck in capitalism:

> Critics of capitalism often imagine that they have discovered some great scandal of the system when they reveal its crucial reliance on luck: its distribution of benefits and attainment of riches by unpredictable and irrational processes—its resemblance at some level to a lottery.

See Gilder, *Wealth and Poverty* (New York: Basic Books, 1981), 254.

13. See, for example: Marcus G. Raskin, "Progressive Liberalism for the Eighties," *The Nation*, 17 May 1980, 577–591; Samuel Bowles, David M. Gordon, and Thomas E. Weisskopf, "An Economic Strategy for Progressives," *The Nation*, 10 February 1992, 145–165.

14. On the general attempt (and failure) of the 1972 platform to express dissatis-faction with traditional liberalism, see Thomas Geoghegan, "Miami and the Seeds of Port Huron," *The New Republic*, 2 September 1972, 16–18.

15. Frank is quoted in E. J. Dionne, Jr., "A Liberal's Liberal Tells Just What Went Wrong," *New York Times*, 22 December 1988, 8. ("There are three not-sa-pos-tas that have hurt liberals. You're not supposed to say that the free enterprise system is wonderful and has worked better than any other. You're not supposed to say that in our era, certainly since the fall of Hitler, Communism has been by far the worst system of government in the world, or that most people who are in prison are bad people.")

16. See, for example: Robert S. McIntyre and Dean C. Tipps, *Inequity and Decline* (Washington, D.C.: Center on Budget and Policy Priorities, 1983); this is also the thrust of Kuttner's *The Economic Illusion.*

17. See, for example: Mark Kelman, "The Ambiguities of Tax Reform" *Working Papers for a New Society* 6 (January/February 1978): 85–88. Kuttner, for his part, touts limited "positive sum bargains" in which, for example, labor unions would agree to wage restraint in exchange for more equal wage scales and government full employment policies. See Kuttner, *Economic Illusion*, 148 et seq. The income-equal-izing potential of these and other schemes is discussed in Chapter 5.

18. Michael Kinsley, "Stat Wars," *The New Republic*, 26 March 1990, 42.

19. "Tilt the balance": Stanley B. Greenberg, "From Crisis to Working Major-ity," *The American Prospect* (Fall 1991): 117. "A good deal more ...": Kuttner, *Eco-nomic Illusion*, 7. "The strong owe a duty to the weak; the privileged have an obliga-tion to the powerless....": Sen. Edward Kennedy, remarks at the John F. Kennedy Presidential Conference, Hofstra University, New York, 29 March 1985. Under-privileged versus overprivileged: Franklin D. Roosevelt, "Annual Message to the Congress. January 4, 1935," *The Public Papers and Addresses of Franklin D. Roosevelt*, vol. 4, *The Court Disapproves* (New York: Random House, 1938), 16.

20. See ibid., 17, where FDR denies exactly this desire ("nor do we seek to divide our wealth into equal shares on stated occasions").

21. See, for example, Kuttner, *Economic Illusion*, 10, 12–13. See also Ryan, *Equal-ity*, 30–31.

22. Tawney is quoted in Ryan, *Equality*, 31. See also Tawney, *Equality* (1938; reprint, New York: Barnes & Noble, 1964), 122–123.

23. Tawney, *Equality*, 121, 112–113. Tawney undoubtedly had a narrow defini-tion of the occasions that justified such "exceptional rewards."

24. Ibid., 56.

25. Ryan, *Equality*, 30.

26. George Orwell, *Homage to Catalonia* (1938; reprint New York, Harcourt Brace, 1952), 5, 104. See also page 113: "'Smart' clothes were an abnormality, no-body cringed or took tips, waiters and flower-women and bootblacks looked you in the eye and called you 'comrade.'"

27. Ibid., 5.

28. Ibid., 113, 114.

29. Ibid., 115.

30. Macdonald is quoted in James Patterson, *America's Struggle Against Poverty 1900–1980* (Cambridge: Harvard University Press, 1981), 159–160. The "mini-

mum" will undoubtedly vary from society to society—it will be higher in the United States than in India. But it remains a *minimum*, not equality.

31. Tawney, *Equality*, 71.

32. Tawney's question is recounted in Richard M. Titmuss's introduction to the 1964 edition of *Equality*. See ibid., 23.

33. Michael Walzer has put it clearly: "This is the lively hope named by the word *equality:* no more bowing and scraping, fawning and toadying; no more fearful trembling, no more high-and-mightiness; no more masters, no more slaves." Walzer, *Spheres of Justice* (New York: Basic Books, 1983), xiii.

Chapter 3
Two Strategies of Equality

1. "Smaller Slices of the Pie," Center on Budget and Policy Priorities, November 1985, 3.

2. More precisely, this book discusses three sub-strategies of what I call Money Liberalism. All seek social equality by manipulating the distribution of income and reducing income differences. They are:

a. Money-egalitarianism—the general pursuit of "more income equality."

b. Solidarity-through-check-cashing—the idea that universal receipt of cash government benefits promotes social equality (see Chapters 6 and 9).

c. "Give them cash"—the attempt to end the indignity of poverty by distributing money to the poor (see Chapters 7 through 9).

These three sub-strategies are logically independent. For example, a Democrat could in theory favor distributing a guaranteed income to the poor (c) but forswear further tinkering with the income distribution (a). Yet the sub-strategies are united by their economism, including, as we'll see, their disdain for non-material distinctions (such as the distinction between workers and non-workers). They all assume that money and its distribution are what is important for achieving social equality. And together, in practice, they form an identifiable tendency in contemporary liberal Democratic thinking.

3. *A note on "equal opportunity"*: I want to explicitly reject as inadequate the more limited goal frequently chosen by Democrats who accept capitalism's money differences, namely "equality of opportunity." For years, neoconservatives have seen liberal social policy as a long twilight struggle between this noble Democratic ideal and the insidious McGovernite idea of "equality of outcomes." The "mainstream Democrats" of the Democratic Leadership Council have on occasion latched onto the same formula. ("We believe the promise of America is equal opportunity, not equal outcomes.")

Money egalitarians traditionally ridicule this notion as, in Tawney's words, "the equal right to be unequal" (see *Equality* [1938; reprint, New York: Barnes & Noble, 1964], 103). So it is. Saying there should be equal opportunities doesn't tell anything about what structure of inequality those opportunities are to be made equal in. It could be an equal scramble for a few positions at the top of a very pointy income pyramid. ("Tadpole philosophy," Tawney cracked.) It could be equal competition for more numerous, less lucrative positions in a "flatter" income structure. Money egalitarians make it their business to try to sculpt the structure's shape. If money equality is what is important, "outcomes" are indeed what count.

If you care about social inequality rather than money inequality per se, then equal opportunity seems far less insubstantial; it's hard to imagine a more direct violation of social equality than class privilege and race discrimination. But for social egalitarians, too, equal opportunity is an insufficient, even perverse, goal. Social equality isn't a process, after all. It's another "outcome." The difference is that this outcome is measured in social rather than financial terms. And equal opportunity can't produce the social-egalitarian outcome by itself. How much does the enforcement of equal opportunity through the antidiscrimination laws affect your personal sense of equality with, say, the billionaire media baron John Kluge? Those who win capitalism's game will, if allowed, act like winners, even if the game is honest and everyone starts off with the same number of points on the scoreboard.

Indeed, emphasizing equal opportunity can make the social-inegalitarian consequences of money inequality much worse (a point discussed in more detail in Chapter 4).

4. See Orwell's "The Lion and the Unicorn," in Sonia Orwell and Ian Angus, eds., *The Collected Essays, Journalism and Letters of George Orwell* (New York: Harcourt Brace, 1969), vol. 2, *My Country Right or Left 1940–43*, 98. See also Tawney, *Equality*, 43: "... a common culture ... is incompatible with the existence of sharp contrasts between the economic standards ... of different classes, for such contrasts have as their result, not a common culture, but servility or resentment, on the one hand, and patronage or arrogance on the other." However, Tawney goes on to define these contrasts *not* by "level of pecuniary incomes," but in terms more compatible with what I've called Civic Liberalism: "equality of environment, of access to education and the means of civilization, of security and independence, and of the social consideration which equality in these matters usually carries with it."

5. Quoted in Robert Kuttner, *The Economic Illusion* (Boston: Houghton Mifflin, 1984), 266.

6. "England is the most class-ridden country under the sun. It is a land of snobbery and privilege...." (Orwell, "The Lion and the Unicorn," *Collected Essays*, vol. 2, 67.)

7. Tawney, *Equality*, 79. Tawney, like many others, feared this might change with industrialization and the demise of the independent farmers and businessmen of our Middle West. Orwell similarly identified social equality with the frontier (see *Collected Essays*, vol. 2, 326).

8. See Robert Kuttner, *The Life of the Party* (New York: Viking, 1987), 14.

9. (New York: Basic Books, 1983). I don't want to saddle Walzer with the variation of his idea presented here. See also Lawrence M. Mead, *Beyond Entitlement: The Social Obligations of Citizenship* (New York: Basic Books, 1986), 238–239; Amitai Etzioni, *Capital Corruption* (New Brunswick: Transaction, 1988), especially 133–135.

10. Tawney, *Equality,* 113.

11. Interview with Senator Hollings, 1983. For the McGovern plan, see Theodore H. White, *The Making of the President, 1972* (New York: Atheneum, 1973), 118.

12. Five million dollars was Long's limit on family wealth. He also envisioned an income limit of $1 million—again, extraordinarily high, given the value of the dollar in 1934. See T. Harry Williams, *Huey Long* (New York: Knopf, 1969), 692–693.

13. By way of contrast, Orwell thought it remarkable enough to note in his diaries when he heard that, in the 1940 retreat from France, a "Lady ————" tried to pull rank and push herself to the front of the line waiting to board a refugee ship, only to be told, "You can take your turn in the queue." Orwell took this as evidence that "England is now definitely in the first stage of revolution." See *Collected Essays,* vol. 2, 341.

Chapter 4
Who Killed Social Equality?

1. Andre Leon Talley, "CeCe Rider," *Vanity Fair,* November 1987, 98.

2. *Architectural Digest,* December 1987, 45 (ad) and 165 (club).

3. *Town and Country,* December 1987, 154–155. Another article revealed that the practice of riding to Saratoga in liveried horse-drawn coaches was "undergoing a revival in the United States" (198–200). Who gets to go on these rides? An expert explained: "Someone with a Honda will not be invited, but someone with a vintage Mercedes would be."

4. This quote was pointed out to me by Nicholas Lemann and cited in Jason DeParle, "Spy Anxiety," *Washington Monthly,* February 1989, 10–11.

5. Simmons Market Research Bureau, Inc. (1991); also Mediamark Research, Inc. (Fall 1991).

6. See DeParle, "Spy Anxiety," 17.

7. Mark Kelman, "The Social Cost of Inequality," *Dissent,* Summer 1973, 292.

8. It's not exactly the same thing to say that "money inequality increased" as to say that the number of people near the middle of the income distribution decreased. In theory, income inequality could increase at the extremes of the distribution, leaving the number of people in the middle unchanged. In practice, as we'll see, rising money inequality has been accompanied by some dispersion of the population away from the middle.

9. See Walter Mondale, acceptance speech before the Democratic National Convention, San Francisco, 19 July 1984.

Robert Kuttner has suggested the link to social equality, arguing in *The Atlantic* that we are becoming "a society in which one half of the work force waits on the other half, and makes a good deal less." See "The Declining Middle," *The Atlantic,* July 1983, 64. On the general split of the mass middle market, see Bruce Steinberg, "The Mass Market Is Splitting Apart," *Fortune,* 28 November 1983, 76–82.

10. See *Background Material and Data on Programs within the Jurisdiction of the*

Committee on Ways and Means (hereinafter referred to as the *Green Book*), 1989 edition, Table 27, 987. The CBO study was important because it corrected two flaws that had previously plagued income inequality data. First, Williams and Primus adopted a new price index that didn't overestimate inflation. Second, they counted *both* individuals and families, weighting each family by the number of people in it.

According to similar data in the *1990 Green Book,* the real, after-tax income of the poorest 30 percent of the population actually declined from 1977 to 1990 in absolute as well as relative terms. But it's not true that those in the middle experienced an absolute income drop, as current Democratic rhetoric occasionally implies. The middle deciles of the population gained a bit of income, both before and after federal taxes, over the 1977 to 1990 period. It's just that the affluent gained much, much more. (For the pre-tax figures, see *1990 Green Book,* Table 92, 1188; the after-tax figure, adjusted for family size and measured by deciles, is unpublished and was obtained from the CBO.)

Those who spotted the money-inequality trend early on included Barry Bluestone and Bennett Harrison (*The Deindustrialization of America* [New York: Basic Books, 1982], 94–98) and Kuttner ("The Declining Middle"). See also Lester C. Thurow, "A Surge in Inequality," *Scientific American,* May 1987, 30–37.

In late 1991 the CBO released figures suggesting that the inequality trend abated somewhat in 1989, with the pretax income share of the richest one percent actually falling from 13.5 to 13.0 percent. But this one-year decline at the very top did not come close to reversing the long-term inequality trend. See House Committee on Ways and Means, *Background Material on Family Income and Benefit Changes,* 102d Cong., 1st sess., 1991, Committee Print, 70.

11. *1990 Green Book,* Table 88, 1180.

12. See, for example: Michael W. Horrigan and Steven E. Haugen, "The Declining Middle-Class Thesis: A Sensitivity Analysis," *Monthly Labor Review,* May 1988, 3; Frank Levy, "Incomes, Families, and Living Standards," in *American Living Standards,* ed. Robert E. Litan, Robert Z. Lawrence, and Charles L. Schultze (Washington, D.C.: Brookings, 1988), 135–137.

13. See, for example: Robert Z. Lawrence, "Sectoral Shifts and the Size of the Middle Class," *The Brookings Review,* Fall 1984, 4; Katharine L. Bradbury, "The Shrinking Middle Class," *New England Economic Review,* September–October 1986, 41–55. See also U.S. Bureau of the Census, *Trends in Relative Income: 1964–1989,* Current Population Reports, Series P-60, no. 177 (Washington, D.C.: Government Printing Office, 1991).

14. Horrigan and Haugen, "The Declining Middle-Class Thesis," 8. This study probably overstates the trend a bit because it is based on the "family" income distribution. "Family" statistics can be deceptive if they leave out the one-fifth of Americans who aren't living in families, including people living alone. Thanks to divorce, and baby boomers' tendency to postpone marriage, a lot of solid middle-class earners who in previous eras might have been heads of families are now single and aren't counted in the "family" distribution. See Horrigan and Haugen, "The Declining Middle-Class Thesis," 4; *1989 Green Book,* 984–985; Bradbury, "The Shrinking Middle Class," 46–47; Frank Levy, *Dollars and Dreams.* (New York: Russell Sage, 1987), 15–16.

Data on consumption (as opposed to income) show the same inequality trend. See David M. Cutler and Lawrence F. Katz, "Untouched by the Rising Tide," *Brookings Review* 10, no. 1 (Winter 1992): 44.

15. For the starting date of the inequality trend, see, e.g., Levy, *Dollars and Dreams,* Table 2.1, 14; Bennett Harrison and Barry Bluestone, *The Great U-Turn* (New York: Basic Books, 1988), Figure 1.3, 7, and Figure 5.2, 119. For the inequality trend among married couples with children, see *1989 Green Book.* Table 30, 994.

The trend to inequality among full-time workers shows up in the studies of "declining middle" proponents (see Harrison and Bluestone, *The Great U-Turn,* 119) as well as their critics (see Marvin H. Kosters and Murray N. Ross, "The Distribution of Earnings and Employment Opportunities: A Re-examination of the Evidence," American Enterprise Institute, Washington, D.C., September 1987, Table 14, 39). See also Gary Burtless, "Earnings Inequality Over the Business Cycle," in *A Future of Lousy Jobs?* ed. Gary Burtless (Washington, D.C.: Brookings, 1990), 97, and Steve J. Davis and John Haltiwanger "Wage Dispersion Between and Within U.S. Manufacturing Plants, 1963–86," Brookings Papers on Economic Activity, Microeconomics 1991, ed. Martin Neil Baily and Clifford Winston (Washington, D.C.: Brookings, 1991), 115–200.

There is, of course, at least one way that tax cuts, like those of the early Reagan era, can affect *pre*-tax income inequality: If the rich take their tax savings and invest them, the earnings on those investments will eventually show up as pre-tax income in later years. Undoubtedly this happened, to some extent, during the 1977 to 1990 period. But it's a second-order effect—a point discussed in more detail in Chapter 5 and the notes thereto.

For a widely publicized attempt to blame "government action" for the "dismantling of the middle class," see Donald L. Barlett and James B. Steele, *America: What Went Wrong?* (Kansas City: Andrews and McMeel, 1992). At one point in the 1992 campaign, Democrat Bill Clinton took to waving the Barlett and Steele book from the podium while attacking the money-inequality trend.

16. The quote is from a notorious 1986 study, in which Bluestone and Harrison claimed to find an "unmistakable trend" that confirmed this "popular perception." (See "The Great American Job Machine," Study Prepared for the Joint Economic Committee, December 1986, 42.) In fact, this report (which used 1984 data) mainly documented wage stagnation: there weren't more rich and more poor, but *fewer* rich and more poor (see Figure 3, 42). This study was also frequently cited by campaigning Democrats for its startling finding that "nearly three fifths" of "net new" jobs created between 1979 and 1984 paid less than $7,000 a year. But the vast majority of those jobs were part-time or part-year. (See Marvin Kosters and Murray Ross, "A Shrinking Middle Class?" *The Public Interest,* Winter 1988, 18.) And Bluestone and Harrison exaggerated the number of "new" bad jobs by counting them in a peculiar way: if someone was working throughout the period in the same job, paying the same dollar wage, his job was nevertheless counted as a "new" bad job if, thanks to inflation, his real wage slipped below a fixed cutoff point between "low" and "middle" class.

17. Even Bluestone and Harrison's alarmist 1986 study showed that 78.5 per-

cent of new *full-time* jobs were in the "middle stratum." (See "The Great American Job Machine," Figure 3, 42.)

18. Early on in the "declining middle" debate, a cottage industry of economists sprang up to debunk the idea that income inequality was rising. For example, Marvin Kosters and Murray Ross of the American Enterprise Institute wrote in 1988 that despite the "superficial plausibility" of the thesis, the slow growth of the economy had *"not* been accompanied by any significant change during the past twenty years in the shape of the distribution of earnings for the work force as a whole." (See Kosters and Ross, "A Shrinking Middle Class?" 3, 23.) See also James Fallows, "America's Changing Economic Landscape," *The Atlantic,* March 1985, 61 et seq. By now, any attempt to deny the money inequality trend has collapsed under the mounting weight of the evidence. The initial defensiveness of the debunkers is revealing, however, because it appears to reflect a closet money-egalitarianism. No less than Bluestone and Harrison, the debunkers seemed to believe that if money inequality really was growing, then something would have to be done to correct the situation.

19. See Bluestone and Harrison, *The Deindustrialization of America,* and *The Great U-Turn;* Kuttner, "The Declining Middle." Actually, to account for all the people who aren't in the middle because they've moved *up,* the "occupational structure" of capitalism must be blamed for a lot of "good jobs" too. But that's easily done. See Robert Reich, "As the World Turns," *The New Republic,* 1 May 1989, 23–28.

20. See Kuttner, "The Declining Middle," 61.

21. See Levy, "American Living Standards," 127. See also Robert Reischauer, statement before the Committee on Ways and Means, U.S. House of Representatives, 19 April 1989, 12.

22. For the demographic explanation, see Lawrence, "Sectoral Shifts." See also Louise B. Russell, *The Baby Boom Generation and the Economy* (Washington, D.C.: Brookings, 1982), 50–90. Significantly, wage competition among unskilled boomers might lower the income of even non-boomers who are in unskilled jobs.

23. Reischauer, statement before the Committee on Ways and Means, 12. See also Lawrence, "Sectoral Shifts," 5 , 9; Levy, *Dollars and Dreams,* 123 et seq, and "Incomes, Families and Living Standards," in *American Living Standards,* Table 4-2, 124; and Fallows, "Changing Economic Landscape," 62.

24. See Fallows, "Changing Economic Landscape," 62, discussing Robert Lawrence's views.

25. Interview with author, 1990. See also Burtless, "Earnings Inequality," 105–109; Kuttner, "Declining Middle," 69; Bradbury, "The Shrinking Middle Class," 60.

It's still possible, of course, that the inequality trend will "cure itself" over time. Perhaps, as Marvin Kosters speculates, future generations will react to the premium paid for education and skills by getting more education and skills. More Americans will learn enough to make it into the middle class (though this development itself would have some ominous consequences for social equality that will be explored later). Kosters also suggests that boomers may advance more rapidly because more of them are in non-union jobs where wages traditionally start low and end high (compared with union jobs). As the non-unionists prosper, the middle of the income distribution might replenish itself.

26. See Levy, *Dollars and Dreams,* 209–210.

27. See, for example, Levy, "Incomes, Families, and Living Standards," Figure 4-4, 123.

28. See Barbara Ehrenreich, *Fear of Falling* (New York: Pantheon, 1989), 211–220. Lester Thurow, Marvin Kosters, and Frank Levy all told me that they suspect "assortative mating" is taking place.

29. See for example, Levy, *Dollars and Dreams,* fn. 8, 20, noting that the richest fifth of all households holds 75 percent of all household assets, and the top 2 percent holds 26 percent. According to the *New York Times,* IRS statistics show that the share of the nation's wealth held by the richest 1 percent grew from 27 percent in 1973 to 36 percent in 1987. See Michael deCourcy Hinds, "The Budget Battle; Reading Lips of the Rich: Spending, not Taxes, Is the Problem," *New York Times,* 20 October 1990, 8. See also John M. Berry, "Detailed Study Finds Wealth Gap Widened in Eighties," *Washington Post,* 7 January 1992, C4; Sylvia Nasar, "Fed Gives New Evidence of 80's Gains by Richest," *New York Times,* 21 April 1992, A1.

30. Source for the rise in the value of homes: National Association of Realtors. This figure is unadjusted for inflation. See also Levy, *Dollars and Dreams,* 68. Inherited wealth, as Kuttner notes, is the "dirty little secret of the yuppie class." See Robert Kuttner, "The Patrimony Society," *The New Republic,* 11 May 1987, 18–21.

31. A fourth potential disequalizing factor is the pattern of births. The birth rate to two-parent families fell in the sixties and seventies. This means that proportionately more babies have been born into families with only one parent, which tend to be poor. Frank Levy notes that a sixth of American children now live in households with less than $10,000 in income, up from a tenth in 1973. In other words, the income distribution has grown less equal, but the income distribution of *children* has grown more unequal more rapidly. This might not mean that money inequality in the future will be greater than it is today; it all depends on whether the circumstances of birth and childhood translate into circumstances of adulthood. But the statistics on children certainly aren't encouraging to those who expect money inequality to decrease in the coming decades. See Levy, "Incomes, Families, and Living Standards," 136–139.

32. Levy, *Dollars and Dreams,* caption to Table 2.1, 14.

33. Tobin is quoted in "If Inequality Is Inevitable, What Can Be Done About It?" *New York Times,* 3 January 1982, sec. 4, 5.

34. See *1990 Green Book,* Table 70, 1147. Sheldon Danziger provided me with income share and Gini figures from Current Population Survey data to supplement the *Green Book* chart, which ends in 1980. See also Harrison and Bluestone, *The Great U-Turn,* Figure 5-2, 119.

35. This possibility might seem to revive Tawney's argument that what matters is "in which direction" we're moving. But the argument that maintaining a money-egalitarian *trend* is the key to social equality has some of the same problems as the argument that maintaining such a trend is itself the "end" of liberal politics. Most obviously, can money keep getting more equal forever? It would seem that either we will actually reach a state of pure equality (which money egalitarians deny is

their goal—and in which case the trend will stop) or else we will have to delight ourselves with rapidly diminishing increments of progress, approaching pure money equality in the fashion of Zeno's paradox.

36. See Ehrenreich, *Fear of Falling*, 14, 200. Ehrenreich calls the signs of class superiority "class cues"; Charles Peters calls them "taste badges." Guilt could play a perverse role here as well: faced with an increasing gap between their standard of living and the living standards of, say, steelworkers, those lucky enough to remain in the upper tier may attempt to justify it by subtly reminding themselves of their own superiority.

37. Under this theory, an inegalitarian distribution might produce greater social equality than an egalitarian distribution, if in the unequal distribution a "critical mass" of average people were clustered at a single level and thus had a standard-setting effect on the culture.

38. The economists' "Gini coefficients" of inequality for the two years are given in Levy, *Dollars and Dreams*, 12. A higher Gini coefficient means more inequality, with a score of 1 representing complete inequality. The coefficient for 1947 was .376. For 1973 it was .356. The low point in the postwar era was 1969, at .349.

39. *A note on stagnation:* This suggests the possibility that economic stagnation, not inequality, should be the real suspect in the death of social equality. Take another look at the chart of income distributions in 1947, 1973, and 1984. Surely the most obvious story it tells is this: from 1947 to 1973, the family income distribution moved dramatically to the right, meaning American families were growing more prosperous. Then, between 1973 and 1984, this growth stopped, so that the later graph is stuck in almost the same place as the graph of a decade earlier.

The idea that stagnation, not money inequality, set the zeitgeist of the eighties has been promoted most forcefully by economist Frank Levy. (See *Dollars and Dreams*, 79.) The stagnation trend, even more than the inequality trend, broke with the early post-war decades when wages were expected to rise each year. "If wages begin to grow again," Levy predicted in 1987, "the issue of the vanishing middle class will itself vanish." (Ibid., 208.)

Would the issue of social inequality vanish? Levy doesn't address this question directly; but his argument is suggestive. He makes much of the idea that by the early eighties, "being in the middle of the distribution no longer guaranteed a middle-class income"; that is, it no longer guaranteed the components of the "middle-class dream," which Levy identifies as a "single-family home, one or two cars, a washing machine and a dryer." Maybe a sense of social equality requires this absolute level of material comfort. The problem, of course, is that if that's true, it doesn't matter whether America is stagnating or not—social equality will be an impossibility, In 1973, when 51 percent of husband-wife families met Levy's $30,000 "middle-class" threshold, they still didn't constitute a majority of all families, let alone all individuals. What about the other 49 percent? Were they really doomed to undignified lives?

There are other theories that might implicate stagnation in social equality's decline. A stagnating economy could sour everyone's mood, drying up avenues of promotion, making money differences look distressingly permanent to those on the bottom, producing degrading feelings of self-pity in those who've been laid off or otherwise seen their fortunes decline. Note that this effect would be exactly opposite to the "growth effect" hypothesized earlier, in which the spread of incomes that comes with prosperity, rather than stagnation, was held to provoke anxious assertions of superiority.

In any case, the stagnation explanation doesn't track with the social-inegalitarian trend of the 1980s. The economy started growing in 1983. Between 1985 and 1990, Americans at every income level saw their incomes rise. (See *1990 Green Book*, Table 92, 1188–1189.) The obnoxiousness of the late 1980s—including the ascendancy of magazines like *Vanity Fair*—coincided with economic growth, not stagnation. Likewise the end of the Reagan boom in the nineties was accompanied by an anti-snob backlash.

40. On anxious middle-class dieting, see Ehrenreich, *Fear of Falling,* 32. On "voluntary simplicity," see ibid., 225–227. By the end of her book even Ehrenreich herself is complaining, a bit snootily, that yuppies don't know enough about Proust (ibid., 241).

41. Ibid., 15.

42. See Gilder, *Wealth and Poverty,* 90–91; DeParle, "Spy Anxiety," 12. It's not far from this insight to DeParle's argument that it wasn't too much money inequality that produced middle-class snobbery, but too much money *equality:* "The relative rise in equality that Frederick Lewis Allen thought would eliminate the differences in choice of razor, cigarette, and home lighting instead made those choices all the more crucial for those eager to make the grade. How else to set oneself apart?" DeParle, "Spy Anxiety," 12. See also Gilder, *Wealth and Poverty,* 90. Ehrenreich, in fact, notes that the egalitarian 1950s were "an era of intense preoccupation with the innumerable little cues distinguishing one layer of taste and achievement from another" (*Fear of Falling,* 24).

43. Ehrenreich even speculates, at one point, that instead of money inequality producing status anxiety the causality runs the other way: the status anxiety of the middle class causes money inequality. "When more is not enough, but only serves as a springboard to further excess, then we have entered a state analogous to physical addiction." Craving more and costlier signs of election, the anxious $150,000 executive demands a raise, or switches to a $200,000 job he doesn't like. Then, faced with "the loss of an intrinsically rewarding profession," he has to compensate with still more consumption financed by higher earnings. That's yet another plausible theory (*Fear of Falling,* 247).

44. Ibid., 128.

45. Indeed, money equality among families was about to reach its post-war peak. See Levy, *Dollars and Dreams,* 14. Wage equality had been increasing rapidly, according to Harrison and Bluestone, and would continue to increase until the mid-1970s. See Harrison and Bluestone, *The Great U-Turn,* 119.

46. Whether it's getting more equal or less equal, the income distribution isn't a fixed ranking. Individuals are constantly succeeding and failing, rising and falling. The University of Michigan's Panel Study of Income Dynamics took a representative group of families and looked at their incomes in 1971 and 1978. Of those in the bottom fifth (in income) in 1971, only a little over half were still in the bottom fifth seven years later. Nearly a quarter had moved into the top three-fifths of the

income distribution. Meanwhile, less than half of those in the top fifth were still there after seven years. All told, only 40 percent of the population remained in the same income quintile. See Greg J. Duncan, *Years of Poverty, Years of Plenty: The Changing Economic Fortunes of American Workers and Families* (Ann Arbor: Institute for Social Research, 1984), 13–14. Despite the anxiety it may produce, this sort of mobility is traditionally considered a major source of social *equality*. It's harder to sneer at people poorer than you if lot of them will soon be richer than you. This chapter considers not only the question of whether "meritocracy" is changing the basis for this mobility, but whether it is reducing the *amount* of mobility, contributing to what Tawney called "permanence of rank."

47. Kurt Vonnegut, *Player Piano* (1952; reprint, New York: Dell, 1980).

48. See Reich, "As the World Turns," 23; see also Davis and Haltiwanger, "Wage Dispersion," 118, and sources cited therein.

49. Reich, "As the World Turns," 26. Technically the phrase should be "symbol analysts," not "symbolic analysts," since these are people who analyze symbols, not analysts who have symbolic value.

50. Nor can we count technology out as a source of inequality. It may simply take more brains to run the machines that now produce cars, pipes, plastics, et cetera. When Davis and Haltiwanger looked at rising wage inequality, they concluded that the evidence points to "skill-biased technical change as the major driving force behind rising wage inequality in the United States." In particular, they note that some forms of wage inequality have been growing steadily, while the trade shocks of the 1980s occurred suddenly. See Davis and Haltiwanger, "Wage Dispersion," 174, 119. The technology question is complicated, however, since it's not physical labor but tedious mental labor that, with computers, is most obviously going the way of the carthorse. (See generally Shoshana Zuboff, *In the Age of the Smart Machine* [New York: Basic Books, 1988], discussed further in Chapter 5.) I've emphasized Reich's trade-driven dynamic because it applies whether or not technology by itself is exacerbating inequality.

51. This is also the affective undercurrent when Democrats lament the loss of "good jobs at good wages." See Levy, *Dollars and Dreams*, 88.

52. In some ways, as Michael Kinsley has noted, yuppies were worse off financially than their parents (at least when it came to being able to afford houses). See "Arise Ye Yuppies," *The New Republic*, 9 July 1984, 4.

53. James Fallows, *More Like Us* (Boston: Houghton Mifflin, 1989), 179.

54. That is clearly the hope, for example, of Lester Thurow in "A Surge in Inequality," 36–37. In 1992, Bill Clinton made this argument one theme of his presidential campaign.

55. Since people lacking these credentials are in effect locked out of many desirable careers, the predictions become more than a bit self-fulfilling. See Fallows, *More Like Us*, 131 et seq; and "Sheepskins Are for Sheep," *Washington Monthly*, March 1980, 9; and "The American Class System and How to End It," *Washington Monthly*, February 1978, 6 (written under the pseudonym Thomas Massey). See also David Owen, "The Last Days of ETS," *Harper's*, May 1983, 21; Nicholas Lemann, "The SATs Are Ruining the GNP" *Washington Monthly*, December 1981, 41–46.

56. In the early years of testing, Fallows notes, students were not told their

SAT scores. The information was thought so important they were better off proceeding to their inevitable fates in blissful ignorance. See Fallows, *More Like Us,* 179. On the use of SAT scores as proxies, see Fallows, "Sheepskins Are for Sheep," 13. ("But in general the kids who know these things know a lot else. A *lot,*" argues an ETS test designer.)

57. See, for example, Stephen Jay Gould, *The Mismeasure of Man* (New York: Norton, 1981).

58. See Ehrenreich, *Fear of Falling.* 30. In Walzer's terms, the pursuit of knowledge can be a "sphere" of life separate from the money sphere, with its own status hierarchy and rewards.

59. Fallows, *More Like Us,* 163.

60. The first SAT test was administered in 1926, but it took until the 1950s for the idea of "merit" to achieve what Nicholas Lemann calls "its psychological dominance of American life" ("The SATs Are Ruining the GNP," 43).

61. "Consider the tortoise and the hare. In the genuine meritocracy of the fable the tortoise won the race, through a combination of modest talent and considerable determination. But in our times the hare would win on form alone." Fallows, "The American Class System," 14.

62. Source: Federation of State Medical Boards of the United States. The total number of "serious" disciplinary actions, including fines, consent orders, and license restrictions, was 3,234. That's still only about 5 doctors out of every 1,000 practicing.

63. Fallows cites sociologist Randall Collins on this point. See "Sheepskins Are for Sheep," 10.

64. Ibid., 15. In the National Football League, Fallows notes, this openness to reevaluation is institutionalized in open tryouts "where the occasional offbeat character (who usually shows up in headlines with nicknames like 'the Place-Kicking Bartender') can demonstrate his ability to catch the pass or kick the ball and win a spot on the team even though he has not come through the normal channels of big-college ball." Is there any doubt that this system produces the best football teams—as opposed, say, to selecting players on the basis of an FSAT exam of general athletic ability in high school?

65. The "Eurailpass" analogy (in a slightly different form) originates in Suzannah Lessard, "The Case Against Tenure," *Washington Monthly.* September 1971, 13.

66. Nicholas Lemann speculates that if now-secure professions such as law and medicine were opened up to ongoing tests of performance, they would become less appealing to risk-averse college students. "[W]e'd stop seeing more than half the graduates of our best colleges becoming doctors and lawyers." Instead, they would pursue less safe, but perhaps more productive, careers as entrepreneurs, engineers, and managers. See Lemann, "Curse of the Merit Class," *Washington Post,* 9 February 1992, B4.

67. See Fallows, "Sheepskins Are for Sheep," 15–16. In at least one important area, teaching, there is already a substantial movement afoot to eliminate a phony credential, the requirement of a teaching degree. (See, for example, William J. Warren, "Alternative Certificates: New Paths to Teaching," *New York Times.* 28 September 1988, B15.) Why restrict the pool of teachers to those who (often for want of any real scholarly interests) majored in "education"?

68. Irving Kristol, "About Equality," *Commentary*, November 1972, 41–47, as cited and discussed in Michael Walzer, "In Defense of Equality," *Dissent*, Fall 1973, 401.

I want to distinguish two concepts, "spheres" and "bells." In Walzer's terminology, spheres are competing hierarchies, each with its own good to distribute on the terms appropriate to it. Examples are the economic sphere (in which those who can make money are rewarded with money), the public sphere, and (for Walzer) the spheres of the arts, of academia, of romance, et cetera.

By "bells" I refer to the various discrete talents and skills that allow you to succeed within one specific sphere, the economic sphere. Thus, there are different talents that help people make money: drive, charm, looks, analytic ability, physical skills, artistic ability, and so on, each with its own "bell curve" measuring its distribution.

I'm not sure Walzer means by "bells" what I mean by "bells." The Walzer quote cited, if read in context, seems to be referring to the "spheres" concept he was to develop in his later book *Spheres of Justice*. So I'm slightly twisting his quote to make a point he may not have intended.

69. "... and may be compatible with the easy movement of individuals, according to their capacity, from one point on the scale to another" (Tawney, *Equality* [1938; reprint, New York: Barnes & Noble, 1964], 71; see also 150.

70. "Task-specific" is Philip Green's term. See his *The Pursuit of Inequality* (New York: Pantheon, 1981), 98. One point of True Meritocracy would be to discover, nurture, and reward these discrete skills.

71. Richard Herrnstein, "I.Q.," *The Atlantic*, September 1971, 43–64.

72. See Geoffrey Cowley, "A Confederacy of Dunces: Are the Best and Brightest Making Too Few Babies?" *Newsweek*, 22 May 1989, 80, for an instance where the second view of Herrnstein is honestly stated in public.

73. See Richard Herrnstein, "The IQ Controversy," *Dissent*, Summer 1977, 297. As for which jobs are "consequential," Herrnstein seems to accept the idea that whatever jobs pay more (or have highest status ratings in public opinion polls) are in fact the most important—a ranking that places PR men among the most vital actors in American today and that generally undervalues people doing real work (e.g., teachers) who should perhaps have their pay and prestige enhanced. See Herrnstein, "I.Q.," 51, and Philip Green, *Pursuit of Inequality*, 105–109.

74. Herrnstein anticipates this point: "[T]here may be other inherited traits that differ among people and contribute to their success in life. Such qualities as temperament, personality, appearance, perhaps even physical strength or endurance, may enter into our strivings for achievement and are to varying degrees inherited. The meritocracy concerns not just inherited intelligence, but all inherited traits affecting success, whether or not we know of their importance or have tests to gauge them" ("I.Q.," 63).

Herrnstein does not claim I.Q. is entirely inherited, or that it is as heritable as, say, height. In his *Atlantic* article, he estimated the heritability of I.Q. at 80 percent ("I.Q.," 57–58). He put the heritability of height at 95 percent. In later writings he claimed only that studies showed I.Q.'s heritability to be "almost invariably ... above 50 percent and more often above 60 percent than below" ("The I.Q. Controversy," 298). See also Gina Kolata, "Study Raises the Estimate of Inherited Intelligence," *New York Times,* 12 October 1990, A22, treating a recent report of 70 percent heritability as surprisingly high.

75. Fallows, *More Like Us,* 153.

76. It doesn't help to point out, as George Will does, that talented people aren't responsible for their "faculties" (including their genes) and really have no right to feel superior. Humans generally feel superior to cows, though they aren't responsible for the difference. See Will, "Taxation Isn't Tyranny," *Washington Post,* 13 April 1989, A31. Michael Young, who invented the word "meritocracy," makes a point similar to Will's in "Is Equality a Dream?" *Dissent,* Fall 1973, 417.

77. Assortative mating will also amplify cultural differences between various income groups, of course. This raises the question of whether intergenerational transmission of "R-factors" is any less ominous for social equality when the mechanism is cultural rather than genetic. The traditional (and I think, correct) answer is yes. The mechanisms of cultural transmission can be blocked and modified, in a way that genes cannot.

Note that a Fallowsian meritocracy would by itself also make assortative mating more difficult. Currently colleges and professional schools are the major assortative mating grounds, filled with people of opposing sexes and similar credentials. If you want to marry at the meritocratic top, just wed your Harvard Med School classmate, with whom the meritocracy conspires to have you spend a lot of time. That selection process might be harder in, say, Randall Collins' start-at-the-bottom medical hierarchy. How would you tell who was going to end up a doctor and who wouldn't make it past orderly? You'd be socializing with all future classes, and you might just fall in love with the orderly.

78. This doesn't mean a *permanent* genetic aristocracy would evolve. The advantage of even highly heritable traits, such as height, is not fully passed on to children. This phenomenon is known to geneticists as "regression toward the mean." See, for example, Herrnstein, "I.Q.," 58. On average, very tall parents will have children who are a little shorter than they are; very short parents will have children who aren't quite as short as they are. This means that, even *with* assortative mating, the genetic advantages of any one family will naturally decay over the course of several generations.

Unfortunately, this heartening tendency doesn't detoxify the Herrnstein syllogism for social egalitarians. Even if genetic advantages last for only a few generations, as opposed to being embedded in permanent dynasties, they're still genetic advantages. Children of successful parents will, *to some extent,* be able to assume they are on average a bit more talented, and more likely to be successful, than children of unsuccessful parents. The more assortative mating there is, the stronger this assumption will be.

79. See Christopher Jencks et al., *Inequality* (New York: Harper & Row, 1972), 213–216. Jencks estimated that for children of high-status fathers, the income advantage of birth had roughly three times the effect of the genetic advantage of birth. But he also concludes that "family background, test scores, and occupation explain relatively little of the variation in income," attributing much of the variation instead to luck (227).

Genetic transmission *itself* involves an element of randomness. Even with full

100 percent heritability, individual children of the same parents will have different gene combinations, and the precise combination is unpredictable.

80. I get this argument from Philip Green, *The Pursuit of Inequality*, 94.

81. See Herrnstein, "I.Q.," 58.

82. See Fallows, *More Like Us*, 158–159.

83. Herrnstein, "I.Q.," 63.

84. I'm not arguing that the Fairness Trap applies at the level of any single occupation. Take Fallows's favorite meritocracy, the National Football League. Let's accept that the NFL "tryout" system provides a true test of "merit." No phony credentials. Instead, continuing tests of performance. Are the losers in this system bitter or humiliated? I think most viewers of local sports newscasts would agree with Fallows that, to a remarkable extent, those who don't make the cut tend to accept the judgment with dignity, and that this is directly related to the system's perceived fairness. But nobody really expects to make the NFL, just as nobody expects to host the "Tonight Show." If you don't get those jobs, there are other things to do, other bells to ring. But what if you ring *no* bells? Even in a Fallowsian "100-bell" society, some people won't succeed at anything. The cumulative effect of all those discrete, oh-so-fair judgments might be devastating, even if each individual judgment could be accepted with equanimity.

85. Samuelson, "An Imperfect Job Machine," *Washington Post*, 18 February 1987, F1–2.

86. Robert J. Donovan, *PT-109: John F. Kennedy in World War II* (New York: McGraw-Hill, 1961), 51–52, 79–80, 111–113, 120. Charles Peters suggested this example to me.

87. See Charles Moskos, *A Call to Civic Service* (New York: Free Press, 1988), 23. See also Timothy Noah, "We Need You: National Service, An Idea Whose Time Has Come," *Washington Monthly*, November 1986, 37.

88. See also Nicholas Lemann, "Community Without Conformity: The Road Back from Narcissism," *Washington Monthly*, September 1983, 20–25.

89. In 1947, the Selective Service Act expired, and though a new one was passed a year later, few Americans were actually drafted again until the Korean War. See Moskos, *Civic Service*, 25, 40.

90. Ibid., 40.

91. William Broyles, *Brothers in Arms* (New York: Knopf, 1986), 135.

92. I got out in the lottery. Would I have served if called? It's a good question. I don't know the answer.

93. By the time the undergraduate deferment was ended (in 1971) the war was winding down. Even then the affluent could often find a sympathetic psychiatrist or doctor to produce some medical excuse, or a priest to write a letter designed to obtain conscientious objector status.

Out of about 27 million men of draft age, about 15.4 million were deferred, exempted, or disqualified. Some 2.2 million were actually drafted. About 8.7 million enlisted voluntarily. (Statistics from *America's Vietnam Experience* [Berlin: Conelsen Verlag 1991], 13.)

94. The less-educated soldiers in Vietnam included many of the participants in Project 100,000, a 1966 scheme by Robert MacNamara's defense department de-

signed to give the benefits of military service to youths who scored below the ordinary cutoff point on the Armed Forces Qualification Test. In practice, many Project 100,000 soldiers were sent into combat in Vietnam. "They were cannon fodder, pure and simple," an Air Force historian later concluded. Project 100,000 was nicknamed "MacNamara's Moron Corps" and is widely considered to have been a dramatic failure. See David Evans, "Losing Battle," *The New Republic*, 30 June 1986, 10–13.

95. Broyles, *Brothers in Arms*, 137. See also Moskos, *Civic Service*, 41, noting that during the Vietnam years, "High school dropouts were twice as likely to enter the service as college graduates."

96. This arrangement provoked the 1863 working-class riots in New York City in which over one hundred people were killed. See Walzer, *Spheres of Justice*, 98–99; Iver Bernstein, *The New York City Draft Riots* (New York: Oxford University Press, 1990).

97. See U.S. Army Recruiting Command, *1988 USAREC New Recruit Survey* (June–August 1988), 897. In 1989, 7.81 percent of American households lived in homes they owned worth at least $200,000; in 1987, the figure was 5.2 percent. There are no 1988 figures. The percentage of families *with draft-age children* who lived in $200,000 homes was probably higher. (U.S. Census Bureau, "American Housing Survey for the United States for 1989 [1987]," Commerce Department Report H150-89 [87]).

Another example: Only 18 percent of 1989 Army recruits had fathers with a college degree, compared with 26 percent in a sample of the general population identified by the Pentagon as comparable. See Department of Defense, Office of the Assistant Secretary of Defense (Force Management and Personnel), Population Representation in the Military Services, Fiscal Year 1989, July 1990, 49.

Definitive statistics on the relative failure of the affluent to serve are hard to find in part because the Pentagon doesn't publicize them. A favorite technique is the use of average figures. In 1989, for example, the Defense Department rated the "socioeconomic status" of recruits' parents on a scale of (roughly) 14 to 90. The average "status" rank for the fathers of recruits was 36.0. The average rank for the comparison group from the general population was 40.1. This is a significant difference, but it doesn't look too bad—until you remember that the military won't accept those testing low on aptitude tests, who tend to be those with low incomes. That means there are relatively few sons and daughters of the truly poor in the armed forces. If recruits were a genuine cross-section of the remaining classes, then, the military "socioeconomic status" average would be far *higher* than the overall civilian average. See 46–47, 54.

The social-egalitarian argument for a draft does not, I think, hinge on such evidence of "class bias." Even if the makeup of the All-Volunteer Force were perfectly representative of the population as a whole, it would still violate social egalitarian principles. The point isn't to spread the risk to all demographic groups. The point (for social egalitarians, anyway) is that *everyone* should bear the risk, that the fighting of wars should be removed from the sphere of things that money buys and included in the sphere of equal citizenship.

98. *Schooling for All: Class, Race, and the Decline of the Democratic Ideal* (New York: Basic Books, 1985), 214.

99. Charles Peters, *Tilting at Windmills* (Reading, Mass.: Addison-Wesley, 1988), 25.

100. *Schooling for All*, 214–215.

101. Even within schools, "tracking"—that is, stratifying the curriculum by expected future occupation—was occurring as early as 1889. See David F. Labaree, "Shaping the Role of the Public High School: Past Patterns and Present Implications," Department of Teacher Education, Michigan State University, March 1987 paper, prepared for presentation at the April 1987 meeting of the American Educational Research Association.

102. Source: U.S. Census, Current Population Reports, Series P-60. See also John R. Logan and Mark Schneider, "Governmental Organization and City/Suburb Income Inequality, 1960–1970," *Urban Affairs Quarterly* 17, no. 3 (March 1982): 312, showing the growth in the inequality of median incomes between cities and their suburbs between 1960 and 1970.

103. See John R. Logan and Mark Schneider, "Racial Segregation and Racial Change in American Suburbs, 1970–1980," *American Journal of Sociology* 89, no. 4 (January 1984): 874–888.

104. Source: 1980 U.S. Census, Vol. 1, Chapter A, Part 1, Table 5.

105. Jargowsky's "sorting index" runs between 0 (perfect integration by income) and 1.000 (total segregation by income). For all races and for a weighted average of 237 metropolitan areas, the index increased from .392 to .399 between 1970 and 1980. However, in the North it increased from .377 to .404 overall, and from .360 to .377 even among whites. It increased more in big cities than small cities. In New York it leaped from .359 to .430. This is unpublished data derived in the preparation of Jargowsky, "Ghetto Poverty: The Neighborhood Distribution Framework" (Ph.D. diss., Harvard University, Malcolm Wiener Center for Social Policy, 1991).

The Massey and Eggers data cited is in "The Ecology of Inequality: Minorities and the Concentration of Poverty, 1970–1980," *American Journal of Sociology* 95, no. 5 (March 1990); 1153–1188, see especially Table 2, 1172–1173. In addition, Massey and Eggers collected (unpublished) data for Chicago, Los Angeles, and New York showing substantial increases between 1970 and 1980 in the overall probability that an affluent family shared a neighborhood with another affluent family. Those statistics reflect both the sheer increase in the numbers of affluent families as well as the tendency of families to isolate themselves in neighborhoods according to their income class. The virtue of Jargowsky's "sorting index" is that it measures only the second factor—the extent to which neighborhoods separate out whatever income classes the economy generates. It demonstrates that public-sphere segregation (Suspect #3) was increasing in many cities quite apart from changes in the income distribution (Suspect #1). See also Michael J. White, *American Neighborhoods and Residential Differentiation* (New York: Russell Sage, 1987), 192, Figure 6.1, showing that residential segregation by *education* level fell from 1940 to 1960, and then rose from 1960 to 1980.

University of Michigan demographer Reynolds Farley dissents from the idea that class segregation increased in the 1970s. See "Residential Segregation of Social and Economic Groups Among Blacks, 1970–1980," in Christopher Jencks and Paul E. Peterson, eds., *The Urban Underclass* (Washington, D.C.: Brookings, 1991), 289. I am unable to reconcile Farley's numbers with Jargowsky's or Massey and Eggers's. But even Farley shows an increase in economic segregation in New York and Los Angeles, within the white community as well as within the black community. And, according to Farley, segregation by education level has increased across the entire population spectrum in cities of the West as well as the Northeast-Midwest.

106. For Boston: According to the Boston mayor's office, 38 percent of the children in the city's public schools are from families receiving Aid to Families with Dependent Children (AFDC). For Seattle: See Timothy Egan, "In Seattle Mayoral Race, a Sense of the Possible," *New York Times,* 1 November 1989, 20; Maralee Schwartz and Elizabeth Hudson, "In Seattle Mayoral Race, Big Issue Is Busing," *Washington Post,* 5 November 1989, A30.

107. Source: Los Angeles Unified School District.

108. For the non-Catholic enrollment figure, see Denis P. Doyle, "The Storm before the Lull: The Future of Private Schooling in America," in John H. Bunzel, ed., *Challenge to American Schools: The Case for Standards and Values* (New York: Oxford University Press, 1985), 154. In general, private school enrollment (grades K through 12) has been growing, but slowly: from 10.5 percent in 1970 to 11.7 percent in 1989. Within that private school figure, however, Catholic school enrollment has declined from 4.36 million in 1970–71 to 3.1 million in 1980–81 to approximately 2.5 million in 1988–89. Figures from U.S. Department of Education, National Center for Education Statistics, Digest of Education Statistics, 1991 (Washington, D.C., 1991), 12, 68.

109. See Labaree, "Shaping the Role of the Public High School," 15.

110. Michael Walzer, "The Pleasures and Costs of Urbanity," *Dissent,* Fall 1986, 472.

111. See Ray Oldenburg, *The Great Good Place* (New York: Paragon House, 1989), 215. Interestingly, many suburban malls have found it in their interest to attempt to recreate a class-mixing sense of community—through concerts, festivals, and other events—in defiance of the argument that lively community spaces are inherently less profitable than single-purpose commercial uses. My impression, however, is that few malls have succeeded in replicating the complex social interactions of a good urban public square. See ibid., 214; Walzer, "Pleasures and Costs of Urbanity," 474.

112. The most notorious case is probably in Morristown, N.J., where a homeless man sued to overturn a library rule that barred "patrons whose bodily hygiene is so offensive as to constitute a nuisance to other persons."

113. Even suburbs that aren't actually surrounded by gates often charge fees to use public beaches or facilities—occasionally banning their use by outsiders entirely. There is also evidence that those who have moved to the suburbs are spending less and less time in the central city. See Elizabeth Kolbert, "Region Around New York Sees Ties to City Faltering," *New York Times,* 1 December 1991, 1; William Glaberson, "For Many in the New York Region, The City Is Ignored and Irrelevant," *New York Times,* 2 January 1992, 1.

114. Elizabeth Rudulph and Elizabeth Taylor, "Old Fashioned Play—For Pay," *Time*, 4 November 1991, 86.

115. For example, as part of the renovation of New York's Times Square, developers are constructing buildings with large indoor shopping areas. These private, indoor spaces are considered commercially viable in part because they can be policed privately without the civil-libertarian strictures that apply in the famous, publicly owned space outside.

116. Oldenburg, *The Great Good Place*, 284.

117. See Paul Gray, "Another Look at Democracy in America," *Time*, 16 June 1986, 99. See also Charles Murray, "Of a Conservative (Created) Caste," *Harper's*, October 1991, 17–18, reprinted from the 8 July 1991 issue of *National Review*. Murray asks his readers to "Try to envision what happens when 10 or 20 percent of the population has enough income to bypass the social institutions it doesn't like in ways that only the top fraction of 1 percent used to be able to do." That begs the question, of course, of whether it's relative or absolute prosperity that enables the bypassing.

Chapter 5
Money Liberalism's Lost Battle

1. See Paul Krugman, *The Age of Diminished Expectations* (Cambridge, Mass.: MIT Press, 1990), 25, for a similar conclusion.

2. Quoted in Robert Kuttner, *The Economic Illusion* (Boston: Houghton Mifflin, 1984), 40–41, citing Julian Le Grand, *The Strategy of Equality* (London: George Allen & Unwin, 1982), 139.

3. The quote is from Paul Blustein, "Compromise on Capital Gains Could Produce Some Pretty Weird Tax Policy," *Washington Post*, 14 June 1989, F3.

4. *A note on taxes and income inequality:* Gramlich, Kasten, and Sammartino's calculations do not include two factors that would increase the estimated effect of recent regressive tax changes: (*a*) They only measure the effect of tax changes in the 1980s. But the "supply-side" tax cut of 1978 also aided the rich. (*b*) They don't attempt to measure the "feedback" effect of the tax code on pre-tax income. That is, you can't say that *pre*-tax income was unaffected by tax cuts, since part of the pre-tax income of the rich was interest they earned from investing the money tax cuts saved them.

If you take into account those two factors, how much of the income shift can be explained by tax changes? The highest estimate I have seen is from Robert S. McIntyre, director of Citizens for Tax Justice. In testimony before Congress during the Democrats 1991 "fairness" campaign, McIntyre claimed that supply-side cuts starting in 1977 explained "some two thirds" of the increased income share of the richest one percent. (See also McIntyre, "The Reaganites and the Renegade," *The American Prospect*, Winter 1991, 13.) But McIntyre's figure is exaggerated in at least four ways:

1. He assumes that the 1977 tax code would have been allowed to claim an ever-higher share of national income, raising over half a trillion dollars more than was actually raised between 1977 and 1990. *All* of this extra revenue would have come from the top 1 percent, as their rising incomes pushed them into higher brackets. If instead you assume the government would have raised the amount it did raise, but done it as progressively as in 1977, the "two-thirds" figure falls dramatically.

2. In 1977 corporate profits were at record highs, and (because taxes on profits fall heavily on the rich) tax progressivity was at a record high. McIntyre assumes this record progressivity would have prevailed in all subsequent years even though *under the 1977 code itself* progressivity would have been lower because corporate profits fell.

3. McIntyre assumes the richest one percent accumulated their tax savings and reinvested them. But the richest one percent are not a fixed set of people, able to pile up such large sums year after year. They are a different set of people each year. Less than half of those in the top quintile in 1971 were in that quintile seven years later, according to the Panel Study of Income Dynamics. There's no reason to think the top 1 percent is any less volatile a group.

4. McIntyre assumes that all the extra money he'd raise from the top 1 percent would find its way into the pockets of the other 99 percent. How? If it would have been rebated to them, then he is testing a tax code that 's much more progressive than in 1977.

In sum, when it comes to the relative income gain of the rich, tax changes since 1977 probably explain a bit more than Gramlich et al.'s 20 percent but a good deal less than McIntyre's "two-thirds." I doubt that under a sensible set of assumptions taxes explain much more than one third of the rise. And that's just for the richest 1 percent. During this period, the top 5 to 15 percent gained in income share. The second-to-the-top quintile gained relative to the second-to-the-bottom quintile. Wage inequality increased. Tax changes don't come close to explaining those things.

See Edward M. Gramlich, Richard Kasten, and Frank Sammartino, "Growing Inequality in the 1980s: The Role of Federal Taxes and Cash Transfers," in *Uneven Tides: Rising Inequality in the 1980s,* ed. Sheldon Danziger and Peter Gottschalk (New York: Russell Sage, 1992)—compare Table 7 with Table 9. See also Mickey Kaus, "Facts for Hacks," *The New Republic,* 20 May 1991, 24, and McIntyre's response in "Correspondence," *The New Republic,* 1 July 1991, 2–3, 42.

5. See Chapter 8 at note 26. Whether we want to transfer money to non-working families is another question, discussed in Chapters 7 through 9.

6. The tax rates used in this calculation include all federal taxes—income taxes, social insurance taxes (including the Social Security payroll tax), corporate income taxes, and excise taxes—but not state taxes. These are Congressional Budget Office figures. See U.S. House of Representatives, Committee on Ways and Means, *Tax Progressivity and Income Distribution,* 101st Cong., 2d sess. 1990, Table 7, 20 (income share) and Table 3, 16 (effective tax rates).

7. For effective tax rates going back to 1966, see Joseph Pechman, "The Future

of the Income Tax," *American Economic Review,* 80, no. 1 (March 1990): 4, Table 3 (showing, as the highest effective rate on the top 1 percent, the 39.6 percent rate in 1966—*counting* state and local taxes).

8. See Joseph Pechman, *Who Paid the Taxes* (Washington, D.C.: Brookings, 1985), 77, and Pechman, *Federal Tax Policy,* 5th ed. (Washington, D.C.: Brookings, 1987), 313.

9. See, for example, Robert Reich's erroneous pronouncement that "In November 1986 the progressive income tax was substantially ended." Reich argues that the code lost progressivity, because starting in 1988, "the federal government claimed no more than 28 percent of the highest personal incomes in the land" (Reich, *The Resurgent Liberal* [New York: Times Books, 1989], 243). In fact, because the 1986 tax reform closed loopholes, its lower marginal rates produced higher effective tax rates on the rich—*more* progressivity. See Committee on Ways and Means, *Tax Progressivity,* 15–16.

10. See Joseph A. Pechman and Gary V. Engelhardt, "The Income Tax Treatment of the Family: An International Perspective" (Washington, D.C.: Brookings 1989, revised 1990), Table 10, 39. The Netherlands appears to have effective rates almost in Sweden's league. See also Edward M. Gramlich, "Rethinking the Role of the Public Sector," in *The Swedish Economy,* ed. Barry P. Bosworth and Alice M. Rivlin (Washington, D.C.: Brookings, 1987), Fig. 7-5, 269.

11. On the effect of the 1990 revisions, see *Background Material and Data on Programs within the Jurisdiction of the Committee on Ways and Means* (hereinafter referred to as the *Green Book*), 1991 edition, Table 28, 1318. On the effective tax rate in 1977, see *Tax Progressivity,* Table 3, 16.

12. For the top marginal tax rate (87 percent) in 1979, see Assar Lindbeck, "Income Distributions in a Welfare State: The Case of Sweden," *European Economic Review* 21 (1983): 243.

13. On the size of the gray market, see Gramlich, "Role of the Public Sector," 270–272.

Another problem for Sweden has been that, faced with high tax rates, some high earners (Ingmar Bergman, the rock group Abba) simply emigrated. As skills become more important and better rewarded, any country that imposes high taxes on high earners may be faced with a brain drain.

14. The loophole I'm talking about is not the tax break for "capital gains" that President Bush was obsessed with reestablishing. That loophole would let the rich pay at a lower rate when they finally sell an asset. The loophole that can't be closed is the one that lets the rich escape taxation for the rise in value of an asset as long as they *don't* sell it. If, for example, a wealthy man puts $1,000,000 in a savings account, he pays high marginal taxes on the income it earns. But if he buys a piece of land or a painting that appreciates in value, or builds up a company he owns rather than paying himself a salary, he pays no income taxes even though his net wealth may rise every year the same as if he were getting income.

Sweden and several other industrialized nations do have a "net wealth" tax that taxes the *total* wealth of the rich. But these nations do not attempt to tax the increase in wealth from year to year. Indeed, most avoid the hassle of valuing assets every year, adopting various rules of thumb and shortcuts. (Sweden, for example, assesses immovable property only every 5 years.) Information on net wealth taxes is in Organisation for Economic Co-operation and Development, *Taxation of Net Wealth, Capital Transfers and Capital Gains of Individual* (Paris: OECD, 1988), 22, 31–32, 36, 61–74.

How much have rich Swedes been legally keeping from the tax collectors? In 1979 economist Assar Lindbeck estimated that thanks to the untaxed appreciation of capital assets, as well as various deductions available for purchasing them, the official income records understated the actual disposable income of the rich by up to 75 percent. See "Interpreting Income Distributions in a Welfare State: The Case of Sweden," *European Economic Review* 21 (1983), 251–252.

15. The $163,000 figure is an unpublished datum from the Internal Revenue Service, Statistics of Income Division. It does not take into account family size. The Thurow quote is from a telephone interview (winter 1987). See also Phillip Moffitt, "When $2 Million Isn't Enough," *Esquire,* May 1989, 79.

16. For ordinary workers, high tax rates probably discourage putting in long hours. That's not necessarily true—faced with lower take-home pay, workers might in theory respond by working harder in order to maintain their incomes, a phenomenon called the "backwards bending" supply curve of labor. But in Sweden, apparently, this "backwards" phenomenon remains theoretical. Gary Burtless estimates that the labor supply of Swedish prime-age workers would have been 6 and 10 percent higher if Swedish tax rates had been as low as U.S. tax rates. See Burtless, "Taxes, Transfers, and Swedish Labor Supply," in *The Swedish Economy,* 241. See also comments by Assar Lindbeck, ibid., 243–249.

17. Pre-tax incomes appear to be growing faster than average for somewhere between the top 10 and the top 20 percent of the income distribution. See *1990 Green Book,* 1188–1189. But this boom at the top itself raises the average against which everyone gets compared. The third-from-the-top decile (the 70th to 80th percentiles) is still gaining when compared to the deciles underneath it. So it's not at all clear that money egalitarians can focus their fire only on the top 10 to 20 percent. If the top 20 percent of the distribution magically disappeared along with all of its income, money egalitarians would look at the remaining income distribution and complain that the richest of those who remained (the current 70th to 80th percentile group) were getting richer relative to everyone else.

18. Some money-egalitarians hope that demographics may yet provide at least a partial cure for income inequality. In this theory, a prolonged post-baby boom shortage of young, entry-level workers will raise incomes at the bottom of the distribution, as desperate employers are forced to increase the pay of unskilled work. "Someone will have to change oil filters and wait on tables in the affluent economy," writes Peter Passell of the *New York Times.* "And as American labor markets tighten, reflecting the decline in birthrates in the 1960s, wages in unskilled jobs are likely to rise sharply" ("Burger Flippers Take the Heat," *New York Times,* 26 April 1989, D2). See also Lester Thurow, "The Post Industrial Era Is Over," *New York Times,* 4 September 1989, 27, which relies on the baby-bust to raise wages at the bottom.

Alas, the skills trend threatens even this limited wage-boosting scenario. One reason skills are becoming more valuable, after all, is that more and more jobs—at least jobs performed competitively in this country—require them. Assembly-line workers must know how to do statistical quality control. Workers in IBM's chip-making factories need to know trigonometry. (See Charles C. Mann, "The Man with All the Answers," *The Atlantic,* January 1990, 60.) "The first rung on the ladder is going to be higher than it ever was before," argues Frank Doyle, a senior vice president of General Electric. Kids who don't already have math skills or computer-operating skills are finding themselves shut out of more and more entry-level jobs.

Where do they end up? In the "unskilled" labor market. Which means there might not be a shortage of unskilled workers at all. Yes, there will be fewer entry-level workers because of the baby bust. But there will be more people looking for unskilled jobs if workers who don't meet the skills requirements of most employers pile up in the unskilled sector. We don't know which of these opposing trends will dominate, economist Frank Levy points out. But Levy suspects "there will be enough people around to do the McDonald's jobs." Doyle, who preaches to corporate leaders about the "coming demographic crunch," agrees: "No more will too many people chase too few jobs," he declares, *"except the low or non-skilled jobs"* (Frank P. Doyle, "People Power: The Global Human Resource Challenge for the Nineties," plenary paper prepared for the World Management Conference, CIOS 21, 23 September, 1989, 3 [emphasis added]).

19. "A Surge in Inequality," *Scientific American,* May 1987, 36.

20. This is what Christopher Jencks in fact wound up proposing in his 1972 book *Inequality.* See Jencks et al., *Inequality* (New York: Harper & Row, 1972), 230.

21. See, for example: Robert Reich, *The Work of Nations* (New York: Knopf, 1991), 247–249; Robert I. Lerman and Hillard Pouncy, "Why America Should Develop a Youth Apprenticeship System," Policy Report No. 5 (Washington, D.C.: Progressive Policy Institute, March 1990). The most prominent recent bipartisan report is *America's Choice: High Skills or Low Wages!* Report of the Commission on the Skills of the American Work Force (Rochester, N.Y.: The National Center on Education and the Economy, June 1990). Clinton advocated what he called a "smart-work, high-wage" economy and generally embraced Reich's ideas.

22. See Robert Reich, *The Next American Frontier* (New York: Times Books, 1983), 236; Michael J. Piore and Charles F. Sabel, *The Second Industrial Divide: Possibilities for Prosperity* (New York: Basic Books, 1984), 273, 301.

23. "Unlike America's old vertically integrated economy, whose white-collar jobs were necessarily limited in proportion to the number of blue-collar jobs beneath them, the global economy imposes no particular limit on the number of Americans who can sell symbolic-analytic services. In principle [i.e., with enough training] all of America's routine production workers could become symbolic analysts and let their old jobs drift overseas" (Reich, "As the World Turns," *The New Republic,* 1 May 1989, 28).

24. See Passell, "Burger Flippers Take the Heat," which makes some of the arguments that follow.

25. Unpublished tabulations for college educated males aged 35 to 44 from Current Population Survey tapes by Gary Burtless, Brookings Institution. The income share of the poorest quintile of this college-educated group fell from 10.2 percent to 7.3 percent. The share of the top quintile rose from 30.2 percent to 35.6 percent, but that figure substantially understates the increase at the top since Burtless ex-

cluded earners in the 98th and 99th percentiles for technical reasons.

26. Even in Hollywood, this phenomenon isn't confined to the famous. I used to play softball in Los Angeles with a group of screenwriters. All were college graduates, and in that sense all had been "trained." But some were struggling. Others became successful and made $100,000 a year. One eventually signed a four-year contract paying him and his wife $15 million. *Fifteen million dollars.* It seems he'd created "The Wonder Years," and that's what the Walt Disney Company thought he was worth. Neither transfers nor training could stop the rising income inequality within this one softball game! See also Sherwin Rosen, "The Economics of Superstars," *American Economic Review* 71, no. 5 (December 1981): 845–858; "The Economics of Superstars," *The American Scholar* 52, no.4 (Autumn 1983); 449–460. See also Gary Burtless, "Earnings Inequality Over the Business Cycle," in *A Future of Lousy Jobs?* ed. Gary Burtless (Washington, D.C.: Brookings, 1990), 115; Robert H. Frank and Philip J. Cook, "Winner-Take-All Markets" (Cornell University, Department of Economics, 1991, mimeographed).

27. See Richard B. Freeman and James L. Medoff, *What Do Unions Do?* (New York: Basic Books, 1984), 78–93. Freeman and Medoff explicitly accept that without unions inequality would increase even among people with identical "training": "Roughly half of the union reduction in inequality takes the form of less pay [inequality] among workers with observationally identical characteristics (that is, of the same age, sex, race, years of schooling, and working in the same occupation, industry, and region)" (87). But see Steve J. Davis and John Haltiwanger, "Wage Dispersion between and within U.S. Manufacturing Plants. 1963–86," in *Brookings Papers on Economic Activity, Microeconomics 1991,* ed. Martin Neil Baily and Clifford Winston (Washington, D.C.: Brookings, 1991), 115–180, especially 137–138, which discounts the effect of declining unionism on wage inequality.

28. *A note on CEO pay:* I don't want to claim that high pay always represents the market's reward for exceptional talent. One entire species of high-earner, the corporate CEO, seems to have benefited from a breakdown in the relationship between high pay and performance. Median compensation (including salaries, bonuses, and long-term incentives) for the CEOs of 352 of America's biggest companies, as surveyed by the *Wall Street Journal,* was about $1.4 million in 1990. This represented a huge relative rise in pay—a tripling within two decades, after inflation, according to compensation specialist Graef S. Crystal. Most famously, Steve Ross of Time-Warner averaged about $16 million a year from 1973 to 1989.

No doubt many CEOs are talented, and undoubtedly part of the boom in executive pay simply parallels the rise in pay at the top of virtually every profession in the country—the Hollywood Effect. But it's hard to argue that such lavish payments represent what America's CEOs are actually worth (in comparison with others who might be able to perform as well for less). Crystal, who has studied executive pay for years and wrote a recent book on the subject, found precious little relationship between CEOs' compensation and how their firms actually performed. Instead, the split between ownership and management of the large public corporation, and the frequently incestuous relationship of CEOs with their boards of directors, seems to have undermined the accountability that is supposed to go with capitalism.

Certainly steps should be taken to restore that accountability. The Securities and

Exchange Commission is moving to make to make it easier for shareholders to challenge executive pay. Crystal has his own set of recommendations, generally designed to give corporate boards more independence, to give shareholders more information, and to encourage executive "incentives" that really do reward long-term performance. Various Democrats have advanced tax changes designed to restrict the ability of corporations to deduct high executive salaries.

But it's also true that the CEO problem is only one part of the income boom at the top of the distribution, and not such a big part. There are only so many huge, unaccountable corporations. Yes, when *Business Week* surveyed the compensation of the two top executives at 356 of the biggest U.S. companies—a total of 712 executives—it discovered about half of them taking home total compensation of more than a million a year. But those 372 executives account for less than one percent of the approximately 62,000 tax returns that show an income of over a million. Crystal notes that at a single law firm, Cravath, Swaine & Moore, 66 partners made $1.5 million each! Steve Ross may have made $34 million in one year, but Bill Cosby is reported to have made $115 million in two years, and Steven Spielberg made $87 million over the same period, all negotiated with people who had real money to lose but who thought that's what Cosby and Spielberg were worth. The vast bulk of the newly rich appear to be those with valuable talents—lawyers, entertainers, writers, athletes, hotshot bond traders and bankers, et cetera—who have been freed to bargain for their full value in something that approaches a market transaction, or else businessmen who struck it rich without the collusion of a chummy board of directors spending shareholders' money. Even Kevin Phillips admits that small-business owners, not bigshot corporate CEOs, make up the bulk of the very rich. (See *The Politics of Rich and Poor* [New York: Random House, 1990], 178.)

See generally Graef S. Crystal, *In Search of Excess: The Overcompensation of American Executives* (New York: Norton, 1991), especially 37 (Cosby and Spielberg), 40 (Cravath), 84 (Ross), 241–252 (Crystal's proposed reforms). For the *Wall Street Journal* survey see "The Boss's Pay," 17 April 1991, R9. For the *Business Week* survey see "Pay Stubs of the Rich and Corporate," 7 May 1990, 56–108. For the 62,000 tax returns showing an adjusted gross income of more than a million, see Internal Revenue Service, *Individual Income Tax Returns, 1988,* Table 1.4, 26.

29. Charles Murray makes this point in "Of a Conservative (Created) Caste," *Harper's,* October 1991, 17. ("... when a percentage point of market share is worth hundreds of millions of dollars, the people who can help you get that extra percentage point will command very large salaries.")

30. Note that, to the extent the Hollywood Effect produces great disparities of income *within* each profession, it makes the Loser Problem nastier: Instead of worrying why I'm only a $40,000-a-year magazine writer instead of a $150,000-a-year investment banker, I now have to worry about why I'm not a $150,000-a-year magazine writer.

31. Robert Kuttner, "The Declining Middle," *The Atlantic,* July 1983, 70. Elsewhere, Kuttner has endorsed training. Indeed, a few paragraphs later in his *Atlantic* article, he praises two labor unions for their training programs. See also "On Civic Liberalism: A Symposium," *The New Republic.* 18 June 1990, 27–28.

32. Robert Kuttner, "The Declining Middle," 61, 70. Harrison and Bluestone

are a bit more realistic (that is, pessimistic) about the prospects for a union revival large enough to affect the income distribution. See Harrison and Bluestone, *The Great U-Turn* (New York: Basic Books, 1988), 186–187.

33. Another unevenly distributed source of union leverage is the ability to benefit from government regulations. The airline and broadcasting industries were once regulated in a way that virtually guaranteed fat monopoly profits; management in those industries could then afford to grant unions plush wage and benefit packages. When these industries were deregulated and began to compete in the marketplace, unionized airline and broadcast workers were forced into a series of dramatic "givebacks" that continue to this day.

34. See Gregg Easterbrook, "Voting for Unemployment," *The Atlantic,* May 1983, 32–33, for a discussion of pattern bargaining.

35. See Robert M. Kaus, "The Trouble with Unions," *Harper's,* June 1983, 25–27.

36. See Kuttner, "The Declining Middle," 70.

37. The "solidarity wage" might seem, on its face, a foolhardy attempt to fight capitalism. But as originally conceived, the Swedish policy was designed only to force employers to pay equal wages for equal work. All unskilled workers, for example, would make the same wage. The effect, the LO reasoned, wouldn't be to fight the market; it would be to achieve free market results faster. Firms that couldn't use unskilled labor productively would not be able to afford to pay the equalized wage. They'd go bankrupt, and unskilled workers would shift to more productive firms. See Berndt Ohman, "A Note on the 'Solidarity Wage Policy' of the Swedish Labor Movement," *Swedish Journal of Economics 1969,* 198–205.

In this equal-pay-for-equal-work sense, Swedish-style unionism might well succeed at eliminating pay disparities—especially disparities of the sort created by American-style unionism! If both garment workers and autoworkers are part of one union, instead of the former making $6 an hour and the latter $18 an hour, the union might negotiate to have each make $12 an hour. Of course, if it simply assured equal pay for equal work, a solidarity wage might still do little to curtail income inequality. It would leave untouched inequality generated by different skill levels (and by the Hollywood Effect).

By the 1960s, Swedish unions shifted to a more money-egalitarian concept of "solidarity": wages would be equalized between workers doing different types of work. This really was an attempt to fight capitalism, at least capitalism's natural tendency to reward higher productivity with higher pay. See Robert J. Flanagan, "Efficiency and Equality in Labor Markets," in *The Swedish Economy,* 149–150.

38. For white-collar workers, "drift" constituted between 45 and 61 percent of earnings increases from 1982 to 1984. See Flanagan, "Efficiency and Equality," 167, 140, 151–153. See also Erik Lundberg, "The Rise and Fall of the Swedish Model," *Journal of Economic Literature* 23 (March 1985): 23; and Kuttner, *Economic Illusion,* 156.

To the extent a solidarity policy did succeed in equalizing wages, free market theory would say it could only come at a cost in efficiency—as workers decide it's not worth their while to acquire new skills. For evidence of concern that this in fact happened, see Marquis Childs, *Sweden: The Middle Way on Trial* (New Haven: Yale University Press, 1980), 87; Lundberg, "Rise and Fall," 25; and Glenn Frankel

"Swedish-Made Economic Model May be Running on Empty," *Washington Post,* 22 March 1990, A1–A26.

39. See Lennart Jonsson and Claes-Henric Siven, *Why Wage Differentials?* Svenska Arbetsgivare Foremingen, Stockholm, 1986, 12; Flanagan, "Efficiency and Equality," 139; Lundberg, "Rise and Fall," 3–4.

40. See Jonsson and Siven, *Why Wage Differentials?* 18. A look at comparative income statistics reinforces the impression that any equalizing effects of "solidarity" were concentrated in the lower rungs of the Swedish income ladder. In 1979, after decades of "solidarity," the top quintile of Swedes made about 1.7 times the national average, before taxes and transfers. In the same year, the top quintile of Americans made about 1.9 times the national average. Not a huge difference. See charts for pre-tax, pre-transfer income ("factor income") in Michael O'Higgins, Gunther Schmaus, and Geoffrey Stephenson, "Income Distribution and Redistribution: A Microdata Analysis for Seven Countries," *Poverty, Inequality and Income Distribution in Comparative Perspective: The Luxembourg Income Study (LIS),* ed. Timothy M. Smeeding, Michael O'Higgins, and Lee Rainwater (Washington, D.C.: Urban Institute Press, 1990), 41. See also Flanagan, "Efficiency and Equity," 139–140, 150. Sweden does appear to have a relatively poorer top *one* percent than we do. But that's precisely the rarefied territory where the effect of unionism is presumably the weakest.

Perversely, to the extent it worked, the "solidarity wage" probably increased the incomes of those who owned Sweden's most profitable business enterprises—they paid less for their most skilled blue collar workers. In addition, their unskilled workers (under the equal work/equal pay doctrine) saw their income restrained to match that of workers in less profitable firms. Indeed, the LO eventually charged that some capitalists were earning what the union called "excess profits." The "wages policy of solidarity," the LO noted tactfully, had "awkward consequences for income distribution." See Childs, *Sweden: The Middle Way on Trial,* 60–61.

41. Source: Sten Johansson, Director-General, Statistiska Centralbyran, Sweden.

42. On the gradual assertion of independent, skill-based power by Sweden's unionized white collar workers, see Flanagan, "Efficiency and Equality," 162–163, Lundberg, "Rise and Fall," 34.

43. See Medoff and Freeman, *What Do Unions Do?* 87 et seq.

44. One of the Writers Guild's first acts, in the middle of the Depression, was to petition President Roosevelt to lift a proposed NRA code provision that would have capped salaries at $100,000 a year. See Nancy Lynn Schwartz, *The Hollywood Writer's Wars* (New York: McGraw-Hill, 1982), 29. More recently, in 1985, when the AFL-CIO proposed unionization of doctors and engineers along Hollywood lines, it made it clear that such unions would only "negotiate minimum guarantees that will serve as a floor for individual bargaining." See Mickey Kaus, "A Union for Yuppies," *The New Republic,* 3 June 1985, 14–16.

45. See Tamar Lewin, "Big Gain in Nursing Students Lifts Hopes Amid a Shortage," *New York Times,* 28 December 1990, A1.

46. *A note on industrial revivalism:* There's also a practical objection to the Union Cure. Even if an 80 percent unionized society *were* more desirable than our current 18 percent unionized society, in order to get to that promised land we'd have to go

through the wilderness of 30, 40, and 50 percent unionism. There we would get to enjoy in full all the negative aspects of American-style collective bargaining—including idiotic work rules and inflationary industry-by-industry wage hikes—without the discipline imposed by all-encompassing Swedish-style organizations. If we never made it to 80 percent, we'd be worse off than if we'd never tried. See Mancur Olson, *The Rise and Decline of Nations* (New Haven: Yale University Press, 1982), 90–92; Robert M. Kaus, "The Trouble with Unions."

But that raises an interesting point. If, in fact, the unproductive habits of American labor and management bear a good deal of blame for our industrial decline, perhaps there is a fairly simple solution to the problem of disappearing unskilled middle-class jobs. Put bluntly, American management and American labor have been so stupid for so long that maybe the Reichian scenario—in which "routine production" jobs go overseas—didn't have to happen. Maybe if we just stopped being stupid we could regain our former industrial position. Reviving American industries, according to this theory, would serve Money Liberalism by creating "good jobs at good wages" for the unskilled as well as the skilled.

Let's tactfully label this revivalist strategy "Beat Japan," in honor of our most formidable industrial rival. It has tremendous political appeal, forming the respectable half of the Democrats' familiar "economic nationalism" pitch. Look at Japan, the revivalists might say. Doesn't its very success show that well-paid, unskilled industrial jobs can be retained even in a prosperous nation? After all, Japanese autoworkers are now actually paid as much or more than American autoworkers. Yet Japan's auto industry isn't crumbling. It's thriving. If Japan can do it, why can't America?

There's something to this. Any industry that spent billions to produce the Chevy Celebrity could obviously do better. But in the long run it's hard to see how we're going to escape the Reichian dilemma, which is not that our industries will disappear, but that they will *either* disappear *or* demand ever more skill on the part of even low-level workers.

The experience of industrial rivals like Germany and Japan confirms more than it confounds this long-term trend, as Michael Piore and Charles Sabel have pointed out. For example, both Germany and Japan have moved out of basic steel into the production of "specialty" steel—fancy alloys, difficult shapes, and small-batch orders requiring quick turnaround. Basic steel production has moved to Korea, Brazil, and other lower-wage countries. It's because "specialty" steel production is difficult that the Third World hasn't gotten to it yet. But because it's difficult, West German steelworkers cannot be unskilled. Instead, they are "given basic courses in metallurgy and plant operation and are briefly apprenticed in all the mill's operating units before they receive intensive theoretical and practical instruction in the area in which they will eventually work. Workers trained in this way are formally regarded as craftsmen, rather than semiskilled production workers" (Piore and Sabel, *The Second Industrial Divide,* 210).

In Japan, even auto production work is only partly unskilled. Yes, some Nissan and Toyota workers do traditional assembly-line jobs. But the Japanese auto giants also depend on a network of small suppliers, which are no longer the unskilled sweatshops they're reputed to be. These suppliers must produce many small batches of various products to keep up with "just-in-time" deliveries. Significantly, they have abandoned traditional assembly lines for something called "U-line" production, in which a variety of machines are arrayed in a U shape around as few as one worker. This enables the worker to shift quickly between producing, say, a taillight for a Toyota Camry and one for a Toyota Celica. It also means the worker must know how to operate all the various machines and how to rejigger them to produce each new part. That doesn't make U-line workers skilled craftsmen, but increasingly they're closer to skilled craftsmen than they are to mere bolt-tighteners. See Masayoshi Ikeda, Shoichiro Sei, and Toshihiro Nishiguchi, "U-Line Auto Parts Production," October 1988 paper for the International Motor Vehicle Program Research Affiliates' Meeting at MIT.

Even so, actual car production is starting to leave Japan. While the Japanese themselves are concentrating on design and on the construction of higher-value items like engines and complex luxury cars (Lexus, Infiniti), the actual assembly of mass-market cars is increasingly farmed out to other, lower-wage countries.

Even if GM president Roger Smith had been a genius, he couldn't have figured out a way to build a minicar cheaper than the Koreans or Mexicans *while employing the traditional number of unskilled Americans*. With autos, as with steel, as with virtually all manufacturing, efficiency eventually means more engineers, more robots, fewer people turning wrenches and more supervising the "process" from computer terminals—in short, skilled workers. Winning the international industrial competition won't restore the high-pay/low-skilled work force structure of the good old days. We can't win without transforming that structure.

47. See Carlos H. Waisman, *Reversal of Development in Argentina: Postwar Counterrevolutionary Policies and Their Structural Consequences* (Princeton, N.J.: Princeton University Press, 1987), 5–7, 124–126.

I'm distinguishing here between two types of trade policies that are called "protectionist." One type—threatening to close our markets until other countries open theirs—is in theory designed to produce free trade eventually. The other, more disreputable form of protectionism seeks to permanently shield existing industries from their fate under the free world market. The point is that, if we want to stop the inegalitarian pay-for-skills income trend, only the second type of protectionism—*real* protectionism—will do. To prevent the global market's effect of rewarding skills, trade barriers would have to be used to avoid going where the market would go.

48. The bargain would be all the worse for social-egalitarians because the unskilled workers protectionism protected might be seen as the culprits in any economic decline.

49. Robert Reich, *The Next American Frontier* (New York: Times Books, 1983), 246.

50. Piore and Sabel, *The Second Industrial Divide.* Piore and Sabel's key examples are "the technologically sophisticated, highly flexible firms in central and northwestern Italy," producing specialty textiles, chemicals, ceramics, even steel and robots. Reich offers his own (not very long) list in *Next American Frontier*, 257.

Many of these firms use computerized general-purpose machines, such as numerically controlled machine tools. Instead of having to be rebuilt in order to turn out a new product, the machines only need to be reprogrammed. But, according to Piore and Sabel, computers aren't the essential element of these organizations. Their structure derives not from technology but from the need to service rapidly changing markets for specialized goods produced in small batches. See *Second Industrial Divide,* 258–263; Reich, *Next American Frontier,* 246.

One reason why flexibility might be highly valued is that mass-produced goods become subject to fast-changing consumer fashions. This is most obvious in the case of textiles. As recounted by Piore and Sabel, the Italian textile industry couldn't compete with cheap mass produced woolens from Eastern Europe. Its response was to create "fantasy fabrics" made of reconstituted threads, with constantly changing designs. Consumers were apparently willing to pay a bit more to get a more stylishly specialized product. (Piore and Sabel, *Second Industrial Divide,* 214.)

51. Shoshana Zuboff, *In the Age of the Smart Machine: The Future of Work and Power* (New York: Basic Books, 1988). At the automated pulp plants Zuboff studies, threatened managers fight back, trying to create jobs for themselves by denying data and authority to lower level operators. See ibid., 278. But it's clear from Zuboff's account that the managers are doomed.

52. See Reich, *Next American Frontier,* 134–135. The whole idea is that the U.S. will have the workers who know how to alter production processes rapidly enough to keep up with changing consumer desires (Piore and Sabel) or to advance the technological state of the art (Zuboff). What if the Koreans develop those skills first? In his most recent book, Reich seems to concede that much flexible-production work will eventually move overseas. (See Reich, *The Work of Nations,* 225–249, especially 248.).

53. Piore and Sabel: "Production workers must be so broadly skilled that they can shift rapidly from one job to another; even more important, they must be able to collaborate with designers to solve the problems that inevitably arise in execution." (*Second Industrial Divide,* 273.)

54. After operating the plant, the workers themselves came to believe that "in the future all factory workers would be college graduates." See Zuboff, *Smart Machine,* 399.

55. Zuboff talks airily of how the informated organization will be "post-hierarchical," staffed by "colleagues" and "co-learners," in which "power is a roving force that comes to rest as dictated by function and need" (See Zuboff, *Smart Machine,* 395). This seems utopian. It's hard to envision an economic enterprise, with owners whose money is at risk, in which "power is a roving force."

56. See Reich, *Next American Frontier,* 135. Judgment and initiative are of course exactly the sort of things that it is difficult to "train" into everyone. Zuboff's predictions—that each worker must be allowed to learn "as much as his or her talent will allow"—should not comfort egalitarians on this score. See *Smart Machine,* 394.

Reich appears to discount the Hollywood Effect on the grounds that in flexible firms individual "tasks are so interrelated" that individual contributions can't be measured separately—"success can be measured only in reference to the final collective result" (*Next American Frontier,* 135). But surely it is possible to assess the contribution of individuals to a collective enterprise.

57. See Zuboff, *Smart Machine,* 274–277, 282.

58. Ibid., 282. Rather than eliminating middle managers, the eventual effect would be to eliminate the unskilled people at the base of the job pyramid, giving skilled manager-types direct hands-on duties at the "data interface."

59. Telephone interview, 1989.

60. See Zuboff, *Smart Machine,* 248–249, and Harrison and Bluestone, *The Great U-Turn,* 73. Piore and Sabel speculate that some communities and regions might succeed at being flexible while others fail. "Such a regime could resemble the old Bourbon kingdom of Naples, where an island of craftsmen, producing luxury goods for the court, was surrounded by a subproletarian sea of misery." Doesn't sound encouraging for money egalitarians. *The Second Industrial Divide,* 279.

61. Zuboff, *Smart Machine,* 285.

62. Ibid., 407–408.

63. Ibid., 408–409. In a passage that reads as if it might have been an outtake from *Player Piano,* Zuboff tells of a "subtle sifting process" within the labor force: "People began to believe that the best and the brightest were those who excelled at the data interface, while others gravitated (or were nudged) toward maintenance work."

64. Ibid., 411; see also 394.

65. Even complete worker-ownership doesn't necessarily alter the day-to-day authority of managers, though it might. Worker-owners often wind up hiring managers, who then run things in fairly traditional fashion.

There are many reasons, other than money-egalitarianism, to encourage worker-ownership and profit-sharing. Most obviously, there is the likelihood that workers are simply more creative, energetic, and responsible when they have a stake in their employer's success—a productivity bonus. Economist Martin Weitzman has also argued that when firms pay wages that vary with revenues or profits, they have an incentive to hire more workers and a disincentive to lay them off. An economy of such firms would have fuller employment and lower inflation, even if profit-sharing didn't boost productivity. But Weitzman's salutary macroeconomic effects require profit-sharing that falls *short* of full worker-ownership. The reason is that worker-owners might restrict hiring to avoid having to give new workers a share of the profit "pot." See *The Share Economy: Conquering Stagflation* (Cambridge, Mass.: Harvard University Press, 1984), 110, 132–133.

For purposes of this discussion, by profit-sharing I refer to any enterprise in which the profit-sharing formula at least potentially offers more money to workers than a straight wage. If the formula is somehow rigged so workers can never earn more than under a straight-wage system, then there is no potential for reducing money inequality. But most profit sharing schemes apparently have raised total compensation. See Daniel J. B. Mitchell, David Lewin, and Edward E. Lawler III, "Alternative Pay Systems, Firm Performance, and Productivity," in *Paying for Productivity,* ed. Alan S. Blinder (Washington, D.C.: Brookings, 1990). Whether productivity has risen enough to pay for that increased compensation is a closer question. See Alan S. Blinder's introduction to ibid., 4. For money equality, it may not matter whether the workers get more by increasing productivity or simply by acquiring the rights to profit-shares previously enjoyed by non-employee owners. In practice, though, unless there are productivity gains neither profit-sharing nor worker-ownership is likely to spread.

66. Even mild forms of profit-sharing effectively distribute *some* of the owners' right to residual revenues—in exchange for what is hoped to be the assumption by employees of an owner's attitude.

67. See Flanagan, "Efficiency and Equality," 164; Childs, *Sweden: The Middle Way on Trial*, 58–65, Lundberg, "Rise and Fall," 30. Swedish unions preferred the "Meidner Plan," in which big "wage-earners' funds" collected profits from all firms, and in which all workers—whether employed by "winning" or "losing" firms—participated.

The money inequality created when some worker-owned firms succeed and others fail is likely to be relatively benign, of course (when compared with the skill-based rewards of, say, Zuboff's "intellective" hierarchy). Unskilled workers will share in successes and skilled workers will share in the failures.

68. See David I. Levine and Laura D'Andrea Tyson, "Participation, Productivity, and the Firm's Environment," in *Paying for Productivity*, 224, and sources cited therein. See also Weitzman, *Share Economy*, 74–75.

69. Levine and Tyson, "Participation, Productivity, and the Firm's Environment," 222–230.

70. Ibid., 218, 228.

71. See Joanne S. Lublin, "Japanese Are Doing More Job Hopping," *Wall Street Journal*, 18 November 1991, B1; but see also John Burgess, "Big Bucks for Executives Finds Some Favor Abroad," *Washington Post*, 20 October 1991, H1 (noting that Europe is joining the trend toward huge pay differentials at the top, while Japan still "remains impervious").

72. See Weitzman, *Share Economy*, 133, especially footnote 4 and sources cited therein.

73. It's also possible that worker-ownership is a productive but unstable form of management, because transferring ownership while maintaining a worker-owned structure is difficult. For example, the employee-owners of a successful company may be best able to realize the full market value of their stock by selling the company to an individual entrepreneur.

74. A 14 September 1990 memo from the Machinist's International President, George J. Kourpias, pledges to "*vigorously resist* any team concept programs" because they "undermine our collective bargaining rights" [emphasis in original]. Copy in author's files. Companies that initiate participation schemes have actually been charged with violating the National Labor Relations Act. See "Precedent Pending: Employee Involvement Programs Face Legal Hurdles," *Wall Street Journal*, 15 October 1991, A1.

Chapter 6
The Public Sphere

1. You could even construct a syllogism, just as elementary and powerful as Herrnstein's:

1. If success requires luck, and
2. If earnings and prestige depend on success;
3. Then social standing (which reflects earnings and prestige) will be based to some extent on luck; and

4. Then social standing will never be entirely deserved.

2. It's not enough, remember, to attract so many hundred thousand warm bodies. The recruits must have the talent and skill necessary to operate complicated weapons.

Figures on the size of the 18 to 21 male cohort are from Richard Halloran, "High School Graduates Revive Volunteer Force," *New York Times*, 11 October 1987, 42. The pool of young men (and women) will begin to increase in size again after the middle of the decade, though it will continue to decline as a percentage of the total population. See Charles Moskos, *A Call to Civic Service* (New York: Free Press, 1988), 146.

3. See Michael Walzer, *Spheres of Justice* (New York: Basic Books, 1983), 168–169. If a risk of death is to be distributed, why not do it "progressively"—i.e., draft the richest first, or in a disproportionate ratio, just as we tax the rich disproportionately? That we find this idea vaguely abhorrent demonstrates, I think, that with war we enter a qualitatively different, non-money domain. We are talking about lives, and the sacrifice of any life (unlike the sacrifice of the rich man's marginal dollar) has an equal weight. Where lives are what's "taxed," equality of sacrifice would seem to require strict proportionality.

4. See Walter Isaacson, *Kissinger: A Biography* (New York: Simon & Schuster, 1992), Chapter 3; also David Landau, *Kissinger: The Uses of Power* (New York: Crowell, 1972), 18–21.

5. Due to the post–Cold War reduction in military forces, the figure for 1995 is lower than for 1991, when the armed forces needed 15 percent of draft-age men. During the Vietnam War, by comparison, the need was for 40 percent. These figures were compiled by Prof. Charles Moskos of Northwestern University in December 1991. They include all draft-age men, whether or not they meet the physical, mental and moral qualifications for service. They take into account the manpower needs of the reserves, national guard, and the officer corps, and assume that women will continue to serve in their current proportions.

6. Kemp is quoted in Timothy Noah, "We Need You: National Service, An Idea Whose Time Has Come," *Washington Monthly*, November 1986, 41.

7. On Hart's views, see Moskos, *Civic Service*, 120, and Randall Rothenberg, *The Neoliberals* (New York: Simon & Schuster, 1984), 210. For a general overview of attempts to pass national service legislation, see Moskos, *Civic Service*, 118–123. For Buckley's plan, see his book, *Gratitude* (New York: Random House, 1990).

8. Buckley speaks of lifting young people out of the "trough of self-concern" (ibid., 161).

9. It's legitimate to ask why a national service should focus on the young. Sen. Bob Kerrey, for one, caricatures NS advocates as adults who are saying, "we don't care enough about our country, and our solution is instead of requiring adults to serve more, we're going to require our kids to serve more." Certainly any national service program should allow adults who want to serve to do so. Even in a voluntary program, though, most participants would be young people, in part because the low-earning years between high school and college graduation are the least economically costly time for an individual to serve.

There are four other good reasons for a mandatory program to focus on youth.

First, young people are presumably more malleable and therefore susceptible to the egalitarian lesson national service would teach. Second, we want them to carry that lesson through their lives, not learn it only when they're middle-aged. Third, if Americans of all ages were suddenly required to serve, nobody would know what to do with them all, and the cost in lost work to the economy would be staggering. Fourth, it would be very difficult to administer a mandatory program that allowed people to postpone service until later in life. Are we really going to take a 45-year-old refrigerator repairman with a mortgage and five kids and *make* him serve for a year, on pain of some huge fine?

For Kerrey's objections, see Albert R. Hunt, "National Service—On the Whole, Not a Bad Idea," *Wall Street Journal.* 25 July 1990, A12.

10. As Timothy Noah reports, even when voluntary service programs aren't explicitly designed as jobs programs for the poor, that is what most of them quickly turn into. The rich, apparently, don't yet see service as an obligation; the poor, meanwhile, need the work. See Noah, "We Need You," 35; Moskos, *Civic Service.* 163. In the much-admired California Conservation Corps, only 40 percent of the participants have high-school diplomas, and only a third of that 40 percent were on an "academic" as opposed to a "vocational" track. See Moskos, *Civic Service*, 72–73, 65.

11. Ibid., 162.

12. Richard Danzig and Peter Szanton, *National Service: What Would It Mean?* (Lexington, Mass.: D.C. Heath, 1986), 223–264. Buckley and Moskos hold out the hope that non-money incentives—idealism, status pressure to fulfill what is perceived as a moral obligation—might move the affluent to join a voluntary national service. Civic Liberals shouldn't dismiss this possibility out of hand. In a 1973 book, *Four Reforms,* Buckley proposed an ingenious, non-governmental way to enhance the attractions of service for the rich (see *Gratitude.* 109):

> I envision a statement by the trustees of the ten top-rated private colleges and universities in the United States in which it is given as common policy that beginning in the fall semester of 1976 ... no one accepted into the freshman class will be matriculated until after he has passed one year in public service.

That would get the attention of ambitious parents in all the right zip codes. Coupled with enough exhortation from opinion leaders, with the example of taste-models like Buckley, and maybe a year of service by Madonna or Tom Cruise, it might be enough to draw a reasonable cross section of the monied into voluntary service. But Buckley's goal of 80 percent participation seems far too high for a voluntary system to sustain.

13. Buckley suggests that those who refuse to serve might lose their driver's licenses (see *Gratitude,* 144–145). De-licensing has become a popular device for influencing the young (for instance, in West Virginia and Arkansas you lose your license if you drop out of school). It seems to me too cute a solution, at least for national service. If we want the program to be mandatory we should probably have the guts to be explicit about it.

14. See Moskos, *Civic Service,* 146. If the plan were broadened to allow service by

older Americans, of course, even more people would wind up participating at any one time.

15. See U.S. Senate Special Committee on Aging, *Developments in Aging: 1987*, vol. 3: *The Long-Term Care Challenge*, 110th Cong., 2d sess., S. Rept. 100–291, 1988, 29; Buckley, *Gratitude*, 97; Moskos, *Civic Service*, 149–151; see also Danzig and Szanton, *National Service*, 24–28.

16. Buckley argues explicitly that it is more important to demonstrate an "attempt of requital" than to provide services. The "redemption of Scrooge," he says, "was more important, in *A Christmas Carol*, than the stuffed goose." This perspective has its pitfalls, however, because it tempts national service advocates to approve projects of marginal significance. Buckley suggests "anti-litter campaigns," and raising "money for charities through walk-a-thons." That is close to makework. See *Gratitude*, 47, 99.

17. Nursing-home care is peculiarly appropriate for national service because the service being provided in a sense requires a negation of the market. What many of the bedridden elderly need are friends, and friends are something the market can't provide, because friendship can't be bought. Perhaps it can't be drafted either. But a national service draftee who *chooses* nursing-care work seems more likely to be a sincere companion than someone who is just doing it for the money. (This point is suggested by Buckley in *Gratitude*, 37.)

18. See Danzig and Szanton, *National Service*, 24–28, cited in Buckley, *Gratitude*, 102.

19. See Michael Kinsley, "Sam Nunn Wants You," *The New Republic*, 6 June 1988, 50; also Democratic Leadership Council, *Citizenship and National Service* (Washington, D.C., May 1988), 32, 50.

20. The DLC would create a "Corporation for National Service" which would hand out funds to "a grass roots network of community service projects," including those run by nonprofit groups. See *Citizenship and National Service*, 10, 42, 50. See also Moskos, *Civic Service*, 120, describing a similar mid-1980s plan from Rep. Leon Panetta.

21. Some projects suggested by Buckley, such as fundraising for art museums, would seem to fall into this category. (See *Gratitude*, 98–100.) Many charities may not have enough experience at training kids for useful work. See comments by Walter Oi in Williamson M. Evers, ed., *National Service: Pro and Con* (Stanford: Hoover Institution Press, 1990), 221.

22. Restricting the list of jobs could also avoid overlap with the separate, guaranteed-jobs program that (I'll argue in Chapter 8) is the only way to break the culture of the "underclass." Conceivably, the two programs could be combined. But it's probably better to keep them distinct. The idea of a guaranteed "last resort" job is that it's a job in which you get paid for work performed. It's the first step into the labor market, not an attempt to "ask what you can do for your country." A public-service ethos might undermine that understanding.

23. Two other ways to combine military and civilian service suggest themselves. Neither seems preferable to the approach recommended in the text:

A draft-powered system. Under this scheme, if his (or her) draft number were called, a teenager could choose to perform a year's civilian service instead of two years of military service. Again, in order to make the longer military tour of duty appealing, the pay for military service would have to be higher. The government would simply keep drafting people by lot until enough chose the military option to satisfy the Pentagon's manpower needs. If the military needed 10 percent of an age cohort it might have to run through 50 percent of them to get its share—in the process pushing 40 percent into civilian service. That would generate a large civilian service corps, drawn from all classes. But service still wouldn't be universal.

Preemptive service. To attract even broader participation, the government might let students put themselves at the end of the draft queue by preemptively performing service before, say, their twentieth birthday. This preemptive service would have to be more appealing—shorter terms or better pay—than any civilian service offered as an option for those who waited to see if they were drafted. (This is similar to a 1979 proposal of Rep. Paul McCloskey's. See the discussion in Danzig and Szanton, National Service, 132–133; Moskos, Civic Service, 121.) The problem with preemptive service is that it forces young Americans to play a sort of game with their lives, deciding whether to serve or not on the basis of whether they think they will be drafted. Some kids would still "luck out" and not serve at all.

24. Of course, the armed forces would also accept volunteers, and these would probably be disproportionately poor (even if the pay were low). That much class division seems unavoidable.

Note that this scheme could accommodate either a military draft that included women or a draft restricted to men. In either case, all citizens, of both sexes, would serve in some capacity.

25. Epstein is quoted in James Fallows, *More Like Us* (Boston: Houghton Mifflin, 1989), 176.

26. Nick Salvatore, *Eugene V. Debs: Citizen and Socialist* (Urbana: University of Illinois Press, 1982), 148, 154.

27. That rule is established in the case of Baker v. Carr, 369 U.S. 186 (1962). Our Constitution's original sin—the malapportioned Senate—stands as the major exception to this rule.

28. On Boies Penrose, see Walter Shapiro, "A House Full of Millionaires," *Harper's,* July 1982, 48. The practice of accepting such "honoraria" proved so embarrassing to Congress that it was abolished, though up to $2,000 per speech may still be given to "charities" designated by Congressmen.

29. Elizabeth Drew, *Politics and Money: The New Road to Corruption* (New York: Macmillan, 1983), 64.

30. The key Supreme Court case is Buckley v. Valeo, 424 U.S. 1 (1976).

The Madisonian strategy of playing factions off against each other is a lot less promising when applied to campaign spending than when applied to voting. Factions start out with equal numbers of votes per citizen, but they don't start out with equal numbers of dollars. When it comes to financing elections, the Madisonian approach must depend, uncomfortably, on a theory of "virtual representation"—the hope that for every point of view, for every class and interest group, there will be *somebody* with enough money to field a representative candidate.

31. And Shapiro was told he could profitably spend hundreds of thousands of dollars more. See "House Full of Millionaires," 49.

32. Primary and general elections count separately for purposes of the $1,000 limitation, so in most campaigns an individual can give a candidate a maximum of $2,000. Individuals are also limited to $25,000 in total contributions to all candidates in any one calendar year.

33. An individual can give $5,000 a year to a PAC, and a PAC can give each candidate $5,000 per election. Unlike individuals, PACs are not subject to a limit on the amount they can contribute to all candidates put together. See generally William T. Mayton, "⅄ PACs Americana," *Washington Monthly,* January 1980, 54–57; Brooks J "Electoral Detox," *The American Prospect* 7 (Fall 1991): 37–48.

Washington wisdom holds that no PAC can "buy" a candidate for a $5,000 contribution. But lobbyists such as Washington lawyer Tommy Boggs, who influence dozens of PACs, may be able to make a substantial down payment. Of course, the arm-twisting often runs in the other direction—politicians extorting money from lobbyists upon the unstated threat of hurting their clients. ("Nice little industry you've got there ...") This introduces a further distorting effect on the one-man one-vote principle, because politicians focus their attention on laws that could help or hurt businesses from whom money can then be extorted. These are the "juice bills" (as California legislators call them).

34. Under the Buckley v. Valeo ruling, a candidate may spend unlimited amounts of both his own money *and* money contributed by others (though the latter are subject to the $1,000-per-person limit). The other major constitutional loophole in campaign spending restrictions involves so-called "independent expenditures." The Court ruled the First Amendment prohibits limiting the amount anyone can spend on political advertisements for or against a candidate, as long as the spending is "independent" of any campaign.

35. The major blemish in this generally happy picture is "soft money," money ostensibly given to state party organizations for general get-out-the-vote campaigns and the like. There are now no federal limits on this sort of donation, a loophole that needs to be closed. See Jackson, "Electoral Detox," 46.

36. The amount could vary with the cost of campaigning in each district.

37. Robert Samuelson, in an otherwise dispositive critique of every campaign reform ever proposed, claims that with public financing "incumbents would become more obsessed—if that is possible—with electioneering as opposed to legislating." But this argument stabs itself to death in mid-sentence. How, indeed, could politicians become more obsessed with their own reelections? Samuelson's complaint is reminiscent of John J. McCloy's argument against bombing the concentration camps in World War II because it "might provoke even more vindictive acts by the Germans" against the Jews. Nor, once the need to raise money was eliminated, would "electioneering" necessarily be bad for social equality. It's another name for trying to win votes which, unlike dollars, are equally distributed. See Samuelson, "The Campaign Reform Failure," *The New Republic,* 5 September 1983, 34.

38. Public financing wouldn't necessarily match the early "seed" contributions dollar-for-dollar. But once the $50,000 threshold was reached, the public subsidy might match private contributions of $1,000 or less, up to, say, a spending limit of $250,000 for a typical congressional primary.

In 1991 both the House and Senate actually passed campaign reform bills, but the bills differed, and were threatened with a presidential veto. As this book goes to press their fate is uncertain.

The idea of relaxing contribution limits for "seed money" is in Norman Ornstein, "Campaign Reform: Breaking the Deadlock," *Washington Post,* 28 July 1989, A25.

39. PACs would then be what they were before the ill-fated reforms of the early 1970s gave them life. (See Mayton, "Nixon's PACs Americana.") Currently, congressional reformers favor lowering the allowable contributions from a PAC to a candidate, and restricting the total a candidate could receive from all PACs put together. But the sums being talked about are still obscenely large—$200,000 in allowable PAC contributions for House races, up to $1.1 million for big-state Senate races.

40. The owners of radio and TV stations, who would lose billions in ad revenue under this plan, would oppose it. But broadcasters don't own the public airwaves (most of their licenses were not paid for), and cable systems are a public utility subject to regulation.

41. See Uwe Reinhardt, "West Germany's Health-Care and Health-Insurance System: Combining Access with Cost Control," report prepared for the United States Bipartisan Commission on Comprehensive Health Care, 30 August 1989, 6. See also 7, 34–35. The Germans call this the "principle of social solidarity." As Reinhardt notes, it embraces the idea that the healthy should subsidize the sick, not just the money-egalitarian idea that the rich should subsidize the poor. Ibid., 34. Reinhardt's report is reprinted, in slightly different form, in *A Call for Action: The Pepper Commission, Supplement to the Final Report* (Washington, D.C.: Government Printing Office, 1990), 3–17.

42. See Robert Kuttner, *The Economic Illusion* (Boston: Houghton Mifflin, 1984), 231. This argument for "universalism" is far weaker when applied to programs that simply send out checks rather than providing a service—a distinction discussed later in this chapter.

43. See *Background Material and Data on Programs within the Jurisdiction of the Committee on Ways and Means* (hereinafter referred to as the *Green Book*), 1991 edition, 1409. The 42 percent figure is for 1989.

44. Henry Aaron reports that excluding employer-financed health insurance from income and payroll taxes cost between $29.6 and $36.3 billion in 1991. Stuart Butler, author of the Heritage Foundation plan discussed below, puts the cost at $48 billion. See Henry Aaron, *Serious and Unstable Condition: Financing America's Health Care* (Washington, D.C.: Brookings, 1991), 66–67; Stuart M. Butler, "A Tax Reform Strategy to Deal With the Uninsured," *Journal of the American Medical Association* 265, no. 19 (15 May 1991): 2542.

45. On the number of uninsured: See Aaron, *Serious and Unstable Condition,* 75–76, and sources cited therein. See also Robert Pear, "34.7 Million Lack Health Insurance, Studies Say; Number Is Highest Since '65," *New York Times,* 19 December 1991, B17.

On qualifying for Medicare: There are two "parts" to Medicare coverage. "Part A" benefits cover hospital expenses. These benefits are free for Americans over 65 who qualify for Social Security or railroad retirement benefits. In essence, the Social

Security "work test" applies to this portion of Medicare. But Americans over age 65 who *don't* pass this work test can still obtain Part A insurance by paying a monthly premium, which was $177 a month as of 1 January 1991.

"Part B" benefits cover other medical expenses. Part B is voluntary and requires payment of a monthly premium. The premium is heavily subsidized, but Part B benefits are not work-tested. All Americans over 65 can get Part B coverage by paying the premium. See *1991 Green Book*, 129; U.S. Department of Health and Human Services, Social Security Handbook 1988 (Washington, D.C.: Social Security Administration Publication No. 05-10135), 418, 427.

46. Apart from emergency rooms, however, many hospitals historically have been split between "private" floors or wings, attended by the private physicians of the patients in them, and "public" areas attended by house staff. I am told this distinction is breaking down somewhat.

47. Medicare pays $30.63 for an office visit in New York. See Physician Payment Review Commission, *Physician Payment Under Medicaid*, No. 91-4, 29.

48. See Lynne Duke, "D.C. General Faces Financial Crisis as More Patients Cannot Pay," *Washington Post*, 11 February, 1990, A14. The cost of giving free services to uninsured patients is causing many urban emergency rooms to close down, which has the effect of concentrating the uninsured in those facilities that remain open.

49. See Aaron, *Serious and Unstable Condition*, 93.

50. "The Health System of the Unites States: Lessons for the Developing Countries," (unpublished; December 1990).

51. See Aaron, *Serious and Unstable Condition*, 80. These numbers are for 1987. The U.S. figure will rise to 14 percent in 1992, according to the Commerce Department and the Department of Health and Human Services.

52. The most prominent of the blue-ribbon panels was the U.S. Bipartisan Commission on Comprehensive Health Care, commonly known as the Pepper Commission, which recommended a mandatory employer-based plan in September 1990.

53. In practice some doctors are also employed by the government under a contract system. See "Surgery Needed," *The Economist*, 6 July 1991, 6.

54. Canadian doctors can choose to practice entirely outside the government system, but they must then opt completely out—they cannot charge some patients outside the system and accept the government's payment for other patients. Not many doctors take this route.

A Canada-style system has been proposed by Representatives Marty Russo and Fortney (Pete) Stark. See Aaron, *Serious and Unstable Condition*, 129; see also Theodore R. Marmor, Jerry L. Mashaw, and Philip L. Harvey, *America's Misunderstood Welfare State: Persistent Myths, Enduring Realities* (New York: Basic Books, 1990), 175–212.

55. See Uwe Reinhardt, "West Germany's Health Care and Health Insurance System," 22.

56. This was the approach suggested by President Bush during his 1988 campaign. See "Beyond Sound Bites," *Newsweek*, 17 October 1988, 27. For a variation, see Uwe Reinhardt, "Toward a Fail-Safe Health-Insurance System, *Wall Street Journal*, 11 January 1989, A16; see also David Ellwood, *Poor Support* (New York: Basic Books, 1988), 106–108, and sources cited therein. Another option is to simply ex-

tend Medicare to cover everybody. With Medicare costs escalating rapidly, this approach seems especially unpromising. See Rep. Edward R. Roybal, "The 'USHealth Act,'" *Journal of the American Medical Association* 265, no. 19 (15 May 1991): 2545–2548.

57. For the Heritage plan, see Stuart M. Butler, "A Tax Reform Strategy," 2542. Bush's initial 1992 plan, unlike Butler's, would not have ended the tax break for employee insurance benefits. It also would not make health insurance mandatory. But you couldn't get the tax credit unless you bought insurance.

58. See John B. Judis, "Cross of Blue," *The New Republic,* 19–26 August 1991, 19–21. Hawaii has implemented an employer-based plan. See Aaron, *Serious and Unstable Condition,* 122–124.

59. Bizarrely, the right-wing Heritage Foundation's scheme is more progressive than the Democrats pay-or-play plan. See Michael Kinsley, "The Right Cure," *The New Republic,* 29 July 1991, 4.

60. See Reinhardt, "West Germany's Health-Care and Health-Insurance System," 2, 19–24.

61. Canada's system does have a safety valve—namely the United States. If the waiting lists get too long north of the border, Canadians with enough money can always travel to private clinics in the U.S. If the U.S. switched to a Canada-style system, its citizens would not have such a convenient alternative. See Michael Walker, "Why Canada's Health Care System Is No Cure for America's Ills" (Washington, D.C.: Heritage Foundation, 13 November 1989), 11.

62. Aaron endorses an ingenious scheme that would start out as an employer-based system but, like a Transformer toy, could slowly turn into a Canada-style system. See Aaron, *Serious and Unstable Condition.* 151.

63. On the cost of expanding Medicaid, see John Holahan and Sheila Zedlewski, "Expanding Medicaid to Cover Uninsured Americans," *Health Affairs* 10, no. 1 (Spring 1991): 54. The cost in 1989 was a little over $1,000 per person for adults, a little under $1,000 for children.

64. This likelihood has led Uwe Reinhardt to suggest that we should consciously abandon "the myth that as an 'egalitarian' nation, we just cannot contemplate a two-tier health system." Since the affluent won't pay for a one-tier system, he argues, "The poor might be better served by a lean delivery system that offers them at least some kindness at a price American taxpayers judge affordable" (Uwe Reinhardt, "On the Economics of Being Kinder and Gentler," unpublished communication, December 1989). Obviously, from a Civic Liberal perspective, this is anathema. To the extent single-payer schemes like Canada's offer even affluent taxpayers an economic benefit in the form of lower medical costs, they may avoid Reinhardt's dilemma. See Kevin Grumbach et al., "Liberal Benefits, Conservative Spending: The Physicians for a National Health Program Proposal," *Journal of the American Medical Association* 265, no. 19 (15 May 1991): 2549–2554.

65. On the importance of technological advance in driving up costs, see Aaron, *Serious and Unstable Condition.* 48–49.

66. Walzer comes to this conclusion in *Spheres of Justice.* 86–91.

67. Another possibility is homemaker services (shopping, cleaning, cooking,

help with dressing) for the incapacitated elderly. Denmark has an elaborate program that serves both affluent and poor, according to Kuttner (see *Economic Illusion*, 254–256). The value of home care, as a social-egalitarian institution, is diminished because (unlike health care or day care) it must be delivered in relative isolation. But, as noted earlier, home care is one of the ideal occupations for a national service, itself a social-egalitarian institution for those who serve.

68. As with health care, the trick would be to make the common day-care services attractive enough for the upper middle class to use alongside the working class and poor. Unlike with health care, there is no hope of simply preventing the affluent from buying separate and better day-care services, because there is no analogous efficiency rationale for supplanting the market. Parents are perfectly capable of policing the quality and cost of day care. You don't need a government "monopsony" to bargain down day-care prices, and you don't need to ration Fisher-Price toys like CAT scanners. Anyway, parents wouldn't tolerate being prevented from sending their children to more expensive centers if that's what they thought best. Yet if communal centers are sufficiently attractive and subsidized, enough of the affluent will presumably take advantage of them.

Day-care centers could either be funded directly, or parents could be given vouchers that could be exchanged for day-care services. The important point is that either type of subsidy would be tied to the actual use of communal facilities.

69. See Kuttner, *Economic Illusion*. 231.

70. Likewise, getting a "family allowance" may involve simply ticking off a box on a tax form. For the contrary view, see Kuttner, *Economic Illusion*, 238–246.

71. Ibid., 231, 240. See generally 230–258. British philosopher T. H. Marshall called this "social citizenship," an unfortunate term because it conflates the provision of services and the provision of cash. As interpreted by Kuttner it also implies that benefits are provided as a matter of right, regardless of whether they are earned through work. The inegalitarian consequences of failing to make this second distinction are discussed in Chapter 9. See also E. J. Dionne, *Why Americans Hate Politics* (New York: Simon & Schuster, 1991), 353–354.

72. The idea that universal cash transfers promote social equality is, to be more precise, the second "sub-strategy" of Money Liberalism, the first being the general pursuit of more income equality (money-egalitarianism). See Chapter 3, note 2.

73. Certainly receipt of "universal" Social Security transfers didn't do much to breed empathy for the poor among the affluent elderly who demanded in 1989 that Congress cancel the "catastrophic care" benefits that helped mainly the non-affluent elderly. Indeed, in the 1980s Social Security transfers to the middle and upper classes reached record levels just as (according to Money Liberals) the middle and upper classes were for some reason callously turning their backs on the poor.

74. Gregg Easterbrook, "How Big Labor Brings Home the Bacon," *Washington Monthly*, February 1981, 40. In 1981, Easterbrook estimated that the Davis-Bacon Act cost the federal government $2 billion a year in construction wages alone. An indication of the continuing importance of Davis-Bacon to the Democratic party's labor supporters came in 1989, when Democrats on the Senate Labor and Resources Committee rejected Debra Bowland as administrator of the Labor Department's

Wage and Hour division because she had opposed Davis-Bacon as a Louisiana state official in the early 1980s. See Frank Swoboda, "Panel Kills Nomination for Labor's Wage Post," *Washington Post*, 2 November 1989, A25.

75. Unfortunately, union officials have a natural tendency to accept the tradeoff of higher pay for fewer jobs. They stand a better chance of being reelected if 90 percent of their members are happy and 10 percent are unemployed than if 100 percent of their members are annoyed at having to take a 10 percent pay cut. See Gregg Easterbrook, "Voting for Unemployment," *The Atlantic*, May 1983, 31–44.

76. Overall, between 1980 and 1987, city and state salaries grew by 59 percent, compared with only 35 percent in the private sector (Rich Thomas and Evan Thomas, "Where Did All the Money Go?" *Newsweek*, 1 July 1991, 25). Then, when revenues fell in the 1990–91 recession, states and cities cut back services even further.

77. *A note on civil service reform and privatization:* Civil service reform thus involves two distinct issues. First, within the civil service, it remains too difficult to fire incompetents. Jimmy Carter attempted to streamline the process, but was stymied, in part, by the Supreme Court's discovery that public employees had "property rights" in their jobs. But making it easier to fire incompetents is not a substitute for restoring a decent number of non-civil service, political appointments—people who can be simply kicked out of office by an electorate dissatisfied with the government's performance.

Charles Peters advocates a "50/50" plan: fill half the job vacancies with civil servants who enjoy a measure of job protection (and who could maintain an institutional memory and blow the whistle on abuses). Fill the other half with patronage workers who will be expected to leave if voters choose a new administration, and who therefore have a strong incentive to make the government work. The key is to have sufficient numbers of dismissable patronage employees at the bottom and middle levels of the bureaucracy, as well as at the top. A lazy clerk or a park worker who doesn't bother to trim the trees can degrade the public sphere as surely as an inept cabinet secretary. The Peters plan would require overturning another perverse line of Supreme Court decisions that says an elected official can fire only "policymaking and confidential employees," and even then only when the Court deems politics (that is, democracy) an "appropriate" consideration. See Elrod v. Burns, 427 U.S. 347 (1976), Branti v. Finkel, 445 U.S. 507 (1980), and Rutan v. Republican Party of Illinois, ——— U.S. ———, 110 S. Ct. 2729 (1990); Charles Peters, *How Washington Really Works* (Reading, Mass.: Addison-Wesley, 1980), 46–51; Robert M. Kaus, "Zbig for Life," *Washington Monthly*, June 1980, 25–32.

The rival of patronage, as a way to improve government performance, is privatization—the "contracting out" of government functions. This practice has increased dramatically in recent years. For an overview see *Privatization 1991* (Santa Monica, Calif.: Reason Foundation, 1991); see also David Osborne and Ted Gaebler, *Reinventing Government* (Reading, Mass.: Addison-Wesley, 1992). The privatization trend seems part of the worldwide advance of what Albert O. Hirschman calls the mechanisms of "exit" (generally associated with the market) against the mechanisms of "voice" (generally associated with politics). The "new paradigm" popularized by Bush aide James Pinkerton champions this shift. Advocates of the market once had to defend reliance on "exit" even in the private economic sphere. Now they've gone on offense, arguing that "voice" mechanisms are less effective than market competition even in the *public* sphere.

When decisions can be devolved to individuals who will bear the consequences—as in the case of school choice—"exit" may make a great deal of sense. The Canadian health care system, for example, gives patients a large measure of "choice" in deciding which doctors to consult. But it is not clear that most government institutions can be so easily decentralized. When it comes to building roads, can motorists be given a "choice" of rejecting badly built highways? In these instances "privatization" means competition by private contractors to please government officials. This sort of contracting-out may be a useful way around bloated, civil-servicized bureaucracies. But is it inherently more efficient than the bureaucracies would be if they were reformed? The very process of negotiating with outside parties imposes a layer of transaction costs. And the success of the process depends, ultimately, on the judgment of the government officials who award the contracts. How can we be sure they will perform well unless they are democratically accountable—that is, unless they can be dismissed when the voters choose a new government? Whatever the role of privatization, restoring the power of "voice" through patronage seems a prerequisite for efficiency. On "exit" versus "voice," see Hirschman's *Exit, Voice and Loyalty* (Cambridge, Mass.: Harvard University Press, 1970).

On civil service reform, see Robert M. Kaus, "How the Supreme Court Sabotaged Civil Service Reform," *Washington Monthly,* December 1978, 38–44; Leonard Reed, "Firing a Federal Employee: The Impossible Dream," reprinted in *Inside the System,* 4th edition, ed. Charles Peters and Nicholas Lemann (New York: Holt, Rinehart and Winston, 1979), 214–226.

Source for the number of patronage employees (in October 1991): White House Office of Presidential Personnel. Source for number of federal workers and number fired: Office of Personnel Management, Washington, D.C. The 2.2 million federal workers do not include employees of the postal service, of Congress, or of the court system. All told, in 1990 only 15,269 federal workers were discharged, a figure that includes (in addition to firings for poor performance) workers discharged for misconduct and for conduct prior to their appointment as well as workers terminated during their probationary period.

78. Good bars, Oldenburg says "serve to level their guests to a condition of social equality." See Ray Oldenburg, *The Great Good Place: Cafes, Coffee Shops, Community Centers. Beauty Parlors. General Stores, Bars, Hangouts and How They Get You Through the Day* (New York: Paragon House, 1989), 25, 42. According to Oldenburg, third places are "levelers" in part because they lay "emphasis on qualities not confined to status distinctions current in the society ... the charm and flavor of one's personality, irrespective of his or her station in life, is what counts" (ibid., 24). This is the same characteristic exhibited by a good, class-mixing school. See Peters, *Tilting at Windmills* (Reading, Mass.: Addison-Wesley, 1988), 25–26, quoted in Chapter 4 above.

79. Oldenburg, *Great Good Place,* 23.

ᐧ). Oldenburg makes this argument. (Ibid., 215.)

81. To the extent that some "third places," like sidewalk cafes, depend on civilized public plazas and thoroughfares, their decline may also be hastened by increases in crime.

82. In 1991, for example, the Chicago White Sox replaced old Comiskey Park with a new $135-million facility containing 90 skyboxes and suites, plus ticket attendants in tuxedos and a special glass-encased atrium for members of the "Stadium Club." See Isabel Wilkerson, "A 16–0 Day to Forget at New Comiskey Park," *New York Times,* 19 April 1991, 1. For a Civic Liberal account of the skybox phenomenon, see Jonathan S. Cohn, "Divided the Stands," *Washington Monthly.* December 1991, 31–34.

83. See Michael Goodwin, "TV Sports; Many Yank Viewers Shut Out," *New York Times,* 8 April 1987, B11; "Schumer Enters TV Fray," *New York Times,* 8 June 1987, C5.

84. On the value of the TV networks as a common institution, see Charles Paul Freund, "Save the Networks!" *Washington Post,* 28 July 1991, C1; also Robert J. Samuelson, "The Fragmenting of America," *Washington Post.* 7 August 1991, A15.

85. The deduction for "luxury skyboxes" was sharply restricted in 1988, but not completely eliminated. See Cohn, "Divided the Stands," 33. If eliminating the deduction failed to suppress the skyboxes, localities might simply ban (or heavily tax) them.

86. In 1980, when the Oakland Raiders decided to move to Los Angeles, the City of Oakland tried to seize the team by eminent domain. The California Supreme Court ruled this was arguably within the state's eminent domain statute, but a lower court threw the case out on other grounds. See City of Oakland v. Oakland Raiders, 32 Cal. 3d. 60 (1982); City of Oakland v. Oakland Raiders, 174 Cal. App. 3d 414 (1985).

87. Michael Walzer, "Dirty Work Should Be Shared," *Harper's.* December 1982, 26.

88. See Walzer, *Spheres of Justice,* 190, and sources cited therein. Walzer's discussion of vacations-versus-holidays ends on a relativistic note: "The right that requires protection is ... not to be excluded from the forms of rest central to one's own time and place, to enjoy vacations ... if vacations are central, to participate in the festivals that give shape to a common life wherever there is a common life" (ibid. 196). I am arguing for affirmatively expanding holidays and holiday rituals, where possible, as part of the general Civic Liberal strategy of *rebuilding* a common life.

Chapter 7
Welfare and the Underclass Threat

1. See sources cited earlier (Chapter 4, note 105 and accompanying text) on the class segregation that has accompanied suburbanization. For an investigation into the possible dynamics of this segregation, see John R. Logan and Mark Schneider, "Governmental Organization and City/Suburb Income Inequality, 1960–1970," *Urban Affairs Quarterly* 17, no. 3 (March 1982): 303–318.

2. "A class must be formed which has *radical chains*. ... a sphere of society which has a universal character because its sufferings are universal ... a sphere, finally, which cannot emancipate itself without emancipating itself from all the other spheres of society, without, therefore, emancipating all these other spheres.... This dissolution of society, as a particular class, is the *proletariat*." Karl Marx, "Contribution to the Critique of Hegel's Philosophy of Right, Introduction," in *Karl Marx: Early Writings,* ed. T. B. Bottomore (New York: McGraw-Hill, 1964).

3. For Wilson's discussion of labor force non-attachment as an identifying trait of the underclass, see his "Public Policy Research and *The Truly Disadvantaged*" in *The Urban Underclass,* ed. Christopher Jencks and Paul E. Peterson (Washington, D.C.: Brookings, 1991), 471–472, citing Martha Van Haitsma, "A Contextual Definition of the Underclass," *Focus* 12 (Spring–Summer): 27–31.

The basic texts on the underclass include Wilson's *The Truly Disadvantaged: The Inner City, the Underclass and Public Policy* (Chicago: University of Chicago Press, 1987); Ken Auletta, *The Underclass* (New York: Random House, 1982); Charles Murray, *Losing Ground: American Social Policy 1950–1980* (New York: Basic Books, 1984); The Staff of the *Chicago Tribune, The American Millstone: An Examination of the Nation's Permanent Underclass* (Chicago: Contemporary Books, 1986); Nicholas Lemann, "The Origins of the Underclass," *The Atlantic,* June 1986, 31–61 and July 1986, 54–68; Myron Magnet, "America's Underclass: What To Do?" *Fortune.* 11 May 1987, 130–150; Leon Dash, *When Children Want Children* (New York: William Morrow, 1989); Ze'ev Chafets, *Devil's Night: And Other True Tales of Detroit* (New York: Random House, 1990); Nicholas Lemann, *The Promised Land: The Great Black Migration and How It Changed America* (New York: Alfred A. Knopf, 1991); Alex Kotlowitz, *There Are No Children Here: The Story of Two Boys Growing Up in the Other America* (New York: Doubleday, 1991).

For a widely accepted behavior-based definition of the underclass, see Isabel V. Sawhill, "An Overview," *The Public Interest* 96 (Summer 1989): 3–15. See also David Ellwood, *Poor Support* (New York: Basic Books, 1988), 203–204.

4. On the other hand, this behavioral definition of "underclass neighborhood" is very strict. As devised by Erol Ricketts and Isabel Sawhill of the Urban Institute, it counts as "underclass" only neighborhoods that are one standard deviation above the mean in each of the four social problems listed.

The underclass statistics are in Ronald B. Mincy, "Underclass Variations by Race and Place: Have Large Cities Darkened Our Picture of the Underclass?" Urban Institute, Washington, D.C., February 1991. See Table 1 (extreme poverty neighborhoods) and Table 3A (neighborhoods with extreme social problems). See also Sawhill, "An Overview," 6. The 2.5 million figure is drawn from all census tracts, a much bigger sample than just the 100 largest cities (though it still omits the fifth of the U.S. population living in "untracted" rural areas).

5. When you look at the experiences of black Americans over time, instead of in a snapshot, the picture isn't nearly as tidy or cheerful. The Panel Study of Income Dynamics reports that of black children born from 1967 through 1969, 72 *percent* had spent at least a year on welfare (AFDC) by the time they reached age eighteen. The comparable figure for non-blacks was 16 percent. More than 40 percent of black children were on welfare for seven years or more, compared with 3.6 percent

of non-blacks. The picture does not improve for later cohorts of black children. Data are from Greg Duncan, Terry Adams, and Deborah Laren of the University of Michigan, contained in a Memorandum written to Bill Prosser of Senator Moynihan's office on 24 August 1990.

6. See Murray, "White Welfare, White Families, 'White Trash,' " *National Review,* 28 March 1986, 30, 31.

7. To say that the underclass is mainly black is not to explain *why* the underclass is mainly black. Certainly there are ample historical explanations—slavery and segregation being the most obvious. Some would add the sharecropping system in the South to the list. See Nicholas Lemann's "The Origins of the Underclass" and *The Promised Land;* and Leon Dash, *When Children Want Children,* 235–262. For criticism of the "sharecropper thesis" see David Whitman, "The Great Sharecropper Success Story," *The Public Interest* 104 (Summer 1991): 3–19; and Lemann's subsequent exchange with Whitman in *The Public Interest* 105 (Fall 1991): 107–122.

But it's also possible that the mere fact of race difference and race hostility allows the development of a minority "opposition culture," a culture that defines itself, in part, by its rejection of mainstream norms and attitudes. In this case, the danger is that succeeding in school, or learning the polite language of commerce, will come to be scorned as "acting white." See Marc Fisher, "Peers Inhibit Black Students, Study of D.C. Schools Finds," *Washington Post,* 14 March 1987, A1.

Whether some sort of race or ethnic hostility (and geographic segregation) is an indispensable element in creation of an underclass is an interesting question. I suspect that "cash welfare plus prejudice" is the worldwide underclass recipe.

8. Unpublished data tabulation from the Panel Study of Income Dynamics, Greg Duncan, University of Michigan. Fifty-five percent is the fraction of individuals averaging below-poverty incomes from 1977 to 1986 who were black. Sixty-three percent is the "non-white" share of those in families for whom AFDC plus the value of food stamps was at least 50 percent of total family income in at least eight years between 1975 and 1984. Virtually all "non-whites" in the PSID survey were blacks. See also Greg Duncan, *Years of Poverty, Years of Plenty* (Ann Arbor: Institute for Social Research, 1984), 49, 80, 52.

9. See Mincy, "Underclass Variations by Race and Place," 5, Table 1, and Table 3A. In 59 percent of the 880 "extreme social problem" neighborhoods, blacks constituted the majority of the population (ibid., Table 4A). Nineteen percent of the neighborhoods were majority-white. These are mainly isolated census tracts scattered around the industrial Northeast and Midwest, with a few clusters in the metropolitan areas of Philadelphia, Baltimore, and Columbus, Ohio.

The statistics are equally striking on the question of family breakup. Black illegitimacy ratios have always been many times higher than white ratios. Then, starting in 1965, about the same time the welfare rolls exploded, the black ratio began to rise dramatically, from its already high Moynihan-report level of about 25 percent to about 65 percent today. White illegitimacy rates have been rising too, but the white rate is still only about 19 percent. That Murray could find one poor town where the white rate reaches less than half the rate for *all* blacks only proves how vast the gap is. For the illegitimacy ratios from 1950 to 1980, see Murray, *Losing Ground,* 262.

10. Mincy's data show that two-thirds of the 880 "underclass neighborhoods" (defined by extreme social problems) were in metropolitan areas of over 1 million population. See Mincy, "Underclass Variations by Race and Place," Table 5.

11. See Kip Viscusi, "Market Incentives for Criminal Behavior," in *The Black Youth Employment Crisis*, ed. Richard B. Freeman and Harry J. Holzer (Chicago: University of Chicago Press, 1986), 343. One recent survey estimated that in the District of Columbia, on any given day in 1991, 42 percent of black men aged 18–35 were either in prison, in jail, on probation, on parole, awaiting trial, or being sought under an arrest warrant. See Keith Harriston, "Going to Jail Is 'Rite of Passage' for Many D.C. Men, Report Says," *Washington Post*, 18 April 1992, B3.

12. For example, Richard Freeman and Larry Katz looked at a survey of poor black and white Boston youths age 16–24. Even among these teenagers who are already poor, those who said someone in their home was getting welfare also reported having been jailed or probated at more than twice the rate of those who weren't in welfare families. (Unpublished data set compiled by Richard Freeman and Larry Katz from the Boston Youth Survey, NBER, 1989.) Another study showed that 20 percent of black men from welfare families have been in jail, compared with 8 percent of those from non-welfare homes. (M. Anne Hill and June O'Neill, "Underclass Behaviors in the United States: Measurement and Analysis of Determinants," (forthcoming), City University of New York, March 1990.) These correlations do not prove causality, of course. But there are a number of obvious possible causal links. Welfare receipt might affect the socialization process, either directly (for example, by removing the discipline of work) or because it correlates with single-parenthood, which in turn produces ineffective socialization. There might also be "neighborhood effects" of the sort posited by William J. Wilson—in which case the correlation would presumably be with growing up in a "welfare neighborhood" rather than with actually receiving welfare.

In fact, there is evidence to support each of these links. Hill and O'Neill found that growing up in a welfare *neighborhood* was significantly related to being in jail for black men and women, even after other factors (such as the unemployment rate, family structure, and mothers' schooling) were taken into account. Growing up in a welfare *family* was correlated with being in jail for black and white women. Being from a fatherless home was strongly related to jail for black men (ibid., 8–9). One way of putting it: The probability of going to jail was 10 percent for young black men. Not having a father added 10 percent to that, and living in a welfare neighborhood added another 6 percent (ibid).

On the connection between single-parent families and crime, see also Sara McLanahan and Karen Book, "Mother-Only Families: Problems, Prospects and Politics," *Journal of Marriage and the Family* 51 (August 1989): 565, and sources cited therein. Interestingly, in a 1986 study Freeman found that among inner-city black male youths, being from a welfare family was significantly related to illegal activity (after taking into account other variables). But being from a female-headed home had no independent effect. (See Richard B. Freeman, "Who Escapes? The Relation of Churchgoing and Other Background Factors to the Socioeconomic Performance of Black Male Youths from Inner-City Poverty Tracts," in Freeman and Holzer, eds., *The Black Youth Unemployment Crisis*, 368, 373–374.)

13. Blanche Bernstein, *The Politics of Welfare* (Cambridge, Mass.: Abt Books, 1982), 5.

14. See Jack Curry, "Tourist Slain in a Subway in Manhattan," *New York Times,* 4 September 1990, B1.

15. "6 Black Teenagers Held in Attacks on Whites," *Washington Post,* 3 July 1991, A2. The Detroit police chief invited the victims to be his personal guests at the next year's celebration. They refused. "You can take Detroit and its fireworks and kiss it goodbye, baby," said one.

16. See Ze'ev Chafets, "The Tragedy of Detroit," *New York Times Magazine,* 29 July 1990, 22; see also Barbara Vobejda, "For Big Cities, Disheartening Census News," *Washington Post,* 14 September 1990, A3. On the growth of tall grass: Isabel Wilkerson, "Detroit Journal: Giving Up the Jewels to Salvage the House," *New York Times,* 10 September 1990, A18.

17. "Competitive" goods are sometimes also called "positional" goods. Education is probably inherently a competitive good, to some extent, because one function of schools is to sort and rank people.

18. And if they're surrounded by kids who plan to go to college they'll probably plan to go to college themselves.

19. See William E. Leuchtenburg, *Franklin D. Roosevelt and the New Deal 1932–1940* (New York: Harper & Row, 1963), 124. In November of 1934, Roosevelt wrote a letter to Col. Edward House, the grand old counselor of the Wilson administration. "What I am seeking is the abolition of relief altogether," FDR wrote. "I cannot say so out loud yet but I hope to be able to substitute work for relief" (ibid., 124).

20. "Annual Message to the Congress. January 4, 1935," *The Public Papers and Addresses of Franklin D. Roosevelt,* vol. 4 (New York: Random House, 1938), 19–20.

21. The WPA's name was changed in 1939 to the Work Projects Administration.

22. Ibid., 20–23. The cash relief programs for those who could *not* be expected to work—the blind, the aged, and dependent children—were to be state programs, subsidized by the federal government. Unemployment insurance was also a joint federal-state program. Those who could work but didn't avail themselves of WPA jobs might fall back on unsubsidized state programs of "general assistance," if they existed. Otherwise, they would have to rely on private charity.

Three years later, Roosevelt's aide Harry Hopkins would reaffirm FDR's decision in public testimony:

> On the question of a work program as against direct relief, it is my conviction, and one of the strongest convictions I hold, that the Federal government should never return to a direct relief program. It is degrading to the individual; it destroys morale and self-respect; it results in no increase in the wealth of the community; it tends to destroy the ability of the individual to perform useful work in the future and it tends to establish a permanent body of dependents. We should do away with direct relief for the unemployed in the United States.

(See Josephine Brown, *Public Relief 1929–1939* [New York: Octagon Books, 1971], 341.)

23. There is a program called AFDC-UP (Unemployed Parent) that extends cash welfare to two-parent families in which the breadwinner is unemployed. The 1988 welfare reform law required all states to offer this program to qualified families for at least 6 of every 13 months. But AFDC-UP is hedged about with restrictions, and has never constituted more than about 11 percent of the AFDC caseload. To get AFDC-UP, a family's "principal earner" must have a fairly substantial work history. Parents who get AFDC-UP cannot stay on the program if they work more than one hundred hours a month. They cannot have more than a specified amount of assets. And most states apply their statutory work requirements more rigorously to the breadwinners of AFDC-UP families.

Other barriers to AFDC-UP expansion are cultural. By all accounts, far fewer of the two-parent families eligible for AFDC-UP actually apply for the program, when compared with the high percentage of eligible single-parent families who sign up for regular AFDC. (See for example, Bernstein, *The Politics of Welfare,* 154.) In late 1991, during a recession, there were about 300,000 families receiving AFDC-UP, approximately 6.5 percent of the total AFDC caseload. See *Background Material and Data on Programs within the Jurisdiction of the Committee on Ways and Means* (hereinafter referred to as the *Green Book*), 1991 edition, 570–572, 620; Jason DeParle, "Fueled by Social Trends, Welfare Cases Are Rising," *New York Times,* 10 January 1992, A16.

24. See, for example: Murray, *Losing Ground;* George Gilder, *Wealth and Poverty* (New York: Basic Books, 1981), 105–127.

25. In part, federalism let FDR get away without making a completely clear choice. Roosevelt didn't declare that the able-bodied poor should not be eligible for any direct relief, only any *federal* relief.

26. See Bernstein, *The Politics of Welfare,* 36.

27. See James Patterson, *America's Struggle Against Poverty, 1900–1980* (Cambridge, Mass.: Harvard, 1981), 27.

28. Ibid. For some early antipoverty activists, this danger was enough to justify dropping the Mother's Aid idea. ("Public funds not to widows only, mark you, but … funds to the families of those who have deserted and are going to desert!") See Winifred Bell, *Aid to Dependent Children* (New York: Columbia University Press, 1965), 6.

29. Patterson, *America's Struggle,* 68. Indeed, the "mere act of receiving a Mother's Pension Grant bestowed prestige, so high were the moral and child rearing expectations" (Winifred Bell, quoted in Mildred Rein, *Work or Welfare?: Factors in the Choice for AFDC Mothers* [New York: Praeger, 1974], 3).

30. See Bell, *Aid to Dependent Children,* 8–9; Rein, *Work or Welfare?* 8. The key definition in the New Deal's ADC program—"dead, disabled or absent"—was lifted directly from state Mother's Aid laws that, in practice, were restricted to "suitable homes." Here again, however, federalism played its historic role as engine of national confusion. The congressional conservatives who might have favored more explicit restrictions on ADC were instead championing "states' rights." They could hardly propose federal "suitable home" limits when they were arguing it was none

of Washington's business. The conservatives won the states' rights battle—but that meant passing a law that in itself imposed no restrictions on aid. There was only an acknowledgement, during the legislative debate, that the states could take into account a mother's "moral character" in determining eligibility. See Rein, *Work or Welfare?* 6. See also Edwin Witte, *The Development of the Social Security Act* (Madison: University of Wisconsin Press, 1962), 162, 164; Josephine Brown, *Public Relief*. 309–312; Bell, *Aid to Dependent Children*. 29.

31. Opponents of "suitable home" restrictions also noted that the vagueness of the term led to horror stories of moralistic meddling—mothers denied aid because a caseworker reported they "spoke gruffly to their children at times," for instance. It was considered progress when by 1939, under prodding from the federal Bureau of Public Assistance, all states technically allowed illegitimate children to receive aid. See Bell, *Aid to Dependent Children*, 35; Rein, *Work or Welfare?* 10–11.

32. Widows of breadwinners who died before retirement were included in Social Security in 1939. Disability insurance was added in 1956. See Patterson, *America's Struggle*, 68, 94. Still other "deserving" disabled single parents were siphoned off the AFDC rolls when Congress created Supplemental Security Income (SSI) in 1972. See Vincent and Vee Burke, *Nixon's Good Deed: Welfare Reform* (New York: Columbia University Press, 1974), 188–204.

33. See Rein, *Work or Welfare?* 10–11. ADC became Aid to *Families* with Dependent Children in 1950, reflecting Congress's addition of a "caretaker" grant for the mother.

34. Patterson, *America's Struggle*, 68, 86.

35. Louisiana attempted to cut off aid to all families in which the mothers, since receiving aid, had given birth to illegitimate children. The cutoffs provoked an international outcry, and three days before the Eisenhower Administration left office in 1961 the lame-duck secretary of HEW decreed that in the future states would not be allowed to deny assistance to children in "unsuitable homes" unless they were actually prepared to remove them and place them in better ones. In 1966 HEW forbade surprise visits to homes. See Bell, *Aid to Dependent Children*, 57–110, 137–151; Patterson, *America's Struggle*, 88; Murray, *Losing Ground*, 162.

Anti-welfare practices were by no means restricted the to South. In 1961 the city of Newburgh, New York, sparked a national furor by requiring, among other things, that applicants for welfare prove that they came to town with firm offers of employment. See Patterson, *America's Struggle*, 107–108.

36. See King v. Smith, 392 U.S. 309 (1968). See also New Jersey Welfare Right Organization v. Cahill, 411 U.S. 619 (1973), holding that cash aid could not be constitutionally denied a family just because all its children were illegitimate.

37. See Patterson, *America's Struggle*, 130–132. Throughout this section I rely heavily on Patterson's excellent account.

38. This was accomplished, in a very limited manner, when Congress passed the AFDC-UP (Unemployed Parent) program in 1961. As noted earlier, this program is hedged with restrictions, and has not been adopted on a full-year basis by all the states. Where it has been tried it appears to have done nothing to curb the formation of single-parent welfare families. Ibid., 130–131.

39. Thus, Richard Nixon's 1969 Family Assistance Plan (FAP), which extended

welfare to cover fully employed-but-poor parents, failed to entirely eliminate the perverse incentive to avoid marriage. Under FAP, if a couple married and one of them found work, their benefits might be reduced and (if the work paid decently) phased out completely. If they stayed unmarried, the mother could go on welfare and her benefits would not be reduced at all by any earnings the father contributed surreptitiously to the household. See Vincent and Vee Burke, *Nixon's Good Deed*, 77.

But maybe the answer was to extend welfare still further! If fathers were remaining unmarried so they wouldn't lose any of their family's welfare benefits if they worked, then the solution was to make it so they *would* lose welfare benefits as they worked even if they were unmarried. But they couldn't lose welfare benefits unless they first got them, right? Reformers inevitably took the step of proposing a universal income guarantee, available to single citizens who didn't work. Such a plan was presented by liberals during the FAP debate, and was included in the initial drafts of Jimmy Carter's ill-fated Program for Better Jobs and Income. No poor person would be tempted to do anything naughty to get on welfare for the simple reason that all poor people would be on welfare from the start. Ibid., 180–181; see Laurence E. Lynn, Jr., and David deF. Whitman, *The President as Policymaker* (Philadelphia: Temple University Press, 1981), 122–124.

The draft Carter plan proved too dole-like for Carter, and its rejection marked the political end of the line for the attempt to eliminate welfare's perversities by expanding benefits. In theory, however, the train could have rolled on for one more stop. After all, even a pure negative income tax—available to every poor American, single or married—wouldn't completely eliminate the incentive to break up a family if doing so made the resulting halves look poor enough to qualify for a check. A welfare plan that would end even this perversity would have to send checks to everyone, poor and middle class and rich alike. But this sort of no-questions-asked universal cash entitlement—called a "demogrant"—would be unthinkably expensive if it were big enough to take Americans with no other income out of poverty.

40. See Milton Friedman, *Capitalism and Freedom* (Chicago: University of Chicago Press, 1962), 190–195.

41. John Kenneth Galbraith, for example, praised Friedman's plan as "one of the two or three new ideas in economics in 25 years" (see Vincent and Vee Burke, *Nixon's Good Deed*, 18). No less than Friedman, many liberals resented social workers, viewing them as the condescending relics of a patrician tradition. This resentment grew after the fiasco of President Kennedy's 1962 Public Welfare Amendments, which tried and failed to cut the welfare rolls through a massive application of social work. See Patterson, *America's Struggle*, 131–133; Gilbert Y. Steiner, *The State of Welfare* (Washington, D.C.: Brookings, 1971), 35–40.

42. Vincent and Vee Burke, *Nixon's Good Deed*, 19.

43. See, for example: Patterson, *America's Struggle*, 188–190, 166–167, 206–207; Vincent and Vee Burke, *Nixon's Good Deed*, 10; Robert Theobald, ed., *The Guaranteed Income: Next Step in Economic Evolution?* (Garden City, N.Y.: Doubleday, 1966), 227–229. Theobald freely conceded that a guaranteed income would, "of course, mean that there will be far more unemployment." But he thought that, thanks to automation, we were moving toward an "abundance economy" in which unemployment would come to be seen as "highly desirable" (ibid., 83–96).

44. The idea that cash assistance is the way to prevent poverty from undermining social equality is the third identifiable "sub-strategy" of Money Liberalism. The first two are: (1) the general pursuit of more money equality; and (2) the idea that universal cash transfers in themselves promote social equality.

45. "You tell Shriver, no doles!" Johnson instructed his aide Bill Moyers (see Nicholas Lemann, *The Promised Land,* 149). LBJ dismissed a jobs program as too expensive, preferring to spend money on his other war. The whole budget of the Office of Economic Opportunity, the Pentagon of the anti-poverty conflict, amounted to no more than $70 a year for each poor person (ibid., 154); see also Patterson, *America's Struggle,* 141, 151.

The key metaphors of the poverty "war" were not military, but architectural. Poverty was caused by "blockages" in the "opportunity structure" facing the poor. The goal was to break the blockages, open the "exits from poverty," and give the poor an assist through the "door" into the middle class. See Lemann, *The Promised Land,* 125; Patterson, *America's Struggle,* 127, 135–136.

46. "Community action" was a famous mess in practice, arousing the ire of local politicians, who resented it as an "end run" around their authority. They demanded, and got, their own Great Society white elephant, the Model Cities program. See Lemann, *The Promised Land,* 164–169, 198; Patterson, *America's Struggle,* 138–141, 145–148; Daniel Patrick Moynihan, *Maximum Feasible Misunderstanding: Community Action in the War on Poverty* (New York: Free Press, 1970).

47. Lee Rainwater and William L. Yancey, *The Moynihan Report and the Politics of Controversy* (Cambridge, Mass.: MIT Press, 1967), 285; Patterson, *America's Struggle,* 186.

Shriver was converted to the guaranteed income idea in 1965, and his Office of Economic Opportunity was soon cranking out give-them-cash plans. See Lemann, *Promised Land,* 170; Patterson, *America's Struggle,* 189; Vincent and Vee Burke, *Nixon's Good Deed,* 20–21.

48. The 1968 Democratic party platform declares that "every American family whose income is not sufficient to enable its members to live in decency should receive assistance free of the indignities and uncertainties that still too often mar our present programs." On the economists' petition, see Patterson, *America's Struggle,* 188.

49. Patterson, *America's Struggle,* 189–190; Allan Sheahan, *Guaranteed Income: The Right to Economic Security* (Los Angeles: GAIN Publications, 1983), 148–149.

50. *A note on the "cash consensus":* Both Patterson (who approves) and Murray (who disapproves) document the emergence of this set of pro-dole ideas—what might be called the "cash consensus." Its basic tenets were these:

1. *The poor are like the rest of us. They want to work. There is no "poverty culture."* By 1966 give-them-cash enthusiasts believed they had "delivered a scholarly coup de grace to the notion that most poor people wallowed in a culture of poverty," as Patterson puts it in *America's Struggle,* 125; see also 189–190.
2. *Giving out jobs instead of money will not work.* It would be too expensive, said the 1969 Heineman Commission, requiring the creation of 9 million jobs at an annual cost of $16 billion, far more than the price of simply handing out checks. What's more, the jobs might be makework. The program would be unwieldy and proba-

bly corrupt. You'd need to decide who could work and who couldn't. That discretion would be "exercised at the lowest administrative level" (Heineman again)—in other words by incompetents. Henry Aaron, the resident welfare expert at the liberal Brookings Institution, declared in 1973 that "It is unimaginable that a large bureaucracy would be capable of sifting millions of individual cases, each fraught with special problems, needs, and ambiguity, all requiring judgment if not wisdom" (ibid., 190); see also Sheahan, *Guaranteed Income,* 148; Aaron, *Why Is Welfare So Hard to Reform?* (Washington, D.C.: Brookings, 1973), 50.

3. *The only real problem facing the poor is their lack of money; the solution is to give it to them.* Once the poor had money, social problems—family breakups, illegitimacy, drugs, crime—would soon disappear too. Cash would come first; work later. "Only when the poor are assured a minimum stable income can the other mechanisms in our fight against poverty—education, training, health, and employment—begin to function adequately" (Heineman Commission, quoted in Patterson, *America's Struggle,* 190). Even Moynihan, once a proponent of jobs programs, soon embraced the cash solution. "Our proposition," he remembers, "was that a condition that was normal and universal would not have the effect of creating dependency" (Auletta, *The Underclass,* 274). But see Lemann, *Promised Land,* 213, for evidence Moynihan didn't really believe this.

4. *A guaranteed income, because it would apply to everybody, would be not be stigmatizing like "welfare."* For social egalitarians, of course, this was the crucial contention. In their headier moments, "cash" advocates simply asserted there was no shame to the dole, that "demoralization came mainly from being unemployed and poor, not from accepting relief" (Patterson, *America's Struggle,* 66). But any lingering stigma would surely be eliminated when the "relief" guarantee was extended to cover everybody.

Not all liberals bought this package. For example, the sociologist Kenneth Clark, who advocated a "Marshall Plan" for the ghettos, resisted guaranteed income schemes. (See Auletta, *The Underclass,* 274.) The first president to endorse the give-them-cash idea, in fact, was Richard Nixon. But among liberals, "give-them-cash" had enough appeal to achieve something close to what Marxists call ideological hegemony among the scholars, columnists, and staffers from whom "new ideas" flow. Nixon's 1969 plan, the Burkes' book demonstrates, was produced largely by Democratic holdovers in the Department of Health, Education, and Welfare. And the leading liberal alternative, proposed by Sen. Abraham Ribicoff, was an even broader guaranteed income scheme. (*Nixon's Good Deed,* 40–67, 180–181.) George McGovern's aborted $1,000-per-person proposal during the 1972 campaign—perhaps the most famous give-them-cash plan of all—was merely a reiteration of the cash consensus. (It was based on a proposal by Professor Tobin.)

Today's Democrats exhibit an understandable tendency to expunge the cash consensus from their party's resume, to deny the conservative charge that an ideological shift in the Great Society years tended to approve of welfare over work. Lemann, for example, has written: "[N]one of these charges against the War on Poverty is true.... Rather than promoting welfare, the War on Poverty explicitly rejected it, in part because Lyndon Johnson hated the idea of government handouts" ("Fighting the Last War," *The Atlantic*, February 1991, 32). That is an accurate description of Johnson, and of the War on Poverty when it started in 1964. But the thinking of liberals (aside from LBJ himself) had changed dramatically by the time the Democrats lost control of the executive branch in 1969.

51. Patterson, *America's Struggle*, 171.

52. Though the female-headed families tended to be somewhat larger and to live in Northern states with more liberal eligibility rules. Ibid., 178–179.

53. Ibid., 179.

54. By 1971, the courts had struck down local residency requirements, restrictions on aid to families with "employable mothers," and they had declared the "man in the house" rule unconstitutional (ibid.).

55. Patterson notes approvingly that federal bureaucrats became "more aggressive and innovative" in what one HEW official called their desire "to maximize the total resources available to the poorest segment of society." The "arrival of a presumably more cost conscious Republican Administration in 1969 made no difference" (ibid., 181–182).

56. Bernstein, *The Politics of Welfare*, 21, citing Charles R. Morris, *The Cost of Good Intentions: New York City and the Liberal Experience* (New York: Norton, 1980). "It became something of a badge of honor for caseworkers to manipulate the regulations to build the largest possible grant for a client," recalls another New York welfare official (ibid.).

57. Lemann cites a memo Pat Buchanan sent Nixon during the 1968 campaign complaining about "community action" programs urging people to apply for welfare (*The Promised Land*, 206).

58. Patterson, *America's Struggle*, 179.

59. The first attempt was Nixon's Family Assistance Plan, in essence a guaranteed income for families with children. FAP failed in the Senate, defeated by a strange-bedfellows alliance of conservatives who didn't like the whole idea and liberals who objected to its low benefits. Congress instead created Supplemental Security Income (SSI), which guaranteed an income only to "deserving" elements of the poor who weren't expected to work—the aged, blind, and disabled. SSI filled up several of the bigger "nooks and crannies" Shriver had complained about, thus undercutting the argument for guaranteeing an income for everyone.

That didn't stop Jimmy Carter from trying in 1976. Carter's Program for Better Jobs and Income was an amalgamation of a give-them-cash approach (favored by technocrats in the Department of Health, Education, and Welfare) and a guaranteed job approach advocated, with little support from the policy establishment, by the Department of Labor. Carter instinctively favored Labor, but allowed the warring bureaucracies to concoct a compromise so complex almost nobody understood it. Basically, it was a modified guaranteed income scheme plus 1.4 million government jobs. The plan never made it *into*, much less out of, committee.

For the story of FAP, see the Burkes' *Nixon's Good Deed*; also Taylor Branch, "Patrick Moynihan's Ship of Fools," *Washington Monthly*, January 1973, 6–19. For Carter's plan, see Lynn and Whitman's absorbing account in *The President as Policymaker*.

Opposition to the give-them-cash plans was both economic and moral, and it focused on the work issue. The "objection is to paying people not to work," Senator Russell Long (in whose committee FAP died) told Nixon (see Lynn and Whitman, *The President as Policymaker*, 27). Then-Governor Ronald Reagan called Nixon's plan a "megadole." It was clear, in this debate, which side the American public was on. "If it had been put to a referendum," one FAP supporter admitted, "the public would have murdered it" (Patterson, *America's Struggle*, 196). Patterson is at a loss to explain the embarrassing "persistence" of these "durable attitudes" on the part of the voters, but admits "they had not changed much in 80 years" (ibid., 109–110, 209). The Burkes, surveying the rubble of FAP, come right out and charge that "In a broad sense, the American public IS the welfare problem" (*Nixon's Good Deed*, 2).

60. Wilson, *The Truly Disadvantaged*, 39–42, citing John D. Kasarda, "Urban Change and Minority Opportunities," *The New Urban Reality*, ed. Paul E. Peterson (Washington, D.C.: Brookings, 1985), 33–67. See also Kasarda, "Economic Restructuring and America's Urban Dilemma," *The Metropolis Era*, vol. 1, ed. Mattei Dogan and John D. Kasarda (New York: Russell Sage, 1988), 61–62; and Kasarda, "City Jobs and Residents on a Collision Course: The Urban Underclass Dilemma," in *Economic Development Quarterly* 4, no. 4 (November 1990): 313–319. David Ellwood also cites Kasarda's research (see *Poor Support*, 206).

61. See Wilson, *The Truly Disadvantaged*, 50–62, 138. Wilson emphasizes the disappearance of middle-class role models who had attempted to enforce "explicit norms and sanctions against aberrant behavior." Lemann describes some of these efforts in "Origins of the Underclass," 35, 51–52, citing St. Clair Drake and Horace Cayton, *Black Metropolis: A Study of Negro Life in a Northern City* (New York: Harcourt Brace, 1945). See also *The Promised Land*, 65.

62. On the "marriageable male" problem, see Wilson, *The Truly Disadvantaged*, 83–92, 95–106.

63. Ibid., 15–16, 77–81, 93–95, 104.

64. Murray, *Losing Ground*, 156–166. See also Murray, "No, Welfare Isn't Really the Problem," *The Public Interest* 84 (Summer 1986): 4. I am using Murray's terminology ("bribe" theory vs. "enabling" theory).

65. Lemann, "Origins of the Underclass," 49.

66. David T. Ellwood and Mary Jo Bane, "The Impact of AFDC on Family Structure and Living Arrangements," report prepared for the U.S. Department of Health and Human Services under grant no. 92A-82 (John F. Kennedy School of Government, Harvard University, 1984); Wilson, *The Truly Disadvantaged*, 78–81, 186; Robert Greenstein, "The Great Society: An Exchange," *The New Republic*, 8 April 1985, 23. (Greenstein also pointed out that Murray miscalculated Harold and Phyllis's hypothetical budgets. See "Losing Faith in 'Losing Ground,'" *The New Republic*, 25 March 1985, 13.)

Subsequent studies, however, have begun to find the connection between high welfare benefits and out-of-wedlock births that Ellwood and Bane did not find. See Shelly Lundberg and Robert Plotnick, "Testing the Opportunity Cost Hypothesis of Teenage Out-of-Wedlock Childbearing," University of Washington, 1990, report prepared for the U.S. Department of Health and Human Services under Grant

88ASPE195A, 66, 77; M. Anne Hill and June O'Neill, "Underclass Behaviors in the United States: Measurement and Analysis of Determinants," City University of New York (forthcoming). See also William R. Prosser, "The Underclass: Assessing What We Have Learned," *Focus* 13, no. 2 (Summer 1991): 12.

67. Dash, *When Children Want Children,* 175, 159, 161–162.

68. See Barbara Ehrenreich and Frances Fox Piven, "The Alarm Clock Syndrome," *The New Republic,* 6 October 1986, 18.

69. These statistics are from David Ellwood, "Targeting the Would-Be Long-Term Recipient: Who Should Be Served?" report to the U.S. Department of Health and Human Services (Princeton, N.J: Mathematica Policy Research, 1986), Table I.1, 5. See also Ellwood, *Poor Support,* 148. If you look at those who, over the course of a year, go on welfare for the first time, the average stay is 6.6 years—still far longer than liberal welfare defenders let on. For example, New York Gov. Mario Cuomo has declared that people in his state only stay on welfare "an average of two years." See Joe Klein, "Mario's Messianic Humility," *New York,* 18 November 1991, 16.

The studies on which liberals rely for such reassuring statistics typically contain two sorts of errors. First, many mothers are mistakenly recorded as having left the rolls, in some cases because AFDC money is inadvertently listed as "other welfare." Second, the studies fail to account for recidivism. If a woman goes on welfare for two years, leaves for a year, and then returns for two more years, should we really count this as two admirably short welfare spells? When Ellwood corrected for these factors, it turned out that only about 30 percent of people who go on AFDC spend less than two years on the program. See Ellwood, "Targeting," 5, 16; see also Charles Murray with Deborah Laren, "According to Age: Longitudinal Profiles of AFDC Recipients and the Poor by Age Group," paper prepared for the Working Seminar on the Family and American Welfare Policy, September 1986, 44–46.

One caveat: Ellwood's data count anyone who gets AFDC for at least two months in a calendar year as being "on" for the year. Ellwood estimates that, under this definition, a three-year "stay" means about 24 months of AFDC receipt, on average. See Ellwood, "Major Issues in Time-Limited Welfare," paper prepared for the Urban Institute's Roundtable on Children, 4 December 1992, 19.

70. Lemann notes that even in Mississippi, a low-benefit state, "a life on welfare … became sustainable when benefits were raised slightly and the food stamp program began" (see Lemann, *The Promised Land,* 320; see also 335, describing a family living in Mississippi on only $168 a month in AFDC—but $368 in food stamps).

71. Murray, *Losing Ground,* 227–228.

72. "Saving the Underclass: Ken Auletta interviews Charles Murray," *Washington Monthly,* September 1985, 20.

73. Lemann, *The Promised Land,* 285.

74. In Lemann's rich non-fiction account of the great black migration, at least one protagonist appears to have an illegitimate child for just this reason (ibid., 298–299).

75. In Lemann's 1986 *Atlantic* article, the thesis paragraph was delivered by Mildred Nichols, an immigrant from Canton, Mississippi, to Chicago: "Most people on welfare here, they were on welfare there, in a sense, because they were sharecroppers.

There they were working hard for nothing, now they're not working for nothing" (see "Origins of the Underclass," 47). Lemann's subsequent book puts less emphasis on the sharecropper-underclass link. See Lemann, "The Underclass and the Great Migration," *The Public Interest* 105 (Fall 1991): 107–108.

76. Kasarda, "Urban Change and Minority Opportunities," 59. Indeed, this is one of the very articles cited by Wilson (*The Truly Disadvantaged,* 39).

77. Kasarda, "Urban Change and Minority Opportunities," 59–60.

78. Ibid., 66.

79. Blacks who do seek jobs outside the ghetto often confront employer prejudices against hiring them. But those prejudices themselves are not unrelated to the "opposition" culture of the underclass. Largely in the attempt to avoid ghetto culture, employers practice "statistical discrimination," choosing whites over blacks, and suburban blacks over inner-city blacks, and even distinguishing between different neighborhoods in the inner city. Joleen Kirschenman and Kathryn M. Neckerman have documented these practices. Blacks with ghetto styles of dress, speech, and attitude are at a particular disadvantage in sales jobs. Such illegal, but not irrational, discrimination in turn reinforces the equally rational perception of inner-city blacks that the mainstream culture is hostile to them—which makes rejection of that culture all the more appealing, completing the disastrous circle of resentment. See Joleen Kirschenman and Kathryn M. Neckerman, "We'd Love to Hire Them, But ...": The Meaning of Race for Employers," *The Urban Underclass,* ed. Christopher Jencks and Paul E. Peterson (Washington, D.C.: Brookings, 1991), 216.

80. Kasarda, "Urban Change and Minority Opportunities," 61.

81. Lemann *The Promised Land,* 29–32. But see William Tucker. "Chronicler Without a Clue," *The American Spectator,* June 1991, 16—noting that very few sharecropper families were actually headed by single mothers.

82. In 1970, 33 percent of black families with children under age 18 were single-parent families headed by women. By 1988, the percentage had risen to 58 percent. The comparable figure for whites in 1988 was 19 percent. See *1991 Green Book,* 951.

Obviously, in the black community single-motherhood is a phenomenon encompassing much more than the underclass. But that doesn't necessarily mean that the underclass, and welfare, aren't implicated in this broader phenomenon. First, as Wilson notes, the pool of "marriageable" black men is reduced for all black women by the large number of black men who are not participating in the labor force—who are in the underclass. See *The Truly Disadvantaged,* 83–92, 95–106. Second, as noted earlier, the exposure of the African-American community to AFDC is much broader than a snapshot of the welfare rolls at any one time would lead you to expect—with almost three-quarters of black children who turned eighteen in the late 1980s having spent at least a year on AFDC. Sources: *Green Book,* 951; *Characteristics and Financial Circumstances of AFDC Recipients: FY 1989* (Washington, D.C.: Department of Health and Human Services, Family Support Administration, Office of Family Assistance), 28, Table 10; Panel Study of Income Dynamics, University of Michigan.

Chapter 8
The Cure for the Culture of Poverty

1. Source: Urban Institute. The national average is 9 percent. In these "underclass" neighborhoods an average of 60 percent of the families with children are headed by women, compared with a national average of 19 percent. See Isabel V. Sawhill, "An Overview," *The Public Interest* 96 (Summer 1989): 5–6.

2. See Congressional Budget Office, *Trends in Family Income: 1970–1986* (Washington, D.C.: Government Printing Office, February 1988), 52, 74. The 65 percent figure includes AFDC, general assistance, and Supplemental Security Income (SSI), but AFDC by far the biggest chunk (ibid., 48). Technically, SSI should not be included as a "welfare" program because it is work-tested—it goes only to the disabled or elderly. The 65 percent figure does not include food stamps, either as "welfare" or in calculating total income. Virtually no single mothers in the poorest quintile have any family members working full-time (ibid., 52).

See also *Background Material and Data on Programs within the Jurisdiction of the Committee on Ways and Means* (hereinafter referred to as the *Green Book*), 1990 edition, 937 (noting that for all poor single-parent families, the three means-tested cash programs [AFDC, GA, and SSI], food stamps, and housing assistance account for about 60 percent of total income.)

3. Christopher Jencks and Kathryn Edin, "The Real Welfare Problem," *The American Prospect* 1 (Spring 1990): 34.

4. Glenn C. Loury, "The Moral Quandary of the Black Community," *The Public Interest* 79 (Spring, 1985): 15; Roger Wilkins, "Not By Bootstraps Alone," *Village Voice*, 4 February 1986, 29.

5. Wilkins, "Not By Bootstraps Alone," 29, 30; Loury, "The Moral Quandary of the Black Community," 15.

6. Richard Freeman, "Employment and Earnings of Disadvantaged Young Men in a Labor Shortage Economy," in *The Urban Underclass*, ed. Christopher Jencks and Paul Peterson (Washington, D.C.: Brookings, 1991), 108.

7. Paul Osterman, "Gains from Growth?: The Impact of Full Employment on Poverty in Boston," in *The Urban Underclass*, 126.

8. Charles Murray, "Here's the Bad News on the Underclass," *Wall Street Journal*. 8 March 1990, A16.

9. Osterman, "Impact of Full Employment," 128.

10. Lemann, *The Promised Land: The Great Black Migration and How It Changed America* (New York: Alfred A. Knopf, 1991), 350.

11. See John R. Berrueta-Clement et al., *Changed Lives: The Effects of the Perry Preschool Program on Youths Through Age 19* (High/Scope Educational Research Foundation, Number 8, High/Scope Press, 1984), 102, 64, 49; see also the exchange in "Correspondence," *The New Republic*, 1 May 1989, 6.

12. Lemann, "Fighting the Last War," *The Atlantic*. February 1991, 28.

13. See Isabel V. Sawhill, Raymond J. Struyk, and Steven M. Sachs, "The New Paradigm: Choice and Empowerment as Social Policy Tools," *Policy Bites* 5 (February 1991): 2.

It's true that, by giving the poor actual assets they can conserve and sell, Kemp's idea adds an interesting wrinkle to the War On Poverty "empowerment" notion. Owning your own apartment is at least conceivably a transformative experience. But in practice, the ghetto poor are too poor to be able to buy and maintain their apartments without a giant government subsidy—between $50,000 and $90,000 per participant, according to the Urban Institute. (Ibid.) At Washington, D.C.'s Kenilworth-Parkside project, the cost may be $130,000 per apartment (see Robert Guskind and Carol F. Steinbach, "Sales Resistance," *National Journal* 6 April 1991, 800). Even with these subsidies, transformation doesn't seem to necessarily follow. It seems to be quite difficult to obtain accurate statistics on the number of Kenilworth residents who have actually left the welfare rolls. "When asked how much welfare dependency had been reduced ... Kimi Gray [Kenilworth's tenant-leader] and her top two managers gave wildly different figures," reports David Osborne, in an otherwise flattering story about the project ("They Can't Stop Us Now," *Washington Post Magazine*, 30 July 1989, 29).

14. On Cochran Gardens, see Jason DeParle, "Cultivating Their Own Gardens," *New York Times Magazine*, 5 January 1992, 46. DeParle notes that the average reported household income in this "successful" project is $4,992!

On Bromley Heath, see Timothy Noah, "Bush 'Empowerment' Self-Help Plans for the Poor Could Prove as Costly as Any Proposal by Liberals," *Wall Street Journal*, 30 January 1991, A12.

15. See, for example, James Patterson, *America's Struggle Against Poverty. 1900–1980* (Cambridge, Mass.: Harvard, 1981), 130–131, 174.

16. *A note on "carrot-and-stick" incentives:* Nor is it enough, if the enabling theory is correct, to tinker with AFDC benefits in order to give welfare mothers various small incentives to get married, postpone childbearing, send their kids to school, et cetera. A wave of this "carrot and stick" type of welfare reform swept the states, beginning in the late 1980s. In Wisconsin, Republican Governor Tommy Thompson's "Learnfare" plan cut the benefits of recipients whose adolescent children didn't attend school regularly. Thompson also proposed paying welfare mothers a small monthly bonus if they married. New Jersey has decided to deny welfare mothers some of the extra benefits they now get when they have additional children; California may soon do the same. As this book goes to press, Ohio is testing out a plan that gives teen welfare mothers a bonus if they attend school themselves. New Jersey may also try out another Thompson suggestion: allowing welfare mothers to marry and stay on welfare even if their husband works and earns some money.

There are particular perversities with each of these programs. Learnfare, for example, transfers power within the home from the mother to the child, who by failing to attend school can cost the mother a chunk of her check. Letting welfare mothers marry and stay on welfare while their husbands work, Murray has pointed out, may give them an incentive to marry workers, but it also makes going on AFDC in the first place much more attractive. Under the New Jersey plan, a two-parent welfare family can keep getting a check even if it has an income of $20,000. But what about sub-$20,000 working couples who never go on welfare? If they don't get a check too, it's grossly unfair. But if you do send them a check, you've recreated Nixon's guaranteed-income plan.

Still, as with Nixon's plan, the greatest defect of the carrot-and-stick reforms isn't the perverse incentives they create. It's that they won't have a significant de-enabling effect on the underclass. Will Thompson's proposed $77-a-month marriage bonus (or New Jersey's denial of a $64 increase for additional children) transform the culture of single motherhood? No. Ghetto girls will be able to go on becoming single mothers. They will just be slightly poorer single mothers.

17. When Roosevelt proposed the WPA in his 1935 address, he said the wage should be "larger than the amount now received as a relief dole, but at the same time not so large as to encourage the rejection of opportunities for private employment or the leaving of private employment to engage in government work."

As noted later in this chapter, some jobs would also have to be offered to mothers younger than age 18—preferably jobs that allowed them to stay in school.

18. *A note on the welfare "triangle":* The technical problem facing any cash dole—a problem that helped kill the guaranteed income—is known in the welfare business as "The Triangle." The phrase refers to the three desirable goals of Money Liberals: (1) decent benefit levels; (2) greater work incentives; and (3) affordable cost. You won't be surprised to hear that these goals are mutually conflicting. What is surprising is how the nasty mathematics of a give-them-cash solution tend to make all the possible compromises unappealing.

Why? Remember that a give-them-cash approach relies on "marginal" incentives to get the poor off welfare. For every dollar earned, a recipient would lose (for example) only 50 cents in benefits. If the basic benefit level for a poor family with no income were set at $5,000, it would lose benefits gradually until it earned $10,000, at which point it would be off welfare.

Now, suppose we feel generous and decide to double the size of the basic benefit, from $5,000 to $10,000. We're willing double the portion of our taxes devoted to welfare, we probably tell ourselves. But we're in for an unpleasant surprise. If we stick to the plan of reducing benefits at the rate of 50 cents for each dollar earned, people will now still get *some* benefits all the way up to $20,000. As a result, our $10,000 plan turns out to cost, not double, but at least *quadruple* what the $5,000 plan costs. Worse, raising benefit levels not only means paying more money to those who were getting benefits before, *it also means paying those benefits to many more people.* There are a whole lot of families making less than $20,000 who would suddenly qualify for a check. The only way to keep down the ballooning cost is to reduce benefits more rapidly as people earn money, but that means throwing the precious work incentives out the window. See David Whitman, "Liberal Rhetoric and the Welfare Underclass," *Society* 21, no. 1 (November–December 1983): 64–65.

The Triangle problem is virtually impossible for guaranteed income plans to solve because of their basic feature: they pay the same benefits to both the poor who can work and the "deserving" poor who can't. This means the benefit guaranteed to people with no earnings has to be relatively generous. After all, it's what the helpless poor will have to live on. But the poor who *can* work get the same amount. To motivate them to work, you have to offer incentives, in the form of retained benefits, on top of this relatively generous guaranteed living standard. But if you do let them keep a big portion of their benefits as their incomes rise, the result is a long, extremely expensive benefit "tail" extending up into the middle class. Compromises designed to avoid this result not only have failed to live up to the give-them-cash technocrats own promises, they have missed their mark by absurd margins. See Henry Aaron, *Why Is Welfare So Hard to Reform?* (Washington, D.C.: Brookings, 1973).

With a WPA-based plan, though, the terrifying Triangle virtually disappears. For those who can't work, cash benefits can be docked a dollar for each dollar earned—these are people who claim to be unable to work, after all. For those who can work, there is no cash dole, and hence no Triangle problem. There *is* a supplement of wages that must be taken away gradually as income rises. But this supplement is so small that it's easily and affordably handled.

A final note: By far the most dramatic work disincentive in current anti-poverty programs is the so-called "Medicaid notch," the point at which if you earn a dollar more you lose free Medicaid coverage. This notch is not eliminated by a neo-WPA, but it is eliminated by another element in the Civic Liberal agenda: national health insurance, which would cover everyone with a system that doesn't require that they stay poor.

19. In other words, current welfare recipients could be "grandfathered," if necessary, to avoid the Take Away problem of ending benefits for those accustomed to getting them. They could still be required to work in return for their checks—"workfare." But new single mothers would not be required to work for their checks. They would not get checks.

20. Sixty-six percent of single mothers are in the work force. Source: U.S. Department of Labor, Bureau of Labor Statistics, unpublished tabulations from the Current Population Survey, March 1991. According to statistics tabulated by David Ellwood, in 1984 about 41 percent of single mothers worked full-time. But over half either worked full-time or said they were looking for full-time work. Half the single mothers who worked full-time did so at jobs paying less than $7.00 an hour. See Ellwood, *Poor Support* (New York: Basic Books, 1988), 143–144.

21. I accept the possibility that it may be best, all other things being equal, for young children to be tended by their mothers full-time. But it's more important, for underclass kids, to end the culture of poverty. And it's not at all clear that mothering by underclass mothers is better than day care. On day care vs. home care generally, see: Deborah Fallows, *A Mother's Work* (Boston: Houghton Mifflin, 1985); Karl Zinsmeister, "Brave New World: How Day Care Harms Children," *Policy Review* 44 (Spring 1988): 40–48.

22. For example, Ohio's LEAP program tries to get teen welfare mothers to attend school by offering subsidized day care. According to one study, "Few LEAP teens have availed themselves of program-funded child care primarily because many teens prefer informal care provided by relatives...." Only "about 14 percent" of the teens used state-funded day care, even though they were enrolled in school and had preschool-age children. See Dan Bloom et al., *LEAP: Implementing a Welfare Initiative to Improve School Attendance Among Teen Parents* (New York: Manpower Demonstration Research Corporation, July 1991), Executive Summary, 13. See also Ellwood, *Poor Support,* 176–177.

23. Other programs might keep "unfit" parents and children together under some sort of supervision. On the need for modern equivalents of the orphanage, see

Lois G. Forer, "Bring Back the Orphanage," *Washington Monthly*, April 1988, 17–22.

24. For a discussion of Long's plan, see Aaron, *Why Is Welfare So Hard to Reform?* 25–27 et seq. For the Burns proposal, see his *Reflections of an Economic Policy Maker: Speeches and Congressional Statements: 1969–1978* (Washington, D.C.: American Enterprise Institute, 1978), 223–224. See also Paul Simon, *Let's Put America Back to Work* (Chicago: Bonus Books, 1987), 135. See also Robert I. Lerman, "JOIN: A Jobs and Income Program for American Families," Studies in Public Welfare, Paper No. 19, Joint Economic Committee of the Congress of the U.S. (Washington, D.C.: Government Printing Office, 1974), 3–67; Lester Thurow, *The Zero-Sum Society* (New York: Basic Books, 1980), 204–206; Timothy Noah, "Bring Back the WPA," *Washington Monthly*, September 1982, 38–46; Robert M. Kaus, "Jobs for Everyone," *Harper's*, October 1982, 11–16; Nicholas Lemann, "The Origins of the Underclass," *The Atlantic*, July 1986, 68; Mickey Kaus, "The Work Ethic State," *The New Republic*, 7 July 1986, 22–33; Irwin Garfinkel and Sara S. McLanahan, *Single Mothers and Their Children: A New American Dilemma* (Washington, D.C.: Urban Institute Press, 1986), 185–187; David Raphael Riemer, *The Prisoners of Welfare: Liberating America's Poor from Unemployment and Low Wages* (New York: Praeger, 1988); Kevin Hopkins, "A New Deal for America's Poor: Abolish Welfare, Guarantee Jobs," *Policy Review* 45 (Summer 1988): 70–73; Philip Harvey, *Securing the Right to Employment* (Princeton: Princeton University Press, 1989). In March of 1992, Sen. David Boren of Oklahoma introduced legislation to establish a WPA-style jobs program. About 75 percent of the neo-WPA jobs would go to welfare recipients who would be required to take them.

25. The supplement currently tapers off for incomes above that, completely disappearing for families making more than about $21,000. Families with two or more children get a slightly larger credit. A two-child family got a maximum EITC of $1,369 in 1992. Add that to a full-time minimum-wage income of $8,840 and the family was still about $1,000 short of the poverty line if it had one parent—$4,000 short if there were two parents. An additional tax credit of up to $400 is available to working families with a child under a year old, plus there's another $450 or so available to low-income families who buy health insurance out of their own pockets. All these separate subsidies make the tax forms much too complicated. They should be combined into a single, adequate EITC. See David Wessel, "Paved with Good Intentions, Tax Writers' Road to Help the Working Poor Turns Into a Maze," *Wall Street Journal*, 11 June 1991, A16.

26. The major defect with the EITC, for our purposes, is that for most low-wage workers it delivers only a once-yearly tax bonus. That may not be a sufficiently immediate payoff in a ghetto culture where time horizons are short. We want young women and men who go to work this week to get an above-poverty wage *this week*, not next April 15. That requires including the EITC in their paycheck. This is already possible, but only a tiny number of workers do it—about 10,000, out of the 12 million families who get the credit. It seems employers don't encourage their employees to apply for this "reverse-withholding," and low-wage workers don't fill out the requisite forms even when notified of their eligibility. A concerted effort to overcome this resistance would have to be mounted.

An alternative to the EITC would be the innovative Wage Rate Subsidy proposed by Brandeis University's Robert Lerman. In 1986, for example, Lerman would have had the government pay half the difference between the family bread-winner's wage and $6 an hour. A $4-an-hour WPA worker would qualify for a $1-an-hour supplement, making his job, in effect, pay $5 an hour. But the $5-an-hour worker in the private sector would get a 50-cent supplement. The great advantage of Lerman's plan is that it helps the working poor in direct proportion to how much they work. The great disadvantage of his plan is administrative—it would require employers to keep detailed records of hours worked. And employers and employees would have a mutual interest in fudging these records to make it look as if someone who worked 4 hours at $6 an hour really worked 6 hours at $4 an hour, thereby qualifying for a subsidy. The EITC avoids this incentive to cheat, and it has the major practical virtue of already existing. See Robert Lerman, "JOIN: A Jobs and Income Program for American Families," and Lerman, "Separating Income Support from Income Supplementation," *Journal of the Institute for Socioeconomic Studies* 10 (Autumn 1985): 101–125.

Simply extending the EITC to the poverty line for current workers, without the rest of the reforms proposed here, would cost on the order of $15 billion a year. I do not think it makes sense, however, to expand the EITC so that it takes large families out of poverty. To take a 5-person family out of poverty on the basis of just one minimum-wage paycheck, for example, the EITC supplement would have to be as large as the wage itself.

27. Studies have shown that welfare mothers are in fact the most employable underclass group. (See Ken Auletta, *The Underclass* [New York: Random House, 1982], 222–230.) If we discover that many Americans in the ghettos are in fact unemployable, that will be dramatic proof of the existence of a culture of poverty. It would hardly provide justification for reinstating the welfare system that helped produce that culture.

28. Compassion, in this sense, is inherently demeaning. But those who can work but don't, and who turn to the government for support, have already lost their claim to full dignity. See Lawrence Mead, *Beyond Entitlement: The Social Obligations of Citizenship* (New York: Free Press, 1986), 43; Mickey Kaus, "Up from Altruism," *The New Republic,* 15 December 1986, 17–18.

29. And because there would be no cash, there would be a large incentive for the destitute to make the most of the counseling and training that was offered.

30. I am indebted to Lemann and to Charles Krauthammer for raising this issue.

31. See, for example, Dolores G. Norton, "Understanding the Early Experience of Black Children in High Risk Environments: Culturally and Ecologically Relevant Research as a Guide to Support for Families," *Zero to Three: Bulletin of the National Center for Clinical Infant Programs* 10, no. 4 (April 1990) and sources cited therein. See especially 4–6. See also Dolores G. Norton, "Diversity, Early Socialization and Temporal Development: The Dual Perspective Revisited," (forthcoming), 9 ("Often these children have mothers who have no work nor anyplace to go, and have little reason to plan or observe time.... The day flows by on a seemingly unscheduled basis, unrelated to any overall division.") See also Robert Haveman, Barbara Wolfe, and James Spaulding, "Childhood Events and Circumstances Influencing High School Completion," *Demography* 28, no. 1 (February 1991): 145–148.

But see M. Anne Hill and June O'Neill, "Underclass Behaviors in the United States: Measurement and Analysis of Determinants," City University of New York, March 1992, 6–8 (concluding that for black men the absence of a father appeared to be more important than family welfare receipt).

32. The breakdown is: 54.5 percent of mothers with children under three are in the labor force (33.5 percent work full-time, 15.5 percent part-time, the remainder are looking for work). For *single* mothers with kids under three, about 47 percent are in the labor force (27 percent working full-time, 10 percent part-time, the rest looking for work). Source: U.S. Department of Labor, Bureau of Labor Statistics, unpublished tabulations from the Current Population Survey, March 1991.

33. California State Sen. Diane Watson, opposing that state's 1986 welfare-to-work plan, actually predicted that her inner-city constituents would "go home and have another baby" if faced with "forced labor."

34. Note that this alternative differs from the time-limited welfare plan proposed by David Ellwood in *Poor Support*. Ellwood's plan would offer 18 to 36 months of cash assistance to all single mothers (and two-parent families) who are poor enough to qualify, whether their children were six months or six years old. The alternative suggested here would offer the time-limited welfare only to poor mothers of children under two years old. Currently about 25 to 30 percent of welfare mothers have children that young—but many of these mothers have already been on welfare for two years and wouldn't qualify for cash aid under this alternative.

35. This would be especially true if the two years of cash assistance came with valuable training designed to provide a "transition" to work. There is also what Isabel Sawhill has called the "falling off the cliff" problem. Time-limited welfare plans would have the government send mothers cash assistance, then cut them off. This may be politically difficult for a government to do. It's also crueler, in a way, than never letting the mothers on the dole in the first place.

36. Even if the objective is helping those individuals who have an illegitimate kid (rather then deterring them) immediate work might be better. It would put mothers into the world of bosses and paychecks without letting them grow accustomed to dependency.

37. Ellwood's proposal contemplates denying mothers with just-born infants any cash assistance if they've already used up their allotted time on welfare. But if these mothers can be faced with zero welfare from the moment of birth, why not all mothers? A possible compromise has been suggested by Lawrence Mead, who advocates distinguishing between mothers who are married when the child is born and those who aren't. Once-married mothers would get two or three years of cash; unmarried mothers wouldn't. See Ellwood, *Poor Support*, 179; Mead, "Work and Dependency, Part II: Past Policies and Proposals" (New York University, Department of Politics, September 1986), 44, written for the Welfare Dependency Project of the Hudson Institute.

A variation on Mead's approach would be a scheme of "divorce insurance." One justification for a "transitional" period on welfare, after all, is that just-divorced mothers may need welfare as a temporary crutch after a bad marriage. Is it really unfair to ask a destitute divorcee to take a low-wage job (with day care), if that's what we expect poor, never-married mothers to do? I'm not so sure. But if it is unfair, the answer isn't to keep on subsidizing the underclass culture in order to help the minority of deserving divorcees. It is to deal with these distinct groups separately. Why not allow poor mothers (or fathers with custody of kids) half a year of cash "divorce insurance" for every two years they've lived in a family in which one member worked full-time—up to a one-year limit on aid?

Finally, what about teenage mothers who haven't even finished high school? They could receive free day care while finishing, and in-kind nutritional assistance, plus training and any special courses (in "parenting skills," for example) that prove effective. But no cash. To obtain any extra money necessary to support a baby, they would have to work, in one of the "guaranteed" government jobs if necessary.

38. *A note on "workfare" and the Ellwood Plan:* The bipartisan trend toward "workfare" in the states during the 1980s (which the 1988 Family Support Act reflects) was a bit deceiving. Virtually all electable politicians now agree, as New York Gov. Mario Cuomo puts it, that "work is better than welfare"—even for single mothers. But pro-work rhetoric is also a cheap way for liberals to gloss over the crucial question of what, exactly, the government will do to produce this desired end. Work is better than welfare—but when does the welfare stop? While Cuomo was talking up work, his welfare chief Cesar Perales was testifying before Congress *against* work requirements. Welfare mothers, Perales said, "don't get much by being assigned to some work site to act as a clerk or empty wastebaskets." Unless they could "get" something extra, in other words, New York would keep sending them AFDC checks. Never mind that millions of Americans earn their livings as clerks or wastebasket-emptiers.

In fact, most state welfare reform plans haven't come close to actually requiring *work.* Some, like Michael Dukakis's once-touted "ET" program, have been purely voluntary job training programs. Even theoretically mandatory "workfare" is often seen as essentially a program to educate and train welfare mothers. This approach, which might be called "soft workfare," is championed by the Manpower Demonstration Research Corporation and embodied in the Family Support Act. Soft workfare enthusiasts ask questions like: What was the net increase in welfare mothers who found private jobs? Do the resulting welfare savings justify the program's cost? It's in pursuit of these incremental, short-term gains that the Softs drastically water down the work aspects of workfare. Welfare mothers are offered elaborate menus of activities, including vocational instruction, "job search," and remedial education. Taking such courses, one after another, can easily become a way to *avoid* going into the labor market. Putting off work can always be justified by the hope that, with a bit more training, a welfare mother may qualify for a "good" high-paying job. See Jason DeParle, "Using Books Instead of Brooms to Escape Welfare," *New York Times,* 9 September 1991, A-1.

Actual public service work, meanwhile, is only one menu choice in most soft workfare schemes, and then it's billed as educational "work experience" and often limited to 12 or 13 weeks. California enacted an elaborate menu-style welfare reform plan in 1986. Five years later, out of over 650,000 California families on welfare, exactly 1,235 recipients were actually working for their checks in "workfare" jobs. Even welfare mothers who do wind up working are excused by the Family Support Act from working (or studying) for more than 20 hours a week if they have children under six—a provision that covers about two-thirds of the caseload.

Perversities abound. "Reformed" welfare systems not only offer AFDC recipients expensive schooling (including post-secondary education)—they also typically provide "transitional" day care and Medicaid for a year if a mother finds work. But these valuable goodies aren't available to the millions of poor single mothers who never go on welfare in the first place, or to the millions of poor women who never become single mothers. Even if this doesn't create an incentive to go on welfare, it's not fair.

In practice, the welfare-to-work plans promoted by the Family Support Act face a major Take Away problem. They first send AFDC mothers checks, *then* try somehow to get them to "participate" in work or training. Mothers are summoned to the welfare office where "employability" plans are negotiated. Day-care slots are lined up. If the mothers don't show up, their excuses must be evaluated. (In California, recipients are excused, by statute, if they are "seriously dependent upon alcohol or drugs" or if they have "an emotional or mental problem.") If the recipient continues to balk, an administrative hearing is held and a limited "sanction" is imposed—loss of a portion of the welfare check. That's assuming the local legal aid office doesn't take everyone to court. In 1985, the Social Security Administration ran an experiment in San Diego to see what would happen if welfare officials really tried to force the entire caseload to do at least *something* (including but not limited to work). After a year, about half the recipients were still "non-participating." They either had excuses—health, drug addiction, another pregnancy—or were "non-cooperative," or were otherwise lost to bureaucratic friction.

Attempts to "get tough" with welfare recipients and actually make them work—"hard workfare"—face an even bigger Take Away problem. Recipients who resist attempts to take away their checks if they don't attend self-esteem classes may be expected to vigorously resist attempts to take away checks if they don't work in low-paying public service jobs. The solution is simply to not send the checks in the first place. In the plan proposed in the text, there would be no need to "require" work. Work would be all that was offered.

But the biggest defect in workfare schemes, "soft" and "hard," is that they do little to employ those in the underclass who have few welfare benefits to work off, namely able-bodied men and women who aren't mothers. Workfare, in a sense, is a backdoor WPA, because "requiring" work means eventually providing a last-resort public service job. But why provide the jobs only to single mothers on the dole? Surely it will be far easier to transform the underclass if above-poverty jobs are available to ghetto men, single and married, and to women who resist having illegitimate children. Even if most underclass men, initially, don't take the jobs, some would, and they would be lifted out of poverty. The pool of "marriageable males" would increase. (For a differing view, see the defense of workfare—and its role in a Civic Liberalism—in Lawrence M. Mead's *Beyond Entitlement*.)

There are proposals that fall in-between current welfare reform efforts and a full-fledged replacement of welfare with a guaranteed job. The most prominent is David Ellwood's. Ellwood is often cast as a liberal critic of Murray, yet he advocates cutting off welfare payments entirely after a mother has been getting cash for 18 to 36 months. Mothers would keep getting a small "guaranteed child support" check ($1,500 to $2,000 annually per child), but to meet the rest of their financial needs they would be offered a last-resort, minimum-wage public service job. If they turned the job down they would be on their own, and they couldn't re-start the 18- to 36-month welfare clock by having another baby. Unemployed men and women in two-parent families would get similar temporary cash assistance, then a public service job. See Ellwood, *Poor Support*. 123, 179; see also *A New Social Contract: Rethinking the Nature and Purpose of Public Assistance*. report of the Task Force on Poverty and Welfare submitted to Gov. Mario M. Cuomo, State of New York, December 1986, 80.

The Ellwood Plan would eliminate much of the clumsy welfare reform bureaucracy. There would (in theory) be no need to evaluate excuses or impose "sanctions." When the time limit expired, cash welfare would simply end, period. Above all, it's hard to see how Ellwood's plan wouldn't have a significant Murrayesque "de-enabling" effect on ghetto culture. Certainly it would change the unconscious background perception that welfare will sustain women who have illegitimate kids. Potential single parents will see plenty of unwed mothers who aren't being sustained because their 18 to 36 months are up. Significantly, an Ellwood-like scheme has been endorsed by such respectable black Democrats as Eleanor Holmes Norton and Vernon Jordan. See *The Common Good: Social Welfare and the American Future* (New York: Ford Foundation, 1989), 63.

But Ellwood's plan still sends mixed signals into the ghetto. Women who become single mothers would still get a "guaranteed child support" check that would (by design) enable them to get by with only part-time work. They would also get the 18 to 36 months of cash benefits, plus "a wide variety of support and training services," plus eventually a guaranteed above-poverty job. None of these benefits would be available to young women who don't become mothers. None would be available to mothers who marry employed men. None (aside from the child support check) would be available to single mothers who go to work without going on the dole first. Faced with this array of choices, many women, again, might see no reason not to have an illegitimate child, get the check and the training, and worry about working later. Nor does Ellwood's plan offer any jobs to single *men* who might then be able to start working families.

Why risk luring young women onto a dole only to cut them and their children off 18 to 36 months later? Why not make the choice clear, and apply it across the board? Work is available to everybody, but everybody is expected to work or live in a working family. No cash doles. No excuses for not working. Women and men. Married and single. If you have a child, be prepared to carry an extra burden. These are the rules the mainstream culture tries to live by, and they are the norms that are in danger of disappearing entirely in the underclass.

39. The "participation" requirement means that, out of 4 million adults on welfare at any one time, 3.6 million need not be doing anything other than getting a check. In practice, in 1991 about 510,000 welfare families were listed as "participating" (see Jason DeParle, "Using Books Instead of Brooms"). For these "participants," the breakdown at the time of DeParle's article was: 33 percent in basic education, 11 percent in post-secondary school, 16 percent learning a technical skill, 15 percent other miscellaneous education, 11 percent in job search, 4 percent in "an actual work setting" (ibid.).

40. For example, Arkansas's mandatory "job search" program, considered wildly

successful, reduced welfare receipt by 18 percent after three years. But Arkansas is a low-benefit state (which means even low-paying private sector jobs are relatively attractive to its AFDC recipients). The San Diego "saturation" experiment, which attempted to force an entire caseload to either train, work, or search for work, achieved a 9 to 13 percent reduction in welfare receipt—about the best a Family Support Act–type reform can expect to achieve in an urban, high-benefit setting. See Judith M. Gueron and Edward Pauly, *From Welfare to Work* (New York: Russell Sage, 1991), 142–143.

41. See Irwin Garfinkel and Elizabeth Uhr, "A New Approach to Child Support," *The Public Interest* 75 (Spring 1984): 111–122; Irwin Garfinkel, Liz Phillips, and Tom Corbett, "A New Way to Fight Child Poverty and Welfare Dependence: The Child Support Assurance System," (Madison, Wis: Institute for Research on Poverty, February 1992); see also Ellwood, *Poor Support*, 155–174.

42. Moynihan broaches the idea of such "compulsory" work, then quickly backs off, in *Family and Nation* (San Diego: Harcourt Brace Jovanovich, 1986), 180–181.

43. Under an "assured child support" scheme, a single mother would also know that even if the father *does* pay his child support she won't see any extra money, at least until the father's contribution exceeds the minimum "assured" payment. Garfinkel concedes this might discourage mothers from cooperating with authorities in keeping track of fathers. But he argues this factor is outweighed by another: mothers couldn't get the assured child support check unless they identified the father in the first place, and obtained a child support award (or voluntary agreement to pay support).

44. See *Beyond Rhetoric; A New American Agenda for Children and Families; Final Report of the National Commission on Children* (Washington, D.C.: Government Printing Office, 1991), 97–109.

45. It's true, as Ellwood points out, that "assured child support" differs from welfare in that a child support check is not reduced by any wages a single mother earns (see *Poor Support*, 168–169). Ellwood claims this is a major virtue, since it preserves the work incentive for single mothers. But it also might have the perverse effect of subtly encouraging women to become single mothers. In a Garfinkel regime, after all, if they have an out-of-wedlock child they not only get cash support, but they get part of that support in the form of a check that won't be reduced if they work a bit. See Charles Murray, *Losing Ground: American Social Policy 1950–1980* (New York: Basic Books, 1984), 163, for a similar point.

The key question, in terms of "de-enabling" the underclass, is whether the "assured child support" check of, say, $1,500 a year is supplemented by AFDC for mothers who have no other income. If it is, then the scheme has done nothing to make a life on welfare less possible. If it is *not* supplemented by AFDC, then the scheme should have a significant de-enabling effect, at least for single mothers with one child, since it's very hard to live on $1,500 a year. The mothers would have to seek other means of support. Of course, this would amount to the abolition of AFDC. Without the provision of guaranteed jobs, it would be a Murrayesque plan far harsher than the proposal offered in the text.

For their part, Ellwood and Garfinkel have endorsed combining child support assurance with either the time-limitation of AFDC or its replacement with guaranteed jobs. (See Ellwood, *Poor Support;* Garfinkel and McLanahan, *Single Mothers and Their Children,* 181–187.) What's wrong with that? The small guaranteed child support check wouldn't be enough to "enable" a life on the dole, yet it would offer some social recognition that mothering is itself work. But if we are going to give mothering a subsidy, it is probably better to do it in the form of a small child allowance, available to broken and intact families alike, rather than a child support payment available only to single parents.

46. During the debate on Carter's welfare plan, Senator Moynihan criticized the idea that welfare mothers might be asked to climb 14-foot ladders or do dangerous work in national parks and forests. See Laurence E. Lynn, Jr. and David deF. Whitman, *The President as Policymaker* (Philadelphia: Temple University Press, 1981), 144–145.

Large neo-WPA infrastructure projects could be ongoing, expanding as necessary in times of high unemployment. Other projects could be planned in advance and put on the shelf, to be taken down in bad economic times.

47. Public schools and day-care centers might also employ a few parents as WPA workers to keep order. Is there any point in offering women free day care and then putting some of them to work in day-care centers? Yes. First, it would still free up a lot of women for employment. Second, and more important, the day-care jobs would exist within the culture of work—with alarm clocks to set, appointments to keep and bosses to please—rather than the culture of welfare.

48. Gregory Hoerz and Karla Hanson, "A Survey of Participants and Worksite Supervisors in the New York City Work Experience Program," Manpower Demonstration Research Corporation, September 1986, 18–19.

49. Could guaranteed-jobholders be fired? Certainly we want a neo-WPA in which people who show up drunk, who show up high, or who pick a fight with their supervisor would lose their jobs (though they could show up again after a decent interval). There is a danger that the courts would declare the WPA jobs to be "property" under the Fifth Amendment and impose debilitating "due process" requirements that had to be met prior to any dismissal. Congress could make this constitutional claim less tenable by providing basic procedural guarantees (such as a rudimentary hearing), and by making it clear that this is all neo-WPA workers have a right to expect.

See Barbara Blumberg, *The New Deal and the Unemployed: The View from New York City* (Lewisburg: Bucknell University Press, 1979), 114, for a description of the sensible procedures for firing workers in the original WPA.

50. In its eight-year existence, according to official records, the WPA built or improved 651,000 miles of roads, 953 airports, 124,000 bridges and viaducts, 1,178,000 culverts, 8,000 parks, 18,000 playgrounds and athletic fields, and 2,000 swimming pools. It constructed 40,000 buildings (including 8,000 schools) and repaired 85,000 more. Much of New York City—including LaGuardia Airport, FDR Drive, plus hundreds of parks and libraries—was built by the WPA (see ibid., esp. 124–146, 266, 301–302). Lester Thurow has suggested that New York's infrastructure is now decaying because no WPA has existed to repair or replace these public works in the half-century since.

51. Interviewed on "CBS Morning News," 23 October 1980. Reagan continued:

"So, if government, instead of inventing these new programs, had a backlog of government projects, and they would say, 'Well, now, this is the time to put those into effect,' I think it could be most helpful."

52. The opposition of "liberal" unions like AFSCME to the sort of jobs program that might help America's poorest communities is one of the dirtier little secrets of the labor movement. American workers in general would benefit from a guaranteed-job program, since full employment tends to shore up wages. But what sometimes goes for labor as a whole doesn't go for individual unions in the industries where a permanent WPA-style presence might bring in new, lower-income workers.

In the 1930s, the American Federation of Labor almost crippled the WPA by demanding that it pay "prevailing"—that is, union—wages. FDR actually broke a strike over the issue in 1939. See Blumberg, *The New Deal and the Unemployed,* 246–249; also 53–57, 115, 138–139; William E. Leuchtenburg, *Franklin D. Roosevelt and the New Deal 1932–1940* (New York: Harper & Row, 1963), 124–125, 147. In the 1960s, union opposition was one reason the War on Poverty didn't include a jobs program. See Lemann, *The Promised Land,* 154, 195. In the 1970s, unions tacitly opposed the jobs component of Jimmy Carter's welfare plan. See David Whitman, "Liberal Rhetoric and the Welfare Underclass, 67–68.

See also Nicholas Lemann, "A Culture of Poverty," *The Atlantic,* September 1984, 37–38; Doron P. Levin, "Many Welfare Clients Don't Seem to Mind Being Forced to Work," *Wall Street Journal,* 28 October 1982, A1; and Peter Perl, "Union Says Growing Use of Workfare Robs Some Public Employes [sic] of Jobs," *Washington Post,* 25 September 1985, A7.

53. It's important to recognize here that the number of jobs in a market economy is not fixed, like the seats in a game of musical chairs. Employment can expand with the size of the work force.

54. That means the Davis-Bacon Act (and similar state laws) would not be applied to the neo-WPA's projects. It does not mean the neo-WPA wouldn't have an internal promotion ladder, in which workers were paid more as they acquired skills or became foremen and supervisors. See the discussion of Davis-Bacon in Chapter 6 at note 74.

55. In other words, the jobs shouldn't be "targeted" to ghetto communities. That's a sure recipe for having work projects captured by the culture of the ghetto. See Nicholas Lemann, "Origins of the Underclass," *The Atlantic,* July 1986, 67–68. Vague-sounding service efforts—arts centers, drop-in counseling for veterans, community organizing, and the like—should also be avoided, not because they aren't valuable, but because their contributions are hard to measure and the possibility of workers spending all day doing very little is high.

56. See Blumberg, *The New Deal and the Unemployed,* 126, 137.

57. Note that even if there were "enough" private-sector jobs—something our capitalism has never provided at all times in all places—we'd still need some residual public jobs. We want to be able to say, with moral certainty, that any able-bodied citizen who is unemployed has chosen that course. But we don't know, *with moral certainty,* that all private-sector jobs available to the unemployed are ones we can fairly expect them to take. That's especially true for the least skilled workers. The jobs available to those at the bottom might be unsafe jobs in sweatshops or hu-

miliating work for petty-tyrannical bosses. Only when the government provides the jobs itself, with safe conditions and a decent boss, can we end what Thurow calls "the endless sterile debate about what fraction of the unemployed are lazy and unwilling to work."

58. *A note on the cost of a neo-WPA:* Welfare cost projections can get quite complicated. This one necessarily makes some simplifying assumptions. But most of these assumptions are pessimistic—that is, they tend to make the estimate higher than replacing welfare with work is likely to actually cost.

The estimate is for a fully implemented plan in 1990. Basically, it assumes the following:

- Two-thirds of former AFDC families would send someone to take a neo-WPA job—yielding about 2.1 million neo-WPA workers. (The remaining adult AFDC recipients are already employed, are disabled, or else will fail to work.)
- 3.2 million additional Americans will claim neo-WPA jobs. (This includes a third of the unemployed, plus a third of those not in the labor force because they "can't find a job.") That makes a total neo-WPA work force of 5.3 million.
- Administrative costs of the neo-WPA will be 20 percent of wages (which are $4 an hour for 35 hours a week).
- Capital costs of the neo-WPA will be another 20 percent of wages.
- Day care will cost an extra $13 billion.
- The Earned Income Tax Credit will bring neo-WPA workers and other low-wage workers (in families of four or fewer) up to the poverty line. It will also pay $8 billion in additional benefits to workers above the poverty line. (That happens because EITC benefits must be taken away gradually as people earn their way out of poverty.)
- Disabled former welfare recipients will receive cash benefits (presumably through the existing Supplemental Security Income program) that bring them up to the poverty line.
- For those who are able-bodied and poor but fail to work, the government will spend at least the amount by which their incomes fall short of the poverty line on "compassionate" in-kind assistance—shelter, counseling, et cetera.
- AFDC will be abolished, for a savings of $21.2 billion.
- Food stamps will be abolished for all potential workers, saving approximately $11.4 billion. The elderly and disabled would continue to get food stamps.

The total gross costs of the plan come to about $84 billion (for the neo-WPA, the EITC, day care, and compassionate assistance). The total savings come to about $33 billion. The net cost is $51 billion. If you figure a 15 percent margin of error, the range of net costs comes to $43 to $59 billion.

That's a great deal of money. But note:

- It represents the cost to both the federal government and the states.
- It includes the cost of relatively generous aid to the homeless and "undeserving" poor who fail to work.
- The $51-billion net cost doesn't take into account any of the value of the work performed by the neo-WPA. The reason is that this value is difficult to gauge. If you assumed, for example, that the neo-WPA workers produce public works worth the wages paid them, then the 5.3 million neo-WPA workers would cre-

ate almost $39 billion in value, reducing the net cost of the program to a mere $12 billion. But you can't make that assumption. First, many neo-WPA workers would be marginally productive employees whose output didn't equal their $4 wage. Second, much of their work would be producing public goods and services that, were it not for the need to provide jobs, the voters would not want to purchase. If WPA workers cleaned the streets, taxpayers might get cleaner streets than they'd normally be willing to pay for. But clearly the neo-WPA's work would be worth *something*—many billions of dollars, if not $39 billion.

* Finally, of course, the $51 billion doesn't attempt to capture any of the indirect, dynamic benefits of replacing welfare, including the revenue that would be raised from would-be welfare mothers who instead joined the labor force and became taxpayers.

This estimate also assumes medical costs are taken care of separately (e.g., by a national health insurance system).

Chapter 9
The "Work Test"

1. "The goal is to get poor families' incomes over the poverty line, not *merely* to change the source of poverty incomes," argues a policy paper from the liberal Economic Policy Institute (emphasis added) (see Max B. Sawicky, "The Poverty of the New Paradigm" [Washington, D.C: Economic Policy Institute, February 1991], 22). This same Money Liberal assumption lies behind the elaborate tables printed every year by the House Ways and Means Committee detailing the "antipoverty effectiveness" of various government transfer programs. ("In 1979, 15.0 percent of all poor individuals were removed from poverty due to means-tested transfers and Federal tax policy. In 1982 this had declined to 5.7 percent. Beginning in 1984 the downward trend reversed...."—*Background Material and Data on Programs within the Jurisdiction of the Committee on Ways and Means* [hereinafter referred to as the *Green Book*], 1991 edition, 1160.)

2. See James Patterson, *America's Struggle Against Poverty, 1900–1980* (Cambridge, Mass.: Harvard, 1981), 66. See also Henry Aaron, "Six Welfare Questions Still Searching for Answers," *Brookings Review* (Fall 1984): 13; Robert Theobald, ed., *The Guaranteed Income: Next Step in Economic Evolution?* (Garden City, N.Y.: Doubleday, 1966), 93–94.

3. The causality may go the other way: welfare bureaucracies are allowed to be callous when the benefits they dispense go to able-bodied people who might be working.

4. The homeless are a group largely distinct from, and much smaller than, the underclass. But their ranks could easily swell in the initial phase of the plan I've sketched out, because some able-bodied Americans who would formerly have supported themselves on welfare will fail to work. The goal would be to give these people compassionate aid that helps them achieve the equal dignity that can only come with work—while at the same time enforcing the rules of civility in the public sphere.

It seems to me the essential steps are fairly obvious: *(a)* Establish an adequate system of shelters, providing food and other in-kind necessities along with a good deal of supervision, counseling, et cetera; *(b)* Make sure the disabled homeless receive the Supplemental Security Income benefits to which they are entitled—though if someone is entitled by virtue of being mentally ill, alcoholic, or drug-addicted, the aid should be accompanied by appropriate paternalistic strings; *(c)* Expand the supply of housing, including Single Room Occupancy rental units, to make sure that people with only a poverty-level income can afford a place to stay; *(d)* Rigorously prohibit sleeping in public spaces, including parks and sidewalks.

With time, the ranks of the homeless would diminish. The government would be assuring that all disabled and working Americans could live decently, off the streets. The consequences of not working would be clear. And living *on* the streets would be unashamedly discouraged.

5. "On Civic Liberalism: A Symposium," *The New Republic,* 18 June 1990, 28.

6. That respect is an overriding concern in ghetto culture is evidenced by the term "dissing," slang for disrespecting.

7. Encouraging this sort of respect is not the same thing as encouraging upward mobility. Indeed there may be some tension between these two goals, because upward mobility is often promoted by denigrating work that doesn't pay a lot. In the mid-eighties, for example, a black jet pilot named Drew Brown gave uplifting talks on ghetto campuses in which he made fun of those who, because they failed to acquire skills, had to go to work as parking lot attendants. ("If you don't learn to do the driving, you'll be taking the parking stubs, and you'll be saying for the rest of your life, '$2.65, please.'") See Karlyn Barker, "Shoot for the Moon, Pilot Urges D.C. Students," *Washington Post,* 10 December 1988, B1.

8. For a left-wing attack on work tests, see Michael B. Katz, *The Undeserving Poor: From the War on Poverty to the War on Welfare* (New York: Pantheon, 1989). For a right-wing attack on a rigorous work test as "crushing and punitive," see Stuart Butler and Anna Kondratas, *Out of the Poverty Trap: A Conservative Strategy for Welfare Reform* (New York: Free Press, 1987), 147. Indeed, in the late 1980s some conservatives began moving down the slippery slope toward a right-wing version of give-them-cash. See Robert Pear, "White House Urges Cash Welfare Aid," *New York Times,* 10 August 1986, 1. Providing cash, they noted, is cheap. It "empowers" the poor—since it "is the form of support to the poor which gives them the greatest flexibility and degree of choice" (Butler and Kondratas, *Out of the Poverty Trap,* 159). You can extend it to two-parent families (ibid., 156). And it lets you wrap all sorts of government programs up into one check. Conservatives just don't want it to be a very big check.

For a defense of the nineteenth-century work tests, see Marvin Olasky, "Beyond the Stingy Welfare State," *Policy Review* 54 (Fall 1990): 2.

9. George Orwell, "The Lion and the Unicorn" in *My Country Right or Left 1940–43* (New York: Harcourt Brace, 1969), 96.

10. Lawrence Mead, *Beyond Entitlement: The Social Obligations of Citizenship* (New York: Free Press, 1986), 12, 254–255.

11. It's not an original observation that the ghetto drug dealer's respect for money is a distorted version of *Vanity Fair*'s respect for money.

12. See David Ellwood, *Poor Support* (New York: Basic Books, 1988), 29.

13. *A note on Social Security's "insurance" analogy:* Generally, to be "fully insured" by Social Security you have to pay taxes on a small amount of wages in one "quarter" of each year in which you aren't disabled. Once you've paid for 40 quarters, you are "fully insured" for life. There is another sense, however, in which Social Security's "insurance" checks are commonly thought to be "earned." Ask an elderly voter why his benefit shouldn't be cut, and he may tell you, not only that he "earned" it, but that it was "paid for" by his payroll tax contributions, that (in the strongest formulation) "It's my money." This is the analogy between Social Security and private insurance plans. Under this theory, Social Security benefits are not only earned in the sense that you can't get them without having worked, they are earned in the more precise sense that they reflect the actual value of the contributions a worker has paid into the system.

Social Security was carefully designed to encourage this idea. FDR himself said contributors could be "likened to the policy holders of a private insurance company." The idea retained its power four decades later, when Jimmy Carter's Counselor on Aging, Nelson Cruikshank, threatened to resign unless he was permitted to denounce a set of very mild benefit cuts as "a breach of faith" between the government and recipients whose benefits were "earned rights people *have paid for* and are entitled to" (emphasis added). See Jerry R. Cates, *Insuring Inequality: Administrative Leadership in Social Security, 1935–54* (Ann Arbor: University of Michigan Press, 1983), 33; W. Andrew Achenbaum, *Social Security: Visions and Revisions* (Cambridge, England: Cambridge University Press, 1986), 35, 69–70.

The only problem with this appealing "insurance" idea, of course, is that it's a lie. The payroll contributions of John Anyworker aren't salted away in an account to earn interest and then get paid back to him decades hence when he retires, as is done with private insurance. Rather, his payroll tax contributions are typically paid out to today's retirees, perhaps without ever having earned any interest at all. When John retires in the future his Social Security benefits must be paid for by taxes imposed on the people then working.

Honest liberals of both the Civic and Money schools necessarily see through the "it's my money" aspect of Social Security's "insurance" analogy. But Money Liberals naturally tend to overlook the real work test that underlies the contribution requirement. Thus Paul Taylor of the *Washington Post* smugly lectures his readers that Social Security's "popularity rests, in part, on the widespread misperception that benefits are earned rights, based on the contributions of individual participants, and therefore are free of the stigma of welfare." Never mind that Social Security's benefits are earned, in an important moral sense, and are based on contributions. (Paul Taylor, "Tax Policy as Political Battleground," *Washington Post.* 18 February 1990, A1.)

At the same time, the "insurance" analogy is often given a somewhat cynical role in the Money Liberal version of Social Security's appeal to the American middle class. The analogy, Kuttner says, is a "politically useful myth" that helps disguise the "substantially redistributive" nature of Social Security from a middle class that has little "ideological support for egalitarianism" (*Economic Illusion* [Boston: Houghton Mifflin, 1984], 237). In this view, the idea of "means-testing" Social Security is dangerous not only because it would take away some people's checks, but also because it blows the program's "insurance" cover story.

14. Payroll taxes may be desirable, even if they are regressive, because they establish a sense of entitlement based not on age but on work.

15. Note that age per se is an ambiguous category in work ethic terms, since it's possible to have lived for 65 years without having worked a day. Programs that pay people on the basis of their age—what might be called generational entitlements—have a correspondingly ambiguous history, sometimes tainted as unearned, sometimes righteously claimed by elderly Americans as their reward for having achieved seniority. It's impolitic to mention it now, but in 1935, when the Social Security Act was passed, its most popular provision was not the old age "insurance" scheme we now know as "Social Security," but the provision to fund state programs of Old Age Assistance (OAA), which would send out cash to needy old people whether they'd worked or not. So popular were the OAA provisions that Roosevelt's strategists placed them at the beginning of the Act, to make sure everyone read them first. (See William E. Leuchtenburg, *Franklin D. Roosevelt and the New Deal 1932–1940* (New York: Harper & Row, 1963), 106; Witte, *Development of the Social Security Act* (Madison: University of Wisconsin Press, 1962), 79; Patterson, *America's Struggle,* 70–71).

The SSI program is the modern, federalized successor to the 1935 programs of Old Age Assistance and aid to the blind. People who today wind up on SSI may have worked quite a bit, just not in jobs covered by Social Security. But because SSI recipients haven't *necessarily* worked in the past, being on SSI is inevitably considered a cut less dignified than being on "regular" Social Security. Congress recognized this distinction by requiring that SSI checks be colored gold to distinguish them from the green, "earned" Social Security checks. See Vincent and Vee Burke, *Nixon's Good Deed: Welfare Reform* (New York: Columbia University Press, 1974), 193.

16. Money Liberals look longingly across the Atlantic to Western Europe, where the hoary work issue that so obsesses Americans is said to be elegantly fudged. See Patterson, *America's Struggle,* 76. Kuttner, *Economic Illusion,* 230–258.

17. Theda Skocpol, "Sustainable Social Policy: Fighting Poverty Without Poverty Programs," *The American Prospect* 2 (Summer 1990): 63. The common formulation of this argument is that "programs limited to the poor are poor programs" because they lack a broad political base of self-interested support.

18. Charles Peters, "A Neoliberals' Manifesto," *Washington Monthly,* May 1983, 10. One possible psychological dynamic might be this: Nobody likes to think they're getting an undeserved "welfare" benefit. They think "I'm not lazy. If I'm getting this check, it must be OK." If you send out enough checks, so that enough people have the opportunity to undertake this felicitous moral reevaluation, it *will* be OK.

19. See Kuttner, *Economic Illusion,* 231; "On Civic Liberalism: A Symposium," *The New Republic,* 18 June 1990, 27 ("Social Security creates a sense of social solidarity as well as redistributing a lot of income.").

20. Elizabeth Wickenden, "Social Security—Why Not a Means Test?" (New York: Study Group on Social Security, Fact Sheet No. 13, August 1984): 6, 4. To prove they are really poor, the argument goes, citizens are required to disclose their family finances to snoopy agents of the state, sacrificing their privacy and opening the door to all sorts of demeaning, paternalistic requirements (not to spend money on luxuries, liquor, and the like). Most humiliating of all are "asset tests"—require-

ments that those asking for aid sell their property, perhaps including their homes, and "spend down" to become poor enough to qualify for assistance.

21. Skocpol argues that only "minimal" service in the Union Army was required (Skocpol, "Sustainable Social Policy," 63). But minimal service is still service.

22. See David Wessel, "Paved with Good Intentions, Taxwriters' Road to Help the Working Poor Turns into a Maze," *Wall Street Journal*, 11 June 1991, A16; Robert Greenstein, "Universal and Targeted Approaches to Relieving Poverty: An Alternative View," in *The Urban Underclass*, ed. Christopher Jencks and Paul Peterson (Washington, D.C.: Brookings, 1991), 447–448.

23. It's because "universal" benefit programs are so expensive that a debate occasionally flares up within the Money Liberal camp over whether universal or "targeted" schemes are the best way to get money to those at the bottom of the distribution. See Skocpol, "Targeting Within Universalism" and Greenstein, "An Alternative View," in *The Urban Underclass*, 411–459. But few liberal champions of "targeting" dare to apply their logic to Social Security.

24. Source: *1991 Green Book*, 75, 98, 614. The 12.4 percent payroll tax rate does not include an additional 1.45 percent tax on both an employer and the employee that goes to fund Medicare.

25. *A note on Social Security's solvency:* The Social Security system is scheduled to build up huge surpluses over the next several decades, which will then be drained rapidly as baby boomers mature and collect benefits. Under the official "middle-of-the road" economic assumptions, the retirement and disability portion of the Social Security trust fund begins to drain around 2016 and runs out of money by 2036.

This limited measure of solvency is due to a series of changes passed in the Social Security "rescue" legislation of 1983. The most significant change was to subject half of Social Security benefits to the federal income tax for couples whose income from other sources is over $32,000 ($25,000 for an individual). This is a mild, backdoor version of means-testing—more acceptable in part because it preserves the fictional analogy of Social Security with private insurance. (Private insurance benefits are already taxed). Significantly, the $32,000 threshold was *not* indexed for inflation. As the years pass and the incomes of more and more elderly Americans spill over the line, a majority of Social Security recipients may find themselves paying income tax on at least part of their benefits.

At least four things could disturb the official projections:

1. Congress could chicken out by indexing the $32,000 threshold when enough seniors discover that, thanks to inflation, they are subject to partial benefit taxation.

2. Congress could raid the surpluses building up in the Social Security accounts, spending them for other benefits and projects—as is currently being done. (Though the process by which "raiding" the surpluses reduces the ability to pay future benefits is actually a bit complicated. See *1991 Green Book*, 86–94.)

3. As noted in the text, the economy could turn out worse than current expectations. For the assumptions underlying the official projections, see *1992 Annual Report of the Board of Trustees of the Federal Old Age and Survivors Insurance and Disability Insurance Trust Funds*, 2 April 1992, 55–61. For a critique of these as-

sumptions, see James Dale Davidson, "Social Security Rip-Off," *The New Republic,* 11 November 1985, 12–14; Philip Longman, *Born to Pay: The New Politics of Aging in America* (Boston: Houghton Mifflin, 1987), 70–72: Peter G. Peterson and Neil Howe, *On Borrowed Time* (San Francisco: ICS Press, 1988), 130–140.

4. Something could go awry with demographic factors, to which the system is peculiarly sensitive. The most important of these factors are fertility rates and life expectancy. Lots of babies, remember, means lots of new taxpaying workers to pay for our retirement. If the fertility rate falls below projections, there is a safety valve: increased immigration. But if the death rate is reduced by 60 percent, instead of the projected 35 percent—if, say, we discover a cure for heart disease—the system is in deep trouble. See *1991 Green Book.* 104.

Although they don't like to talk about it in public, even Social Security's most ardent defenders admit we may well have to fix it again down the road. "It could happen," says Robert Myers, the longtime chief actuary of Social Security. "We can make some adjustment," says Robert Ball, one of the system's architects. Plenty of time to make changes, these experts say, if after a decade or three the pessimistic scenarios seem to be coming true and the surplus we're building up doesn't look big enough to do the job.

But wait a minute. That would put the burden of rescuing Social Security—of cutting benefits or raising taxes—on the generations that have yet to retire, the same generations who are demonstrably getting the lousiest deal from the system so far and who bore the brunt of the fixes adopted in 1983. If we do need to save some money, is it fairer to make their deal even worse, or to place the burden on those who have so far made out like bandits—namely, current recipients who paid into the system during the early, low-tax years and drew pensions vastly greater than their contributions? See Longman, *Born to Pay.* 62–76; Neil Howe and Phillip Longman, "The Next New Deal," *The Atlantic.* April 1992, 98; Geoffrey Kollmann, "How Long Does It Take New Retirees to Recover the Value of Their Social Security Taxes?" (CRS Report for Congress, Congressional Research Service, 15 January 1992), 11.

Generational justice is at war here with the Take Away principle, which says you never, ever, reduce the benefits of anybody already receiving them. Here a sense of equity says: cut the checks of current recipients. If that violates their expectations, limiting the cuts to the rich is the way to minimize the sacrifice involved. See Walter J. Blum and Harry Kalven, Jr., *The Uneasy Case for Progressive Taxation* (Chicago: University of Chicago Press, 1953), 49–52.

26. These rough estimates are derived from the *1991 Green Book,* Table 13, 28.

27. Among politicians, the most prominent means-tester has been former Arizona governor (and 1988 presidential candidate) Bruce Babbitt. The means-testing of Social Security was also suggested by Ronald Reagan's Treasury Secretary, Donald Regan. President Bush's budget director, Richard Darman, repeatedly suggested a "general means-testing principle" for government programs—"except with respect to Social Security."

The Kirk flap is recounted in Keith Love and Karen Tumulty, "Top Democrat Stirs Fuss on Social Security," *Los Angeles Times.* 18 April 1985, sec. 1, 1. (Kirk advocated means-testing at breakfast. By bedtime he had put out a statement saying: "I was wrong. Our party ... is unalterably opposed to any cuts in Social Security benefits. I should not have mentioned the subject of a means test.")

The Kennedy speech is Sen. Edward M. Kennedy, remarks at the John F. Kennedy Presidential Conference, Hofstra University, New York, 29 March 1985, 6.

28. Guaranteed-income schemes must be means-tested because it would be inconceivably expensive to mail everybody—rich, poor, and middle class—checks big enough to ensure the poor a decent income.

29. Cohen is quoted in Cates, *Insuring Inequality,* 11.

30. See Elizabeth Wickenden, "Paying for Social Security: Why the Payroll Tax?" Fact Sheet 17, Study Group on Social Security, New York, September 1986, 3; see also *1991 Green Book,* 46. For a Money Liberal defense of Social Security against means-testing—based in part on the need to defend this redistributive feature—see Robert Kuttner, "The Social Security Hysteria," *The New Republic,* 27 December 1982, 18; and Kuttner, *Economic Illusion,* 242.

31. Indeed, the progressive "skew" in benefits is counterbalanced by other factors that tend to make Social Security harder on the poor—the regressive payroll tax, the tendency of affluent retirees to enjoy a bigger windfall of benefits over contributions, the tendency of poor workers to die younger (and therefore collect fewer retirement checks). See Cates, *Insuring Inequality,* 5–10, and sources cited therein; also Gary Burtless, "Public Spending for the Poor: Trends, Prospects, and Economic Limits," in *Fighting Poverty: What Works and What Doesn't,* ed. Sheldon H. Danziger and Daniel H. Weinberg (Cambridge, Mass.: Harvard University Press, 1986), 27.

32. Cates, *Insuring Inequality,* 11.

33. See, for example, Democratic Rep. Jim Cooper of Tennessee quoted in David Broder, "Who's the Fairest of Them All?" *Washington Post,* 13 February 1991, A19.

34. Nor, apparently, is Social Security popular because most Americans have bought the myth that, like private insurance, it has been "paid for." In 1981, for example, a Louis Harris poll asked "As far as you know, do the Social Security taxes working people pay today get set aside in a fund for their own future retirement, or are they used to pay Social Security benefits for retired people today?" Seventy-five percent gave the right answer ("Are used today"). Only 9 percent said the taxes are set aside.

35. Nor would a means-test necessarily be mean. It could allow the elderly a decent retirement income before gradually taking away benefits as incomes rose. The vast majority of the middle class would still be getting Social Security. Any "asset test" could also be quite liberal, avoiding the need for a humiliating "spend down" in order to qualify for a retirement check.

In fact, Social Security's defenders have it backwards. The nasty means test doesn't turn nice programs into humiliating "welfare." Rather, programs that are unearned welfare tend to encourage nasty versions of the means test. Taxpayers see AFDC recipients as freeloaders, because AFDC recipients *are* freeloaders, in that they get benefits without necessarily having worked. And when you're giving somebody a benefit you regard as a temptation to idleness, you're going to make damn sure he doesn't get more of it than he absolutely needs. If you're administering a program that is earned through work, this motive evaporates.

It turns out that the architects of Social Security knew perfectly well that a "nice" means test was possible. In the early days of the New Deal, many states tried to humanize the means-tests they imposed on the indigent elderly under the Old Age Assistance program. They were stopped by none other than the Social Security Board, which feared that if the states made Old Age Assistance dignified, it would undermine support for the fledgling Social Security "insurance" system. The Social Security Board actually required that the states adopt the most intrusive, demeaning restrictions possible. This is documented in damning detail in Jerry Cates's *Insuring Inequality,* 112–117.

36. See Henry J. Aaron, "Social Welfare in Australia," in *The Australian Economy: A View from the North,* ed. Richard E. Caves and Lawrence B. Krause (Washington, D.C.: Brookings, 1984), 354–355. The income limits in the Australian system are set relatively high, so that most people qualify for some benefits. About half Australia's aged get full pensions; only the richest 25 percent receive no benefits at all. (Source: Office of the Minister for Social Security.)

37. *A note on European "universalism":* Kuttner says Western European welfare states are characterized by generous "universal citizen entitlements" that serve both rich and poor, workers and non-workers, "without subjecting them to the indignity of a means test" (*Economic Illusion,* 242–243); see also Timothy M. Smeeding, "Cross National Perspectives on Income Security Programs," Testimony before the Joint Economic Committee, U.S. Congress, September 25, 1991. Kuttner relies on the work of two Columbia professors, Alfred J. Kahn and Sheila Kamerman, for his description of these entitlements, which include family and housing allowances. "A single parent with no job in France collects a combined family allowance and housing allowance package equal to about 79 percent of the average worker's wage," Kuttner declares. "In Sweden the figure is 94 percent" (ibid, 246).

Sounds impressive. But Kahn and Kamerman's own figures show that in France 52.4 percent of this single mother's income is, in fact, means-tested public assistance. In Sweden, the figure is 36.1 percent. In both Sweden and France this assistance comes with paternalistic strings. In France the allowance is "discretionary and time-limited." In Sweden "local welfare committees" review eligibility. See Kahn and Kamerman, "Social Assistance: An Eight-Country Overview," *The Journal* 8, no. 4 (White Plains: Institute for Socioeconomic Studies, Winter 1983–84), 101, 106, 110; see also Kahn and Kamerman, *Income Transfers for Families with Children: An Eight-Country Study* (Philadelphia: Temple University Press, 1983), 67.

Moreover, Kahn and Kamerman tell us, much of the remaining aid in both countries, while not "means-tested," is "income-tested." What's the big difference? "Income-tested" programs, in Kahn and Kamerman's definition, do not have an "asset test." But they are hardly universal. In Sweden, it turns out, another 22 percent of the aid Kuttner cites comes in the form of a housing allowance available *only* to the poorest third of the population (see *Income Transfers,* 67). In France, another 38.2 percent of the aid is from two separate "income-tested" programs. Only 9.4 percent is actually in the form of the "universal" family allowances, available to rich and poor, that Kuttner touts (ibid., 76).

Kahn and Kamerman claim this "income-tested" aid is "nonstigmatized" because the programs "cover people sufficiently high into the income distribution so as not to carry stigma" ("Social Assistance," 100, 112). But that's just the sort of mild income test Money Liberal Democrats such as Kuttner have furiously resisted applying to Social Security. Kahn and Kamerman's study, far from demonstrating the evils of cutting benefits to the rich, proves exactly the opposite—that a means-test can be thoroughly detoxified. "Given what we have seen," they conclude, "it would appear possible to use income-testing without stigma" (*Income Transfers*, 318).

38. See Skocpol, "Targeting Within Universalism: Politically Viable Policies to Combat Poverty in the United States," and Greenstein, "An Alternative View." If the argument of this chapter is correct, neither universality nor the extra redistributive efficiency of "targeting" is a source of political legitimacy. If a program passes the work test, it can be targeted—means-tested—without depriving it of public support (see ibid., 450). At the same time, a "targeted" cash benefit, no matter how affordable, will be politically vulnerable if it fails the work test.

39. About 19 percent of the elderly apparently get slightly bigger checks because they have unusually large shelter expenses (*1991 Green Book*, 743).

40. *1991 Green Book*, 743–744. About 46 percent of SSI recipients get some state supplement (ibid, 740).

41. This would not end poverty among the elderly, because only about 55 to 60 percent of the eligible elderly participate in SSI. That is in part because SSI retains some distasteful "welfare" connotations. This stigma, as noted earlier, is ineradicable. The innuendo isn't that anyone on SSI should "get a job." It isn't that if someone needs SSI he failed to save for his retirement years—few of us would begrudge a minimum income to an elderly sucker who blew his nest egg in bad investments. The incriminating question is: "Why isn't he getting regular Social Security?" Being on SSI seems to imply that a senior not only didn't save, he didn't *work*—or marry someone who worked.

In the past, this innuendo has had a weak basis in fact. Many people wound up on SSI after working in jobs (often backbreaking agricultural jobs) not covered by Social Security. SSI is also the last resort of many elderly women who grew up in an era when women weren't expected to work. But the logic behind the stigma is likely to become stronger, not weaker, over the coming decades. Since 1983 virtually every job in the economy has been covered by Social Security. And women are now widely expected to work. If somebody manages to live 65 years in this new regime without earning enough Social Security insurance (or forming a family with someone who has) what has he or she been doing?

The truth is SSI will always remain slightly tainted in a Work Ethic State. If any American is too proud to claim this ambiguous "entitlement," that's his choice, and it should be respected.

See generally Sheila R. Zedlewski and Jack A. Meyer, "Toward Ending Poverty Among the Elderly and Disabled: Policy and Financing Options" (Washington, D.C.: Urban Institute, February 1987). They note that the SSI asset test could also be liberalized at very low cost.

42. See *1991 Green Book*, 46. He would also qualify for food stamps, of course.

43. Calculation from *1991 Green Book*, 25.

44. The $460 a month does reflect a "special minimum" Congress enacted in

1972 for the benefit of full-time, life-long, low-wage workers. Unfortunately, the provision is inadequate.

45. The bulk of the $10 billion would be for the increases in SSI. Raising the special minimum for low-wage workers to $600 per month would actually require less than $1 billion. The cost is so small because relatively few of those receiving low Social Security benefits are low-wage earners who have put in thirty years of work.

46. Ken Auletta, *The Underclass* (New York: Random House, 1982), 283.

Chapter 10
An Ecology of Equality

1. The same idea is suggested by the title of Douglas Massey and Mitchell Eggers, "The Ecology of Inequality: Minorities and the Concentration of Poverty, 1970–1980," *American Journal of Sociology* 95, no. 5 (March 1990).

2. What needs to be explained, it should be noted, is not why neighborhoods of similar houses are occupied by members of the same economic class. In a market, after all, similar houses will sell for similar prices and will tend to be purchased by people of similar incomes. What needs to be explained is, first, why this rule sometimes doesn't hold—why a neighborhood can suddenly become desirable to affluent professionals, and therefore more expensive, simply because other affluent professionals live there. More important, why are neighborhoods built with similarly sized houses in the first place, instead of a mix of the small and the luxurious?

3. George Gilder, *Wealth and Poverty* (New York: Basic Books, 1981), 90–91.

4. Barbara Ehrenreich, *Fear of Falling* (New York: Pantheon, 1989), 14–24. Charles Peters suggests yet another possible cause of snobbery: "The mobility of postwar Americans meant that people were moving every few years and having to reestablish their identities in new communities. This was easiest to do by using demonstrations of taste as the means of indicating their social class" (*Tilting at Windmills* [Reading, Mass.: Addison-Wesley, 1988], 220).

5. When advocates of "affordable housing" proposed building some moderately priced apartments and townhouses in suburban Loudon County near Washington in 1990, local homeowners made the usual noises about traffic and congestion. But they also complained vociferously that their children might wind up mingling with moderate- and low-income children—so vociferously that, according to the *Washington Post,* the developer actually volunteered to bus children in the proposed development to a school out of the neighborhood. The project was killed anyway. See Kirstin Downey, "Suburbs Support Cheaper Housing But in Someone Else's Back Yard," *Washington Post,* 12 November 1991, A1.

6. This calculation, which underlies the national debate over "equity" in school financing, works quite independently of the underclass. But if poorer people require *more* spending, either to handle increased crime or to provide various remedial educational services, that makes the tax benefits of secession vastly greater. See John R.

Logan and Mark Schneider, "Governmental Organization and City/Suburb Income Inequality, 1960–1970," *Urban Affairs Quarterly* 17, no. 3 (March 1982): 303–318, for evidence that income inequality between suburbs and cities is in fact greater when suburbs rely on property taxes to fund local services.

7. These figures were obtained from the assessor's offices of Princeton and Trenton.

8. A counterfactor once neatly frustrated this cozy game: industrial property. Factories pay a lot of taxes, but rich suburbs traditionally didn't want to be anywhere near them because they were dirty. The poor neighborhoods that got stuck with them also got the benefit of their taxability. Unfortunately, smelly industries are now less important and service and information industries more important. Rich suburbs may be quite happy to have a neat row of shiny offices filled with lawyers and systems analysts if it helps pay for the schools. See John R. Logan and Reid M. Golden, "Suburbs and Satellites: Two Decades of Change," *American Sociological Review* 51 (June 1986): 436.

9. The great temptation will be for Civic Liberals to file inventive constitutional lawsuits and get the courts to cram class-mixing down suburban throats. That—as the New Jersey Supreme Court discovered when it tried to force suburbs to accept low-income housing—is a surefire way to get the suburbs' backs up. The New Jersey court's 1975 Mount Laurel decision, in 16 years, produced fewer than 8,000 affordable units. See Rachelle Gabarine, "A Mt. Laurel Ruling Backs Impact Fees," *New York Times*, 3 February 1991, sec. 10, 9. Of course, resistance to the Mount Laurel decision was bound up with resistance to the underclass. Were the underclass assimilated, the political environment would be changed. Still, social-egalitarians should be loath to use anti-democratic institutions like the courts to impose their agenda on voters.

10. The underclass issue, needless to say, made Florio's plan even less popular. Not only were the suburbanites getting socked, they were getting socked mainly to fund the decaying inner-city schools in Newark, Trenton, Paterson, Camden, and Jersey City. Given the social disorganization of the ghetto, taxpayers reasonably feared their money was not even going to do any good. See John Judis, "A Taxing Governor," *The New Republic*, 15 October, 1990, 22–31.

11. In 23 states liberal school-funding lawsuits (including one that prompted Florio's action) seek this separate-but-equal outcome. See also Jonathan Kozol, *Savage Inequalities* (New York: Crown, 1991).

12. The deal would be even harder to refuse if the alternative to direct class-mixing was some sort of school-funding equalization, with its attendant loss of local control. See Peter Schrag, "Savage Equalities," *The New Republic*, 16 December 1991, 18–20.

13. By what political coalition would the rich suburbs get "rolled"? Presumably by a coalition of all the people in poorer districts who want relief from unequal tax burdens, or who want to be able to share the superior facilities and services the rich now enjoy exclusively. This coalition cannot form now, because even relatively poor working-class suburbs and municipalities fiercely defend suburban autonomy as a means of insulating themselves from the underclass. Once the underclass is assimi-

lated, however, they will have nothing to lose by class-integration, and much to gain.

14. See Kirstin Downey, "Advocates See a Way to Achieve More Low-Cost Housing: Mandate It," *Washington Post,* 12 November 1991, A12; George Judson, "Connecticut Developers Challenge the Power of Local Zoning," *New York Times,* 24 November 1991, sec. 4, 1.

15. *Politics, Markets, and America's Schools* (Washington, D.C.: Brookings, 1990).

16. Ibid., 220–221. An "equalization" formula would ensure that rich districts subsidized adequate scholarships for students from poorer districts. Chubb and Moe also hope to encourage schools to admit "at risk" students by giving those students "add-on" scholarships (ibid.). It seems more probable that such scholarships would serve as a red flag to schools and parents, signaling which kids to avoid.

17. That is how Chubb responded when I asked him.

18. Chubb and Moe would also allow districts to collectively boost their "scholarships"—Beverly Hills, California, could tax itself to provide, say, a $5,000 scholarship, once it was through subsidizing the $4,000 scholarships of poorer districts through an "equalization" formula (ibid., 220). Wouldn't specialized schools crop up that only kids from districts with big collective scholarships could afford?

19. Chubb and Moe presumably depend on competition for high-school admission to spur students to study harder. Competition could indeed have this effect— but that may only mean that maximizing student effort sometimes conflicts with social equality.

Choice advocates occasionally argue that merit would not be the dominant factor in admissions. Students, they say, will group themselves by interest and philosophy rather than academic success. Some parents will want schools that emphasize discipline and "fundamentals," and those parents will be both rich and poor, with dumb kids and smart kids. Some parents (again, of all species) will want "progressive" schools, or an emphasis on science, or on the arts, et cetera. In desegregation cases, school boards routinely resort to similarly specialized "magnet" schools to attract students of various races. The magnet school "mixing effect" is real, and should be used in any attempt to integrate schools by class and ability as well as race. But colleges are specialized too. The example of higher education shows that, given pure "choice," the impulse to merit-based stratification is likely to overwhelm the "magnet" effect.

20. John Coons, a Berkeley law professor and prominent choice advocate, proposes another method of controlling "choice." He would require schools to set aside at least 25 percent of their spaces for "children from ... the bottom twenty-five percent of the income scale." Any "add-on" charges (beyond the basic voucher) would have to be levied according to ability to pay. To prevent schools from admitting low-income kids and then dismissing them on a pretext, a student could only be dismissed for misconduct, not "for academic reasons unless he or she were acquiring no substantial benefit." But while Coons's plan might mix income classes, it would still let merit segregation flourish as the better schools siphoned off the "gifted and talented" low-income kids to fill their 25 percent quotas. John E. Coons, "Making Schools Public," in *Private Schools and the Public Good: Policy Alternatives for the Eight-*

ies, ed. Edward McGlynn Gaffney, Jr. (Notre Dame: University of Notre Dame Press, 1981), 96–98.

21. Also, the imperatives toward merit-based stratification are so strong that in many cities (New York and Chicago, for example) magnet schools impose sub rosa merit tests, looking at applicants' achievements and disciplinary records. See Donald R. Moore and Suzanne Davenport, *Excerpts from The New Improved Sorting Machine: Concerning School Choice* (Chicago: Designs for Change, February 1989), 93, 97. See also Nicholas Lemann, "Magnetic Attraction," *The New Republic,* 13 April 1987, 16–19.

22. Moore and Davenport, "School Choice: The New Improved Sorting Machine," in *Choice in Education: Potential and Problems,* ed. William Lowe Boyd and Herbert J. Walberg (Berkeley: McCutchan Corp., 1990), 211.

23. In the Cambridge plan, students who live within half a mile of a school, or who have a sibling at a school, are given priority. Beyond that, as long as racial balance is maintained, everything is by lot. See Christine H. Rossell and Charles L. Glenn, "The Cambridge Controlled Choice Plan," *The Urban Review* 20, no. 2 (Summer 1988): 80–92; Abigail Thernstrom, *School Choice in Massachusetts* (Boston: Pioneer Institute, 1991), 12–16.

24. In 1984, about 51 percent of Cambridge students were classified as low income. But after two years of choice, 76 percent of the students at the Kennedy elementary school were low income—a higher percentage, actually, than before choice was initiated. The other previously low-income school, Roberts, remained 74 percent poor. Kennedy was also the school least likely to be a parent's first choice, and it has among the city's lowest scores on the "basic skills" test.

Meanwhile, on the other side of town, only 13 percent of the children at the Agassiz school qualify as "low income"; 31 percent at the Peabody School. These are also two of the schools most often chosen by parents. Remember that these class and merit disparities persisted even in the face of total *racial* desegregation, which you'd think would tend in itself to even things out. Source: unpublished data prepared by Michael Alves, February 1985; Rossell and Glenn, "The Cambridge Controlled Choice Plan," 86, 90.

On the possibility that parents are subtly "steered" by school admissions personnel, see Thernstrom, *School Choice in Massachusetts,* 3.

25. Nineteen percent of the students in Montclair are poor enough to be eligible for free or reduced-price school lunches, and these students seem to be fairly evenly dispersed. See Beatriz C. Clewell and Myra F. Joy, *Choice in Montclair, New Jersey: A Policy Information Paper* (Princeton, Educational Testing Service, January 1990), 10. Montclair has not yet had to resort to a lottery—the vast majority of parents are said to get their first choice. Racial desegregation is complete. But in Montclair, again, even requiring all parents to make a choice didn't necessarily mean that the poor exercised their choices as diligently as the affluent. "[S]ome parents, particularly those of Head Start students, are still late signing up and may not get their first choice" (ibid., 8).

Note that these experiments involve elementary schools. The experience of class-mixing in high school might be expected to have a more lasting impact. (Who remembers the class of the kids they played with when they were five years old?) Yet, more or less precisely for that reason, it's a lot easier to get affluent parents to send a 5-year-old to kindergarten with working-class kids than to get them to send a 14-year-old to a working-class high school. Exclusionary pressures are also maximized in high school because it's closer to the "meritocratic moment" of college admission.

26. According to Rossell and Glenn, "the decline in school age children in Cambridge increased from twice the national average between 1970 and 1980 to almost 10 times the national average from 1980–1984." See "The Cambridge, Controlled Choice Plan," 89. Between 1978 and 1988, the city's student population declined by more than 20 percent (source: Cambridge School Department). Some of this "avoidance" may be a reaction to the period of mandatory desegregation before 1982. But some of it may also be flight from "controlled choice" itself.

27. Might the city-suburb line be broken down by expanding "controlled choice" to include privately run schools? That sounds appealing in theory, because t' e ew schools would come without political jurisdictions attached. And private schools are accustomed to drawing students from a wide geographic area. But remember, such a system would have to require use of lotteries for admission (otherwise you wind up with Chubb/Moe-style merit stratification). You'd also have to prohibit parents from "adding on" to their kids' vouchers. This would be a very difficult radical reform to pull off in the face of affluent parents who are content with current arrangements. I doubt it is politically feasible unless dissatisfaction with even suburban public schools greatly increases.

28. That goes double, of course, for any attempt to force class integration through non-"choice" mechanisms such as mandatory busing. Interestingly, the town of La Crosse, Wisconsin, is currently attempting to bus students in order to achieve income integration. It is encountering the same sort of resistance that accompanied b˙ ˙in˙ for racial integration, even though La Crosse is 85 percent white. Parents, ap, ˙˙ , simply hate seeing their children forced to take a bus when there is a neighborhood school close by. See William Celis III, "In Effort to Improve Schools, Pupils to Be Assigned on Basis of Income," *New York Times*, 22 January 1991, A18.

29. This possibility was suggested to me by Abigail Thernstrom. The elimination of assigned "neighborhood" schools in the Montclair, New Jersey, choice system appears to have had the effect of removing some of the motive for housing segregation by race.

30. See Jeannie Oakes, *Keeping Track: How Schools Structure Inequality* (New Haven: Yale University Press, 1985), 33–34.

31. Ibid., 34.

32. Orwell actually thought it counterproductive to deliberately mix the classes, lest it "drive the bourgeois, who has idealised the proletariat so long as he knew nothing about them, back into frenzies of snobbishness." See Orwell, *Wigan Pier*, 162–169.

33. See Stuart Elliot, ˙ s of 80s Excesses Yield to the Basics of the 90s," *New York Times*, 21 October 1991, 10.

34. *A note on the "servant problem"*: Servants are the troubling exception to this general egalitarianism. But the employment of servants has declined dramatically in recent decades. In 1960, 29 percent of American families reported expenditures for

"domestic service," for example. By 1972 the percentage had declined to 11.6 percent, and by 1980 it had declined to 5.1 percent. There was, however, a slight rise during the eighties, with 6.73 percent of families spending for "housekeeping services" in 1989 (source: Bureau of Labor Statistics, Consumer Expenditure Surveys).

The possibility that rising money inequality might allow the rich to employ increasing numbers of Americans in demeaning roles—as butlers, maids, valets, et cetera—presents a difficult problem for Civic Liberalism. As Christopher Jencks has argued, "The rich are rich because they can afford to buy other people's time. They can hire other people to make their beds, tend their gardens, and drive their cars" (*Inequality* [New York: Harper & Row, 1972], 6).

But note, first, that only some personal services are demeaning—generally, roles that require fawning or the performance of intimate personal tasks. Just because Americans now spend a lot of money hiring "other people's time" in the form of aerobics instruction, Smokenders sessions, and marriage counseling doesn't mean social inequality has increased, because those service-providing roles aren't demeaning. Similarly, as two-worker couples increasingly farm out tasks formerly performed in-house—cooking, washing laundry, and tending gardens, for example—the performance of those services becomes more routine and less demeaning.

Second, Civic Liberalism is not without remedies should the employment of butlers and valets begin rising to dangerous levels. The hiring of personal domestic servants could be discouraged directly, through taxation, or at the very least through a crackdown on the evasion of existing Social Security taxes. Strict enforcement of the immigration laws would deprive the affluent of the easily intimidated workers who are (in many areas of the country) the only people willing to take servants' jobs. Nor do I think it's crazy to suggest that some especially demeaning jobs could simply be banned—as shoeshine stands were in Washington, D.C., until a misguided right-wing lawsuit overturned the ordinance.

Ultimately it is the attitude of Americans that will determine the prevalence of demeaning jobs. My impression is that most Americans—even affluent Americans—don't like being on *either* side of the master-servant relationship. Given the other pleasures capitalism affords, bossing people around just isn't that much fun. No less an authority than Miss Manners has noted the growing phobia of Americans about being served:

> Drivers continue to pump their own gas even when there is not a big difference in price from the so-called full-service lanes.... In hotels, where there are still alert bellmen, guests may go to some trouble to circumvent them. At transportation terminals, luggage carts are chosen over porters, regardless of the rental fees.... ("Self Service with a Smile," *Washington Post*, 11 June 1989, F1)

Yes, one can envision a degree of money inequality that might, over time, erode these healthy instincts, and with it the ability of a Civic Liberalism to cope with the "servant problem." But it would take a lot more money inequality than we have now, a level of inequality that perhaps defies a realistic estimate of the distribution of human talents.

See also Michael Walzer, *Spheres of Justice* (New York: Basic Books, 1983), 174–177.

35. William Ryan, *Equality* (1938; reprint, New York: Barnes & Noble, 1964), 87.

36. In fact, the culture shift both Tawney and Civic Liberals envision might result in greater money *in*equality. Once money becomes less important, businesses may find that they have to offer still more of it in order to induce highly skilled employees to stay on the job.

37. See Walzer, *Spheres of Justice*, 20.

38. This perception will be enhanced by the assimilation of the underclass. Once our most conspicuous pool of unutilized talent is tapped, the insinuation that Americans who don't make a lot of money just aren't as good will be harder to avoid.

Chapter 11
Winning

1. That is not to say the Civic Liberal agenda wouldn't have an important and positive impact on American prosperity. Though it's a topic beyond the scope of this book, I think at least three economic benefits of Civic Liberalism can be readily identified.

1. By providing guaranteed jobs, a neo-WPA reduces the temptation of fiscal and monetary policymakers to overheat the economy in order to fight unemployment. This was, in fact, what attracted Arthur Burns to the idea. See *Reflections of an Economic Policy Maker* (Washington, D.C.: American Enterprise Institute, 1978), 221–224; see also Robert M. Kaus, "Jobs For Everyone," *Harper's*, October 1982, 16.
2. Assimilating the underclass would have a huge economic payoff. The number of potential engineers, scientists and businessmen who are now dying or wasting their lives in our ghettos represents a loss of GNP that dwarfs the cost of a program that might harness their talents.
3. National health insurance—and to some extent, I think, the entire public sphere—would encourage mobility. Workers wouldn't have to worry about losing medical coverage were they to switch jobs. Those who moved to new locations would be guaranteed, if not a new set of intimate friends, at least a community sphere where they would be treated as an equal.

Of course, compared with Money Liberalism, Civic Liberalism promises far less interference with the normal incentives of the market. More speculatively, to the extent it offers all Americans a social "floor" of civic dignity, it might even allow governments to avoid some of their more costly attempts to shield individuals from downward mobility in the marketplace—rent control, for example, or elaborate legal protections against discharges in both the private and public sectors.

2. A Canada-style national health insurance could easily transfer $300 billion in medical expenses from private-sector budgets to the tax-financed government budget.

3. See William Schneider, "Tough Liberals Win, Weak Liberals Lose," *The New Republic*, 5 December 1988, 13.

4. Even so, I wouldn't expect most urban black politicians, many of whose constituents have at some time relied on AFDC, to embrace a jobs-not-welfare plan. That wouldn't necessarily hurt its chances. To voters who fear Democrats are already too solicitous of black leaders—and suspect that the party will never actually put welfare mothers to the test—loud complaints from inner city congressmen might offer some reassurance that Civic Liberals meant business. Monolithic African-American opposition, however, would turn the debate into a racial one, and probably doom the plan's chances of success.

Fortunately, not all black leaders represent areas with significant welfare populations—and at least some who do have shown a willingness to take dramatic steps in order to push welfare families into the mainstream. Wayne Bryant, the Democratic majority leader in the New Jersey state assembly in 1991 and architect of his state's controversial welfare changes, represents the ghetto town of Camden. Eleanor Holmes Norton, the delegate to Congress from the majority-black District of Columbia, has endorsed a Ford Foundation plan that would put time limits on welfare receipt. As more blacks move into the middle class, and as the problems of the ghetto poor are discussed more openly, one would expect more Bryants and Nortons to emerge.

5. As of 1992, Thomas Edsall has pointed out, suburbanites (rich and poor) will probably constitute an absolute majority of the *voting* public.

6. See Robert Kuttner, "On Civic Liberalism: A Symposium," *The New Republic*, 18 June 1990, 26–27, and "The Poverty of Neoliberalism," *The American Prospect* 2 (Summer 1990): 9–10.

7. Kuttner, "The Poverty of Neoliberalism," 10.

8. Likewise, by embracing the public sphere Republicans could steal voters from the Democrats' lower income base.

9. I do think there is an argument, for example, that the rich needed a little soaking in the late eighties, not for distributional reasons, but for solid social-egalitarian reasons—to remind them that they lived in a democracy where they must share burdens with everybody else. This point was effectively made by the 1990 tax increases. It doesn't mean an ongoing redistributive campaign is the basis on which Democrats can mobilize a majority over the long haul.

10. As noted earlier, Democratic politicians have long exploited these competing justifications for progressivity—supporting progressive taxes in the name of "ability to pay" while accepting Money Liberal applause for their redistributive effects. See Walter J. Blum and Harry Kalven, Jr., *The Uneasy Case for Progressive Taxation* (Chicago: University of Chicago Press, 1953), 73.

11. "Which Taxes," 9 May 1990, A26. Similarly, a 50-cent-per-gallon gas tax would bring in $50 billion and encourage conservation to boot—but Money Liberals can be expected to denounce it as regressive (as Bill Clinton did during the 1992 presidential campaign).

12. "Throw away the search for the center" is in Robert N. Bellah's contribution to "What Is to Be Done?" *The New Republic*, 20 May 1991, 28; see also John Kenneth Galbraith, ibid., 29.

13. They may also feel liberalism has failed to uphold civic equality by endorsing reverse discrimination.

14. But see James Bennet, "The W-2 Step," *Washington Monthly*, June 1991, 29–32, making the Money Liberal case that taxing only the top 20 percent or so isn't redistributive *enough*.

15. See "Gore, Downey Offer Working Family Tax Relief Act," press release from office of Sen. Al Gore, 6 May 1991. The $300-per-child tax credit was championed by Sen. Lloyd Bentsen (D.-Tex.), the $350 credit by Sen. Bill Bradley (D.-N.J.), and the $200-per-worker credit by Rep. Dan Rostenkowski (D.-Ill.). For a Money Liberal analysis of the distributional consequences of various early nineties tax-relief plans, see Robert Greenstein, "The Kindest Cut," *The American Prospect* 7 (Fall 1991): 49–57; and Marian Wright Edelman, "The Right Middle Class Tax Cut," *Washington Post*, 2 March 1992, A17.

16. See Thomas Byrne Edsall, *The New Politics of Inequality;* Thomas Byrne and Mary Edsall, *Chain Reaction: The Impact of Race, Rights and Taxes on American Politics* (New York: Norton, 1991); Thomas Byrne Edsall, "The American Dilemma," *The New Republic*, 27 May 1991, 35–38.

17. One way to try to get around the problem, exemplified by Rep. Rostenkowski's payroll tax cut, is to avoid the underclass issue by limiting the redistribution to workers. Of course, this means abandoning the give-them-cash part of Money Liberalism.

18. That sort of "top-down" coalition, as Thomas Edsall labeled it, produced the 1989 debacle of "catastrophic" health care insurance. Democrats designed and enacted a program financed by a surcharge on the richest 40 percent of the elderly. Very progressive—until the richest 40 percent formed a coalition and got the program killed.

19. "What's Wrong with the Democrats?" *Harper's*, January 1990, 47.

20. In 1990 the Democrats quite consciously dropped the "millionaire's surtax" from their budget proposal so that they'd have something to demand in the ensuing years' debates.

21. "[A] coalition supportive of taxing and spending policies beneficial to those in the bottom half of the distribution of American income," as Thomas Edsall puts it. See "The American Dilemma," 38. See also Stanley Greenberg, "From Crisis to Working Majority," *The American Prospect* 7 (Fall 1991): 109, 111, arguing for the re-creation of a "bottom-up" coalition.

22. Elshtain, "Issues and Themes in the 1988 Campaign," 114–115. See also Gary C. Jacobson, *The Politics of Congressional Elections* (Boston: Little, Brown, 1983), 146, and sources cited therein; also Steven Kelman, "Why Public Ideas Matter," in *The Power of Public Ideas*, ed. Robert B. Reich (Cambridge, Mass: Harvard University Press, 1990), 42–43, and sources cited there.

23. That is not to say there isn't a large constituency with an immediate pecuniary interest in replacing welfare with a guaranteed jobs program. Quite apart from those on welfare, this constituency includes all the unemployed and discouraged workers who would take the neo-WPA jobs, plus over 10 million low-income working families who would benefit from an expanded Earned Income Tax Credit,

plus all the other low-wage workers who would benefit when the neo-WPA tightened up the labor market.

24. New York Gov. Mario Cuomo's rhetoric, for example, routinely sets up a contrast between Republicans, who say "We can't make it with compassion; it's mushy headed and liberal. We have to be hard and macho," and Democrats who "look beyond our own welfare to the good of all and ... reach down to those at the bottom of the ladder and help them up, if only a rung or two." This sort of talk makes liberals feel satisfyingly righteous, but it should also depress them—because it means that only a sudden tidal wave of new compassion will get the liberal agenda enacted.

25. The demeaning aspect of compassion is most evident in private, individual do-gooding, with its self-satisfied patrons and awed supplicants. This is what the anthropologist Marcel Mauss meant when he said "Charity wounds him who receives...." It's one reason turn-of-the-century labor unions talked of "rescuing" their members "from demoralization at the hands of sentimental almsgivers." See Michael Walzer, *Spheres of Justice* (New York: Basic Books, 1983), 93; Josephine Brown, *Public Relief* (New York: Octagon, 1971), 43–44. See also Sean Wilentz's comments in, "What Is to Be Done?" *The New Republic,* 20 May 1991, 31; Mickey Kaus, "Up from Altruism," *The New Republic,* 15 December 1986, 17–18.

As a basis for antipoverty policy, the trouble with compassion is that it makes few distinctions. We have compassion for the working poor. We have compassion for the unmotivated punk who would rather smoke dope than work. The whole point of "compassion," as commonly used, is to override moralistic distinctions in the name of undifferentiated human need, which is why it leads naturally to the indiscriminate remedy of "give-them-cash."

26. For a definition of social and interpersonal goods, see Robert Paul Wolff, *The Poverty of Liberalism* (Boston: Beacon, 1968), 167–195.

27. In 1987 researchers asked citizens in several countries: "Is it the responsibility of government to reduce the differences in income between people with high incomes and those with low incomes?" In the U.S. only 29 percent answered "yes," compared with 44 percent in Australia, 61 percent in West Germany, 64 percent in Great Britain, and 81 percent in Italy. See Everett Carll Ladd, "The American Ideology: An Exploration and a Survey of the Origins, Meaning, and Role of American Values" (American Enterprise Institute Conference Paper, March 1992), A22.

28. See, for example, Joseph Califano's defense of welfare on these grounds in *Governing America* (New York: Simon & Schuster, 1981), 327 ("less than 1 percent of the welfare population ... could be expected to work").

29. See Califano's euphemistic discussion, at a briefing for President Carter, of the "problems ... in creating jobs for this kind of population," cited in Lynn and Whitman, *The President as Policymaker,* 102. Less euphemistically, one liberal state welfare commissioner argued against work requirements by telling me that many of his department's clients were "so fucked up they couldn't hold down a job if their life depended on it."

30. For the percent of AFDC mothers who are working, see *Background Material and Data on Programs within the Jurisdiction of the Committee on Ways and Means,* 1991

edition, 624. On the Democratic argument that welfare mothers "don't get much" by emptying wastebaskets, see Mickey Kaus, "Revenge of the Softheads," *The New Republic*, 19 June 1989, 26.

31. Greenberg said this in a clip shown on the "NBC Nightly News," 20 October 1991. Similarly, reporters and polltakers from both parties tend to rather blithely treat anti-welfare sentiment as anti-black resentment. See, for example, E. J. Dionne, Jr., and Thomas B. Edsall, "Bush Caught Between Conflicting Constituencies," *Washington Post*, 20 October 1990, A1.

32. Oregon's Measure No. 7 was approved in 1990 by a 57 to 43 percent margin, despite opposition from the AFL-CIO and the Oregon Public Employees Union. In six counties, for three years, it would replace AFDC, food stamps, and unemployment compensation with a system of public and private sector jobs paying 90 percent of the minimum wage. Significantly, the jobs would be available to anyone over eighteen, not just to current aid recipients. Measure 7's sponsors argued (erroneously I think) that their program could be operated "at no additional cost" beyond the money now spent on the programs being replaced. As of this writing, Measure 7 has not been implemented because the state has avoided getting the necessary waivers of federal welfare rules.

Former Gov. Pete du Pont of Delaware also proposed to replace welfare with a neo-WPA in his 1988 presidential campaign. Du Pont lost badly, but not because of the welfare plan.

33. In particular, Senator Moynihan, who hyped the 1988 law shamelessly, will have some explaining to do.

For a poll that confirms AFDC's unpopularity, see the National Opinion Research Center's General Social Survey for 1972–1991. Each year this survey asks citizens whether too much or too little is being spent on "welfare." Consistently, from 40 to 60 percent of the respondents say "too much," and 14 to 24 percent say "too little." Only space exploration and foreign aid get less support. (By way of comparison, almost 70 percent say we spend "too little" on education.) When "assistance to the poor" is substituted for "welfare," public approval shoots up dramatically—suggesting that voters object not to antipoverty measures but to spending that violates the work ethic. See also Keith Melville and John Doble, "The Public's Perspective on Social Welfare Reform" (Public Agenda Foundation, New York, January 1988), 4–6; Lawrence M. Mead, *Beyond Entitlement* (New York: Basic Books, 1986), 240 n. 57.

34. Cuomo's quote is from a speech at the Kennedy School of Government at Harvard on February 12, 1992. See Theodore R. Marmor, Jerry L. Mashaw, and Philip L. Harvey, *America's Misunderstood Welfare State* (New York: Basic Books, 1990), 95. See also Greenberg, "From Crisis to Working Majority," 116.

35. For example, Stanley Greenberg chastises fellow Democrats for ignoring a middle class that "hungers" for "leadership that honors work." But within a page he's arguing that Democrats should get elected so they can raise AFDC benefits! Greenberg, "From Crisis to Working Majority," 113–114.

Chapter 12
Conclusion

1. See, most famously, Francis Fukuyama, "The End of History," *The National Interest* 16 (Summer 1989): 3–18.

2. Supporters of the "millionaire's surtax" estimate that about 30,000 taxpayers would be affected by the provision.

INDEX

7979878R0

Made in the USA
Lexington, KY
28 December 2010